THE LIFE
YOU WERE
BORN TO
LIVE

Selected Books by Dan Millman

The Peaceful Warrior Saga

Way of the Peaceful Warrior
Sacred Journey of the Peaceful Warrior
The Journeys of Socrates
The Hidden School

Core Teachings

Wisdom of the Peaceful Warrior
The Four Purposes of Life
No Ordinary Moments
The Life You Were Born to Live
The Laws of Spirit
Everyday Enlightenment

Writing Guidance

The Creative Compass

Training Guidance

Body Mind Mastery

Inspiration for Children

Secret of the Peaceful Warrior
Quest for the Crystal Castle

For information about Dan Millman's work,
including the Life-Purpose Calculator,
online courses, books, and audios:

peacefulwarrior.com

25th Anniversary Edition

THE LIFE YOU WERE BORN TO LIVE

A Guide to Finding Your Life Purpose

DAN MILLMAN

H J Kramer

published in a joint venture with

New World Library
Novato, California

An H J Kramer Book

published in a joint venture with

New World Library
14 Pamaron Way
Novato, California 94949

Text design by Tona Pearce Myers

Library of Congress Cataloging-in-Publication Data
Names: Millman, Dan, author.
Title: The life you were born to live : a guide to finding your life purpose / Dan Millman.
Description: Revised 25th Anniversary Edition. | Novato : H.J. Kramer, 2019.
 | "An H J Kramer book published in a joint venture with New World Library."
Identifiers: LCCN 2018023084 | ISBN 9781932073751 (alk. paper)
Subjects: LCSH: Spiritual life.
Classification: LCC BL624 .M48 2019 | DDC 204/.4--dc23
LC record available at https://lccn.loc.gov/2018023084

First printing of the 25th Anniversary Edition, August 2018
ISBN 978-1-932073-75-1

Printed in Canada on 100% postconsumer-waste recycled paper

New World Library is proud to be a Gold Certified Environmentally Responsible Publisher. Publisher certification awarded by Green Press Initiative.
www.greenpressinitiative.org

10   9   8   7   6   5   4   3

Dedicated to all those searching for
their life path and higher calling

CONTENTS

Part Three: The Paths of Destiny

Part Four: Laws That Change Lives

Part Five: Applied Wisdom

ACKNOWLEDGMENTS

I first learned the core elements of the Life-Purpose System, as well as some of the spiritual laws detailed in Part Four, from a man I met in 1984 — I'll call him "the warrior-priest" — who had a significant influence on my life and work.

Abiding thanks to respected friends and colleagues who reviewed this manuscript decades ago — and to Hal and Linda Kramer, my first publishers and longtime friends, and to the team at New World Library, who initiated this new edition and who continue to support my books. My longtime freelance editor, Nancy Carleton, provided skillful developmental editing and copyediting for both the original edition and this revised 25th Anniversary Edition.

And, always, love and gratitude to my wife, Joy, whose keen intuition and support have helped shape my writing and enrich my life.

PREFACE TO THE
25TH ANNIVERSARY EDITION

*What lies before us and what lies behind us
are small matters compared to
what lies within us.
And when we bring what is within
out into the world,
miracles happen.*

— Henry David Thoreau

We all share an innate desire for meaning, direction, and purpose — a desire as important to our psychological growth as eating is to our biological survival.

Yet few of us consciously recognize that we even *have* a specific life path or purpose. Meanwhile, our potential and destiny call out to us, sending messages through dreams, intuitions, and our innermost longings — hidden drives that define our personality, shape our careers and relationships, and influence the quality and direction of our life.

Until we recognize and live in accord with our underlying purpose, life may feel like a puzzle with missing pieces, as if there's *something* we're here to do but we can't quite grasp it. As actress Lily Tomlin once quipped, "I always wanted to be *somebody*, but maybe I should have been more specific." Lacking these specifics, we work and rest, eat and sleep, make money and spend it, and experience our share of pleasures and difficulties, even as clarity about our life purpose eludes us.

Over the years, I've written a number of books about the peaceful warrior's approach to life — facing our inner battles with courage, compassion, and higher wisdom. *The Life You Were Born to Live*, one element of my work, presents the Life-Purpose System, a tool for insight and a map that reveals your life path up the mountain you're here to climb and the most direct route to reach the summit.

The Life-Purpose System enables you to expand your awareness of not only your path but the paths of friends, loved ones, clients, colleagues, and others. The insights and guidance provided can help psychotherapists, physicians, physical therapists, bodyworkers, social workers, managers, teachers, coaches, and other helping professionals enhance the effectiveness of their ongoing work, adding a measure of compassion and insight.

Beginning in 1985, I applied, tested, and refined this system by working with thousands of people. The system's strength lies in its relative simplicity and directness, and its demonstrated effectiveness over time. The enthusiastic responses I've received inspired me to write this book and to expand and revise it.

Many systems of personality typing exist in both psychological and spiritual traditions. While self-analysis can generate the *impulse* to change, the Life-Purpose System provides the *means* — namely, specific spiritual laws keyed to each life path to help us transform our health, our relationships, our work, and every other facet of our life.

For this 25th Anniversary Edition — the first major revision since the original publication — I've added new life-path information to include all those born in the twentieth and twenty-first centuries. While the original edition addressed the thirty-seven life paths of those born in the twentieth century, this edition includes all forty-five life paths now possible. I've also added new insights about those working single-digit birth numbers, which only began appearing in the new millennium, and I reveal more about the origins of this particular system and how I came to share it with you. Other refinements reflect the added knowledge of twenty-five more years of real-life experience of many thousands of individuals working with the system. Even those familiar with earlier editions of the book can gain new insights.

The Life-Purpose System has illumined my life and the lives of many others, bringing new levels of clarity and compassion. I trust that this book will bring fresh appreciation and empathy, generating an impulse to make a positive difference for friends, family, and maybe even our planet. In the meantime, may this book guide you toward the fulfillment of your personal destiny — the life you were born to live.

— Dan Millman
Summer 2018
Brooklyn, New York

HOW TO READ THIS BOOK

Nearly half of this book (in Part Three) consists of reference material about the forty-five life paths for all those born from 1750 to the present day and into the foreseeable future. But you need only read relevant sections of the book to gain a sound grasp of the Life-Purpose System and the material directly related to your personal life path. You'll also find information providing insight into the lives of well-known historical figures as well as friends, family, and colleagues as you read more of the book. I suggest the following process as a starting point:

1. Skim through the Contents for an overview.
2. Read Part One to access the Life-Purpose Calculator to determine your birth number and absorb basic information about the Life-Purpose System.
3. Refer to Part Two to grasp the essential meanings of the digit or digits that make up your birth number.
4. Turn to the life-path material specific to your birth number in Part Three. (Over time, you can calculate the birth numbers of significant people in your life, and look up related information among the forty-five life paths described here.)
5. Turn to Part Four to study the spiritual laws key to your life path. (Read about the other spiritual laws at your leisure. They all apply to everyone, but some are particularly pertinent depending on your birth number.)
6. If you wish, refer to Part Five to gain insight into key relationships in your life, and to study the nine-year cycles of life as they apply to you or to others.
7. Read the Epilogue for final words.

THE LIFE-PURPOSE SYSTEM

If we don't know what port we're steering for,
no wind is favorable.

— Seneca

Keys to Part One

ORIGINS OF THE LIFE-PURPOSE SYSTEM

For centuries, observers of human nature have sought common denominators to better understand the forces that shape human personality and destiny. Numerous tools of insight from both psychological and mystical traditions have emerged at different times and in different cultures. All of these methods and maps of consciousness represent our attempts to demonstrate that our universe and our individual psyche aren't random or chaotic, but have a certain structure and order.

This book, introducing the Life-Purpose System, provides a clear, objective method for understanding any individual's life path and purpose — providing that individual has a known and accurate date of birth and was born after 1750, when the modern calendar was widely adopted.

This system's ultimate source is veiled in mystery, but its origins most likely date back to the Pythagorean school of ancient Greece. Pythagoras is best known as a mathematician, one of the founders of geometry. According to *World Book Encyclopedia*, "Pythagoras taught that *number* was the essence of all things. He mystically associated numbers with virtues, colors, and many other ideas that he may have embraced during travels in the East." As the *Encyclopedia Britannica* states, "More probably the bulk of the intellectual tradition originating with Pythagoras himself belongs to mystical wisdom rather than to scientific scholarship."

Like other holistic thinkers, Pythagoras embraced many facets of human consciousness in the same way modern physicists now enter realms once relegated to mystics, philosophers, and theologians. He spoke of cycles, patterns, and waves that existed long before the dawn of humanity, and of how our life paths reflect great and eternal laws, whose origins and purpose remain hidden within the mystery and mechanics of existence. In exploring the fundamentals of form and frequency, he discovered relationships between mind and matter where before no such order had appeared to exist, and he pointed to hidden numerical patterns that served as keys for unlocking secrets of the psyche.

Although the Life-Purpose System resembles some other numerology systems — in the sense that it works with numbers to derive meaningful information — you may find the material in this book especially clear, specific, and applicable to everyday life. The following section describes where I first learned the core elements of this system.

Inceptions of the Life-Purpose System

Despite many decades devoted to exploring the human psyche, insight traditions, and metaphysical models of reality, I remain an empiricist at heart. The scientific method — using controlled experiments to test theories — helped pull humanity out of the dark ages of superstition. I apply critical thinking and skepticism to magical thinking and untested notions. Still, the mind is like a parachute; it works best when open.

I hadn't even considered the existence of a higher calling or life path until 1984, when I met a man — the warrior-priest I mentioned in the Acknowledgments — who became my mentor, colleague, and friend. He had read my first book, *Way of the Peaceful Warrior*, and we shared our experiences and compared perspectives, while he offered his own unique guidance.

Not long after our initial encounter, this warrior-priest offered me an hour-long life-purpose reading. He revealed in-depth information that clarified my past, present, and potential future, including details that rang true and proved amazingly accurate. It was as if his words removed a veil that had previously obscured my vision, and revealed to me the life I was born to live.

I was astonished that he could have such insight into my life but had no idea how he gained access to such information. I was well versed in the cold-read techniques used by so-called psychics. But the warrior-priest claimed no psychic abilities, stating only that he'd been trained to know "where to look" for such information. He would say no more about it at that time.

In the months following that session, I began to learn life's lessons with greater ease and openness, and to engage with life in a way consistent with a new sense of clarity, as if a hazy picture had come into sharper focus. Understanding what I was here to do, I set out to do it. My family's financial situation improved as I refined an approach to living that I called *the peaceful warrior's way*.

Meanwhile, I remained fascinated with the warrior-priest's method. So when he announced an advanced training he was offering in Hawaii, where he would teach, among other things, the basic elements of the system that gave him such uncanny insight into people's lives, I was the first to sign up. I could hardly believe that I might learn to do for other people what he'd done for me.

At the training, I sat with about twenty other participants as he began a series of lectures on this mysterious system. The first thing he revealed was an objective method of adding up the digits of anyone's date of birth, and then deriving meanings that provided insight into that individual's life.

I was initially disappointed by this revelation, the way we sometimes are when a magician shows how a wondrous illusion is accomplished with mirrors or sleight of hand. Besides, using people's birth dates seemed like numerology, an occult art that had never attracted me. It made no sense that adding the digits of someone's date of birth could yield accurate information about central qualities of that person's life.

The warrior-priest explained that such methods had been passed down in various cultures over the centuries, but that they differed in their focus and degree of accuracy. He added, "Once you learn more about this approach, you can determine for yourself the validity of the method." He then spent several evenings presenting basic information that pinpointed key issues for each life path, highlighting innate drives, challenges, and gifts, which for most people remain unseen or obscure.

I took careful notes from the warrior-priest's lectures, outlining in about twenty typewritten pages the fundamental elements of the system. As soon as I returned home, I offered free life-purpose readings to family and friends, using the basic information from my notes. Within a few weeks I had internalized the information and no longer needed my notes. Eventually, after working with many hundreds of people and providing recorded readings (which I called Spiritual Law Alignments), my insight deepened and expanded.

Eight years later, I trained a small number of therapists, health professionals, and life coaches in the fundamentals of what I came to call the Life-Purpose System, and eventually I went on to write the original edition of *The Life You Were Born to Live.*

I can't claim that the Life-Purpose System is based on a scientific theory, nor can I logically explain how people's seemingly arbitrary date of birth on the modern calendar could possibly reveal valid, reliable information about their life path and purpose. I only know, with a confidence based on years of empirical testing, that the material in this book can bring people's lives into focus.

The Life-Purpose System is distinctly different from the Tarot, I-Ching, or Runes — traditional oracles that offer symbolic images or poetic generalities that might apply to anyone, and on which individuals then project their own meaning and wisdom, applying it to their particular situation. Certainly someone could use this (or any) book in a similar way, flipping open to any page to find something meaningful. But the life-purpose material isn't intended as an oracle, nor does it contain vague, generalized information. Rather, it offers specific and distinct insight into the issues of each life path. The more you study your life path and the paths of others, the more you can appreciate this material's power to enhance insight, self-knowledge, understanding, compassion, and transcendent humor.

Perhaps the validity of the Life-Purpose System stems from the holographic nature of the universe, in which each part mirrors and contains the whole, and in which the individual psyche fits within a larger pattern of order. By distilling complex variables into essential patterns, this system reveals the hidden forces behind our personality, furnishing a clear lens from which to view the bigger picture of our life. Trying to explain it in logical terms is like attempting to derive the square root of a sonnet. I can only feel a sense of awe and wonder at laws yet undiscovered.

In Part One, you'll learn how to determine and begin to interpret birth numbers, the key to the Life-Purpose System.

DETERMINING BIRTH NUMBERS

At birth, our parents gave us a name;
the universe gave us a number, or frequency.

The Life-Purpose System adds together the digits in a person's date of birth according to the current-day calendar to determine a birth number or frequency pattern consisting of one digit, three digits, or four digits, and then translates that birth number into meaningful information about that person's life purpose. The information revealed by the birth number, along with application of the spiritual laws especially related to that number, can bring your life into greater focus.

You can choose either of two methods to determine your birth number, the key to your life path. The first is quicker and more accurate.

Method One: Use the Life-Purpose Calculator Online

1. Go to peacefulwarrior.com.
2. In the menu, click on Life Purpose to access the Life-Purpose Calculator.
3. Enter your day, month, and year of birth. You'll then see your birth number, along with a paragraph of summary information about your life path. Make note of your birth number, return to this page, and read on.

NOTE: If you wish, you can also purchase the Life Purpose App for iOS or Android devices, or find it on the web at lifepurposeapp.com. The app provides the Life-Purpose Calculator as well as key information from this revised edition to have at your fingertips.

Method Two: Do the Math

If you prefer to do the math, you can find a step-by-step method for calculating any birth number using an accurate date of birth in the Appendix at the end of this book. Once you've completed the calculation (and checked your math), make note of your birth number, return to this page, and read on.

Possible Birth Numbers for the Twentieth Century

Different birth numbers change over the centuries. The following list shows the thirty-seven possible birth numbers (or frequencies) for anyone born between 1900 and 1999:

12/3, 13/4, 14/5, 15/6, 16/7, 17/8, 18/9, 19/10
20/2, 21/3, 22/4, 23/5, 24/6, 25/7, 26/8, 27/9, 28/10, 29/11
30/3, 31/4, 32/5, 33/6, 34/7, 35/8, 36/9, 37/10, 38/11, 39/12
40/4, 41/5, 42/6, 43/7, 44/8, 45/9, 46/10, 47/11, 48/12

In the general population, certain birth numbers (such as 28/10, 29/11, and 30/3) appear more frequently than others in a given time period, forming a bell curve. Other birth numbers closer to the beginning and end of this list appear less frequently. At the extreme ends, the last 12/3s were born on 1-10-1900, and the first 48/12s didn't appear until 9-29-1999.

Additional Birth Numbers for the Twenty-First Century

Whether or not you were born in the twenty-first century and have a single-digit birth number yourself (or know someone who does), the following information sheds new light on all birth numbers and life paths.

Most people born after the year 2000 have the same birth numbers and life paths as those born in the twentieth century. But in the year 2000, new frequencies began to appear. For the first time in centuries, some children were born on birth dates that result in single-digit birth numbers: 4, 5, 6, 7, 8, and 9. Such single-digit birth numbers are rare, but this doesn't make these individuals superior (or inferior) to those with three- or four-digit birth numbers; it simply makes them different in ways we can now explore. Below are some examples:

January 1 in the year 1000 resulted in a single-digit birth number of 3, which no longer appears. Beginning in 2000, the lowest possible single-digit birth number was 4.

1-1-2000 or 1-10-2000 = 4
1-1-2001 or 1-10-2001 = 5
1-1-2002 or 1-10-2002 = 6
1-1-2003 or 1-10-2003 = 7
1-1-2004 or 1-10-2004 = 8
1-1-2005 or 1-10-2005 = 9

While not comprised of a single digit, two other new birth numbers appeared after 2000: 10/1 and 11/2. (After 11/2, we see 12/3, 13/4, 14/5, and other three-digit birth numbers already included among the twentieth-century numbers.) You'll learn more about these new numbers in the following chapters.

If You Don't Know the Date of Your Birth

In order to pinpoint your birth number (and corresponding life path), I've mentioned the importance of having an accurate date of birth. For some of us, an accurate date of birth isn't available. Not having this information represents a challenge but also an opportunity, prompting you to study all the material carefully (or at least the material relevant to several likely dates of birth), striving for the insight to accurately determine your life path. Or you could use the book as an oracle and learn from every path, even as you home in, through self-reflection and intuition, to find your own path.

If You Were Born at or Near Midnight

It's rare to be born *exactly* at midnight; more likely, a person is born a few minutes (or even seconds) before or after the hour, but birth records may not always reflect this. Some identical (or fraternal) twins have different birth numbers, since one might have been born a few minutes before midnight, and the other just after.

If you were born around noon — between 11:00 AM and 2:00 PM — you're solidly within that day of birth, so your birth number is clear. But if you were born within a few minutes or even hours of midnight, you may feel a resonance with the birth number (or frequency) of the previous (or next) day, depending on whether you were born just before or just after midnight. If you wish to explore that secondary life path, check the Life-Purpose Calculator at peacefulwarrior.com for that secondary date to be sure (or carefully do the math, as instructed in the Appendix). Those born on 2-20-1982, for example, would be working the 24/6 life path. But if they were born the day earlier — on 2-19-1982 — they would be working the 32/5 life path. For those born just before midnight, the same principle would apply. These individuals would tend to have a resonance with the frequency (life path) of someone born the following day.

In contrast to astrology, your location at your time of birth isn't relevant. You don't need to compare or compute Greenwich Mean Time or work out the time zone. The time and day that count are what it says on your birth certificate. Period. Whether you're born when expected, whether you're premature or late, whether you're an induced or a C-section baby, it's all the same. When you as an infant took your first breath, wherever and whenever that may be, local time (whether standard time or daylight savings), marks your frequency (birth number) and life path.

No Birth Number Is Any Better or Worse

There are no inferior or superior frequencies (or life paths) for individuals or for relationships (see Part Five for material about how the Life-Purpose System applies to relationship dynamics between two individuals). There are only different issues that stand out. Each of us, and every relationship, has its potential strengths, vulnerabilities, and hurdles. Your life and relationships are shaped not merely by the numeric characteristics on your path, but by the way you (and your partner) express those qualities — in a more (or less) positive, constructive, evolved, mature manner.

If we live many lifetimes, then perhaps we eventually work through all the numbers, issues, and paths of life as the soul evolves. In a sense, we do something similar within one lifetime as we gain compassion for the paths and challenges of others. As Plato wrote, "Be kind, for everyone is fighting their own battles."

The Pitfalls of Labeling

When approached with respect and understanding, birth numbers can help us understand ourselves and others in the context of the full range of our experience and potential. In language, however, we often take shortcuts and tend to simplify or summarize complex issues and personalities in order to grasp them more easily. In so doing, we sometimes mistake the menu for the meal and summarize our personal identity with our birth number just as we do with our name. Just as we might say "I'm Alicia" or "I'm Roberto," we might also say "I'm a 27/9" or "I'm working 30/3," distilling our complex identity into a numeric label.

We need to avoid viewing our life or other people's lives through a single numerical filter. Birth numbers shed light on our key issues and potential; they don't describe our totality. Labels and categories serve us only as long as we remember their limits. José, Bettina, Hiroko, and Johann may all share the same birth number and life path, but other factors such as gender, culture, role models, genetic heritage, parenting and childhood history, body type, appearance, values, beliefs, and interests influence their common life path in different ways.

While I use numeric labels as a convenient shorthand, I want to acknowledge and emphasize, with complete and total respect, the unique character and qualities within each of us. All of us, even twins, meet with different lessons and life experiences, and develop unique filters through which we perceive the world.

We can probably agree that no two trees on the planet are precisely alike, and yet we can make accurate generalizations about how redwoods differ from pines or birches. In the same way, although each of us is unique — and our precise life story is unlike any other on the planet — those sharing the same life path share a common pattern, which we work out in our own way, experiencing at different times both the positive and negative sides. So the lives of two people working the same birth number may look entirely different, even opposite, if one person addresses the challenges in a more positive way, while the other responds in a less positive way. Moment to moment, the choices we make and actions we take remain a primary factor shaping our life.

MOUNTAINS TO CLIMB: THE LIFE PATHS

We meet ourselves time and again
in a thousand disguises on the paths of life.

— Carl Jung

The entire birth number indicates, in pure mathematical form, the particular blend of qualities comprising each individual's life path. This path doesn't just lead us forward; it leads us up the mountain we're here to climb. The final or right-hand digit (or digits) of our birth number indicates the summit of this mountain — our primary life purpose. (In the case of single-digit numbers, that one digit represents our life path, as well as the challenges along the way.) In order to reach this summit and experience the fulfillment of our personal destiny, we necessarily encounter the tendencies, drives, and hurdles represented by the digits on the left and bring them to maturity.

Viewing our life as a journey up a mountain path leads to an important discovery: *Our life purpose — what we're here to do — isn't what comes easiest.* This statement, which I repeat as an emphatic reminder throughout the book, suggests that although life need not involve unnecessary suffering, this world does present challenges and tests that allow us to learn and evolve. In particular, on the mountain path of personal evolution, as we work to fulfill our life purpose, we engage in a creative struggle with negative or undeveloped tendencies related to our life purpose. Climbing up a mountain path and rising to greater heights requires courage, commitment, and directed effort. If we've prepared well for our climb, our journey is less difficult than if we're unprepared; either way, it's still a climb.

We each begin down at the base, and as we ascend through childhood, adolescence, and adulthood, we encounter periods of preparation, initiation, and training, including challenges that allow us to recognize and improve our weaknesses and develop our strengths. Those of us who become disheartened or discouraged when life feels like an uphill climb have forgotten that the effort and challenge create fires that temper and strengthen our spirit.

The paths of life hold adventure and danger, pleasure and difficulty. Your path, or that of a friend or loved one, may seem clear and direct for a time, then turn sharply in a surprising direction. At certain points on our journey, the road forks and we make choices that influence the rest of our life; we may choose to push onward and upward, to coast downward, or to remain where we are. Each path has its own challenges, each challenge contains a lesson, and each lesson leads toward the summit of the mountain we were born to climb. The higher we climb, the better the view.

We may sometimes seem to lose our way, but ultimately we can't fall off the path — wherever we step, it appears beneath our feet. It may twist or curve, but eventually it leads us upward, because that's the clear call and direction of our evolutionary journey. Our birth number points to an internal path to the higher realms of human experience. But how we climb, and the time we take, are up to us. No path is better or worse than any other, except to the degree we make it so.

Supporting and guiding others who are facing the same or similar issues helps us progress on our own path. We know this subconsciously; thus, we often teach what we most need to learn.

When at last we reach the summit of our mountain, we make the wonderful and startling discovery that it's not the end of the journey. We're not just here to achieve our life purpose; we're here to transcend it. In other words, when we reach the top of our mountain, we keep on rising.

What the Numbers Mean

The Life-Purpose System, like any new way of seeing, takes a little time to learn, so we begin gradually, with a summary look at the life issues associated with each primary digit that makes up the birth numbers.

Qualities and Issues of Each Primary Number

1: Creativity through Security
2: Cooperation through Balance

3: Expression through Sensitivity

4: Stability through Process

5: Freedom through Discipline

6: Vision through Acceptance

7: Trust through Openness

8: Influence through Authority

9: Integrity through Wisdom

0: Inner Gifts

When I write about 1s, 2s, 3s, and so on, I'm referring to the individuals working that particular life path as their final, right-hand number (their primary life purpose), or as their only number (in the case of single-digit birth numbers). No matter what our birth number, to some degree we confront *all* of the issues associated with the primary digits 1 through 9, but the issues and challenges associated with our life-path number hold the most influence.

Those familiar with prior editions of *The Life You Were Born to Live* may notice that in the 25th Anniversary Edition the second key word to describe the 1 life path has changed from "Confidence" to "Security" and the two key words to describe the 8 life path have changed from "Abundance and Power" to "Influence *through* Authority." This change came about because, on reflection, these key words better expressed the core qualities of these two life paths.

In all previous editions of this book, two key words that best indicate the essential purpose(s), potential, and challenge associated with each digit of the birth number were connected by *and*, implying equal importance. In a sense, this remains true — but, significantly, a new and recent insight led me to replace the connector *and* with *through* in order to convey a different relationship of the two defining key words. In other words, the second defining term becomes a key quality that, when mature, enables the first and defining purpose to flourish. You'll find further clarification when I further define each of these digits of the birth number.

Degrees of Influence

Each digit of our birth number uncovers hidden meanings related to our life purpose. The qualities of the digits that make up our birth number *all* contribute to the texture of our life, similar to the way the individual colors of a painting contribute to its totality, or the instruments in an orchestra produce its sound. Certain colors may shine more brightly on our individual canvas; certain instruments may predominate in our symphony.

If each digit 1 through 9 were a different color, then each birth number would consist of a blend of different pigments, with less pigment for digits to the left of the slash mark and more pigment for digits to the right. (In the case of single-digit birth numbers, that one pigment covers the entire canvas.)

A 0 in the birth number, which indicates potential inner gifts, has no pigment, but serves as a color enhancer to amplify or intensify the energies of the other digits. We end up with forty-five different hues, or life paths, for all of those born in the twentieth and twenty-first centuries.

Within this system, the order or position of each digit in the birth number determines its degree of influence: Digits to the left of the slash mark generally have less influence, and digits to the right of the slash mark have more influence. And most people need to work through, or mature in, the issues and challenges represented by the left-most digits before manifesting the full potential represented by the right-most digits. For example, someone working birth number 24/6 needs to find ways to balance giving and receiving (2) and work a careful process (4) before they achieve a practical vision of possibilities (6).

Issues, Obstacles, and Opportunities

Our birth number points to issues and to potential. We have to resolve the issues before we can fulfill the potential. Since, as mentioned, our life purpose isn't what comes easiest, many 1s at first lack the sense of security to be creative; many 2s overcooperate and then withdraw; many 3s have inhibited expression due to self-doubt; many 4s lack stability due to ignoring process; many 5s lack freedom due to a lack of focus; many 6s feel criticized while judging others against perfectionist standards; many 7s don't trust themselves (or others) enough to open up; many 8s feel ambivalent toward abundance, which inhibits action; and many 9s don't yet foresee the consequences of unwise action or slips of integrity.

We all have universal access to talents; no primary number has a monopoly on particular qualities. For example, 1s don't have a monopoly on creativity, 3s don't have a monopoly on expressiveness, and 8s don't have a monopoly on influence or abundance. Because the digits of our birth number also point to obstacles, people who don't have a particular digit in their birth number may (due to fewer obstacles) demonstrate easier achievement in a given area than those actively working through issues related to their life purpose.

The numbers reflect inborn promise. With each birth number come deeply rooted psychological drives toward the fulfillment of that destiny; i.e. 1s *need* to be creative; 3s *need* to be expressive. Along with the intrinsic drives associated with your birth number come subconscious fears of success — fears of abusing what we're here to express. The dynamic tension between our drives and our fears creates the theater of our life.

When you're given a particular mountain to climb, you're also given the capacity to make the journey. Even if you begin down in the swamp, you'll eventually rise to the heavens. And once you discover your life path and dedicate yourself to the climb, you'll find the power to strive toward the summit. Armed with the hard-earned wisdom of experience, as you clear the hurdles on your path you can begin to fulfill your life purpose.

Overview of the Primary Numbers

As we continue our progressive introduction to the dynamics, issues, and meaning of each digit, bear in mind that the drives and abilities associated with any primary number may already be clearly evident, or they may remain hidden for the present. Factors such as family history, personal habits, and self-worth influence how and when these primal energies manifest in our life.

1: Creativity through Security

Energy, when unobstructed, flows naturally into creative endeavors. An abundance of such vitality gives 1s the ability to generate creative work in any endeavor; that same energy, like a surging river, demands movement and expression and can manifest as destructive addictions if blocked or not properly channeled. Security, for 1s, helps them to take creative risks.

2: Cooperation through Balance

The characteristics of 2s make these individuals a source of strength, support, and cooperative service. But first they have to define their limits, boundaries, and levels of responsibility, or they tend to overhelp and then withdraw. They need to avoid the extreme of servitude, which turns to resentment and resistance. Balance, for 2s, helps them establish cooperative relationships.

3: Expression through Sensitivity

The life purpose of 3s entails bringing emotional expression into the world, as they share emotions and ideas in a direct, positive, and honest manner. They need to find ways to apply their sensitivity and expressive abilities to uplift rather than tear down. The sensitivity of 3s eventually enables them to express themselves skillfully.

4: Stability through Process

As in building a house or anything else, 4s need a sound and stable foundation, followed by a patient, step-by-step process toward their goals. Balancing strength with flexibility and analysis with intuition, 4s can progress patiently toward their goal. By mastering process, 4s can establish a stable foundation for life.

5: Freedom through Discipline

The Renaissance individuals working 5 seek freedom through a wide range of direct or vicarious experiences. This sometimes leads them to take on too much. They're here to achieve depth of experience through discipline and focus. They tend to swing from extremes of dependence to independence until a healthy discipline leads to a sense of inner freedom.

6: Vision through Acceptance

The vision of beauty, purity, and high ideals of those working 6 can become tainted by judgments about self, others, and the world. Their purpose lies in recognizing the higher or transcendent perfection in everyone and everything, and aiming for high ideals while accepting themselves and others in the present. Once 6s accept life unfolding, their vision expands.

7: Trust through Openness

Those working 7 have an incisive mind that can read between the lines. They enjoy solitude and the natural world: earth, sea, flowers, wind, and sky.

They're here to trust the wisdom and love inside themselves — to trust Spirit working in them enough to come out of hiding and share themselves openly. Openness — sharing their desires and values — enables 7s to establish trust.

8: Influence through Authority

Most 8s strive for (but also resist) influence and authority, money and power, control and recognition. In this arena lie their greatest challenges and greatest satisfaction. They're here to apply influence and authority in service of a higher purpose, not as an end in themselves.

9: Integrity through Wisdom

The life purpose of 9s calls for the highest integrity — in fact demands that 9s align with higher principles so that they inspire others by their example. With natural depth and charisma, they're often placed in leadership positions, serving as examples of integrity, balance, and wisdom or as examples of the lack of these qualities. Thought they're at first clueless about reality and lost in concepts, 9s' hard-earned wisdom eventually enables them to become role models of integrity.

0: Inner Gifts

We all have access to inner resources — qualities such as sensitivity, strength, expressiveness, and spiritual discernment. But people with a 0 in their birth number — 10/1s, 19/10s, 28/10s, 37/10s, 46/10s, 20/2s, 30/3s, and 40/4s — have gifts or special potential. In such individuals, these inner gifts intensify the dynamics of the primary life purpose. For example, the 0 in 30/3 intensifies the 3 qualities of expression through sensitivity. Since what we're here to do doesn't come easily, those with 0 in their birth number may encounter challenges in these areas until their gifts mature. In another example, a 37/10 needs to establish trust and security before their intuitive gifts blossom.

ESSENTIAL POINTS OF
UNDERSTANDING

Each of us is meant to have a character all our own,
to be what no other can exactly be,
and do what no other can exactly do.

— William Ellery Channing

Now that we've explored the basic dynamics and qualities of the primary numbers 1 through 9, including 0, we turn to additional keys to deeper understanding. The dynamics and issues represented by each primary number can manifest in positive (constructive) or negative (destructive) forms. Therefore, the lives of two people working the same birth number may look radically different if one person is working the positive aspects of that life path and the other person is working the negative aspects.

For example, some 26/8s may be unable to cooperate with others (negative 2); may feel blocked, frustrated, and discouraged by perfectionist ideals (negative 6); and may experience poor financial health due to negative beliefs and subconscious fears about influence and abundance (negative 8). Other 26/8s may work smoothly with others (positive 2); appreciate and apply their high standards doing excellent work (positive 6); and come to achieve a degree of abundance and influence (positive 8).

The preceding example shows the two extremes; most of us work certain aspects of our birth number (frequency) in the positive but confront more negative issues with other aspects. These differences account, in part, for the wide variety in the lives of people working the same birth number.

As I've said before, no birth number or life purpose is inherently superior or inferior to any other. Each presents its own unique strengths and its own unique hurdles. The important question isn't which path we take, but how we travel — in other words, whether we work our life purpose in the positive or the negative.

The following chart summarizes the central issues linked to positive and negative expressions of each primary number.

Positive and Negative Aspects of Primary Numbers

Number	Life Purpose	In the Positive	In the Negative
1	Creativity through Security	Channels high energy and inspiration into creativity and service; feels secure with self.	Feels blocked, stuck, frustrated; feels inferior, ill, lethargic, insecure; may self-medicate.
2	Cooperation through Balance	Has clear sense of personal boundaries and limits; supports self and others in equal measure.	Feels overwhelmed; resistant and reactive; starts out overly helpful, then suddenly withdraws.
3	Expression through Sensitivity	Engages in heartfelt, uplifting expression; communicates with inspiration, sensitivity, and joy.	Feels depressed and disappointed; overly sensitive; complains and criticizes; filled with self-doubt.
4	Stability through Process	Prepares well and progresses step-by-step; patiently follows through; balances logic and emotion.	Wants it all now; skips steps; ambitious, impatient, confused; lacks stability or follow-through.
5	Freedom through Discipline	Uses multifaceted talents in a focused way; applies discipline to achieve independence.	Swings from extreme dependence to independence; scattered; tries to do too much; bluffs and pretends.

Number	Life Purpose	In the Positive	In the Negative
6	Vision through Acceptance	Sees the bigger picture; forgiving and patient; does excellent work without falling into perfectionism; accepts self and others.	Hypercritical; judges self and others against perfectionistic standards; lost in petty details.
7	Trust through Openness	Trusts innermost feelings; trusts others enough to open heart, take emotional risks, and share feelings.	Feels bitter, betrayed, paranoid; uses mind as shield; doesn't trust self or others; forms conspiracy theories.
8	Influence through Authority	Active and strategic; creates abundance and influence without concern or abuse; shares blessings generously and wisely.	Suspicious of, yet preoccupied with, issues of money, power, control, and authority; sabotages self.
9	Integrity through Wisdom	Lives in alignment with higher principles; leads by example; manifests depth, charisma, and wisdom.	Has lost sight of higher purpose; feels lonely and cut off; locked in the mind; out of touch with heart and intuitive guidance.
0	Inner Gifts	Uses gifts of sensitivity, strength, expressiveness, and intuition in service of others, for higher purpose.	Hypersensitive and nervous; stubborn; sarcastic, caustic expression; confused by dreams, emotions, or intuitions.

Although no particular number has a monopoly on challenges or potential, we can summarize typical or more common tendencies and qualities associated with each of the primary numbers. The tendencies can manifest for those with these digits anywhere in their birth number, but they manifest most powerfully for those individuals working the digit as a right-hand number or life purpose.

Evolving Energies

Each primary number has a range of qualities, ranging from negative tendencies (liabilities) to positive traits (strengths):

- Those working 1 can mature from insecurity and addiction to creativity and security.
- Those working 2 can mature from codependence and resentment to balance and diplomacy.
- Those working 3 can mature from depression and manipulation to expressiveness and intuition.
- Those working 4 can mature from instability and indecisiveness to reliability and organization.
- Those working 5 can mature from melodrama and dependency to astuteness and self-reliance.
- Those working 6 can mature from disappointment and criticism to expansive vision and acceptance.
- Those working 7 can mature from paranoia and isolation to insight and openness.
- Those working 8 can mature from self-deceit and opportunism to altruistic influence and inspiring authority.
- Those working 9 can mature from hypocrisy and fanaticism to integrity and wisdom.
- Those working 0 can mature from inner fears and hypersensitivity to attunement and service.

The Masks We Wear

What we feel on the inside — including subconscious drives, desires, and fears — doesn't always show on the surface. Most of us have developed a persona or social mask quite different from, and in fact often the polar opposite of, what we feel inside. Such masks lead to misunderstandings and make it difficult for people to connect with one another at an authentic level; these masks have a clear impact on our health, relationships, and work.

Each of the primary numbers reveals inherent qualities that color our life. But the masks we wear often appear very different from our internal reality.

Many 1s present a confident, calm, or even aloof appearance to mask an underlying insecurity. Their competitive nature stems from their fear of inferiority. They may act independent, but they may fear that they can't make it on their own and need someone to lean on.

Many 2s appear to others to be balanced and analytical, but inside they feel internal contradiction and mental conflicts that can create stress. They may appear rigid when they say no because they're counteracting internal pressures to acquiesce. They find fault with others because, like resonant 4s, they feel responsible inside.

Many 3s present a confident, upbeat persona that hides haunting feelings of self-doubt and depression. They can appear logical and intellectual to veil deep and sensitive emotions.

Many 4s appear to have everything figured out, but behind their cool, analytical exterior hides a whirling mind ready to make impulsive decisions based on their internal sense of confusion or disorientation.

Many 5s appear independent, but they often feel or become dependent or create dependencies. Those 5s who appear focused are often fighting a tendency to be scattered; their river of knowledge may run wide rather than deep, due to an internal thirst for many experiences and a fear of boredom.

Many 6s may project a pleasant public persona that's cool, smiling, nice, and considerate, doing the right thing even as they experience a thinly veiled tendency to judge self and others against sky-high standards. So anger and disappointment at the many faults and wrongs of the world lie just beneath the surface.

Many 7s appear very sure of themselves, making decisions impulsively and without consulting others, but their certainty is a reaction to an underlying lack of faith in themselves. Their social mask and quick mind help them hide while they guard their privacy and their inner world.

Many 8s appear passive while subtly seeking control. They often send mixed messages. They seem indifferent even as they overcompensate for frustrated ambition and an innate drive for authority, recognition, influence, and success.

Many 9s have a certain depth, magnetic charisma, and strong opinions that belie their unsure sense of identity and vulnerability to other people's opinions. Often put in leadership positions, they have trouble living in line with the higher principles they believe in or seek outside themselves.

The preceding paragraphs paint a general picture. They aren't meant to be accurate for everyone, but they point to the play of polar opposites in operation within and without, demonstrating that some of our deepest life issues and fears rarely show on the surface.

We need to recognize and confront our underlying issues if we're to transcend them. Our social masks may help us present our best face to others, but only when we accept the fallible, vulnerable being beneath the mask can we form honest bonds of understanding and come alive to our deeper needs, desires, and humanity.

As we grow into wholeness and authenticity, we can then reveal and integrate all of our qualities; we find out that our life is not positive *or* negative, but positive *and* negative. With this realization, earned through courage and insight, the qualities we bring into life become a matter of choice rather than of reaction.

Chronology of Issues

So far, we've learned that each digit of our birth number represents issues and potential and that the influence of each primary number depends on its relative position in the birth number, with the right-hand digit (or digits), having the greatest impact. A special section on the unique qualities of single-digit birth numbers follows.

We tend to encounter or work through these numbers in a kind of chronology from left to right, and from negative to positive. In childhood, our life usually centers more on the left-hand digits as we begin the hike up our mountain path, meeting challenges and opportunities along the way, making mistakes and learning as we go. The right-hand digits of our birth number represent the summit of the mountain, and the other digits to the left are smaller mountains we have to scale on the way to the highest peak. For example, 26/8s can't fully manifest abundance and recognition (8) in the positive until they achieve cooperation with self and others (2) and work through issues of perfectionism and self-worth (6). Likewise, 29/11s need to work through enough of the issues of 2 and 9 before they can fully tap into the creativity of the double 1.

Most children explore negative or less-developed aspects of their birth numbers before mastering the positive aspects. For example, as a child, Matthew, working 33/6 with its issues of expression and perfectionism, frequently complained (negative 3) and criticized (negative 6). As an adult, his expression tends more toward positive enthusiasm, and he's far more accepting of himself and others. It took time and experience for Matthew to transform his negative tendencies into positive ones.

In other words, we experience the positive aspects of our primary life purpose only to the extent that we've worked through the numbers and issues that come before, left to right. Whether this work takes days, years, or even a lifetime, it's what we're here to do.

An Inside Look at Single-Digit Birth Numbers

An exploration of the unique qualities of single-digit birth numbers is one of the significant additions to the 25th Anniversary Edition. And the key to understanding these new single-digit birth numbers (as well as new millennium digits of 10/1 and 11/2) lies not only in what they represent, but in what they *don't* represent.

To clarify, let's use the three-digit birth number 26/8 as an example. As I've emphasized, each digit in a birth number points to different strengths *and* challenges. Summarizing the basic elements for 26/8, we find 2, representing a need to balance giving and receiving; 6, representing high standards and vision; and, most important, 8, representing a desire to influence others along with challenges around abundance.

Let's now look at the primary numbers *not* associated with 26/8 — namely, 1, 3, 4, 5, 7, and 9 (and 0). What significance might these absent numbers have to someone working the 26/8 life path? Keep in mind that each digit represents both innate strengths and challenges. Our birth number indicates not just a drive and potential, but also hurdles and difficulties along the way. But we don't encounter special challenges represented by numbers *not* found in our birth number. For example, 26/8s have no 1 (centered around creativity) in their birth number. This doesn't mean that someone working 26/8 (or any other birth number without a 1) can't be creative. Rather, it means that if we don't have 1 in our birth number, we won't face the same challenges in the arena of creativity, such as insecurity and a need to prove ourselves. In other words, 26/8s (or those working any other birth number without a 1) don't have a *need* to climb the 1 path up the mountain in order to feel fulfilled. They can take the escalator up the mountain path or choose other directions, as they wish. But 1s don't have that take-it-or-leave-it option.

Similarly, although 26/8s don't have a 3 in their birth number, relating to expression, they may be quite self-expressive in the arts or other areas — and, like 3s, they may also encounter self-doubt at times, but not to anywhere near the degree of those with a 3 or double 3 in their birth number.

This brings us to the key to understanding single-digit birth numbers: People working single-digit birth numbers neither confront the rich complexities and drives of three- or four-digit numbers, nor do they face the challenges of the other numbers. It's as if everyone else is juggling multiple balls in the air, while those with single-digit birth numbers only have one ball to focus on.

All the energy and intensity — the gifts, qualities, tendencies, drives, strengths, and challenges, which expand to fill the life paths of those working three- and four-digit birth numbers — are compressed and consolidated into that one digit for those working single-digit 4, 5, 6, 7, 8, or 9. These individuals thus focus their life energy with a certain concentration. They're also likely to have fewer internal contradictions or complications, and fewer doubts or insecurities, than their three- or four-digit companions.

The unique aspects of single-digit birth numbers don't mean we need to project otherworldly abilities on the individuals working these birth numbers, or consider them the so-called indigo children idealized by some believers. All of us, no matter our birth number or life path, have a unique life but with shared patterns, as we climb our own mountain in our own way.

Understanding Master Numbers

Previous editions of this book have focused on the clearest, most reliable elements of numerology. In the interest of clarity, the Life-Purpose System hasn't specifically addressed until now the issue of so-called master numbers: 11/2, 22/4, 33/6, and 44/8 (to which I would now add 10/1, 20/2, 30/3, and 40/4). The reason I've chosen to address this notion of master numbers now is because insight into the unique qualities (and focus) of the single-digit birth numbers — and the freedom of those working such numbers from the complications of the *absent* digits — provides us with clues about *why* some birth numbers are referred to as master numbers.

Simply put, most birth numbers, which consist of three or four digits, reflect a complex array and interaction of issues represented by each of the digits. But the birth numbers 10/1, 20/2, 30/3, 40/4, 11/2, 22/4, 33/6, and 44/8 only have two *different* digits. And every one of these birth numbers contains the intensity represented by a double 1, 2, 3, or 4. And since they only have two different digits, they each have seven absent digits — or challenges and complications associated with those absent digits. (Birth numbers 10/1, 20/2, 30/3, and 40/4 each have eight absent digits, since the digit 0 is associated with spiritual gifts, not life-path issues.)

The summary point is that birth numbers with both a double digit and *only* two different digits have both an intensity and lack of complicating factors represented by seven (or eight) absent digits; these are sometimes referred to as master numbers for this reason. Less affected by the hurdles and complications of the three- or four-digit life paths, they may manifest a certain effectiveness, assertiveness, and accomplishment, depending on other environmental and experiential factors they meet along the path.

Since we have only recently begun exploring single-digit numbers, we don't yet have enough data for the relatively young individuals working the 4, 5, 6, 7, 8, or 9 life path to determine whether the single-digit alone might indicate a master number. Only time and further research will tell.

Life Gives Us What We Need to Learn

Many of us have noticed that life provides lessons about what we need to learn, and the lessons repeat themselves until we learn them. This phenomenon also applies to our life purpose. If life is a school, the digit(s) in our birth number indicate our major (and minor) areas of special study. To cite a few examples, some 1s who are here to learn about creative healing but who avoid this out of insecurity may end up dealing with physical issues that force them to explore a range of healing methods. If 5s lack discipline, some may have to deal with a physical ailment that forces them to find the discipline to achieve greater freedom and mobility. I've met 6s who had a variety of physical challenges or who were disabled as children, which forced them to reexamine their perfectionist tendencies and see the bigger picture. Some 8s and 9s may get more than their money's worth from a day in court as they learn about honesty (8) and integrity (9).

The more we see problems as potentially invaluable lessons or challenges that we may not want but might just need, the more we can face life's ups and downs with greater equanimity and even with gratitude.

Birth Numbers as Career Guides

We each have innate abilities, some of which haven't yet manifested; inside a bricklayer may lie a brilliant pianist; within the heart of a homemaker, a therapist may be waiting to emerge.

People working different birth numbers can be found in the same career, but they approach the work in different ways according to the tendencies and drives of their birth number. Using acting as an example, we might note that 1s, working in the positive, take a creative approach, while 3s may bring a special depth of emotional expression to their roles, and 6s may work diligently to bring a high standard to their craft (like 33/6s Meryl Streep and Robert De Niro); 7s may share their inner selves in the safety of their roles, while 8s may particularly enjoy the recognition and 9s may bask in the deeper meaning of the role.

Those with the same birth number can be found all over the career map, in every occupation or sport or art, as demonstrated by the Well-Known People sections for most of the birth numbers. For example, Kirk Douglas, Claude Debussy, Harry Houdini, Henry Kissinger, Booker T. Washington, Shirley Temple, Ramakrishna, Edgar Allan Poe, and Wolfgang Amadeus Mozart all have the same life path (29/11).

An interesting note for casting directors: 35/8 Gary Busey, in a knockout performance, portrayed Buddy Holly, another 35/8. Similarly, 32/5 Denzel Washington, in an uncanny performance, became an inspiring Malcolm X, another 32/5.

Although people working the same life path may cluster around certain kinds of fields, such as social service work for 2s and 4s or research and scholarship work for 7s and 9s, too many factors intervene to predict the work of any one person.

Most of us choose our occupations based on self-concept; socioeconomic background; desired income; education level; exposure; influence of other people, beliefs, and values; and other factors. Sometimes we compromise — sacrificing an activity we love for work that pays more or that gains approval.

Ultimately, what we choose to do for a living is best left to our deepest intuition and values as well as to our needs and circumstances. However, birth numbers highlight some inherent drives, issues, and talents that may predispose individuals toward certain kinds of work.

No single occupation is the sole or perfect work for a particular individual. We can grow and evolve through a variety of careers, and in large or small arenas. For example, 3s can bring out self-expression within a relationship, among friends or colleagues, or through acting, singing, politics, or teaching, to name a few possibilities; 8s can find recognition on a world, national, or local level, or even among a few friends or colleagues. Our responsibility is to allow our deepest drives and talents to find expression through whatever form of service or career we choose, in the most positive, altruistic way we can.

In any case, whether our career satisfies us and how we perform or succeed in a particular occupation depends less on the kind of work we do than on whether or not we overcome our hurdles, align our actions with the spiritual laws relevant to our life path, and express our frequencies in positive ways.

In Part Three, I list a few possible occupations for each life path to indicate general kinds of work well suited to the qualities and abilities of those working that birth number. This doesn't mean that the occupations fit every person following that life path. The career paths listed serve as illustrative examples and aren't intended to limit anyone's choices. They simply outline certain kinds of work that provide an archetypal means of expressing that set of characteristics. No matter what work we do, we express that occupation in our own unique way — a way that also reflects the issues we came here to work through.

If the Life-Purpose Information Doesn't Seem to Fit

As you begin to grasp the material related to each birth number and check it against your own experience, you may find that it explains and clarifies much about your life and the lives of others you know. For a relative few, all or some of the material may not seem to apply to your case or to someone you know. Since the Life-Purpose System outlines tendencies and drives associated with each life path, not every specific applies to every person in the same way. Perspective is key: Keep your vision on the overall pattern; in this way, you can derive the greatest benefit.

There's no need to accept this system on faith. Awareness may take time. In sending recordings of the life-purpose material to people all over the world in the late 1980s and early 1990s, I received a number of reports from people like Ken, who, upon hearing his tape, called it "total hogwash." A year later, however, after engaging in considerable insight work while seeing a psychotherapist, Ken happened to listen to his life-purpose tape again and reported to a friend, "I can't believe this — this recording covers everything I've been working on in therapy for the past six months!"

If the issues attributed to people you know don't seem to fit, consider asking them about it. For example, you may know people whose birth number indicates they have issues with insecurity but who appear confident to you. If you ask them if insecurity is a real issue in their life — if, despite appearances to the contrary, they experience insecurity inside — they may well confirm it. The birth numbers and the life-purpose material have more to do with our inner reality than with our outer appearance. Nevertheless, if the material doesn't seem to fit, a number of possibilities exist:

- The date of birth may not be accurate, especially if the birth was close to midnight.
- The lack of fit may be a matter of interpretation. For example, if I point to a tree and say, "That's a tree," we'll probably agree, but if I say, "That's a beautiful tree," you may have a different interpretation.
- The system may be describing a negative issue you've already worked through.
- The system may be describing a positive trait or quality you haven't yet manifested.
- You may have miscalculated your birth number if you did the math yourself.
- You may not yet have confronted a particular issue; it may not yet

have surfaced in your life if you're still working out earlier issues in the chronology of numbers — left to right.

- Sometimes we block, resist, or remain unaware of our deepest issues. If you feel any emotional charge regarding an issue, or strongly disagree about it applying to you, discuss the issue with close friends or relatives who know you well.

- You may be avoiding certain material you're not yet ready to see. I respect this protective mechanism and see no reason to push such information on anyone until they're ready to explore it.

- Finally, the material may not apply to you. No system is perfect.

The information presented in the Life-Purpose System can save us some time and some difficult lessons; it also reminds us that we have company on our journey — that we're not lone travelers. In any case, we're wise to keep our mind open to new insights and discoveries.

If the information doesn't seem to fit, another possibility is to ask yourself, "Even though this doesn't apply to me, if it did apply — if this really were my life path — how would this information affect my life?" Then put the material aside, let it simmer, and come back to it later; it may make more sense on a second or third reading.

Over time, we all discover old parts of ourselves we'd tucked away in childhood. By accepting and reintegrating the shadow sides of our psyche — those parts, motives, and qualities we had previously rejected — we release trapped energy and access new power and creativity. Tools of insight, such as those presented in this book, help us accept ourselves as we are, in our totality. Although we may discover a wealth of information about ourselves, our psyche may let in only a little at a time in order to better process it. This is a healthy mechanism that protects us from overload. You may find you discover something new each time you go through the material. Life situations, relationship difficulties, and challenges serve as mirrors that don't lie. In the reflection of our daily life, we come to know ourselves.

Fundamental and Fabricated Meanings

Ancient roots and modern interpretations have refined the meanings and implications of each of the digits from 1 through 9 (and 0) as presented in this book. Yet some people find or invent unintended and unreliable meanings that aren't part of the Life-Purpose System. We humans endlessly invent meaning without any basis in reality, for example, attributing meaning to the digits in a home address, to dates like 11-11 (November 11), to birth dates like 2-22-2002, or to the fact that two or more family members share the same birth number and life path. Such coincidences are fun to contemplate, but they go beyond the focus and scope of this system.

THE SEEDS OF DESTINY

If I were to begin life again,
I should want it just as it was;
only I would open my eyes a little more.

— Jules Renard

Keys to Part Two

ACCESS AND INSIGHT

Before we can forgive one another,
we have to understand one another.

— Emma Goldman

This section of the book is composed of ten chapters, the first nine of which are devoted to the primary numbers 1 through 9, with their related issues and energies, and a final section covering 0: Inner Gifts, for those with 0 in their birth number.

The primary numbers 1 through 9, along with 0 for inner gifts, all operate within each of us. However, the digits that make up our specific birth number have the deepest impact and influence on our life in terms of core drives, beliefs, fears, issues, talents, and potential.

Part Two prepares readers for all that follows by providing a clear sense of the foundational elements of each life path according to the Life-Purpose System. Once you understand the nine primary numbers plus 0, and have an accurate date of birth, you then hold a master key that unlocks the door to your life purpose and helps you understand and have compassion for the lives of others.

1: CREATIVITY THROUGH SECURITY

Creative energy, flowing in waves —
the nourishing sun, the flash of lightning.
Breathe it in; feel its force.
It can create, nourish, or destroy.
How do you channel creative energy in your life?
Is it blocked or flowing?
How does it manifest in positive ways?
How does it manifest in negative ways?
What would life be like if you
unleashed the creativity within you?

Individuals working 1 as their life purpose are here to bring positive creative energy into the world. However, because our life purpose offers special challenges, 1s have to overcome insecurity and associated tendencies to block, to withhold, or to discharge energy through addictive behaviors.

The creative energy of 1s can be channeled into any field: classical arts, such as music, theater, dance, writing, painting, sculpture, and other fine arts or crafts, or into healing, business, gardening, problem-solving, design, construction, sports, having and raising children, or any other form of innovation.

In order to manifest their creativity most fully, all those with 1 as their primary life purpose (10/1s, 19/10s, 28/10s, 37/10s, 46/10s, 29/11s, 38/11s, 47/11s, and, secondarily, 39/12s and 48/12s) and all those with a 1 in their birth number need to overcome an innate sense of insecurity to take risks and dare take the road less traveled.

The Essence of Creativity through Security

The entire universe is made of energy, manifesting in and flowing through all of the varied forms of creation. Even stones have energy stored within them. But only living creatures, from plants to human beings, have the mysterious spark of life energy that allows them to move, reproduce, respond, and grow. All humans have life energy, yet the life purpose of 1s points to issues and potential in the realm of creative energy. Whether we speak of life energy, sexual energy, or personal magnetism, the dynamic nature of energy demands expression and release. Individuals working 1 either learn to channel this dynamic force or may block it and feel repressed.

Creative energy is a double-edged sword: On the one hand, the powerful force of creative energy breaks new ground, driving past old barriers and old perspectives the way a surging river pushes obstacles out of its path. On the other hand, the river of energy has a compelling force that can't be stopped; it must be channeled for constructive use or it turns destructive.

Creativity flourishes best in an atmosphere of inner security, which enables individuals to open up, risk mistakes, and step off the beaten path — even dare to be considered odd, strange, or outlandish by conventional standards. Because 1s face obstacles in the area of security, developing this quality is key to the fruition of their life path. As Erich Fromm wrote, "The task we must set is not to feel secure, but to be able to tolerate insecurity."

Challenges on the Path

The creative energy at the core of someone working 1 needs to find expression. So 1s create in the positive, or they create in the negative, but in either case they create. These individuals benefit by applying responsibility and the power of choice in how they manifest this energy (see the Law of Choices).

Positive creativity, as already noted, manifests as originality and innovation. Negative creative energy may still display signs of originality, but it tends to create problems for self and others. Creative minds can develop new apps or other technological or aesthetic advances, or find solutions to business quandaries, or such minds can plan bank robberies to use a negative example.

People without 1 in their birth number may also be creative, but not to the same degree or potential as 1s, who experience an uphill climb toward creative expression (as I've noted before, our life path involves special challenges). Until 1s work through issues related to creativity and security, they may feel lethargic, ill, frustrated, or held back; they may just go through the motions.

Often, due to insecurity or the need for approval from others, 1s repress their creative energy until the pressure builds to the point where frustrated energy gets discharged indirectly, most often through addiction to, or abuse of, alcohol, tobacco, other drugs, food, or sex. Although anyone with blocked energy can have a problem with addiction, 1s are especially prone to this due to their amplified energy.

When creative energy is blocked, it can turn back upon itself to create inner turbulence in the form of psychological or physical symptoms. Because creative and sexual energy are so closely aligned, 1s often have sensitive, vulnerable reproductive areas, generally including the lower abdomen and lower back. Blocking or resisting the flow of creative energy can also affect elimination, resulting in physical as well as energetic constipation, lower back pain, and other symptoms. Recurring or chronic problems in these areas often indicate blocked creative energy.

Creativity and innovation require a willingness to be on the cutting edge; this means acting and even feeling original. Most 1s can develop a different way of looking at and experiencing life; they focus on what's unique. They may manifest this quality as early as infancy or as late as middle age.

Due to their sense of being different, 1s (and especially double 1s) can feel like outliers or oddballs, somehow inferior, resulting in a drive to prove themselves, thus making many endeavors more stressful than they need to be, since their sense of worth seems at stake. Some 1s show this insecurity openly, but most often they veil or hide it behind a self-assured persona; they may also demonstrate either an aversion to competition or an extremely strong competitive drive because they fear losing or looking foolish. The competitive drive of 1s can manifest as quick or cutting repartee to stay on top of conversations; 1s may sometimes seem to have a chip on their shoulder, which tends to block or diminish creative impulses, just as an insecure writer's self-criticism or fear of failing blocks the flow of writing.

Insecurity in 1s can also manifest as a concern about having enough money to meet basic needs or feeling unsure about standing on their own feet. Some 1s (such as 28/10s) may feel emotionally needy and look for someone to lean on, a partner to serve as their strength. This emotional neediness sometimes clashes with a deeply rooted independent streak; 1s often display a maverick quality — they aren't usually joiners who run with the herd.

When 1s align themselves with the Law of Action, acknowledging, confronting, and, despite their fears, moving past their innate sense of insecurity (which they may mistakenly attribute to a parent or a childhood experience), they discover, in the light of awareness, that their perceived or imagined lack of security represents a hurdle for them to overcome. Then 1s can come alive in a way they hadn't experienced before.

Other Qualities and Issues

We all have primitive, childlike subconscious tendencies and qualities, but these tendencies lie closer to the surface in the case of 1s, who may experience enthusiasm, vitality, drive, and inspired playfulness, but also suppressed guilt, anger, or petulance, more acutely than other people. People working 1 also tend to be emotionally defensive and hypersensitive or very pushy, but not usually in-between.

In order to open the doors to their innate talents, 1s need to appreciate the difference between *creativity* and *skill*. Creativity involves a new way of looking at life — an expression of originality; it's also a matter of generating the energy necessary to break through old barriers and explore new territory. Because of this capacity, 1s can generate astonishing and delightful creativity from the outset of any venture. Skill in any field, however, takes time and practice. The creative potential of many 1s gets nipped in the bud because they try something — whether a craft, cooking, drawing, or playing a musical instrument — and because it takes time and practice to nourish what talents they have, they give up prematurely.

When 1s continue practicing in the face of mistakes, difficulties, and setbacks on their path, their skills develop and improve over time, enabling their creativity to find its fullest expression. Whether their creativity takes the form of writing poetry or weaving place mats, creating fine art or making films, the process delights them, and, most likely, so do the results.

In the area of health and healing, most 1s gravitate toward dense foods that include concentrated protein and even fats. Excessive weight in the case of 1s may serve as psychic insulation, reflecting blocked creative energy, although other causes also contribute. When feeling repressed, frustrated, or insecure, 1s put on weight, especially when they don't exercise.

A number of years ago, Dottie, an extremely insecure and obese woman working 1, came to see me for a life-purpose consultation; I asked what she did for a living. She replied, "I'm an auditor for the Internal Revenue Service" — not necessarily an occupation that allows for abundant creative expression. Dottie and I discussed options, and I saw her eyes brighten when I suggested she might do very well in some form of healing work. About a year later, I happened to see Dottie again, now a hundred pounds lighter and beaming with newfound physical and psychological security. She was working as a massage therapist — a hands-on healer — applying her creative energy to make good money, doing what she enjoyed, while serving other people.

Even though a vegetarian diet has health benefits for many people, 1s tend to feel light-headed on a pure vegan diet consisting solely of fruits, vegetables, and grains. People working 1 need to experiment to find what dietary lifestyle works best for them but may notice that they need a more grounding diet.

Due to the strong but sensitive energy field of 1s, if they feel ill or out of balance, they seem to respond well to subtle, energetic forms of healing to complement, or sometimes replace, standard drugs and medicines. Of course, we're all wise to consult physicians or other health professionals for a diagnosis, but in terms of treatment, 1s may find modalities such as acupuncture or acupressure, dietary experimentation, hands-on healing, working with the subconscious through hypnosis or visualization, and other complementary means to be valuable adjuncts to standard medical treatment.

Most 1s have a close connection to the realm of nature, especially to the animal kingdom. Exercise in the outdoors can have a purifying, healing, nourishing effect for 1s. In fact, most 1s tend to need more exercise than the average person, as a means to relieve energetic congestion in the reproductive and eliminative organs and to avoid physical symptoms and addictive behaviors associated with blocked energy.

Most 1s have a high degree of sexual energy unless inhibited by guilt or insecurity, or because they channel their sexual energy into creative activities; some 1s may alternate between periods of higher activity and abstention or even celibacy.

Those working 1 as their life purpose naturally encounter periods of uncertainty or feelings of inadequacy as they travel their mountain path to full creative expression, but their kindhearted, trustworthy, compassionate natures, as well as their magnetism, power, and dignity, can help them make the journey and inspire others with the radiance of their life energy. But before 1s can inspire others with their creativity, they have to find the confidence to allow their energy to flow into the world.

At the Summit: Potential and Destiny

Individuals working 1 have within them potential that often lies untapped; creative ideas, projects, and energy flow like an underground stream, waiting to be discovered. As 1s establish a self-contained confidence, not based on the approval of others, they open the floodgates of energy within them; after that, there's no stopping the river of creativity and inspiration that surges forth.

When 1s feel secure within themselves and interested in their work, they need less sleep than most people; no matter what their physical stature, they have an unusually large energy field.

The summit of the mountain path for 1s is a joyful, passionate, confident expression of personal magnetism and productivity that borders on magic. In addition to high achievement in the classical fine arts, 1s can excel in any form of work that involves some form of healing or creativity in the broadest sense; whether decorating a house, telling a story, making a cake, or composing a symphony, confident 1s have unique perceptions and styles. They also have a sense of aliveness that attracts others; their attractiveness goes beyond the shape of the body or face.

At the highest levels, 1s become a pure, nonresistant channel, a clear conduit through which an unlimited amount of creativity flows into the world.

Action Checklist

If you're working 1, the following actions can make a difference in your life:

- Overcome insecurity by seeing it as a hurdle that challenges you to leap over it.
- Find positive ways to channel creative energy through your work or hobbies.

- Establish a daily exercise routine to liberate trapped energy and to help clear away other addictive behaviors.
- Find inspiration by creating ways to serve in the world.

Accessing Creativity through Security

1. Think of someone you know, or imagine a film, literary, or historical character — a role model who exhibits abundant creativity and security.
2. Imagine yourself as that person — secure in your abilities, confident enough to take risks, a dynamo of creativity. In what specific ways can you put these qualities into practice and bring more creativity into your life?

2: COOPERATION THROUGH BALANCE

Imagine two hands, one open and offering,
the other clenched in a fist of resistance.
Which hand do you put forward most?
Do you hold out both hands in equal measure?
Do you allow yourself to receive as much as you give?
Do you overhelp and then resent it?
Where does your responsibility end and that of others begin?
Have you found a balance in your life?

Individuals working 2 as their life purpose are here to clarify the limits of their responsibility and learn to work with others in a spirit of harmony, balance, and mutual support. Because our life purpose is an uphill climb, those working 2 as a primary life purpose (11/2s, 20/2s, 39/12s, and 48/12s) and all those with a 2 in their birth number face the challenge of balancing their compelling sense of responsibility to others with their own inner needs and limits.

Balance is a key issue in the life of 2s: balance between giving and receiving, between saying yes and saying no, between the value of thoughts and the value of feelings, between the needs of self and the needs of others. In order to achieve outer balance, especially in terms of cooperation, 2s first need to resolve their internal conflicts and contradictions.

Inner cooperation can pose special difficulties for 2s. It's as if they have two people inside them, sitting side by side in a rowboat in the middle of a lake. One of the people is rich, and the other is poor; one is a Republican, the other a Democrat; one is tall, the other short; one is male, the other female; one is heavy, the other thin; one is a puritan, the other a hedonist; one is a believer, the other a skeptic; and so on. Despite all of their apparent differences, these "two people in the boat" — the values, beliefs, opinions, ideas, and motivations so often in conflict — are going to have to learn to row together and cooperate if they want to reach the other shore. One simple way 2s can start creating an internal sense of balance and integration is by wearing bright, contrasting colors that are coordinated.

The Essence of Cooperation through Balance

Imagine for a moment what the world might look like if cooperation didn't exist: Isolated humans working alone, with all of their potential, would produce practically nothing; in fact, they probably wouldn't survive very long. Erecting even a single building requires a cooperative network of architects, engineers, builders, and secretaries — specialists in many fields. Human civilization is founded on people working together in relationship, cooperating toward common goals.

For 2s (like resonant 4s), true cooperation and support often involve doing less and allowing others to do more and thereby discover their own abilities, their own strength, and the boundaries of their responsibility in a given situation. For example, Hiroko somehow managed to raise three young children, work part-time, and also volunteer as combination secretary, vice president, and treasurer of her neighborhood association. She wrote the neighborhood bulletin, invited speakers, and cooked for and helped organize block parties. Whenever neighbors needed information or assistance, they would call Hiroko, who had a bad case of overcooperation — and people rarely complain about someone who gives to the point of exhaustion. One memorable weekend when two of her children were ill, it seemed that everyone in Hiroko's world needed help with something. She finally snapped, and she was forced to recognize her general state of imbalance. She told her older child he would have to help take care of the two younger ones for the next few days, something she wouldn't have dreamed of before; she called some neighbors and started to delegate responsibility; and she contacted all of the other people who had made requests of her, took a deep breath, and said no. To her surprise, the sky didn't fall; the Earth, and the neighborhood, went on spinning. Hiroko learned that in resigning as "general manager of the universe," she not only found her balance and retained her health, she also served others by empowering them to take their fair share of responsibility.

Challenges on the Path

The same qualities that make 2s such great potential assets to society can be their own undoing. Wanting so much to be helpful, they may chronically subordinate their own needs to the needs of others, going beyond loving sacrifice and healthy altruism into servitude. They ignore or discount their feelings and needs and end up doing what they or someone else thinks they "should" do.

Most 2s start out in overcooperation — codependent or enabling behavior patterns. If they continue in this manner, when 2s die they may see someone else's life pass before their eyes. Feeling responsible for other people's happiness and lives, having trouble saying no, overcommitting, ignoring their limits and boundaries, they take on more than they need to, and then may feel resentment for a situation they created themselves. Not all codependents are working 2, but where others are amateur enablers, 2s are professionals — if they haven't yet defined their boundaries and limits of responsibility. Guided by the Law of Responsibility, 2s can find a renewed sense of inner peace and of joy in mutual support.

As with resonant 4s, the word *should* is a significant force in the life of 2s, who, as I've noted, think in terms of what they "should" do, what others "should" do, and what situations "should" be like. Vulnerable to other people's needs and demands, 2s often feel confused about the right decision or action. They often ask, "What do you think I should do?"

Until 2s learn to act on the basis of what they truly feel, their service won't last long. If they don't feel good about what they're doing, cooperation will eventually turn to conflict as even the most accommodating 2s begin to feel overwhelmed and shift into undercooperation. In the early stages of working 2, these individuals swing from give-give-give to stubborn resistance. Resenting both themselves and those they helped, they may shut down; at this point, they want things their own way or else — with no compromise. In fact, some 2s who have overcooperated most of their life can later get stuck in a state of chronic resentment, sullenly doing what they think everyone else expects.

Friends or loved ones may wonder what happened to cause the sudden change in attitude and may perceive such 2s as stubborn, unfair, or self-centered. But behind their stubbornness lies a feeling of helplessness, a fear of being overwhelmed by others — a core belief that if they give an inch, others will take a mile. And because our beliefs influence our experience, others sometimes do take that proverbial mile.

Emma, a young woman working 2, used to make her college roommate's bed every morning, even after her roommate's boyfriend had stayed over. Often she would lie very still in her bed, trying to go to sleep, while six feet away her roommate and boyfriend were making love. Emma said nothing about this situation, except to offer to find someplace else to sleep, so as not to disturb the couple — a clear case of overcooperation. Eventually, Emma requested another room — a constructive solution — but Emma might have benefited more had she stated her feelings and her rights and put more responsibility on her roommate for working out her romantic situation without intruding on Emma's privacy. Emma hadn't established her boundaries, so people treated her as a doormat; in ignoring her own needs, she unknowingly encouraged others to do the same. The key for finding cooperative balance for 2s is learning the difference between support and servitude.

In relationships, partners may unintentionally take advantage of 2s by asking or expecting them to do more and more, until they react. After that, 2s may continue to make dinner or take out the trash, but they shut down emotionally.

In the sexual arena or in relationships in general, when 2s start out overcooperating — doing what someone else wants without considering their own needs or desires — one imbalance soon creates another. Where they started out giving and giving, 2s later withdraw, resist, or take a rigid stance. Sexually, this may manifest as frigidity or impotence, as if their subconscious is saying, "I'm not going to give anymore."

Until 2s establish healthy boundaries, they need to avoid situations of physical, emotional, or sexual abuse, and to remember that anyone of any age has the right to say no at any time when it comes to bodies and feelings. If something doesn't feel right to them, 2s need to honor their feelings and communicate that as strongly as necessary.

Other Qualities and Issues

The battle cry of 2s is "It's their fault!" Many people who live with 2s perceive them as judgmental, but what they're really saying is "It's not my fault!"

Assigning blame helps 2s relieve their own internal pressure, since 2s can feel responsible for everything from floods to earthquakes.

In order to succeed in resolving outer conflicts and achieving balanced cooperation, those working 2 first need to resolve internal discord. Due to their exaggerated sense of responsibility, most 2s overthink in the form of obsessive worry or overanalysis, then bounce from mental preoccupation to reactive emotions ("Oh my God! What are we going to do?").

Achieving mental and emotional equanimity poses a major challenge for 2s; when they weigh and sort opposing values to make a decision, they have trouble choosing one over another.

Most of us have potentially conflicting beliefs, values, and desires filed away in our mind — reasons to get out of bed and reasons to pull the covers back up; reasons to get married or have children and reasons to stay single or remain childless. The list is endless. For most of us, these apparent opposites somehow coexist, but for 2s, the opposing values are like two children who both want to ride in the front seat. Resolving these conflicts poses a challenge for 2s, who hate to disappoint anyone.

As they learn to take responsibility for their own life instead of feeling responsible for everyone else's, 2s stop blaming others for their own inner conflicts and begin to establish healthy limits. They find a balance between what's okay and what isn't — between what they'll gladly do and what they won't. They learn when to say yes and how to say no.

Emotional stress happens when the mind resists what is; when 2s resist changes, which tend to make them feel out of control, they may also feel mental conflict, emotional stress, and physical tension. Racing thoughts impose general muscular tension, which compromises the lymphatic system and the immune system. Although 2s don't often get ill due to their robust constitution, allergies can become a problem, especially in times of stress.

Those working 2, whether they have a wiry, muscular, or wide body, have intrinsic physical strength and sturdiness, as well as internal fortitude, vigor, and perseverance. But their strength can also manifest as stubbornness, rigidity, or tension. Because of this, 2s benefit from meditation practice, dance, hatha yoga, and martial arts, such as tai chi — all of which can help them relax, respond, and flow in life.

Anything we do, we can overdo or underdo, so 2s in particular need to develop a higher balance as they fulfill their life purpose. Balance, as outlined in the Law of Balance, is the essential catalyst that leads 2s toward the summit of their mountain.

At the Summit: Potential and Destiny

Those working 2 form the foundation, the very underpinnings, of every society. They often serve as the unsung heroes and heroines who make all the difference in the world; they ensure the success of great undertakings and achievements.

Because 2 is a very strong service number, people working 2 have the desire and drive to serve and help, to assist and support. When working in positive ways, they generally have a reputation as bighearted people. They tend toward loyalty and responsibility; they're the kind of people others can count on. When the going gets tough, make sure you have 2s in your corner; when you need someone to talk to, these individuals can be very good listeners.

With intrinsic inner and outer strength, 2s work hard to improve situations and support people. Once they find a clear goal, they cooperate for the common good. Many 2s have strong ambitions, and they can become leaders in any field, but they most often serve a larger cause in a support capacity, in cooperation with others. They find the most fulfillment when supporting others, because such a role is aligned with their life purpose. This supportive characteristic doesn't by any means relegate 2s to subordinate positions. The essential quality of 2 conveys an attitude about life, not a role in life; 2s can become, and have become, presidents of companies and nations.

At the highest levels, 2s transcend the concept of cooperating with others and see others as a part of their larger Self. This realization dissolves resentment, allows 2s to take complete responsibility for their life, and results in their having equal respect for self and others. They truly become a source of loving service in the world.

Action Checklist

If you're working 2, the following actions can make a difference in your life:

*   Understand the difference between support and servitude; learn when to say yes and how to say no.

- Learn to flow with change, relax into life, and stay flexible, letting go of what isn't your responsibility.
- Spend some time each day stretching, meditating, and relaxing.
- To determine a course of action, use your head but go with your gut.

Accessing Cooperation through Balance

1. Think of someone you know, or imagine a film, literary, or historical character — a role model who exhibits a clear, cooperative balance and who honors equally the needs of self and others.
2. Imagine yourself as that person — feeling inner harmony, responsible for yourself and supportive of others, cooperating toward mutual goals within clear and appropriate limits and boundaries. In what specific ways can you put these qualities into practice and bring more balance into your life?

3: EXPRESSION THROUGH SENSITIVITY

Imagine a rosebud with its petals closed
over a glowing heart,
filled with passionate feelings,
but not yet showing itself in its full beauty,
not until the blossom opens.
It remains closed by doubt.
How does self-doubt affect your life?
Do you express your feelings openly, or do you hide,
like the heart in the rosebud?

Individuals working 3 as their life purpose are here to utilize their emotional sensitivity to bring positive, heartfelt self-expression into the world. Because our life purpose entails challenges, 3s first need to confront issues of blocked or distorted expression, as well as emotional oversensitivity and associated self-doubt.

People with 3 as their primary life purpose (30/3s, 21/3s, and 12/3s) and all those with a 3 in their birth number come into this world with powerful expressive drives. Since our life purpose isn't what comes easiest, 3s also face distinct issues associated with their sensitive emotional nature, such as self-doubt, fear of expression, and a tendency to manipulate rather than state their feelings directly.

The expressive quality of 3s has a strong social component; 3s reach out to other people and depend on other people. Whether 3s express by speaking, painting, singing, sculpting, acting, writing, or any other means, they usually start out one-on-one; then, as their confidence in their ability grows, they discover the satisfaction of reaching out and expressing themselves to groups of people — family, friends, or the public at large.

The Essence of Expression through Sensitivity

Throughout history, people have used expression for both positive and negative ends — to uplift, instruct, and inspire as well as to belittle, demoralize, or even destroy. Expression takes many forms, from verbal language to body language, ranging from a look or a sigh to a full-blown sermon. Humans also express themselves through the languages of art and architecture, of music and mime, to name a few examples.

Although expression takes many forms, the most common one involves talking with other people. When 3s wish to express themselves, they need someone willing to listen. When they have listeners, they need to apply sensitivity to tailor their communication to the needs and interests of others while expressing their authentic feelings and needs.

In human society, we normally think of communication as a means of transferring information. This may be so, but *expression* has a different tone from *communication*; it involves not only sharing our own emotional reality but encouraging others to do the same. For anyone, but especially for 3s, the fulfillment of expression comes through the emotions. Therefore, emotional self-expression — sharing authentic feelings honestly and directly and encouraging others to do the same — is central to the life purpose of 3s. Expressing feelings offers its own reward and releases emotional energy that might otherwise become frustrated.

Whether expressing for the sake of self, others, or both, sensitivity and expression go hand in hand. People working 3 need to acknowledge and honor their own feelings and inspire others to do the same.

Challenges on the Path

Those 3s who haven't yet hit stride may find the idea of public speaking, or of expressing their sensitive emotions, distinctly uncomfortable or even frightening. The nature of our life purpose involves overcoming obstacles; because of this, 3s inevitably encounter difficulties expressing themselves. These difficulties range from speech impediments to chronic shyness, from struggling with English as a second language to speaking eloquently but without an emotional component, which remains repressed. Many 3s seem very quiet, as if gathering courage to speak, but when they finally start talking, those around them had better be good listeners.

Just as 1s create no matter what — whether in the positive or in the negative — 3s express in positive or negative ways; either way, their drive to express manifests. The Law of Choices applies strongly to 3s, because they always have a choice of expressing in positive, constructive ways or in destructive ways. In other words, they have a powerful ability to lift you up or to cut you down.

Positive expression often includes verbal enthusiasm and constructive, creative, inspiring speech or some other form of communication. Because such expression is their life purpose, 3s have a strong drive to express in quality or else in quantity (the motormouth pattern).

Early on their life path, 3s share a tendency to see (as well as express) the negative side of things. Negative forms of expression include whining, complaining, badmouthing, and criticizing. Such negative expression most often arises in childhood and adolescence for 3s. But over time, with further insight, 3s learn to ask themselves, "What positive aspect does this situation have?" — then they can express in more productive ways.

Because our life purpose isn't what comes easiest, 3s may not express much at all; they may clam up, feeling reluctant to speak due to self-doubt, or they may have difficulty being understood. Often they have concerns about, and sometimes problems with, getting the words right or finding the words to express what they mean or feel.

Once 3s get rolling, however, they have much to say and an abundance of energy to say it. Just as 1s have creative energy that can build up as pressure that must be released, 3s have a similar emotional pressure to express not just what they're thinking but what they're feeling — no small task, but a rewarding one.

Most 3s feed on emotions, and they can feed others as well. Just as 1s have a large physical energy field, 3s have a large emotional field — an extended emotional nervous system of energetic feelers reaching out into their environment, leaving them wide open and extremely vulnerable to other people's emotions, whether or not they show it. When someone nearby feels upset or exalted, 3s can feel this state as if it were coming from inside themselves. Similarly, when 3s are upset or inspired, anyone at all sensitive who happens to be nearby can feel their emotional power.

Virtually all 3s, due to their sensitivity, tend to become emotional sponges to other people's upsets or negativity. As a form of self-protection, many 3s present a controlled, logical persona, or mask. But their inner life reveals a deep well of emotions. No matter what their chosen career, when the expressive drive of 3s emerges, they have a passion for helping awaken other people's feelings.

Most 3s are hypersensitive to criticism, always ready to be misunderstood; all but the most gentle criticism leaves most 3s feeling as if they've been hit with a blunt instrument or stabbed in the heart. Learning to view criticism as a form of caring helps 3s move past hypersensitivity into a deeper understanding: Criticism always entails a degree of emotional risk on the part of the critic because the person criticized may become hurt or angry, or may criticize back. Whether or not our critics deliver their criticism in a gentle fashion, they show they care because if they didn't care at all, they wouldn't even bother. The recognition of this caring can help 3s tolerate criticism and see the grains of love within any form of feedback.

Because of the large and sensitive energy field of 3s, they commonly confront hidden or overwhelming self-doubt as another primary issue in their life. Whereas the insecurity of 1s relates to a fear of inferiority or inequality, the self-doubt of 3s deals more with not feeling up to a task. Just as 1s make the best addicts and 2s the best codependents, 3s make the best manic-depressives; due to their sensitivity, they can fall into slumps and experience acute self-doubt, or they may become manic, lack a way to express that energy, and then swing into depression and feel sorry for themselves. Teaching, writing (as in a journal), and physical exercise all allow 3s means for expressing their powerful emotions.

The public persona of Hillary Clinton during her presidential bid provided an example of someone who appeared extremely confident but whose self-doubt compelled her to stick with a safe, well-rehearsed script, rarely showing a vulnerability that might have increased her sense of authenticity, popularity, and likability. Whenever she let down her guard, her popularity seemed to rise correspondingly.

Those working 3 often flip-flop between confidence ("I can do anything!") and a sense of feeling overwhelmed ("How did I ever think I could handle this?"). Confident one day, they may take an emotional nosedive the next. Self-doubt — feeling unqualified, unprepared, or generally unable — manifests in a variety of forms. For example, some 3s become perennial students, eternally preparing, picking up advanced degrees, and changing course, but never venturing into the marketplace — never fully committing themselves for fear of failure. If 3s have problems in any area of life, they can look first to self-doubt and apply the exercise for overcoming insecurity outlined under the Law of Action.

Issues of expression combined with acute sensitivity result in an inherent tendency for 3s to misrepresent their feelings and needs to others and even to themselves; manipulation forms a major hurdle for 3s — either manipulating others or getting manipulated. Unless they've done specific work clearing this tendency, 3s have trouble saying directly what they want or need; they hint or connive instead. They may fall into depressive beliefs: "If they really cared, they'd know how I feel." They may manipulate others emotionally with a look or a sigh, and then wait for someone to make them feel better or give them what they need. They also sometimes get manipulated due to their emotional ties to others.

Those working 3 often hate emotionally needy people, because they're nearly always emotionally needy themselves, hungry for emotional support and nurturance. Only the most mature 3s also give back in kind and provide emotional support for others.

The Law of Honesty applies strongly to 3s and can help in clarifying and revealing the importance of direct and honest communication. As 3s come to recognize that not everyone is as sensitive as they are, they learn to appreciate the necessity of clearly expressing who they are, how they feel, and what they need. The Law of Honesty can help 3s turn their relationships and life around in dramatic ways.

In the positive, 3s find enjoyment and satisfaction in acting, teaching, and managing people, and they also abound in paths involving social service. If a cause or calling brings out their positive, nurturing feelings, they do well to follow it. Their sensitivity enables 3s to tune into other people's feelings when they're paying attention, and to engage in fine teaching and counseling work. In the highest sense, their acute intuition can open them to clairsentience — clear feelings to the point of extrasensory perceptions.

Other Qualities and Issues

A key for 3s is to cultivate empathy but avoid sympathy; the subtle difference between the two applies to us all, but especially to those working 3, because of their tendency to get drawn in by other people's emotions. When we sympathize with others who call to us from a dark hole, we end up jumping in with them and experiencing their distress. When we empathize with them, however, we remain centered in a clear space, and from there we can throw them a ladder. As sometimes happens, they may cry, "No, I don't want a ladder; I want you to jump down here with me!" From our compassionate, empathic space, we can respond, "I can serve better from here. I've done what I can, and I respect your decision to either climb out or sit in the darkness a while longer." Remembering the difference between sympathy and empathy, 3s can more effectively help others while helping themselves.

Due to their sensitive emotional nature, 3s may need to assert themselves and learn to express anger or aggressive energy constructively; otherwise, they may remain inhibited or frustrated in manifesting the full range of their powers. Martial arts, dance, or other focused athletic activities can help open this arena, and 3s generally find great joy in such expansiveness.

In contrast to 8s, who sometimes use sexuality for power, or 1s, who use sex to release pent-up energies, 3s can occasionally find themselves in promiscuous sexual situations where they get emotionally involved and later ask themselves, "What happened?" or "How did I let myself get into that?" Self-doubt can also affect their sexual expression, or they may repress sexual energy out of guilt or feel inadequate and inhibited until they come to appreciate the importance of balanced sexual expression.

Most 3s also benefit from and enjoy organizations that give them a chance to speak to a group of people. The Dale Carnegie training in public speaking or other similar courses can give 3s opportunities to develop their expressive skills and all-important confidence.

Physically, 3s tend toward sensitive stomachs; when under stress, they may experience more butterflies or diarrhea than those with a thicker-skinned emotional disposition.

Although most of us, including 3s, have practical challenges in the financial arena, individuals on this life path have no *inherent* financial difficulty; mainly, 3s just need confidence. When they get past self-doubt, abundance flows naturally, almost without effort.

At the Summit: Potential and Destiny

Sensitive expression, entailing carefully chosen words spoken from the heart, has the power to move people to tears or laughter — to inspire action that can change the world in ways large or small.

Every great culture has had leaders with the power of expression and the sensitivity to feel when and how to use their words to greatest effect. No warrior or world leader could stand long without the power of expression; the pen may indeed be mightier than the sword. According to the Judeo-Christian Bible, even before Light came the Word (sound or vibration).

Waiting at the summit of 3 is the power of expression combined with the compassion of sensitivity. Near the end of their journey, 3s open to the full emotions of their being; filled with passion and love and using the entire palette of emotional color, they reach out and embrace others within their large emotional field, reminding us of the essence of our humanity, the potential of our spirit, and the longing within each of us to wake up to our feeling dimension, for in so doing, we wake up to our full humanity.

The emotional connection 3s can feel to life and to others generates a rising energy that, once expressed, can uplift everyone around them. These individuals have the potential to revel in emotions the way dolphins swim in the sea. At the highest levels, 3s serve as an open channel of loving energy, moving others to joy and inspiration, becoming a force of light in the world.

Action Checklist

If you're working 3, the following actions can make a difference in your life:

- Form the practice of asking yourself, "What am I feeling and what do I need right now?" Express your feelings and needs directly.
- Take a course in public speaking or find another opportunity to explore self-expression, such as acting, art, or dance.
- Find a physical activity — such as a martial art, weight lifting, or aerobic dance — that helps you feel and express your assertive, expansive side.
- The next time you confront self-doubt, face it squarely and move through it.

Accessing Expression through Sensitivity

1. Think of someone you know, or imagine a film, literary, or historical character — a role model who expresses himself or herself clearly,

honestly, and powerfully, while staying attuned and sensitive to listeners.

2. Imagine yourself as that person — secure in your abilities and articulate enough to express yourself artfully and with sensitivity, sharing the full range of your feelings and fears, your joys and sorrows. In what specific ways can you put these qualities into practice and bring greater expression into your life?

4: STABILITY THROUGH PROCESS

Imagine a house under construction,
the foundation poured and set,
the structure and framework rising,
one step at a time.
How is this house like your life?
What does it reveal to you about reaching your goals?
Have you strengthened your foundation?
Do you build your life step-by-step?

Individuals working 4 as their life purpose are here to achieve stability and security by patiently following a gradual process toward selected goals. Achieving security — a solid foundation — is a desirable goal for anyone; for 4s, however, it forms the core of their life purpose. Since what we're here to do doesn't necessarily come easily, those with 4 as their primary life purpose (single-digit 4s, 40/4s, 22/4s, 31/4s, and 13/4s) and all those with 4 in their birth number confront significant issues in the areas of stability, commitment, patience, clarity, and willingness to follow a sometimes slow or arduous process to their goals.

Before 4s can establish stability in the world, they need to create a sense of inner stability — physically, emotionally, and mentally — as the first, essential step toward reaching their goals in the world. The saying "Proper preparation prevents poor performance" serves as a good reminder for 4s, whose preparation may include clearing unspoken issues with parents or other family members who served as their foundation early in life. Their preparation may also require them to commit to a relationship, commit to a present location, or commit to a line of work; in other words, to stay put, because a tree can't blossom until it grows deep roots. Putting down roots isn't the first inclination for those 4s who haven't yet begun integrating their life purpose.

The Essence of Stability through Process

If dynamic forces, such as creativity, cooperation, and expression, lack stability and direction, they serve no useful end. Individuals working 4 need to ground themselves in the world and progress in practical, incremental ways toward achievable goals.

Human civilization is a record of the history of achievement. Whether we pursue achievement in the form of material success, loving relationships, higher education, humanitarian service, or spiritual enlightenment, we need to start from a firm foundation and proceed step-by-step to our goals and to the fulfillment of our destiny.

Achievement flows from clear intent and focused effort over time. In order to achieve, we have to start where we are, find out what we need, have a plan, and follow it through, persisting through challenges until we reach our goal.

The image of a house under construction reveals virtually all the secrets that 4s need to know to reach their goals: In order to build a house, we first need to prepare and plan. We then have to dig deep and pour a strong foundation; only when this is complete can we begin to build. Then, no matter how ambitious or impatient we may feel, we must build in an orderly manner if the house is to remain standing.

Many 4s experience opposing tendencies to skip steps, on the one hand, or, at other times, to get obsessed with or stuck on a single step and lose momentum. To avoid such tunnel vision, 4s need to see each necessary step as part of a flowing, dynamic process. In other words, 4s need to complete each step before proceeding to the next — in other words, do it right or do it over. Or, as Henry David Thoreau wrote, "If you have built castles in the air, your work need not be lost. Now put foundations under them."

Once they have built strong foundations, 4s can build as high as they want. If they skip important steps, the house will fall down around them in the first earthquake or high wind. Even though people don't always appreciate the importance or beauty of a house foundation, a house can't stand for long without one.

Foundation energy reflects issues with family — either the family 4s came from or one they produce. A stable foundation also has to do with money, business, and financial security; it implies physical strength and vigor.

Challenges on the Path

Because 4s are here to develop stability and strength, they may experience difficult trials and experiences to test their stability. If they don't learn lessons quickly, the experiences repeat themselves in more dramatic forms. The most stable foundations are not only strong, they're flexible, like the earthquake-resistant buildings that sway but don't fall. Those 4s who lack physical flexibility often have psychological rigidity as well, manifesting as stubbornness in the form of self-deception or tunnel vision. They put blinders on, they listen to but don't really hear other people's feedback or advice, and they cling to blind beliefs that things will just work themselves out without their going through the steps to make sure. They end up feeling regretful, reevaluating who they are and seeking a new and larger identity consistent with their typically high ambitions.

Building secure foundations requires a careful process. But special challenges arise for most 4s, who have difficulties with process. They either resist it, rush it, or get so fixated on one step that they never take the next one. Those 4s who have practiced anything over time, such as a sport, a craft, or playing a musical instrument, have a kind of inner model; they know what it takes to succeed. Many 4s who were once good athletes later become successful in business or other fields because they learned to apply the same kind of process essential to achievement of any kind.

Doing things slowly and patiently in little steps over time can make many 4s feel a little crazy. They want it now, preferring bursts of energy, enthusiasm, and attention — getting something started and quickly getting it done. Built-in impatience sometimes leads 4s to prefer a magical approach to life. In contrast to the stability of their life path, some 4s can seem among the least grounded in reality.

My friend Miguel, who had written one draft of a screenplay, once told me, "I was flying to L.A. when I happened to sit next to a man who's the cousin of the head of a Hollywood studio! Isn't that incredible? He's going to tell his cousin about my script, which he said sounds terrific, and I gave him my card." In Miguel's mind, the screenplay was as good as sold. This kind of magical thinking — looking for a big score, such as winning the lottery, getting discovered, or getting lucky — is fairly common among 4s until they recognize the necessity of preparation, training, and a process of gaining experience (instead of gaming the system) to reach their goals.

Eventually 4s learn that skipping steps in the short run nearly always means failure in the long run — getting halfway or even all the way up the mountain, then tumbling down.

Most 4s drive hard to reach their goals, but if they don't achieve success as quickly as they want or had hoped for, they tend to become discouraged and say, "What's the use?" or "Forget the whole thing."

They may approach relationships in much the same fashion, with the enthusiasm and intensity of instant friendship or rapid intimacy ("It's as if we're long-lost friends!" "I must have known you in a past life!"), only to abandon the relationship when problems surface.

Such tendencies don't mean 4s are disloyal or fickle — actually, they can be immensely loyal and reliable when working in the positive — but until they align themselves with the Law of Process they aren't always good at persisting through difficulties, and they tend more toward enthusiastic, if temporary, efforts.

Most 4s need to ground their energy; otherwise, they tend to change jobs, change relationships, or change homes without giving themselves the chance to discover the real magic that happens when they commit to a direction in life. Once they understand the necessity of persevering through a sometimes long process, 4s focus their strength, and very few obstacles can stop them.

Related to the potential strength and persistence of 4s is an innate stubbornness of action and of thinking — a rigidity bordering on obsession. "Should" is a core idea for 4s; they have strong expectations about what they (and others) "should" do, and friction can result. Most 4s can benefit from a lyric by David Roth: "Don't should on me and I won't should on you."

Many people working 4 may wonder how or why they ended up with their particular parents; 4s frequently face charged family issues, either with one parent or both, or with a sibling, ranging from getting lost in a large family to moving all the time and lacking stability, from having a parent with a drinking or drug problem to feeling abandoned by a parent who died or left when they were young. They may have had a domineering parent who verbally abused them, or they may have been subjected to emotional, physical, or sexual abuse. Whatever the form, a difficult family history is common for many 4s, but not all. Some 4s face subtler family issues, which nevertheless have a large impact on their life.

The family 4s grow up in represents a stable foundation (or lack thereof). Working out family issues and rebuilding their foundation forms an integral part of the work 4s confront, and 4s who open deeper lines of communication with living parents reach new levels of maturity. While this principle also holds true for non-4s, familial challenges take center stage. By working through rather than avoiding family issues, 4s stand to benefit immensely. Reaching an understanding with parents may not result in agreement or approval, but they gain clarity as they take a stand about who they are — airing secrets and putting family life on a new footing. Even if one or both parents have died, going through a private inner ceremony with them — stating what they wish their parents had said or been like — enables 4s to acknowledge their feelings and reality.

Some 4s who don't believe they had a healthy upbringing can reinvent a happier childhood by becoming the parents they wish they'd had. In general, 4s make good parents, not because they always say or do the ideal thing, but because family is a priority for them. Even 4s whose marriage dissolves may want to maintain a close relationship with their children. Although raising children isn't necessary for everyone, most 4s find child-rearing satisfying on deep levels, whether they parent their own children or take responsibility for other children.

A stable foundation and careful process form the strength of any enterprise. And 4s, like 2s, are born with a predisposition to internal strength, vigor, and fortitude. This strength can also manifest in the negative as stubbornness and resistance, and many 4s find it difficult to let go of the past. Many 4s bowl people over with their bull-in-a-china-shop quality. They suffer from regret and tend to obsess on old relationships, mistakes, or failures, rather than seeing them as lessons and getting on with their life.

Any form of exercise that helps 4s breathe deeply and easily, relax, and let go — such as dance, yoga, or tai chi — makes a big difference by teaching them to embody the Law of Flexibility.

Physical and financial security are especially important for 4s. This doesn't mean they need a million dollars in the bank; as long as they know the rent or mortgage is covered and there's plenty of food on the table, 4s feel secure. Saving some money for a rainy day is another priority.

No matter what external foundations 4s may build, the trinity of body, mind, and emotions forms the most important internal foundation. When in balance, this trinity becomes the solid bedrock of their life. In the positive, 4s exemplify the kind of solidity that others can count on for support no matter what.

Once 4s get a taste of responsibility, even though it brings its burdens and obligations, they thrive on it, because it provides the stability they may avoid but ultimately need. Similar to 2s, 4s can take on so much responsibility that they get overwhelmed.

When working in the negative, 4s tend to be either overly responsible or overly irresponsible, sometimes wavering between the two. On the one hand, they can act like general managers of the universe and, like 2s, meddle beyond appropriate boundaries. Yet 4s can also have problems with the very commitment and constancy required to create secure foundations. Responsibility may take time to develop; it, too, involves a trial-and-error process. So 4s require the same patience from others that they need to develop in themselves. Similarly, although 4s are here to support others, they also need to feel supported — either emotionally, financially, or both. If they feel they lack support, they may go into a slump until they come to trust their own inevitable process of learning and growth.

Support may also take the form of clear expectations because, whether they're children or adults, 4s also need guidelines and limits, to know what is expected of them. If they don't know the rules, 4s tend to feel confused.

Nearly all 4s experience conflict rather than harmony between their mind and emotions. On the positive side, 4s have an extremely powerful analytical ability; on the negative side, they tend to overanalyze when making decisions. Confusion is a significant issue for 4s because they can get stuck in mental loops as they weigh every factor, look at every side of every issue, and bounce between pros and cons, then feel like they don't understand and have trouble making decisions.

The tendency of many 4s to swing from obsessive overanalysis to confusion often leads to impulsive action — impulsive relationships that start hot and end cold, impulsive spending, and other sudden decisions.

Many 4s tend to be reactive rather than responsive; they make champion hysterics. Even when they're able to maintain a controlled demeanor, inside they may be saying, "The sky is falling!" or "Oh my God, what am I going to do?" Some 4s waver between staying in control and a tendency toward nervous episodes or even breakdowns. Due to their sturdy dispositions, however, they usually recover quickly.

Sometimes 4s experience a sense of confusion that blocks their process because they overanalyze until they go into mental paralysis and can't see the right or best next step. It's important for 4s to realize they aren't really confused, they just tend to feel that way — a small but important distinction. When 4s have a decision to make, they do best to write the pros and cons down on paper, rather than letting the variables whirl around too long in their heads, and then go with their gut feelings. If they feel confused or discouraged about reaching a goal, they can break down big tasks into small steps — an action checklist. By making small commitments, 4s find it easier to follow through.

It's important for 4s to keep the perspective that although their progress may be slow, they can reach their goals by following a clear path. Once they stop overanalyzing, trust their gut feelings, and achieve a sense of clarity, they access their innate inner strength, which leads to commitment and persistence, and become a moving force in the world.

Other Qualities and Issues

In the positive, because of their refined ability to structure material and ideas and to break tasks down into their component parts, 4s can become exceptional decision makers or advisers in real estate or business. If mature, they make excellent, practical businesspeople as well as dynamite secretaries, assistants, counselors, or other support people. When in support positions, 4s (like 2s) aren't necessarily subordinate; Pope Paul I and President Grover Cleveland were both working 4, and each, in his own way, viewed himself supporting (and feeling responsible for) others.

If 4s skip steps, they make the same mistakes over and over, start and stop the same projects, and repeat failures. As Mark Twain reputedly once quipped, "Quitting smoking is easy; I've done it hundreds of times." The Law of Process can help 4s stop repeating undesirable habits from the past. The

Law of Patterns can also remind 4s that they will tend to repeat the same mistakes until they use their analytical abilities to notice the cause of patterns and do something different.

In the positive, 4s are reliable; in the negative, they can be undependable and uncommitted. Yet they do want to help in some way, and they can apply their strength and capacity to support others. Their need for support can surface in relationships in the form of "Don't leave me!" If 4s haven't learned to make commitments, they may be the ones to do the leaving.

Generally, 4s are vital and earthy in the sexual arena. But if they shift, like 2s, into a pattern of resistance, they can distance themselves emotionally, blaming their withdrawal on the other person or on circumstances.

In summary, 4s need to stabilize their life, focus on clear goals, and patiently follow a step-by-step process toward their destiny.

At the Summit: Potential and Destiny

Their innate ambition, strength, and fortitude help 4s reach their destination. However, as much as 4s want to become or look successful, if they fail to take all of the necessary steps to accomplish their goal, their success may be short-lived. Once 4s form a clear plan and commit to a process, they can achieve any goal.

Modest goals require few steps and a simple process; larger, more far-reaching goals require a long and sometimes arduous process. In either case, mature 4s have the capacity to analyze the path from where they are to where they want to be — to break it down into small, manageable steps and follow through to achieve their goals. Once 4s form clear goals and follow through, they're experts at helping others to do the same.

Those working 4 thrive in the business world as builders and founders of corporations or empires that support many other people, as dealers in real estate, and as producers of tangible goods and services.

At the highest levels, 4s let Spirit take responsibility and are content to manage their own life, doing their best, trusting the process, and recognizing that they're not in charge of the time frame of achievement. They base their life on the stable foundation of careful process and faith, from which flow clarity and patience.

Action Checklist

If you're working 4, the following actions can make a difference in your life:

- Break down big goals and commitments into small steps; divide and conquer.
- Balance your strength with physical and mental flexibility.
- Whatever you undertake, prepare well, commit, and follow through, step-by-step.
- When making decisions, trust your gut feelings.

Accessing Stability through Process

1. Think of someone you know, or imagine a film, literary, or historical character — a role model who has achieved stability and security by preparing well and following a process to reach a goal.

2. Imagine yourself as that person — stable, grounded, clear in your directions, taking things one step at a time, knowing it's only a matter of time before you achieve what you wish. In what specific ways can you put these qualities into practice and bring greater stability into your life?

5: FREEDOM THROUGH DISCIPLINE

Imagine a bird soaring high above, feeling one kind of freedom.
To experience life fully,
it must land and go through
the arduous task of building a nest.
Through this discipline comes another kind of freedom,
to experience the depths of its life.
How have you felt free,
and how have you felt trapped?
Can you apply the discipline in your life
to explore the depths and, in those depths,
to find another kind of freedom?

Individuals working 5 as a life purpose are here to manifest freedom through discipline, focus, and depth of experience. However, because the path to our life purpose can be steep and rocky, those with 5 as their primary life purpose (single-digit 5s, 32/5s, 23/5s, 41/5s, and 14/5s) and all those with a 5 in their birth number experience difficulties in the areas of both freedom and discipline; they swing between extremes of dependence and independence. And while they may apply temporary, even heroic, discipline at times, they can easily get bored with routine and stir up or manufacture drama to keep things exciting or larger than life. The quest for freedom and independence leads most 5s to seek a *breadth* of experience; yet they're also here for *depth* of experience.

Ultimately, an experience of inner freedom stands paramount for 5s. Without that internal sense of expansiveness, they feel like prisoners no matter what their circumstances, but with it, nothing can truly bind them. Such inner freedom manifests in the world as healthy self-reliance, not absolute independence.

The Essence of Freedom through Discipline

For 5s, freedom manifests as a thirst for a broad range of experience and adventure on physical, emotional, mental, social, sexual, financial, and spiritual levels. These individuals find experience out in the world or in vicarious adventure through books, films, television, or video games, or they may rely on their active imagination. The more mastery or at least experience 5s achieve in various arenas of life, the less they feel bound or controlled by other people or by their circumstances.

Most 5s feel empathy for the freedom fighters throughout history who have battled against tyranny, unlawful imprisonment, and servitude. In their own life, 5s feel degrees of freedom ranging from extreme restriction to nearly unlimited options.

From a transcendent view, freedom means liberation from the conventions of life — entry into spiritual dimensions of experience. In everyday life, issues of freedom for 5s color their relationships, work, and finances.

Discipline provides 5s with the focus, commitment, and inner strength to overcome limitations and achieve the freedom of optimal health and financial independence, providing them the ability to travel and avail themselves of the many experiences they seek.

Most 5s resonate to the characteristics of Mercury, the winged messenger. Quick minded, they want to reach out and touch many areas of life. They make good salespeople because they've gathered a wealth of knowledge as well as breadth, so they can look at things from different angles. They may answer questions and then wonder, "Where did that answer come from?"

Challenges on the Path

Freedom for some 5s can degrade to mere self-indulgence, the absence of external restrictions, or extreme independence. But the transcendent freedom they seek only comes by finding a focus and setting priorities, as an antidote to their tendency to be all over the map with varied interests. Such discipline leads to a sense of internal freedom, broad and deep experience, and the ability to make daily life an adventure, like the literary character Zorba the Greek.

"Don't tie me up; don't lock me down!" is the battle cry of 5s, as they take up the call of freedom fighters everywhere. It's as if they belong to a spiritual search-and-rescue mission. These 5s may hardly notice people who are getting along pretty well. But if someone needs rescuing or saving, 5s will answer the call. In this way, they may take on some of the codependent tendencies of 2s and 4s — not because they feel responsible, but because of the call to adventure.

Theirs is a dramatic calling, and if they don't encounter or create that sense of drama in daily life, they stir it up in their relationships or in their professional life. They fear being tied down by anyone or anything, and they may have trouble committing to a relationship, depending on whether they view it as liberating or restricting.

At one time or another, nearly all 5s encounter issues to work through in the area of freedom by involving themselves with someone who restricts, or who seems to restrict, their independence, provoking, in turn, their tendency to swing from extreme dependence to reactive independence. And just as 2s may habitually overgive and then resent the recipient of their service, and as 8s give away their power, 5s may end up resenting a partner who seems to restrict them, before they realize that they are the causal force behind this repeated pattern.

Sophia, an older woman, had created for herself a state of almost complete dependence on her husband, Georgio. Suppressing her inner urges for freedom and adventure, Sophia stayed home all day, waiting for Georgio to come home. She did the housework, watched soap operas for emotional adventure, and centered her life around making meals for her husband. Georgio even had to take Sophia to the market to shop, because she had never learned to drive. Sophia's dependence was so extreme that she came to resent Georgio for trapping her, and she felt she would leave him if she could.

More recently, however, I learned that Sophia had a liberating experience: She took up a new discipline; at sixty-five years of age, Sophia learned to drive. She did indeed leave her husband — to drive to the park, then do some shopping. She even went to a movie — quite an adventure, on a scale perfect for her. We're never too old to start living. Sophia was born at sixty-five years of age to a life of greater freedom.

At the other extreme of rigid independence, Kordell cuts his own hair even though he could easily afford a barber; he just doesn't want to become dependent. He also fixes his own car and repairs plumbing and electrical problems himself to avoid dependence on other people. He spends most of his time alone because he doesn't want to become dependent on a relationship. Kordell seems independent without a doubt, but this kind of independence is only one extreme, a kind of independence that stems from a fear of dependence — and fear is the real prison.

Freedom and responsibility go together, as do independence and discipline. Nobody really holds 5s back but themselves; they're volunteers, not victims. When 5s take responsibility for choosing that person or that situation in their life, they realize they have been free all along; they've been the director and writer of their own movie, not merely extras or bit players.

People working some of the other birth numbers focus mainly on one or two issues or goals in their lives. But 5s have a natural drive and curiosity to know something about almost everything, which is why their attention gets scattered. "So many possibilities, so little time" expresses a common sentiment of 5s. Multitalented, with an ability to pull inner resources and abilities out of a hat, 5s reflect a kind of Renaissance dynamic. The trickster, the jester, the juggler, and the jack-of-all-trades but master of none are common 5 archetypes.

As noted, some 5s may not engage in real-world experiences but find adventure in novels, television, movies, or online life-and-death video quests to the point where they live through these media. But once they've tasted adventure through direct experience rather than from the living-room couch, they want more, going from one adventure to another as time and finances allow, taking risks to escape boredom or getting involved with drugs for the experience.

Addiction to adventure doesn't fulfill the destiny of 5s any more than making a lot of money satisfies the life purpose of 8s. The goal isn't about exploiting or avoiding the issues of their life path, but instead transcending them. For 5s, this means finding that sense of inner freedom while living a simple, functional, disciplined life, tolerating a modicum of routine.

Until 5s find their true focus, they develop skills in many areas but rarely hit high gear in any one field. They skim across the surface of life, touching down briefly in many areas, without reaching the depths. Such 5s need to remember that when drilling for water, one hole a hundred feet deep works better than ten holes, each ten feet deep. And that by deeply knowing one thing, we can know many things. To master many fields, 5s need to go into one field so deeply that they break through into the space where all fields connect. When 5s stay with something past the point of boredom, they experience the freedom that waits in the depths of life.

Most 5s are versatile, vivacious, and quick thinking. As noted, they can make good salespeople. (That apocryphal person who could sell snow to Eskimos is probably a 5.)

Paradoxically, 5s either obsessively focus on one topic to the exclusion of other business that may need their attention, or they spread themselves too thin while juggling many interests because they don't want to miss out on any experience. Such 5s flirt with burnout, constantly perched on the edge of adrenal exhaustion. Learning to choose priorities — letting go of one thing so they can focus on another — can be lifesaving for some 5s. They need to learn that they can do anything, but they can't do everything (at least not at the same time).

While 4s meet with external tests in the world, the greatest challenges for 5s are internal. Those given to negative thought processes can feel imprisoned by their own fears and doubts. They find freedom by unlocking the shackles of their imagination. People in our world experience bondage in many ways; some are bound by chains of hunger or economic blight, others are politically repressed or limited by physical handicaps or circumstance, and still others may find themselves in real-world prisons. Yet even when limited by physical circumstances, we can experience a sense of internal freedom. Others, even in expansive physical circumstances, feel trapped by people or stifled by surroundings. Eventually, 5s need to learn and completely appreciate that human bondage is a state of mind, and that no one can bind the imagination.

Setting priorities can open the door to a more liberated existence of life. The Law of Discipline can make all the difference in the destiny of 5s. Jack LaLanne, a 32/5 fitness pioneer who performed prodigious feats of strength into his eighties, once remarked, "I hate to exercise, but I love the results," exemplifying what discipline can accomplish.

Many 5s develop discipline through physical training, while practicing cross-training within their set routine — engaging in different activities each day. Variety will better serve 5s than running six laps around the same track every day, putting their feet in the same prints they made the day before.

Other Qualities and Issues

Some less mature 5s unconsciously choose forms of limitation, ending up with injuries, or choosing smothering spouses or partners, or financial pressures — figurative or literal imprisonment. In such circumstances, their inner life and imagination remain their last strongholds of freedom, their own world to control.

It's only when 5s feel insecure or "too ordinary" that they identify with roles they consider larger or better than their perceived mundane selves. An archetype for the roles 5s play is the central character portrayed by Tony Curtis in the film *The Great Imposter*, the true story of a man who impersonated a prison warden and a priest, and who even performed an emergency appendectomy while impersonating a ship's surgeon.

These role-playing 5s can only hope that others won't pull back the curtain (as Dorothy did in the Emerald City of Oz) to discover an ordinary person instead of a great and powerful wizard. They develop chameleonlike qualities, with a life tending toward the intense and episodic, opening one chapter for a while, then closing it and moving on to other people, other lives, building bridges and then burning them, all the while seeking a larger family, connection, and home in their quest for greater freedom.

But when 5s bluff their way through life, they fall into their own traps; for example, they may play the role of a healer by putting on the clothing and taking on the airs without actually knowing much about healing. Such role-playing further undermines their confidence in their core identity, essential nature, and emotional reality.

Those 5s who have applied discipline in their life, having established a depth of experience, can master their role of surgeon, attorney, writer, martial arts instructor, engineer, or teacher while maintaining and valuing their authentic self beneath the role. They come to realize that the roles they play are only costumes they can don and then remove, like those worn by actors; they're the actors, not the characters they animate (or that animate them). They're truly the star of their own movie.

Most 5s are born with agile hands and nimble fingers that can sew, quickly learn to play musical instruments, work well with gadgets, and fiddle with and fix things. Quick-witted and quick learning, 5s try something once or twice and they seem to have it down. They get bored easily — so they need to remember that boredom means they're just starting to get it.

Many 5s pull off amazing accomplishments — winging it, flying through life by the seat of their pants, faking, living by their wits, keeping one step ahead of the creditors. In the long run, by applying the Law of Honesty, expressing what they want in an open way rather than finagling or jockeying for position, their life works out far better.

Financially, 5s aren't overly concerned with money in the bank; in fact, many 5s tend to spend money before they get it. If they have to choose between money in the bank or a real-life experience, they're going to go for the experience. They need to be careful about spending what they don't have, as that just adds pressure to a life that already tends to be dramatic enough. This drama can stress the sensitive nervous system and adrenals of 5s, who may also experience circulatory problems if they haven't achieved a degree of dietary discipline.

With their quick-minded, visual capacity, many 5s have refined intuitive, even clairvoyant, potential. *Clairvoyance* means "clear seeing," and 5s have a vivid visual imagination. While other people may get intuitive feelings or visceral hits, these 5s get pictures. When they start paying attention to these pictures and discovering their meaning, they develop a very good internal guidance system. For all 5s, life's message is "Ask (for a sign), and you will receive."

At the Summit: Potential and Destiny

Those working 5 represent the explorers and adventurers on a quest to true freedom. At the summit of their mountain, 5s have reconciled discipline and freedom, using one to achieve the other, delving into the depths of life by focusing on one activity at a time.

These quick-witted and vivacious individuals can inspire others to find their own freedom. These 5s also recognize that outer freedom is always relative, and usually limited, if we are to live within human society and interact with others, but inner freedom can't be compromised.

Individuals working 5 speak with an authority based upon depth of experience. They have demonstrated the discipline that leads to excellence, and they have balanced independence and freedom, even while fulfilling their responsibilities in daily life.

At the highest levels, 5s realize total and complete internal liberation;

they realize that they've always been free and that any dependence or restrictions they've experienced they also helped arrange for their highest good and learning.

Action Checklist

If you're working 5, the following actions can make a difference in your life:

- Develop some form of simple daily routine to establish discipline; be sure to mix variety within the routine.
- Don't let boredom stop you from going deeply into a subject or activity.
- Find a balance between the extremes of dependence and independence by observing when you slip into each side.
- Strive to be direct in stating what you want or need.

Accessing Freedom through Discipline

1. Think of someone you know, or imagine a film, literary, or historical character — a role model who has achieved a measure of freedom and depth of experience through consistent discipline over time.
2. Imagine yourself as that person — focused and feeling free even in the midst of duties and responsibilities. In what specific ways can you put these qualities into practice and bring greater discipline and freedom into your life?

6: VISION THROUGH ACCEPTANCE

Imagine the scales of justice and equality,
perfectly balanced,
representing fairness and high ideals.
Do ideals guide your life,
or do they rule it?
What is your vision?
How can you manifest it in practical ways?
Do you accept yourself and others,
or do you compare the world against the scales of perfectionism?
Do you appreciate the hidden beauty in your life?
Do you appreciate the perfection of imperfection?

Individuals working 6 as their life purpose are here to reconcile their high ideals with practical reality and to accept themselves, their world, and the present moment through an expanded vision of life's inherent perfection. Those with 6 as their primary life purpose (single-digit 6s, 15/6s, 24/6s, 42/6s, and 33/6s) and all those with a 6 in their birth number need to overcome their perfectionist tendencies by remembering the bigger picture and their true priorities rather than obsessing over petty details. Our life purpose represents a mountain to climb, and 6s have specific issues and challenges in the areas of idealism and perfectionism, including judgments about and disappointment with themselves and others.

Within 6s shine the highest archetypes, the utopian world vision toward which we're all evolving. These visionary individuals keep the flames of idealism alive and burning brightly, calling us to our best and beyond. Without the vision of 6s, we might be doomed to fatalism, nihilism, short-term outcomes, and tunnel vision. Their high ideals involve a cost, however, because they aren't always grounded in reality; looking to higher possibilities, 6s tend to lack perspective and patience. Because they measure themselves and others against such lofty standards, 6s set themselves and everyone else up for failure. Everyone falls short because no one ever satisfies perfectionists, least of all themselves. Therefore, the Law of Flexibility and the Law of Perfection remain foremost for 6s.

The Essence of Vision through Acceptance

As Plato saw it, our ideals come from essential archetypes within human consciousness, reflecting our highest vision and possibilities of justice, of relationship, and of spiritual advancement, which lead and inspire us onward and upward. It's hard to imagine what humanity would be like without such dreamers and visionaries who remind us of our potential, expressing possibilities essential to our evolution and perhaps our survival. They inspire us with hope and direction.

Those working 6, who inspire us with hope and possibility, include icons such as 33/6 H.G. Wells and 24/6s Isaac Asimov, Lewis Carroll (who took us through the looking glass into Wonderland), singer John Denver, inventor Thomas Edison (who brought his visions into the world), Ralph Waldo Emerson, Galileo, Friedrich Nietzsche, Jean-Jacques Rousseau, J. R. R. Tolkien, and even Michael Jackson and Charles Schulz — all of whom, in their own ways, provided doorways to a better world.

We all have vision and hope, for seeds of idealism are planted in each of us, but 6s experience these more acutely as well as feel the pangs of disappointment when these ideals aren't met. Before 6s can guide us and reveal the possibilities, they have to come down to earth and appreciate the perfection of here and now, accepting themselves and others in the present moment.

Acceptance forms the bridge into a more joyous life for 6s, because only by completely embracing everyone and everything as they are can 6s make practical and effective contributions in the world. If they stubbornly reject whatever falls short of their high visions, they grow sad or angry, disheartened by reality. But the moment 6s accept the inherent, transcendent perfection of life unfolding, they find the heart and patience to share their higher vision. They then allow themselves and others to evolve according to life's pace, not their own.

Challenges on the Path

Just as 2s and 5s tend to bounce from one extreme to another, 6s tend to see the world and other people as either perfect or flawed. When they first meet new people, 6s most often project their idealized image on them, surrounding them with a rosy halo of perfection: "He's such a terrific man." "She's absolutely perfect for me." Lacking discrimination or perspective due to such idealized views, 6s set themselves up for later disappointment. As time passes, their laser vision homes in on human flaws, and they feel disappointed. While 6s start out by seeing the beauty in themselves and others, they often fail to appreciate the imperfections they and others came here to work out.

Living with 6s can be difficult, because in their eyes, no one is ever quite perfect enough. Part of their life path drive is to improve themselves and others in their sphere of influence. So it's a personal-growth experience just being around them! The judgments and critiques of 6s can be projected outward, into seeing the flaws in other people and in the world — and there are always plenty of flaws to find — or they can direct their criticisms inward, never feeling good enough.

Many 6s live in a state of emotional denial, not knowing how they feel because they focus so hard mentally on what they "should" feel in some ideal sense, and then convince themselves that they actually feel that way. For this reason, 6s do well to take a good look at what they *really* feel and truly want. They may benefit from working with a therapist or counselor who can help them get back in touch with their real (rather than ideal) self.

Because 6s gravitate toward the ideal and are sensitive to any shortfall, they tend to sort for the lone flaw. Because of their incisive judgments, they can get lost in petty detail — for example, feeling despair over an otherwise brilliant musical piece they played with one tiny error. They do twenty things right and one thing wrong, then obsess about the one thing wrong. They see a good film but talk about that line of dialogue that didn't quite work. They go to a museum and remember the one painting that seemed substandard. They do well on an exam but suffer over the one question they missed. Two important words in their vocabulary: "If only." Perhaps they see a new house: "Wow, what a beautiful house. *If only* they had painted it a different color (or moved that tree, or put in a fountain)."

I had a friend named Roger who single-handedly organized a large convention. The logistics were incredibly complex: He had to arrange for speakers, security, catering, and promotion. Everything seemed to run smoothly. But when the convention ended, during cleanup, I heard him mutter, "Man, I really screwed up." Puzzled, I asked him what was wrong. "Well," he replied, "someone said he would have liked a pitcher of water at his table. Damn! *If only* I had remembered the water pitchers, it would have been perfect!"

Perfectionists always lose; that's their game. They see a glass (or pitcher) of water as half-empty instead of half-full. They judge others against their high standards, and then they judge themselves for judging others. They feel pressure to be the best, or else they avoid an activity because they hate to fall short. If, for example, 6s take up classical guitar and someone tells them, "Your fingers aren't as long as a master guitarist's," their response tends to be "Well, then, I'll stop playing, because if I can't be as good as Segovia, I don't want to do it."

Once 6s begin to apply the Law of Flexibility and the Law of Perfection, the burden of perfectionism lifts from their shoulders, and they learn that the only perfection is perfect flow and perfect fun.

Most 6s face internal pressure from their high standards, which they may project on others and then experience these expectations as coming from outside. As children, many 6s feel such pressure to do well in school that they sometimes develop asthma or asthmatic stress around the chest area, as if the world is pressing in on them. Other young 6s, never feeling good enough, and believing that their parents or teachers think poorly of them because they think poorly of themselves, tend to withdraw and give up ("I can't fail if I never really try").

Comparison is another big issue for 6s; they may start a new project with the grace and enthusiasm of a beginner, but then they start comparing themselves with others, most often to students who seem to be learning faster. Such 6s then collide with their own elevated expectations and become discouraged. These individuals might consider the Buddhist wisdom that comparison is a form of suffering (or dissatisfaction) — because there will always be people who are more (and less) skilled or talented or tall or attractive or intelligent. And comparing ourselves represents a profound disrespect for who we are, right now. As Sir Walter Raleigh once put it, "I cannot write a book commensurate with Shakespeare, but I can write a book by me."

The tendency to compare makes 6s acutely sensitive to being judged by others. When 6s stop comparing, that single change creates a quantum leap in the quality of their life. The Law of Intuition and liberation from the burden of comparison can bring more fun and ease to their life.

Many 6s appear detached or even cold, all the while they're trying to "do it right." But it's not the outward scenario that matters; it's the emotional content of the moment. Sexually, as in other areas of life, 6s tend to focus on doing the right thing and being a good performer, but they may miss the deeper levels of emotional vulnerability and enjoyment that come with accepting and experiencing the emotions that arise, relaxing and loosening up and even feeling comfortable looking foolish now and then. After all, nobody is perfect — or needs to be. And yet, in a higher sense, each of us is unfolding perfectly — a higher truth it takes 6s time and maturity to realize.

All 6s benefit greatly as they come to realize that it's who they are that matters, not how well they do or what they know. They could walk into a party, trip on the step, and fall on their face in front of everyone, then get up and knock over the drinks. But who cares? People like and care about them, not how well they do every little thing. Those working 6 have a certain purity radiating in their energy field due to their high ideals. They're here to let the light they carry shine through their actions, not to become preoccupied with them. To loosen 6s up, I sometimes suggest that they go on a date to an Italian restaurant and eat spaghetti with their hands instead of trying to say and do everything so perfectly.

As they mature, 6s gain new appreciation that while we are innately perfect in a transcendental sense, we're not yet perfected from a conventional view. So while we're all perfect as we are, we can become even more so.

Self-worth is a sensitive and usually problematic area for 6s. Deep down, the core directives of 6s involve being a good person and doing the right thing. There's nothing wrong with doing the right thing, except that other people are often ready to define *good* and *right* for 6s, and to manipulate or pressure them through the medium of their own high ideals.

Ironically, those of us with the highest vision and the highest standards sometimes hold back because we're always measuring ourselves against our ideals. People with low standards often feel that they measure up just fine. Those working 6 need to bring their standards at least down into the stratosphere; they benefit from considering the phrase "I may not be perfect, but I'm good enough for now, and so are other people, and so is the world."

Those working 6 who imagine themselves judged or criticized by other people need to realize that by their choices they invited these people into their life. They wear the costumes and play the roles that 6s may need to confront their own judgments about themselves. As 6s begin to release their own judgments, they find the world and other people a warmer, friendlier place as the coldness or harshness of others evaporates.

The key for 6s is to remind themselves that there's no perfection in this world; excellence is the best we can achieve, and it takes time and practice.

The Law of Process also applies to 6s, because, even though they're more willing than 4s to do things step-by-step, they tend to rush to completion. Feeling impatient, 6s like to get to the bottom line; they read books to get to the end or eat a meal to finish it. Like some golfers who love hitting the ball, they forget to appreciate the walk between swings.

Along with applying the Law of Flexibility, 6s benefit from aligning themselves with the Law of the Present Moment, which reminds us all that *only now exists*. The slow-motion martial art of tai chi serves 6s well in teaching patience and an enjoyment of the eternal present.

Since 6s tend to strive for ideals, they usually do very good work and find success in any field once they clear their self-worth issues and perfectionist tendencies.

Other Qualities and Issues

Money issues for 6s arise in two areas: First, 6s may wait forever to put their product on the market, until their work meets their impossibly high standards. If Babe Ruth, the home run (*and* strikeout) king of his era, had waited until he didn't make any mistakes, he never would have made it out of the dugout. Second, the self-worth issues of 6s may hold them back from placing sufficient value on their work and charging what it's worth. Once they get past these stumbling blocks, 6s move quickly forward and upward due to their high standards and excellent work.

Those working 6 do well to remember the idea of spiritual weight lifting; when life gets difficult or doesn't go as planned, these difficulties are the weights they can lift to strengthen their spirit and learn some perfect lessons. They can apply the Law of Perfection by asking, "How is this perfect?"

Many 6s get bogged down in a never-ending search for the perfect soul mate or work. But as they come to accept who they are, and where they are, and who they're with, and what they're doing right now, they experience the perfection of this passing moment.

The more 6s dwell on their own (and our own) innate perfection, the more they can grasp the beauty of the world even as they work to make the world a better place. When they're working in the positive, 6s can help others see their own beauty. And in the process, they discover a perfect light shining through the world of form.

At the Summit: Potential and Destiny

At the highest levels, 6s become practical visionaries, pointing the way to a more ideal world. They can do this most effectively after they have come to accept themselves, others, and the world in the present. This acceptance builds a bridge to future potentials as 6s release the judgments that follow ideals and perceive the perfect justice in the present moment, operating as universal wisdom and laws. When working in the positive, 6s can help all of us see our own perfection, pointing out how problems are actually opportunities in disguise.

As 6s come to apply more patience, realism, and flexibility in their life, guided and inspired by their visions of what can be but no longer using their visions as yardsticks against which to measure the world, they come to appreciate the bigger picture of life. No longer lost in petty details, they achieve more, have more fun, and worry less. They can finally feel less pressure and more enjoyment in everyday life.

Free of the never-ending self-improvement program generated by a feeling of not being enough, they continue to improve in a more relaxed way of learning. They experience more frequent moments of joy.

At the highest levels, 6s see divine perfection everywhere, even in the crowded streets of the city; they perceive that everything has a purpose and that the challenges and difficulties of life serve perfectly to spur us on toward realizing and manifesting who we are and who we're becoming.

Action Checklist

If you're working 6, the following actions can make a difference in your life:

- When confronting perfectionism, remember the words and the perspective "I am (this is) good enough."

- Remember that it's not what you do that counts; it's who you are.
- Learn to accept and make the best use of whatever happens, and accept your response, no matter what.
- Allow your vision of what you may become to inspire you and call you onward while you enjoy your life here and now.

Accessing Vision through Acceptance

1. Think of someone you know, or imagine a film, literary, or historical character — a role model who displays self-acceptance and acceptance of others and who holds a high vision while maintaining a good sense of perspective.

2. Imagine yourself as that person — feeling good about yourself, others, and the world, accepting the higher justice and perfection in everything as it is. In what specific ways can you put these qualities into practice and bring greater acceptance into your life?

7: TRUST THROUGH OPENNESS

Imagine seeing a dark cave
with a large and luminous flower
floating in the darkness,
shining with the light of inner wisdom.
The flower remains hidden, for it doesn't appreciate
its own beauty, and in revealing itself,
in opening to the light, it fears it may be destroyed.
In what ways might you be like that flower?
Do you invite others into your private spaces?
What if you trusted enough to come out of the cave,
to reveal your heart, your vulnerability,
your own inner light?

Individuals working 7 as their life purpose are here to trust their body, mind, emotions — their inner light, intuitive wisdom, and destiny — so they can open up and share their inner gifts with the world. What we're here to do doesn't usually come easily, however, so those with 7 as their primary life purpose (single-digit 7s, 16/7s, 25/7s, 34/7s, and 43/7s) and all those with a 7 in their birth number encounter issues in the arenas of trust and openness.

The energy of 7s flows inward. Even though they may find success in the world in numerous fields, their deepest drives and destiny involve inner processing rather than external achievement. Whereas 8s can center their life around their work in the world, for most 7s career is part of a larger, deeper search, whether or not they're fully aware of it. Many 7s have jobs so that they can earn the money to pursue other interests, including their sense of self-discovery.

Most 7s need a lot of private space or time; they tend toward independence and are sometimes described as loners. Even if they appear gregarious, they rarely share their private inner process due to fears of being shamed. Some 7s who lack boundaries share everything, then later feel suspicious (even paranoid), violated, betrayed, or misunderstood.

The Essence of Trust through Openness

For most of us, trust means a feeling of physical and psychological safety from shame or betrayal. For 7s, trust can at higher levels become a profound faith in themselves, in others, and in the universe — a faith stemming from a direct knowledge, not just belief, that a higher order of evolution is working in us and through us. This realization engenders a state of relaxation, ease, and openness. It replaces fear with a sense of communion, or mystical fulfillment like that of the Indian saint Ramakrishna, who could look at bird droppings on the street and experience ecstasy, because they reminded him of Spirit.

When 7s come to trust their feelings, thoughts, instincts, and intuitions — to trust Spirit working through them and everyone else — then even as they continue to evolve and stumble and learn over time, they open up to the point of becoming transparent to a spiritual sense of love, wisdom, and justice operating within themselves and everyone else. This doesn't mean that they naively allow themselves to be exploited by others; rather, it means that they let their light shine outward, instead of hoarding or protecting it. In this way, they become insightful guides for others.

Challenges on the Path

Trust for 7s begins with self-trust. But since our life purpose always involves special challenges, self-trust doesn't come easily for 7s. They may *think* they trust themselves, but that's part of the problem; they trust the thinking mind — stored information, theories, and ideas of other people — over their inner knower, or intuitive wisdom. True self-trust has to include physical, emotional, mental, and spiritual levels.

Even though some 7s can appear to trust *only* themselves, almost to the extreme, in the sense that they avoid or ignore the advice of others, they shut out others because they feel so vulnerable to other people's ideas due to their own limited faith in their inner resources.

Most 7s seek to gain knowledge through the minds of others — through books, seminars, teachers, and experts. They try one or another diet, experiment with nutritional supplements and systems of exercise, or with different forms of healing, and follow various teachers and spiritual practices — all the while looking for someone else's theory or method that will work for them. Such exploration and testing has its benefits, and eventually creates an experience base so that 7s can serve as resources for others. But 7s tend to fit themselves into other people's approaches to life rather than tailoring the ideas others have to fit their own needs and circumstances.

Most 7s do well to measure the experts, books, and methods against their own inner knower — their instincts and intuitive sense of what's right or best for them.

For 7s, physical trust involves the willingness to rely on their own body wisdom rather than on someone else's notions. They can learn self-trust through physical practice, such as dance, martial arts, or the study of music or acting. When 7s have a question about how much to exercise, or what foods to eat, or how to express their sexuality, they do best to consult their body rather than look for the nearest expert or guru. Even though experts know a great deal about their particular field, 7s need to remember that *they* are the experts on their own body and life.

Self-trust doesn't simply involve accessing the ideas of others stored in our mental filing cabinets, but rather in accessing cell-level (subconscious) knowledge until 7s discover that they can know more than they've read or have studied. It's fine to study the wisdom of experts, but 7s must find their own truths. Such trust remains a challenge for 7s because their mind gets in the way. For 7s, the intellect feels safer than swimming in emotions ("Here I am, and like it or not, what you see is what you get" isn't easy for these individuals). They tend to maintain a private life because they may not feel enough trust or safety to share what's really in their heart.

In order to open the way for their kind, helpful, insightful qualities to manifest fully, 7s have to clear away fears of betrayal by others and even by themselves. Because of these underlying fears, 7s tend to be very private individuals with mild paranoia, either spending most of their time in isolated work, where they can relax, or spending time with other people but feeling alone due to an invisible mental or verbal shield to protect themselves from being shamed by others.

Most 7s have an innate expectation of, and sensitivity to, being betrayed or misunderstood by others. Since our expectations influence our experience, many 7s interpret misunderstandings (in part because they didn't share what they really expected) as betrayals. They feel like Charlie Brown in the *Peanuts* comic strips: He's about to kick the football held by Lucy as she assures him, "Come on, kick it! I won't pull it out of the way!" But then she does just that. Like Charlie Brown, 7s tend to start out trusting totally, with an almost naive, blind faith; they set themselves up for misunderstandings, and someone ends up walking over their heart with combat boots.

Although many 7s may not immediately relate to this description, a part of them knows and understands. That understanding is a good beginning, a leverage point from which 7s can first examine their issues and then transcend them, arriving at a place of trust and relaxation they didn't know existed — opening themselves and their view of the world and even changing the course of their life.

The Law of Expectations helps 7s clear the often subliminal expectation that they will be betrayed, opening the way for new, positive expectations, based not on blind faith or naïveté but on clear communication and trust in self, in others, and in life. It often helps if they open up and share their doubts: "Excuse me, but my level of trust has slipped a few notches for some reason. Could we clarify what's going on?" They begin to discern the degree to which they can trust certain individuals; they establish clear boundaries of trust rather than naive assumptions.

Work, relationships, and other challenges serve an extremely valuable, deeper purpose for 7s as they confront the issue of trusting Spirit working through them and others. Even those who say they trust themselves completely might do well to take another look. Studying the Law of Faith can serve as a primary catalyst for 7s.

Those working with 7 issues gain self-trust through direct experience — through trial and error — using their work, relationships, and challenges as a bridge to deeper understanding, and using daily life to grow and evolve. At some point in that evolution, 7s access a kind of X-ray vision that links the known and the unknown.

Until that point, 7s fear the unknown, even in themselves, which can bring on a sense of anxiety, confusion, or frustration driven by inner forces they don't understand. This creates a nervous quality; many 7s find it hard to concentrate or stay in one place for very long. They often find it difficult to look into anyone's eyes for any length of time, because they're extremely self-conscious.

Those 7s inclined to spirituality and metaphysics may preoccupy themselves with the mysterious and hidden forces of nature while detaching themselves from the physical realities and responsibilities of everyday life. A few end up as spiritual tramps — vagabonds who put on a backpack and travel the world, never quite touching down, perhaps following one or another teacher, or joining an ashram. They can get lost in the ethers and in realms that promise a connection to heaven, but they may need grounded practices to connect them to planet Earth. The natural world of parks and beaches, of rivers, lakes, and mountains, provides a needed respite and healing for 7s, who can resonate deeply with the spirits of nature.

Other 7s function very well in everyday life but remain in a world of their own and appear distant, disconnected, or emotionally unavailable. Because 7s have such strong issues with trust, others may not perceive them as trustworthy.

Those 7s who contact their own depth also discover the depths of the world. They become mystics who can also remain in the world but not of the world, focusing their astute mind in constructive areas. Such self-actualized mystics express the higher calling of 7. Although difficult for the average person to understand, such 7s offer valuable insights and knowledge of life's mysteries. Their path is built on faith and trust that include but may sometimes go beyond reason or logic.

The less they rely solely on mental processes, the more 7s know. When their mind is disciplined, it pierces the depths of life to find the interconnected threads in the fabric of existence and becomes an important tool to interpret mysticism to the world. Those 7s who spend time meditating in caves or forests, in deserts, on mountains, or by the sea, may feel they're taking a kind of refresher course, accessing and reconnecting with the power and light working through them.

In the arena of relationships, most 7s need and want a partner for companionship and to help them feel a sense of completion, harmony, and balance in their life. But that very companionship means a demand for intimacy, for opening up, and for trusting. Whenever they commit to a caring, interdependent relationship, the possibility of betrayal exists. Therefore, most 7s have mixed feelings about intimate relationships. They long for companionship, but they can at times be cold or distant, with a strong need for their own space where they feel safe. Relationships thus become an arena of negotiation as 7s maintain rigid boundaries until they find a loving, trusting relationship with themselves and with the spirit inside them. As 7s learn to trust their own self-contained wholeness, they can share that wholeness with another, instead of looking for completion through another.

When an active passion calls to them, such as hiking, skiing, ballroom dancing, or a sport or martial art, they can do quite well, as exemplified by accomplished 25/7s like Muhammad Ali and Bruce Lee. Continuing training in a martial art, sport, or musical instrument, for example, provides an avenue for 7s to develop deeper levels of self-trust — not only in ideas or philosophy, but in trusting their training, their instincts, and the process of improvement and evolving skill.

The experience of trust, openness, and communion that lies at the heart of life purpose for 7s has little to do with sectarian religious rituals. Rather, this sense of communion results from a personal, internal faith leading to a direct union with the sense of love and trust we might identify as Spirit. In the natural world, 7s open to more expanded levels of awareness and experience, where the eagle, the brook, and the wind all speak to them. Their deepest longing is to be held in the embrace of the universe. As 7s come to feel that spiritual presence, they can hear that whispered voice within them that says, "I'm ready to find my way home."

Other Qualities and Issues

Nearly all 7s have a sharp mind that can read between the lines of life. They have the potential to be world-class thinkers, writers, mystics, or researchers. Many are inclined to research and scholarship, philosophy, mathematics, physics, religion, metaphysics, or psychology, to learn how they work, how others work, and how life works. They seek deeper lessons not revealed to the casual eye. Those 7s who have contacted their inner knower find out, often to their surprise, that they understand far more than they had once believed. They know things without knowing how they know them, and they have a wealth of internal resources waiting to be tapped.

Many 7s, on the other hand, want nothing to do with metaphysics; they may reject, ignore, or make fun of spiritual ideas. Many 7s work as bank presidents, carpenters, printers, teachers — people in the world who don't look or act at all like metaphysical types. Nevertheless, one way or the other, they eventually are called upon to dig deeper into their life; this drive emerges through circumstances that force deeper self-examination and lead eventually to self-trust.

Most 7s need regular time alone. Even if they appear gregarious, they maintain a fortresslike inner privacy. They have strong inclinations toward solitary activities, such as writing, research, or the arts. Even when in the public eye, such as in acting — for example, in the case of 25/7 Marilyn Monroe — they protect that private space within. Many 7s are excellent dancers, singers, musicians, or even businesspeople, but whatever they do for a living they find the most fulfillment when their work feels connected to a higher good.

Children usually like 7s, and the affection is mutual, because 7s have a childlike heart that is in touch with Spirit at the deepest levels. An important practice for 7s is to appreciate the part of spirit inside them and to feel connected to a larger sense of Spirit in their life.

At the Summit: Potential and Destiny

At the summit, when 7s have ceased looking for evidence of betrayal, they see the deeper wisdom and order emanating from everyone and every circumstance. What they might previously have experienced as deceit or betrayal, they now see as a valuable lesson. They feel a sense of gratitude even while confronting the difficulties of life. Any misunderstandings become lessons about the need for 7s to open up and share what they really feel — to communicate, to work things out, to confront, and to learn. In some cases, where the bridge of understanding has collapsed, the lesson may be to end one relationship and open the space for another.

Near the summit of their own mountain, 7s see wisdom and beauty everywhere — not just in the splendor of the natural world, or in holy places, but in the littered streets of the city, among friends and adversaries alike.

At that point, the relationships, work, experiences, and challenges of 7s all become grist for the mill of wisdom, as 7s learn, stumble, and fall, rise again, confront themselves, and find their way back to the Source. Whether or not they relate to spiritual terminology, they open to a profound trust that evolves into faith in themselves and in life, and may feel more fulfilled than they might ever have imagined.

Action Checklist

If you're working 7, the following actions can make a difference in your life:

- When you have questions, ask yourself, "What if I knew?" See what answers come.
- Do your best to share what's really in your heart, not just your mind, and form clear agreements with others.
- Honor your need for privacy, but take small risks in sharing your feelings openly.
- Trust your own instinct and intuition; you're the expert on your body and your life.

Accessing Trust through Openness

1. Think of someone you know, or imagine a film, literary, or historical character — a role model who expresses the ability to feel trusting and relaxed with other people, who reveals deep thoughts and feelings without concern or fear, and who trusts intuitive knowledge.
2. Imagine yourself as that person — feeling safe with and connected to other people, relaxed, and open. In what specific ways can you put these qualities into practice and bring greater trust and openness to your life?

8: INFLUENCE THROUGH AUTHORITY

Picture a scepter of authority and abundance,
a horn of plenty filled with colorful fruit and precious stones,
shining with a powerful light,
radiating blessings for all those
who take action and make the journey.
How do you feel about such empowerment and abundance?
How might you gain recognition in the world?
Might that influence and abundance already exist within you?

Individuals working 8 as their life purpose are here to own their authority and use their influence to create abundance through action, eventually gaining recognition and using influence and authority in service of a higher purpose. However, since our life purpose offers inherent challenges, those with 8 as their primary life purpose (single-digit 8s, 17/8s, 26/8s, 35/8s, and 44/8s) and all those with an 8 in their birth number have to work through issues related to authority, power, influence, money, and control. All 8s must reconcile their inner drives with their opposing reluctance toward (and fears about) achieving material success.

For some 8s, issues with money predominate; other 8s confront issues of authority, power, or control. All of these areas need to be examined, balanced, and cleared as 8s journey up the mountain path. People working 8 need to experience *inner* abundance, power, and respect before they can effectively manifest these qualities in the world.

Those working 8 as a life path can experience all of the qualities related to worldly success and influence in large or small ways. Whether 8s have an influence worldwide, nationally, locally, or among their family and friends doesn't matter, because our destinies can find fulfilling expression in small arenas as well as large.

Eventually, 8s can transcend their fears and mixed feelings about money, influence, and authority by dedicating these qualities to a higher purpose, with generosity, wisdom, and compassion. People working 8 range from wealthy and powerful celebrities to poor and nameless hermits.

Fulfillment of their life purpose isn't proportional to how much wealth or authority 8s achieve, but most 8s need to enter the arena and face their challenges before they can transcend them.

The Essence of Influence through Authority

Many kinds of success, such as reaching a goal, helping other people, or finding inner peace, may not involve money at all. But work and material success are central to the destiny of 8s. Thus, money issues inevitably arise for 8s in one form or another, but money is only one way of keeping score; it's a form of energy — a kind of mercury in the thermometer of their lives.

Those working 8 aren't just here for money, however; they're here to influence others in positive ways, and to grow into their own sense of personal power, which expresses itself in a broad range of possibilities. Abundance and influence flow from an attitude and expansive sense associated more with an inner state than with worldly achievement. People of modest means may count their blessings in life and feel a sense of abundance. In contrast, some millionaires may have money stress and debt because of overextending themselves and may not experience anything like abundance.

Empowerment, which also manifests as control or authority, works in much the same way as money, and in our culture, money and power are often linked. Influence can manifest in negative ways, such as trying to overpower or control other people, or it can become inner power and self-control. As stated before, 8s experience abundance, power, influence, and respect in the world only to the degree that they feel these qualities inside.

Challenges on the Path

Some 8s who value inner work and spiritual practices may feel disappointed to learn that their life path and purpose involve something as worldly as money, power, influence, or recognition. These 8s need to understand that we can achieve and apply material success in positive, even spiritual ways. We can make good money, doing what we find meaningful, while serving other people. As a 26/8, I've been blessed to earn a good living serving others by writing books and teaching seminars that involve spiritual (or big-picture) themes. Money and spirit can support each other; they don't have to represent polar opposites. But it takes a while for idealistic 26/8s to realize this!

Most 8s experience strong drives for money, power, and recognition, along with an equally strong suspicion of those very things. This attraction-avoidance dynamic may be subconscious or fully conscious; in either case, the contradictions and concerns create issues central to their life path.

Many 8s consciously want to earn more money, gain recognition, or exercise more influence over their circumstances or environment, but these goals remain elusive due to inner reluctance to take decisive action. This may be true for any life path, but both the drive and suspicion are more acute for 8s. As boxer Joe Lewis once said, "I don't really like money, but it quiets my nerves."

Because I work the 26/8 path, I want to share an incident that revealed one of my own negative beliefs about wealth and helped me make an important shift. At the time, I was working two jobs as a typist, struggling unsuccessfully to support my family, and going deeper into debt. While downtown, I noticed two well-dressed young women get into a Mercedes convertible. A dark cloud passed through my psyche as I stared with animosity at these "little rich girls." Suddenly, as if I'd been slapped, I was struck by a realization: I'd never met these young women, who might be kind, intelligent, compassionate people, dealing with their own challenges in the world. Yet I felt negative toward them *just because they appeared to have a lot of money*. In that instant, I realized that if that was how I felt about money, I wasn't likely to attract much of it. Not long after this realization, my material life began to turn around.

Those working 8 play out issues of influence and abundance in a variety of ways: Some 8s remain relatively passive and live on as little money as possible, associating too much wealth with exploitation or unethical behavior, as if affluence were incompatible with ethics; they may, as in my example, initially feel resentful of the wealthy. Other 8s, who perhaps came into money, may feel guilty about their wealth. They never know whether people like them for their money, and they may have less motivation to apply their efforts and test themselves.

Those working 8 need to stop holding themselves back through a lack of follow-through, and take clear and direct action to reap the fruits of material success so they can share their largesse with others. A key to unlocking the gates of abundance and influence, and enabling 8s to take action, is a larger, philanthropic mission. This doesn't mean, however, that all 8s need to become wealthy to fulfill their life path. Perhaps the truth is best expressed by this proverb: "If you have much, give of your wealth; if you have little, give of your heart."

Most 8s need to learn to take influence and abundance in stride, keeping them in balance and in perspective. They come to recognize money as neither god nor devil. Those who tend to overvalue money might want to review the Law of Intuition and substitute the "god of money" for the "god of opinion" in the exercise outlined there.

The Law of Honesty also reminds 8s never to make recognition, influence, or money their goal. Doing so is like training for years in sport only to make medal collection your goal — it misses the point. Let the rewards of excellence flow naturally from striving to do well, and to do good in the world. If 8s do good work and provide a useful service, a sense of abundance will follow, no matter what the income level. Of course, what constitutes making good money varies, depending upon the need. Supporting a large family in an expensive area requires far more money than living as a single person with no one else to support.

While 4s have trouble seeing the light at the end of the tunnel, 8s can see the light, but they may disregard the importance of their own labor in reaching it. The Law of Action is also key for 8s because they encounter inertia to begin and to persist in the work necessary to make their vision manifest. To reap the harvest, 8s have to sow the seeds; no one can sow seeds for them. As the proverb goes, "Success is sweet, but it usually has the scent of sweat about it." And 8s may miss opportunity because, as Thomas Edison said, "it's dressed in overalls and looks like work."

Some 8s appear to have fewer issues with money but face major challenges in the arenas of power or a drive for recognition, influence, and respect. Many other 8s say they prefer to stay out of the limelight, yet arrange in subtle ways to attract notice (or at least not be ignored) when in a group.

Although outwardly courteous and seemingly receptive, many 8s can intimidate or frighten others who feel their unexpressed power, resulting in mixed messages. Some individuals working 8 energy (such as 35/8s) experience a subtle sense that they are, or could be, bad people, further re-pressing their raw assertive power, which they might otherwise use for posi-tive pursuits, such as world-class leadership or philanthropic work. Before 8s can channel their power in positive directions, however, they have to contact and acknowledge it.

Those 8s working through such power or authority issues experience the same tug-of-war other 8s have with money. They either strive for authority, controlling by intellectual or, more rarely, physical intimidation, or act like wimps and give their power to others, who often abuse it and them. They may choose authoritarian mates who abuse or dominate them until these 8s learn how to bring forth their own power. They also let employers, parents, or others treat them with a lack of respect until they learn to stand up inside themselves and reclaim their power.

Some 8s may also exhibit passive-aggressive behavior by suppressing rather than expressing their influence. They may seem timid, subdued, or conciliatory, anxious to avoid emotional or social confrontations. Their chal-lenge may lie not so much in controlling others as in not letting others control them. Eventually, they learn more about when to stand firm and when to let go, and come to recognize that the most useful form of control is self-control. Until then, they tend to play games of dominance or submission. The point isn't to stifle their authority, but to use it for a higher good.

Because of their issues with authority, most 8s prefer making rules rather than following them. In rising above the crowd, they may also imagine that they can rise above the law, that rules somehow don't seem to apply to them — that they're too smart, too aware, or otherwise an exception. If this occurs, they learn rules from the consequences of their actions. Just as the issues of 8s aren't subtle, neither are the lessons they learn. If they act dishon-estly or lose their way long enough, life will send them lessons they can't ig-nore, perhaps in the form of a jail term, until eventually they learn that there are no exceptions to spiritual laws.

Those 8s (such as 26/8s) with low self-worth may self-sabotage to the degree that they flaunt the Law of Honesty in pursuit of fame or influence or wealth. For example, they can be on the verge of major success or recognition when their subconscious mind arranges a traffic accident or illness, an expen-sive divorce, or a business partner who robs them, or they gamble or squander their money or receive another one of life's left hooks. Their conscious mind, with all of its desires, then asks, "How could this happen to me?" The subconscious knows the answer, and the sabotage represents its best, if misguided, effort to keep 8s from misusing power.

Yet 8s have a powerful way of manifesting money and opportunity in ways that may seem mysterious. "Ask and ye shall receive" applies strongly to 8s, but if they only hold up a thimble, they'll only get a thimbleful, even if an ocean of abundance is raining down upon them.

The Law of Honesty keeps 8s from putting on blinders of denial and taking shortcuts to money or power. Like 9s, those working with 8 (especially 18/9s) need to maintain the highest integrity in areas of money, fame, and influence, and avoid petty disputes over money. When 8s do act dishonestly, they usually deceive themselves and rationalize their actions, hypnotized by the glitter of money or seduced by the promise of power.

These 8s can turn their life around through service in the form of giving their time, energy, or money without expecting anything back. Such selfless service can raise their level of self-worth and counter the tendency to self-sabotage, changing their life in unforeseen ways. When they make service the center of their life, they embrace their destiny in the most positive sense, combining money and worldly power with the power of the heart. The Law of Higher Will can remind 8s of the bigger picture and show them how to best use material success as a means to make a positive difference in the world.

Other Qualities and Issues

When 8s work in the positive, all they need eventually manifests because they open to a sense of inner abundance. Nevertheless, 8s will sometimes meet with frustration along the way, calling for patience and persistence. These 8s can find spiritual fulfillment as it manifests in the world, in concrete, observable forms — especially if they remember that whatever we can do ourselves, we can also help others to do. So 8s can share their abundance with generosity. Whatever their income level, they can share abundant friendship, compassion, and support. They learn that money and authority are only forms of energy that makes them more of who they already are. If 8s act from greed, they become greedier; if they act from love, this love amplifies and expands. The more energy they have, the more they can share with other people.

The 8 path works almost like a double 4, so 8s can also have their own brand of family issues to work out, such as dealing with an alcoholic parent as they also establish secure foundations.

The central work for 8s involves owning their authority. Once they find it within, they extend a benign influence and abundance in the world.

At the Summit: Potential and Destiny

Those 8s nearing the summit of their mountain may be very wealthy, or they may live modestly. They may demonstrate a high degree of influence, or they may seem quiet and unassuming. They may have achieved a certain celebrity status and command respect and recognition, or they may remain relatively unknown in the larger world. They're notable, however, in their lack of concern, because they feel their influence, authority, and abundance inside. In this way, they no longer have attachments to external achievements. They have enough. They're content. They have fully lived their life path to the point of transcending it.

In addition, evolved 8s feel happy and grateful to share their blessings in appropriate ways, and to encourage others to achieve their own sense of abundance, power, influence, and recognition if that's what they desire. Many 8s who have broken through their limits become philanthropists, finding causes they believe in and supporting others as they share their wealth.

At the highest levels, 8s experience the outpouring abundance of life, the cornucopia of nature, and the fullness of Spirit, and feel moved to share with others. Their sense of empowerment changes to grateful and loving surrender to a higher power as manifested in the intricate intelligence and web of life.

Action Checklist

If you're working 8, the following actions can make a difference in your life:

- Contact your power and assertiveness through a martial art or another avenue that allows you to express these qualities in a constructive way.
- Take responsibility for any abundance or lack of abundance in your life.
- Consider how you really feel about authority and recognition.

•   Count your blessings, and appreciate the abundance you have in your life right now; share a portion of your blessings with others.

Accessing Influence through Authority

1. Think of someone you know — or imagine a film, literary, or historical character — a role model who demonstrates a quiet authority and sense of abundance, who shares generously and can act assertively when necessary.
2. Imagine yourself as that person — feeling your power to influence others in a positive way. In what specific ways can you put these qualities into practice to influence others?

9: INTEGRITY THROUGH WISDOM

Imagine a lone sage walking down a dark road
just before dawn, holding a lantern
as a light for others to follow.
Such sages, lighting the way for others,
can only lead where they're willing to travel.
If they fall off the path, so will those who follow.
If you were such a sage, could you lead by your example?
Could you inspire others with your integrity?

Those working 9 as a life purpose are here to live with high integrity, to align their life with their heart's intuitive wisdom and serve as role models for others. Because our life path holds special challenges (as well as potential), those with 9 as their primary life purpose (9s, 18/9s, 27/9s, 36/9s, and 45/9s) and all those with a 9 in their birth number confront obstacles in the areas of integrity and wisdom.

Although most of us have the potential to lead others, 9s demonstrate leadership in its purest form — by example. Those working 9 come into this world with a charisma that draws others, so they end up either leading or misleading others. They need to recognize that the example they set and the life they lead, for good or ill, will be followed by others. As 27/9 Mahatma Gandhi said, "My life is my teaching." If 9s speak or act unethically, engage in questionable sexual conduct, or demonstrate unhealthy habits, they need to consider what they're teaching by their example — because whether they know it or not, people are paying attention.

Since our primary life purpose also presents our primary life challenges, most 9s rise and fall in their struggle to live in accord with higher principles of integrity. Early on the path they may ignore higher principles and not take responsibility for, or even recognize, the consequences of their actions. So 9s need to remember that lessons repeat themselves until we learn them — and if we don't learn easier lessons, they get more dramatic. Life throws Ping-Pong balls before it throws bowling balls.

Spiritual laws lie at the heart of 9s' destiny. In Part Four of this book — and in a companion book titled *The Laws of Spirit* — I articulate key spiritual laws. But for 9s, it's also important to connect with their inner lawgiver though the wisdom of the heart, the intuitive dimension. But to connect with the god or goddess of their heart, 9s need to transcend the "god of opinion," which I cover later in this section.

The Essence of Integrity through Wisdom

The writer James Baldwin observed, "Children rarely listen to what their parents tell them, but they never fail to imitate them." The same applies to adults. Our conscious mind hears words, but for the subconscious mind, which generates change, actions do indeed speak louder than words. We learn by imitation, and we teach by example. Those working 9, in particular, need to consider their relationships, their business dealings, their parenting, their friendships, and their lifestyle in light of the question "What example does my life provide for others?"

Some eloquent individuals can inspire others with uplifting words. They may speak with authority, brilliance, or wisdom, expressing lofty ideals. But only those who actually *live* what they talk about have the spiritual authority and integrity to generate real change. Although 9s have a natural attraction to higher wisdom, they need to follow it, not just know it; they need to pay close attention to whether they practice what they preach. In a positive example of integrity, Mahatma Gandhi once declined to tell a young boy to stop eating sugar, suggesting instead that his mother bring him back in two weeks. When she did so, Gandhi advised the boy to stop eating sugar. When the mother asked why he'd waited two weeks, Gandhi replied, "Two weeks ago, I was still eating sugar."

Historically, 9s such as Mahatma Gandhi or Henry David Thoreau, who practiced civil disobedience, have always looked beyond the laws of society toward a higher integrity based on spiritual laws. When 9s unify their mind and heart, their words and actions — when they base their actions on a higher order of law and submit their thoughts and impulses to their heart's intuitive wisdom — they embody the essence of integrity.

Challenges on the Path

Although some people are born with physical, emotional, or mental issues, the underlying challenge for 9s lies in the arena of spiritual law — the higher principles of living. The basic dynamics of some 9s has links to the unconscious archetypes of sin and salvation, spiritual offenses and repentance. Examples of spiritual offenses include taking your own life when things get too painful rather than staying around, accepting the consequences, and learning from them, or failing to respect other people's process or path, or misusing your will to dominate others, or presuming to speak in the name of God (like some televangelists who fall from grace, and fall hard).

Historically, some 9s trusted their mind rather than listened to their heart. From the viewpoint of reincarnation, these individuals seem to have past-life archetypes as overzealous monks or nuns with secret lives, or others who lived by their own laws. Perhaps they burned people at the stake or broke them on the rack to save their souls. Perhaps they persecuted others and were persecuted themselves, playing interchangeable roles until they began to trust the guidance of their heart, where Spirit speaks.

Some 9s have found consolation, forgiveness, and inspiration by associating themselves with a mainstream religion or engaging in Eastern spiritual practices and submitting or surrendering to a teacher or to a teaching. Many 9s have rejected all religious belief. In either case, since birth, the heart of 9s has cried out for the inspiration that comes when they know and live in accordance with universal law and lead by example.

Many 9s don't relate to religious or spiritual themes, yet at the deepest recesses of their being, 9s resonate with an ancient, global lineage of sages, priests, and priestesses searching for inspiration and sometimes getting lost on the way.

In one form or another, because our life purpose doesn't come easily, 9s tend to ignore the very laws they seek to know. Because they live through their mind, they often have difficulty doing what they intuitively know is best. Most 9s have had special difficulty with the law of cause and effect, or action and reaction. Examples of this include having children when too young, and then feeling burdened; eating an unhealthy diet; avoiding exercise; and abusing tobacco, alcohol, food, or sexuality, and then suffering the physical consequences. Such 9s often feel that they're being punished instead of understanding that they have reaped precisely what they have sown — that they've created their own situation.

Often, 9s unconsciously ignore their inherent wisdom in order to learn the lessons of life so that they can better guide others by sharing these experiences. But 9s eventually come to understand that they can't escape the necessity to teach by example. As 27/9 Dr. Albert Schweitzer once said, "In influencing others, example is not the main thing; it is the only thing."

Those working 9 face a demanding path that takes them beyond the distractions of the material world into the heights of spiritual law. Whatever happens in the life of 9s will lead them (or compel them) upward on the path to greater wisdom and integrity.

Not all 9s take on roles as teachers or guides; some are cabinetmakers, carpenters, musicians, secretaries, or mail carriers; they follow every walk of life. Yet when they meet with others and have relationships, whether in the larger society or within family and friends, people tend to look to them as leaders whether they like it or not.

One good example of how 9s are thrust into positions of leadership was told to me by a woman named Gerta. She had been feeling tense and so got a book on hatha yoga. After looking at the pictures, she began imitating some of the stretches and postures. She also began meditating to relax. Soon, however, Gerta felt she needed some instruction, so she found a yoga class at a local community center. A little self-conscious, Gerta walked in and saw about ten people waiting for the teacher. Gerta wanted to warm up, so she went into a corner and did a few postures. The teacher was late, so she did a few more. Finally, someone said, "Well, I guess our teacher's not coming. We might as well go."

Someone else said, "Since we're here, why doesn't one of us lead the class? How about you?" she said to Gerta.

"Me?" Gerta replied. "But this is my first day; I don't really know anything about yoga."

"You look like you do," the woman replied. "Come on, lead the class."

"No, really," Gerta protested. "I was just warming up."

"But you really look like you know what you're doing," said another student. "You can lead us." So Gerta led the yoga class, and it went well.

The next week, she received a phone call from the regular teacher, who said, "People tell me they enjoyed your class so much, why don't we teach it together?" A surprised Gerta ended up coteaching a class, leading by her example.

As 9s awaken to their life purpose, they connect with their deepest feelings, and they look beyond the rules of society to higher law for guidance. If they can't yet contact their own deep intuitive wisdom, they try to create their own law. And if 9s can't live up to their own law, they begin to judge themselves and internalize their pain and mistrust their own feelings. If their frustration is directed inward, 9s may seek to destroy their body through alcohol, drugs, or other means out of guilt.

Many 9s swing from extremes of righteous moral responsibility to ignoring moral guidelines altogether. They sometimes feel confused by their own behavior, feelings, or unarticulated purpose, not realizing or trusting that they're following a deeper guide than the conscious mind. Until 9s understand and trust their higher purpose, they may end up as a kind of rebel without a cause and get punished by the very thing they seek to elevate: human law. When 9s end up in court cases, human laws teach them about spiritual laws.

Spiritual laws are not about right or wrong; they're about truth or consequences. For 9s to align with these laws involves a complete surrender to that part of them that's compassionate, courageous, and wise — call it their higher self. The Law of Higher Will can serve to reawaken and remind 9s of their inner calling. Whatever form or appearance their life takes, this calling whispers to them; it underlies every search, whether for money, fame, love, or meaning. Once 9s start paying attention to the higher will they're here to serve, life doesn't always get easier, but it does become more joyous and meaningful, as 9s connect to a new lightness of being.

As 9s mature and reconnect with higher will, they're like lanterns for others on a dark night. Their inner depth and longing gives them an inborn charisma or presence. Others can look to 9s for guidance, because they sense the profound love, compassion, and wisdom 9s possess, even if these qualities are still hidden, even to themselves.

Those who work 9 in negative ways tend to mistake their opinions for the word of God. They can become well-intentioned fanatics, proceeding to mislead, going astray and taking others with them, reaping painful consequences until they surrender their small mind to the larger will and wisdom that speaks to them in the intuitive dimension.

Those working 9 don't have to be a perfect example of integrity, just a good one. To make spiritual laws a priority and do their best each day to live according to those laws — in their business dealings, in their personal relationships, and in the areas of diet, exercise, and health — 9s need to ask internally, "What is the higher principle here?" To put it another way, they might ask, "If I were courageous, altruistic, generous, compassionate, and wise, what would I do now?" The answer reveals the highest direction, whatever their personal preferences, desires, or vested interests. But the answer doesn't come from the mind, which tends to make up answers that serve its own ends and immediate desires; the answers come from what I can only call the heart's wisdom.

Since the laws of Spirit are written in the heart, how do 9s get in touch with their heart? The Law of Intuition reminds 9s that we can't get in touch with our inner wisdom while depending on the world outside ourselves for answers — the "god of opinion."

Paradoxically, those same 9s who so depend on the opinions of others end up acting as if their opinions carried the weight of absolute truth. Many 9s tend to act like fanatics who are locked into their own views to the exclusion of others; this blocks the transcendental wisdom and guidance available to them when they lose their mind and come to their senses.

As soon as 9s find their own center, they become more secure in their connection to reality. Guided by the heart, they give others the space to follow their own truths. Their life becomes more effortless, powerful, and meaningful.

Eventually, at a certain point in their own awakening, 9s can serve as a beacon of light and lead others, not like a fanatic, but through their depth, their wisdom, and their inspiring example.

Other Qualities and Issues

Many 9s live a life that looks enviable from the outside, but inside themselves they feel a depth, a weight, and a longing for something they can't name. Consciously or not, 9s long to know, and to live in accordance with, life's higher laws, and to experience a deeper connection with others, fulfilling the destiny that calls to them.

When they lose their way, working in the negative, some 9s can on occasion experience strange chronic diseases, rare afflictions, energy illnesses, long-standing suffering, back problems, or crippling arthritis. These maladies don't come from an external source, but from their own subconscious, which responds to ancient memories of sin and repentance.

Healing methods and forms of therapy that work with the subconscious, ranging from hypnosis to faith healing, can be effective for 9s, based on their own system of beliefs.

When 9s try to heal themselves, very little seems to help, but as soon as they turn outward to serve and completely accept their condition, their healing begins. By forgiving themselves, they open the door to healing. And as 9s work their life issues in positive, uplifting ways, most physical maladies drop away as if of their own accord.

Most 9s experience relief as they consider the Law of No Judgments, which tells us that Spirit never judges us but only gives us opportunities to balance and to learn. Judgments only hold the patterns in place. As with 6s, but with an even more profound effect, releasing judgments generates a deep healing for 9s; they feel as if a heavy burden has been lifted from their shoulders. The process can be as simple as taking a deep breath and consciously releasing old judgments, saying internally with each exhalation, "I release all judgments I've placed on myself," and with each inhalation, breathing in forgiveness and healing light.

In moments of openness, 9s discover their connection with Spirit has never been absent, even for a moment, from their life. The Law of Faith reminds 9s, as it reminds all of us, of the direct and intimate connection they have with the mystery and wisdom of Spirit.

At the Summit: Potential and Destiny

Although not all mature 9s necessarily teach or counsel, they always lead by inspiration and example. They may lead many other people or relatively few, but they make a difference in the world as role models of integrity, demonstrating the wisdom and perspective they've gained through their own life experience — finally, becoming light to us all.

When 9s approach the summit of their mountain, they may lecture and teach, their words rich and flowing with the spiritual force and authority of integrity in action. Or they may not speak at all; it doesn't matter. Like Gandhi, they realize that their life is their teaching. The inspiration of such 9s comes from a feeling connection and complete surrender to higher principles of love. In ways large and small, they become movers of humanity. Their life becomes living proof of the wisdom of integrity.

Action Checklist

If you're working 9, the following actions can make a difference in your life:

- Respect the opinions and choices of others, but above all, listen to your own heart.
- Before acting or making an important decision, ask yourself, "What would my higher self do?"
- Remember that whatever your role in life, and whether you like it or not, you're leading others by your example.
- Find what inspires you in life, and follow it.

Accessing Integrity through Wisdom

1. Think of someone you know, or imagine a film, literary, or historical character — a role model who leads by example, someone whose life, integrity, and wisdom inspire others.
2. Imagine yourself as that person — living in accordance with higher principles, happy to serve a higher purpose. In what specific ways can you put these qualities into practice and bring higher wisdom and integrity into your life?

0: INNER GIFTS

Imagine a hidden spring
flowing in depths unseen,
carrying within its current secrets,
ready to burst forth in abundance,
nourishing, giving life,
for anyone willing to dig deeper.
How are you like that hidden spring?
What resources wait for you just beneath the surface?
What gifts might you find?
In what practical ways do you need to balance your life
before your inner sight opens?

The primary numbers 1 through 9 describe the most fundamental arenas of destiny. The 0, however, doesn't involve a life purpose as such, but rather points to inner gifts or potential resources. These resources tend to enhance the energies of the other number as well as signal refined or amplified qualities of the inner gifts of sensitivity, strength, expressiveness, and intuition.

We can all draw on inner resources, including the four gifts just noted, but individuals with 0 in their birth number (10/1s, 19/10s, 28/10s, 37/10s, 46/10s, 20/2s, 30/3s, and 40/4s) tend to experience these gifts with greater intensity. As with the issues of the primary digits 1 through 9, the gifts represented by 0 can manifest in positive or negative ways — or remain latent — depending on the degree to which individuals with 0 in their birth number have worked through their life issues. Because what we're here to do isn't necessarily what comes easiest, individuals with 0 in their birth number may at first seem to have less sensitivity (or strength or discernment) than other people, until they've progressed further up their inner mountain and the gift blossoms.

Those who have these inner gifts may enjoy them, share them, misuse them, or ignore them, depending on their individual level of awareness. As with all other qualities, they grow with use, with inspiration and love, and with an individual's commitment to use them for a higher purpose and the common good.

Sensitivity

The inner gift of sensitivity appears in many forms: It can become profound empathy — an ability to tune in to people at a feeling level (as in counseling or teaching). Those working with inner gifts are more likely to walk into a room and notice, "This room feels very strange" or "This room feels happy" (or sad or troubled or serene), although other people with them may not notice anything unusual.

In the negative, people with this resource can feel hypersensitive and pick up on other people's problems; they can get sucked in or manipulated by others' feelings, become an emotional sponge, or display codependence. They may also feel hurt easily, because their emotional nervous system is wide open.

Strength

The inner gift of strength can appear as unusual physical capacities, including vigor and vitality, or as inner strength in the form of fortitude and persistence. Those with this resource can serve powerfully in supporting others, and their strength may lend itself to leadership.

In the negative, strength can turn to stubbornness, aggressiveness, or resistance if those with this resource rely on their strength instead of blending and balancing it with their sensitivity and other resources.

Expressiveness

The inner gift of expressiveness bestows a silver tongue, a way with words. The words of people with this gift convey special feeling, enabling these individuals to uplift others through enthusiasm and inspiration. Whether or not they're simply glib or clever with words, their communications — which may come through art, music, or other media — are effective because they touch others at an emotional level.

In the negative, the same expressive abilities can cut others to ribbons, so along with this expressive resource comes the clear responsibility to use it in line with higher principles.

Spiritual Discernment

The inner gift of spiritual discernment — sensing where the light leads — dissolves conventional barriers between the material realm and subtler dimensions of perception and experience, enabling those with this resource to follow a kind of inner vision or intuitive decision-making. In the positive, individuals with this gift make excellent counselors and healers; they sense or know things without knowing how they know them.

In the negative, people may block this intuitive gift, this sense of subtle discernment, due to internal interference from other people's opinions, from subtle influences or energies unnoticed by others. They need to check out any internal message by asking if it is for the highest good of all concerned.

How Inner Gifts Manifest

Not everyone with 0 in their birth number will manifest all four inner gifts in equal measure; in some, sensitivity and expressiveness predominate; in others, strength or intuition. Inner gifts tend to amplify and refine the qualities of the birth number, especially the dynamics of the right-hand number indicating primary life purpose.

Inner gifts don't usually mature fully until individuals reach the age of thirty-five to forty-five. They may arise earlier, even suddenly, in the face of a crisis or emergency, or they may develop slowly, over the years. These gifts remain throughout a lifetime, but they only manifest to the degree individuals working 0 have cleared the life issues or obstacles that may block them; the higher the commitment to service, the more powerfully these gifts manifest.

Contemplating Inner Gifts

1. Consider your sensitivity: How have you used this gift? How has it used you? In what ways might you apply this resource in service of others?

2. Consider your strength: Has it manifested as inner strength, outer strength, or both? Do you appreciate this gift? How might you use it more fully in your life?

3. Consider your expressiveness: How has it moved into the world — in your relationships and work? Have you felt aware of this gift, or have you doubted it? How might you use expressiveness in the most positive way?

4. Consider your intuition: Do you trust your clear intuitive capacities when making decisions or when guiding others? Do you notice that when you contact your heart, your intuition opens wide?

THE PATHS
OF DESTINY

*I think one must finally
take one's life in one's arms.*

— Arthur Miller

Keys to Part Three

THE LIFE-PATH MATERIAL

*The great and glorious masterpiece of humanity
is to know how to live with a purpose.*

— Michel de Montaigne

P art Three, designed as a reference section for the Life-Purpose System, is
organized so that you can refer to any birth number and related material
without having to read through the entire section.

Over time, many readers turn repeatedly to this section to review material about their own birth number and the birth numbers of their family,
friends, partners, and peers, in order to better understand them or to offer
useful guidance.

The information related to your life or the lives of others may appear to
change over time, because a second, third, or fourth review several months
later may reveal insights you didn't previously grasp. The material hasn't
changed; you have.

I've grouped all birth numbers (life paths) according to the most influen-
tial digit(s) indicating the primary life path or purpose. Note that I've placed
10s under 1: Creativity through Security, because creativity is their core life
purpose. Those working 11 follow immediately, with their double drives for
creativity and security. I've placed 12s following 2: Cooperation through Balance, since 1 and 2 combine to form creative cooperation.

Each birth-number chapter covers the following topics:

- Each chapter begins with a summary of the life purpose of people working that birth number, reflecting the interaction of all of the numbers and elements that make up that life path.
- Working the Birth Number in the Positive and in the Negative provides contrasting images of the lives of people working the same birth number in positive and negative ways.
- Life-Path Issues describes tendencies and issues in specific areas of health, relationships, talents, work, and finances.
- The Well-Known People section lists accomplished individuals who serve as examples of that birth number, and demonstrates how famous people have expressed the same birth number in different fields of endeavor. Some new birth numbers appeared in the year 2000; future editions of this book will include examples as people working these birth numbers grow into adulthood and begin to show notable accomplishments.
- Keys to Fulfilling Your Destiny helps readers turn understanding to action by revealing laws to overcome hurdles on each given life path.
- Spiritual Laws: The Leverage to Change Your Life outlines key laws for each birth number, which, if followed, guide readers toward the summit of their mountain path and the fulfillment of their destiny.

1: CREATIVITY THROUGH SECURITY

Creativity is a flower
that praise brings to bloom,
but discouragement often
nips in the bud.

— Alex F. Osborn

The following birth numbers describe life paths for people working 1 as their primary life purpose, including 10/1. In the case of the birth numbers ending in 10 — 19/10, 28/10, 37/10, and 46/10 — 1 is intensified by 0: Inner Gifts. Double 1s (11: Double Creativity) follow in their own subsection.

10/1

1: Creativity through Security
10: Creativity through Security with Inner Gifts

Those on the 10/1 life path are here to channel their abundant creative energy in positive, constructive ways, applying intuitive gifts to inspire others through an energy-driven sense of charm. However, since what we're here to do isn't what comes easiest, before 10/1s can fulfill their life purpose, they have to mature and overcome hurdles and negative tendencies of the double 1 — particularly insecurity (feeling inferior to other people) and needing to prove themselves. These issues may spur them to find their talents early on, and focus their efforts on the areas that come to them more easily rather than taking a risk to try new endeavors.

Like those with single-digit birth numbers (single-digit 4s, 5s, 6s, 7s, 8s, and 9s), and 20/2s, 30/3s, and 40/4s, those working 10/1 follow a life path relatively uncomplicated or uncluttered by the challenges of multiple-digit birth numbers. So 10/1s are likely to experience a one-pointed challenge and potential in the arena of creative energy. Specifically, to the degree they apply creative thinking and innovation in any aspect of life, they feel on track and experience a sense of satisfaction or fulfillment of their purpose, even if they still face practical challenges in everyday life in areas of relationship, health, or career.

Even as 10/1s grow, mature, learn life lessons, and come to trust the gift (0) of spiritual discernment — that is, being able to see, feel, or otherwise sense where the light calls them — their innate drives, fears, values, life path, and purpose consolidate around the double-1 challenge of channeling their abundant creative energy.

This energy is a double-edged sword, since it can be used in positive (constructive) or negative (destructive) ways, just as a fire can warm a hearth or burn down the house. Those working 10/1 need to attend closely to the principle that their creative energy can't be denied indefinitely, and they can either create in the positive or create in the negative, but they *will* create.

Some talented coders invent helpful new apps, while others choose to create software viruses; some tech-savvy software engineers help build internet security while others undermine it — demonstrating how upbringing, environment, experiences, and other variables can influence how or why some individuals use their abilities in the positive and others in the negative. These polarized drives to build or to destroy are mirrored in the modern world of politics and social order.

Spiritual laws aren't based on human concepts of morality, but on action and consequence. Even those 10/1s who apply their creativity in negative or destructive ways can learn from the consequences of their actions to others and to themselves, and make fundamental shifts — changes in behavior and goals — to reap a harvest of positive fruits. One example might be a computer hacker and prankster who ends up applying creative solutions to improve a company's network security.

You've already read in Part Two about the number 1 and have a basic understanding of the central purpose of 1s. Here, with the 10/1, we double down on both the drive and potential to create. Since 10/1s can choose to channel their creative energy in constructive or destructive ways, they need to remember that they have the power of choice as stated in the Law of Choices, and that every choice has consequences. And because 10/1s, with the double 1, tend to compete with and compare themselves to others, the Law of Intuition can guide them to follow their own heart and respect their process.

Working 10/1 in the Positive

Individuals working 10/1 in the positive are guided by a clear inner compass, attracting and inspiring others with energy, originality, and innovative approaches to work and play. Fun to be around, they call those around them to new ways of looking at their lives and possibilities. They have a directness and confidence in dealing with others — a sense of good luck — and other people follow them, drawn to their dynamism. They favor improvisation and spontaneity over repeated routines, and love to create and innovate in any area of life, whether art, business, or hobbies.

Working 10/1 in the Negative

Competitive and insecure, these 10/1s ignore their intuitive inner voice and accept less than they may deserve; fearing embarrassment or looking foolish, they play it safe to avoid mistakes. They tend to approach life as a paint-by-numbers project, and are strategic rather than improvisational. Feeling inferior, they tend to be quiet; they struggle with addictions to comfort food, alcohol, or other drugs in private, and in public strive to prove themselves with an intense desire to win and come out ahead in the struggle for survival. Or, alternately, overwhelmed by insecurity, they may avoid the competitive fray altogether for fear of disappointing outcomes.

Life-Path Issues

Health

Due to the double 1, individuals working 10/1 need nutritious food, including protein — such as eggs, fish, or poultry — which may better help them feel grounded than a pure vegan diet.

They thrive on regular but varied exercise, especially cardiovascular or aerobic exercise such as running, brisk walking, biking, or swimming — not just for standard health reasons, but to channel their abundant energy in positive ways. Otherwise, they may be prone to lowering their energy level through addictive behaviors. These individuals have a sensitive energy field that doesn't tolerate alcohol or other nonprescription drugs. Some 10/1s may have a sensitive reproductive area, so normal practices and precautions about reproductive health apply.

Relationships

Like those working other birth numbers, 10/1s are here to create a strong, supportive relationship with themselves so they can then form authentic bonds with others. A need to constantly prove themselves, whether in winning at a game or sports contest, or in relation to the skills of others in a chosen field of endeavor, doesn't make for secure and supportive relationships. So 10/1s need to understand their innate sense of insecurity — of not being as good as other people — by turning attention away from the self and bestowing that bright energy and attention on others, going beyond self-preoccupation.

This, like nothing else, helps build intimacy and bonding, as well as stable relationships, where confidence is developed over time, both in self and in relation to friends and loved ones.

Talents, Work, and Finances

While the creative arts — including painting, collage, design, sculpture, writing, music, and acting, to name a few — offer distinct forms of creative expression, 10/1s can apply fresh, out-of-the-box ideas to problem-solving and troubleshooting in business, education, politics, construction, architecture, or any other field. And since each digit represents the promise of a different sort of intelligence, we can say that the double 1s possess a creative intelligence parallel to but not the same as the ability of 6s to envision a more perfect world; in actively applying that intelligence they can make scenes, solutions, and ideas appear where there were none before. Combined with the intuitive discernment of 0, magic can happen when 10/1 juice is flowing.

Some Well-Known 10/1s

Sasha Obama, daughter of the forty-fourth U.S. president, is currently the only well-known 10/1 we could find. As of 2018, and publication of the Revised 25th Anniversary Edition, the oldest 10/1s are eighteen years old — not generally enough time for many to become well-known. In later editions of this book, as more 10/1s come of age and make notable accomplishments, more names will appear here.

Keys to Fulfilling Your Destiny

If you're working 10/1, this section can help you manifest your life purpose by focusing your attention on core issues and by generating specific action to transform key areas of your life.

Guidelines and Recommendations

- Do something creative every day; practice looking at people or things or problems from a different angle.
- Overcome insecurity by seeing it as a hurdle that's begging you to

leap over it, and strive to behave with confidence, as an actor might, whether or not you happen to feel secure in that moment.

- Find positive ways to express and channel creativity through your work or hobbies.
- Establish a varied daily exercise period to liberate trapped energy and to help reduce or eliminate addictive behaviors.
- Find creative ways to serve in the world.

Useful Questions

1. Reflect on the following questions:

    - How do I use my creative energy?
    - How am I expressing my inner gifts?

2. If these questions generate insights, how might you put these insights into practice?

Deepening Your Understanding

1. Turn back to Part Two, and reread the main sections covering the digits that make up your birth number: 1 and 0.
2. You may wish to review birth numbers of family and friends and, if they're open to it, discuss similar or different issues in your lives.

Spiritual Laws: The Leverage to Change Your Life

1. Read about each of the following laws in Part Four:

    - **THE LAW OF CHOICES:** We can choose to create and express ourselves in positive or negative ways.
    - **THE LAW OF ACTION:** To overcome insecurity or self-doubt, we can accept our feelings yet behave with confidence.
    - **THE LAW OF INTUITION:** No longer monitoring other people's opinions, we connect with our heart's intuitive wisdom.

2. Do the exercises for each of these laws.
3. Consider how you might apply each law to your life.

19/10

10: Creativity through Security with Inner Gifts
9: Integrity through Wisdom
1: Creativity through Security

Those on the 19/10 life path are here to work through issues of creative energy and integrity, learning to channel their magnetic energy, intuitive wisdom, and inner gifts into positive forms of creativity as they guide or inspire others by their example. However, since what we're here to do isn't what comes easiest, before 19/10s can fulfill their life purpose, they have to overcome hurdles and negative tendencies in a number of areas. These individuals are prone to insecurity, addictions, and physical maladies due to blocked energy. Until they find their confidence and overcome hypersensitivity, they also demonstrate a false bravado and often appear angry when they actually feel defensive or hurt. Until they find the wisdom to live in accord with higher principles of integrity, 19/10s learn life lessons as a gymnast often learns balance — by taking some hard falls.

Using the method outlined in this book for determining birth numbers, we don't add together the final two digits of four-digit birth numbers. However, *if we did* add them together (1 + 0), we would end up with 19/10/1 — indicating triple creativity (1) intensified by the inner gifts of sensitivity, strength, expressiveness, and acute intuition (0).

The forms of creative service 19/10s provide may range from intuitive healing work to making handmade greeting cards for friends. The creative endeavors of famous 19/10s range from the cartooning genius of Walt Disney to the whimsical rhymes of Dr. Seuss. Florence Nightingale became a healer, Jim Croce a performing artist, Jacques Cousteau a marine explorer, and Mikhail Gorbachev an inspiring world leader. The magnetic energy, natural charisma, and inner gifts of 19/10s converge to create almost unparalleled ability to inspire others. The more 19/10s allow their creative energy to flow, the better they feel.

Due to innate insecurity, 19/10s are highly sensitive to the opinions of others, which they either rely on or resist. At the same time, because 19/10s have an unsure sense of identity, they often identify with their own opinions and tend to impose them on others. The Law of Intuition helps 19/10s feel secure with their own feelings and find the beautiful heart beneath the bluster; they can then hear other people's opinions without feeling threatened or defensive, and without imposing their own will or ideas on others.

To overcome their innate hypersensitivity and insecurity, 19/10s need to acknowledge these traits, accept them, and find the confidence to push through them, as stated in the Law of Action.

Like all those working 1, 19/10s can choose to channel their creative energy in constructive or destructive ways. They need to remember that they have the power of choice, as stated in the Law of Choices, and that every choice has consequences.

As 19/10s recognize and open to their acute sensitivity, guided by intuitive gifts, they discover that they can tune in to other people. Their resource of strength gives them the fortitude to persevere through hardships.

Whether or not 19/10s choose to practice a form of creative healing, such as massage, psychotherapy, painting pictures, or telling stories, they can, by their very presence, become a natural force of healing and inspiration when acting with integrity and working their energy in expansive ways.

Once 19/10s reconnect with the line of light and dynamism that is their birthright, and find the courage to live the life they came here to live, the energy surges and they come alive in ways they hadn't experienced before.

Working 19/10 in the Positive

Individuals working 19/10 in the positive have a magnetic personality that attracts others. They use their intuitive wisdom in counseling, healing, problem-solving, and other forms of creative endeavor. Having made peace with themselves, they offer guidance by example rather than through dogmatic opinions, and they respect other people's opinions without being dependent on them. They have accepted, even embraced, their sensitive natures, resulting in fulfilling relationships. These 19/10s enjoy regular exercise as a means of balancing their energy, and they have avoided or overcome destructive addictions. They energize, influence, and inspire those around them.

Working 19/10 in the Negative

When the abundant energy of 19/10s is bound or held in, this can generate physical discomfort, tension, and pent-up, explosive anger, as well as problems with tobacco, alcohol, other drugs, or food. Rigidly opinionated, these individuals zealously identify with causes, beliefs, or philosophies. Such 19/10s are usually unmarried, divorced, or just difficult to live with. They alternate between acting shy and bossy, opinionated and insecure. When inhibited, they repress sexual energy; when frustrated, they exploit or abuse sexuality. Their dogmatic opinions reflect their underlying insecurity.

Life-Path Issues

Health

The very large and sensitive energy field of 19/10s often generates an unusual physical appearance in the body, eyes, or face, with unusual physical issues. Individuals working 19/10 don't usually require as much sleep as most other people, especially when they're feeling excited or inspired. In order to serve others, 19/10s need to live a balanced life, keeping everything in moderation and taking their sensitive nature into account.

If blockages occur, 19/10s may have difficulties with their prostate or ovaries, lower back, or heart. Illnesses affect the reproductive area and lower back and result in constipation, psychosomatic problems, or a tendency toward addictions. The energy field of 19/10s is so sensitive that they don't tolerate drugs or alcohol well at all; they tend to crave and then abuse them and so do well to avoid them altogether. When ill, most 19/10s respond better to energetic methods of healing, such as massage, hypnosis, and visualization, than to standard prescription drugs. Even acupuncturists must use special care, given the highly sensitive energy field of 19/10s.

A healthful, grounding diet works best for 19/10s. Even those who generally follow a vegetarian diet may need to include a little fish or poultry on occasion.

All 19/10s thrive on a balanced, moderate exercise program, including walking, stretching, or light calisthenics, which serve to release blocks and general negativity, such as pent-up frustration or anger, so that they don't discharge energy in self-destructive ways.

Many 19/10s display a kind of exceptional luck or special protection, like the proverbial cat with nine lives.

Relationships

Those working 19/10 sometimes feel cut off from others to the degree that they live alone, up in their head. All 19/10s need to pay attention to balancing their mind with their heart; in other words, they only feel their heart when they move out of their head.

Anger is a major issue for 19/10s. Alternately repressed or explosive, timid or bossy, they can act charming with strangers and abusive with family or friends. They can also act self-abusive when they're angry at themselves, reflecting the shadow side of the love that wants to shine through.

This life path doesn't really center around relationships, which can challenge both 19/10s and those who live with them. They can have good relationships, but intimacy doesn't come easily. Their anger at intimates, whether suppressed or expressed, comes when they feel hurt or bossed around. They have to confront and clear a tendency toward shyness or shame before intimacy and openness can blossom. But 19/10s, like anyone else, can change, and when they trust and feel the love in their heart, sexual relationships become a form of healing for all involved.

Talents, Work, and Finances

Those working 19/10 have a very strong call to service — to expressing their creative spirit through a variety of endeavors. Due to their inner gifts of sensitivity, strength, and discernment, plus the magnetic energy surrounding them, 19/10s have an indefinable charm and charisma. When they feel confident, they can manifest uncanny insight and practical wisdom. This life path is one of the most naturally insightful. Although they're by no means limited to such fields, the intense and unique qualities of 19/10s make for intrinsic talents in any form of creativity, intuitive work or healing, community leadership, counseling, or service. When called to the field, they can be gifted healers.

Many forms of healing exist, however, ranging from counseling friends informally, to doing massage, to practicing as a licensed professional. Even those 19/10s in fields unrelated to healing can become a healing influence due to their magnetic energy; this healing doesn't necessarily have to manifest in dramatic ways.

Many 19/10s express their creative energy by drawing on greeting cards, writing poems for friends or relatives, or other forms of creative expression. They're so inventive that, given the space to create, 19/10s come up with their own unique ways to serve and inspire.

With practice, 19/10s can become gifted and creative writers, musicians, actors, gardeners, directors, or other creative artists. They do wondrous energetic bodywork, with intense energy working through their hands. Whether or not they choose healing or creative arts, 19/10s can manage people, lead, or serve.

Many 19/10s shy away from healing out of fear of misusing their gifts or out of insecurity. When they learn to apply their gifts in service of others, for the highest good of all concerned, their life blossoms.

Their level of financial success reflects the degree to which they have overcome insecurity and learned to trust their intuitive gifts.

Some Well-Known 19/10s

Susan B. Anthony, Jacques Cousteau, Walt Disney, Betty Friedan, Theodor Geisel (Dr. Seuss), Dick Gregory, L. Ron Hubbard, Rupert Murdoch, Bhagwan Shree Rajneesh (Osho), Spencer Tracy

Keys to Fulfilling Your Destiny

If you're working 19/10, this section can help you manifest your life purpose by focusing your attention on core issues and by generating specific action to transform key areas of your life.

Guidelines and Recommendations

- Establish a daily exercise routine to release tension.
- Do something creative every day.
- Trust and cultivate your intuitive abilities.
- Open up to your heart; let your feelings and sensitivity show.

Useful Questions

1. Reflect on the following questions:

    - How do I use my creative energy?
    - In what ways can I create a healthier body?
    - Can I let go, surrender, and show my vulnerability?
    - Have I found the courage to be different?

2. If these questions generate insights, how might you put these insights into practice?

Deepening Your Understanding

1. Turn back to Part Two, and reread the main sections covering the digits that make up your birth number: 1, 9, and 0.
2. You may wish to review birth numbers of family and friends and, if they're open to it, discuss similar or different issues in your lives.

Spiritual Laws: The Leverage to Change Your Life

1. Read about each of the following laws in Part Four:

    - **THE LAW OF CHOICES:** We can choose to create and express ourselves in positive or negative ways.
    - **THE LAW OF HIGHER WILL:** Our willingness to serve a higher purpose empowers us to inspire others.
    - **THE LAW OF ACTION:** To overcome insecurity or self-doubt, we can accept our feelings yet behave with confidence.
    - **THE LAW OF INTUITION:** No longer monitoring other people's opinions, we connect with our heart's intuitive wisdom.
    - **THE LAW OF FLEXIBILITY:** Staying flexible, we make the best use of changing circumstances.

2. Do the exercises for each of these laws.
3. Consider how you might apply each law to your life.

28/10

10: Creativity through Security with Inner Gifts
8: Influence through Authority
2: Cooperation through Balance

Those on the 28/10 life path are here to work through issues combining material success and creative energy, applying their creative energy and intuitive gifts in service of others, guiding with authority and compassion. With the combined influence of creativity and the inner gifts of sensitivity, strength, expressiveness, and refined intuition, the authority of 28/10s comes to full power once they overcome their life issues and obstacles. The sense of abundance and authority they achieve may center around family or the world at large, and it manifests as they step forward with confidence and with a clear motivation of service.

Using the method outlined in this book for determining birth numbers, we don't add together the final two digits of four-digit birth numbers. However, *if we did* add them together (1 + 0), we would end up with 28/10/1, underscoring the potential influence of double creative energy (1) and need for security, intensified by the inner gifts of sensitivity, strength, expressiveness, and intuition (0), but will also need to prove themselves due to insecurity.

Nearly all 28/10s have healing hands; using them with sensitivity, they can intuitively feel where to direct or channel life energy. If they give back rubs to friends, both they and their lucky recipients will experience something special.

Because many 28/10s have subconscious resonance with an ancient lineage of wizards, sorceresses, or enchanters, some of whom misused their abilities, 28/10s may fear using their powers. The Law of Higher Will plays a central role, as it inspires them to use their abilities for a higher purpose and thereby releases subconscious fears.

The 28/10s' innate drive to accept the mantle of authority can manifest only when 28/10s overcome their resentment for (and rejection of) authority figures such as teachers, employers, supervisors, and self-proclaimed experts. The bumper sticker "Question Authority!" reflects the attitude of someone on the 28/10 life path. (Their mixed feelings about authority figures mirror the ambiguity most 8s feel about money.)

The powerful creativity of 28/10s is accompanied by equally powerful insecurities. These insecurities, amplified by mixed feelings about power and a tendency to disown their own power, create challenging hurdles for 28/10s to overcome on their life path. As a result of these tendencies, most 28/10s feel they need someone to lean on. They often feel insecure about standing on their own feet and taking care of themselves; yet in the long run, they find great satisfaction when they become self-sufficient and take control of their own life.

When not taking leadership roles, 28/10s can often become the power behind the throne, cooperating with one or more people to create useful forms of service for a better world. In such roles, they need to be careful about getting too serious and preachy.

The insecurities and related passive-aggressive tendencies associated with 1s and 8s contribute to the tendency of 28/10s to control others emotionally or mentally rather than state what they want honestly and directly. The Law of Honesty can help 28/10s heal or improve their relationships.

When these gifted, inspiring people grow into a sense of security, they can assume the mantle of authority. Avoiding a tendency toward didacticism or preachiness (which all 8s are prone to), they can then use their gifts and energy to lead and uplift others.

Working 28/10 in the Positive

These individuals working 28/10 in the positive serve as authority figures whom others admire and respect. They serve as intuitive advisers to friends, loved ones, and other people in their life. Having overcome insecurity, such 28/10s make good money in service of others, feeling the healing force that flows through them. Independent, self-sufficient, even enchanting, they attract others to their energy field. They know that whatever difficulties or challenges arise, they have the power to deal with them. Intuitive and inspiring, they provide clear counsel for the highest good of all concerned.

Working 28/10 in the Negative

Insecure, trapped in negative beliefs about money and authority, feeling needy and dependent, these 28/10s control and manipulate others. They resent authority figures and haven't yet taken on their own authority. Suffering physically with symptoms of suppressed anger and frustration, they fear the dark images that appear in their imagination; they're unable to discriminate between negative impressions and clear intuitions. Such 28/10s haven't yet experienced or contacted the inner and outer guidance available to them.

Life-Path Issues

Health

Because they're here to become healing influences, 28/10s sometimes learn about healing through their own physical issues, energy illnesses, and eating disorders. Physical symptoms of repressed anger appear primarily in the area of the solar plexus (abdomen), down to the perineum (around the base of the spine) and lower back. If their energies are blocked or they're working in the negative, 28/10s may experience symptoms in their ovaries or prostate, lower back, or coccyx, which can result in genital infections, diverticulosis, and problems with the lower intestinal tract. The reproductive area of 28/10s is sensitive and sometimes overstimulated. When 28/10s learn to view their body as a channel of energy, this awareness provides the key to healing themselves and others.

Applying the key spiritual laws for this number will help 28/10s overcome insecurity, allow emotions to flow, and open the way to a greater sense of well-being.

The compulsive eating disorders of some 28/10s, such as bulimia and anorexia, often reflect control issues, with opposing tendencies to overcontrol and undercontrol. Careful attention to a balanced, grounding diet and active, powerful exercise opens channels to new strength and confidence.

Although some may tend to avoid exercise initially, nearly all 28/10s thrive on exercise once they get in shape; exercise can improve their life dramatically by providing a release for withheld emotions, allowing blocked creative energies to flow, and relieving pressure in the reproductive area. Exercise for 28/10s also helps refine the instincts and stimulates a healthy appetite.

While exercise is good for nearly anyone, 28/10s especially thrive on aerobic exercise; active dance and martial arts are ideal.

Relationships

A major issue for 28/10s is suppressed anger, which they tend to intellectualize, acting didactic and aloof instead of passionate. They often hold in anger due to concern about other people's opinions or because they fear the power of their own anger. They may appear shy or quiet, storing negativity that needs to be discharged. In the positive, 28/10s can be very honest and direct in confronting authority figures. Working with the Law of Honesty helps 28/10s express feelings openly and directly.

Self-worth, self-sufficiency, and self-contained power are keys to healthy relationships for 28/10s. When they feel needy and want someone to lean on, 28/10s may fall into games of control and manipulation. But when they approach others from a secure place inside themselves, appreciating their own attractive energy, 28/10s see that manipulation is unnecessary and counterproductive, and they stop giving away their power.

Due to their creative energy and sensitivity, most 28/10s have sensitive and powerful sexual centers. They may experience problems associated with sexuality if they abuse or overuse it. Most 28/10s need to monitor carefully how they express their sexual-creative energy in accordance with the Law of Choices. They need to avoid using sexuality for control, identity, or self-worth, and to engage in sex only when they feel open, loving, and giving.

Talents, Work, and Finances

Those working 28/10 possess high energy, healing hands, and sensitive intuition. They make excellent counselors who grasp important subtleties. In addition, when their inborn leadership and authority shine through, they can inspire others. Most 28/10s find fulfilling work in the field of healing or in a business that helps people. Many forms of healing exist for body, mind, and emotions, including hands-on bodywork or energy work, counseling, writing, teaching, and motivating others. Some 28/10s get involved with the business of personal growth. We find 28/10s in every walk of life, but no matter what their livelihood, they enjoy it most if given the opportunity to use their inner gifts, creative energies, and natural sense of authority.

These individuals need to practice utmost honesty with regard to money. If they value money over service, they end up feeling unfulfilled even if they're making very good money. If they face problems with money or integrity, 28/10s do well to ask themselves, "What do I *really* need?" When under the influence of negative beliefs about money, 28/10s struggle to get it but unconsciously fight or sabotage their own efforts. When their creative energy flows onward with courage and with love, they manifest money naturally; they enjoy it and channel it creatively. When 28/10s feel personally secure and are willing to claim their own authority, they create abundance on every level and make as much money as they allow themselves to. No one stops them but themselves; when they understand this, they get out of their own way and make significant contributions in the world.

Some Well-Known 28/10s

Maya Angelou, Eminem, Steve Jobs, Janis Joplin, Martin Luther King Jr., George Lucas, Ralph Nader, Jack Nicholson, Shakira, Sarah Vaughan, Tiger Woods

Keys to Fulfilling Your Destiny

If you're working 28/10, this section can help you manifest your life purpose by focusing your attention on core issues and by generating specific action to transform key areas of your life.

Guidelines and Recommendations

- Express and clear anger toward authorities; then assume your own authority.
- Exercise daily with strength and vigor.
- Move through insecurity to get where you're going.
- Find ways to use your creativity and inner gifts.

Useful Questions

1. Reflect on the following questions:
   - How can I apply my creative energy to make good money, doing what I love, serving other people?

- How do I feel about authority — my own and other people's?
- When do I feel strong and independent?
- Do I sometimes try to manipulate or control others?

2. If these questions generate insights, how might you put these insights into practice?

Deepening Your Understanding

1. Turn back to Part Two, and reread the main sections covering the digits that make up your birth number: 1, 2, 8, and 0.
2. You may wish to review birth numbers of family and friends and, if they're open to it, discuss similar or different issues in your lives.

Spiritual Laws: The Leverage to Change Your Life

1. Read about each of the following laws in Part Four:

   - **THE LAW OF HONESTY:** Honesty is founded on self-awareness of our emotional reality.
   - **THE LAW OF INTUITION:** No longer monitoring other people's opinions, we connect with our heart's intuitive wisdom.
   - **THE LAW OF ACTION:** To overcome insecurity or self-doubt, we can accept our feelings yet behave with confidence.
   - **THE LAW OF CHOICES:** We can choose to create and express ourselves in positive or negative ways.
   - **THE LAW OF HIGHER WILL:** Our willingness to serve a higher purpose empowers us to inspire others.

2. Do the exercises for each of these laws.
3. Consider how you might apply each law to your life.

37/10

10: Creativity through Security with Inner Gifts
7: Trust through Openness
3: Expression through Sensitivity

Those on the 37/10 life path are here to work through issues of creativity while learning to trust the wise and beautiful spirit in themselves and others, and to apply their inner gifts to create more harmony in the world. These individuals sometimes fulfill their life path in the world at large, as did famous 37/10s Jean Renoir, Aldous Huxley, and Leo Tolstoy, but lesser-known 37/10s can fulfill their destiny equally well within a circle of friends or a smaller community. However, since our life purpose rarely comes easily, 37/10s may take time to open up and trust themselves or the process of their life. They have a sensitive, private disposition and first need to overcome deeply rooted insecurity.

Using the method outlined in this book for determining birth numbers, we don't add together the final two digits of four-digit birth numbers. However, *if we did* add them together (1 + 0), we would end up with 37/10/1, underscoring the potential influence of double creative energy (1) intensified by the inner gifts of sensitivity, expressiveness, strength, and intuition (0).

A sense of trust is important and useful for all of us, but for 37/10s it becomes the touchstone of life. Due to a lack of self-trust, most 37/10s seek knowledge outside of themselves rather than trusting their intuitive depths.

To the degree that 37/10s subconsciously expect betrayal, they encounter betrayal in others and in the world. Many 37/10s learn useful lessons about the human foibles of spiritual teachers and the importance of trusting their own inner knower.

When they recognize that they helped create the drama of past betrayals,

37/10s learn to appreciate the roles played by others in their own long-range evolution, whether intentional or not. They may not feel grateful to the specific individuals who broke a trust, but these 37/10s come to feel gratitude to a larger Spirit for their new awareness as a result of their experience.

As 37/10s apply the Law of Expectations, and come to recognize the power of their hidden expectations, they change their assumptions; in doing so, they change their life. They no longer need to encounter betrayal in the external world because they've learned to trust the larger process of their life.

All 37/10s, deep down, are wise and healing spirits; they can express themselves like angels in human form once they align themselves with the higher energy and will that manifest within them. These sensitive, refined individuals need to maintain a balanced, moderate lifestyle that includes inner work, such as contemplation or meditation, to create a safe, peaceful space in which they can feel nourished and refreshed.

As they come to discover their essential connection to the mystery and beauty of existence, they realize that whatever has happened to them, whether they call it good or bad, easy or difficult, pleasurable or painful, has served their highest good and learning.

Working 37/10 in the Positive

In the positive, 37/10s bring a lightness and dynamism to those around them. Trusting themselves and the energy working through them, they walk forward confidently and lightly, with the faith that even if they make a mistake, it's a natural part of their path. They have the courage and openness to express their deepest feelings and communicate their inner needs directly and clearly, creating trust based on understanding. They feel joy in their expanding gifts and creativity, which enables them to do refined work in healing or other fields as they tune in to other people and feel a deepening connection with the natural world. This healing may take many forms, such as art, music, drama, or other aesthetic forms of expression.

Working 37/10 in the Negative

Starting out as naively trusting seekers, these 37/10s withdraw from others out of insecurity and fear of being embarrassed, and the very betrayal they fear comes true. Not revealing their feelings, they find or perceive that people misunderstand or even mistrust them. Angry or depressed with themselves, they have disturbing dreams, which reveal the shadow side they fear. They also feel repressed bitterness about relationships, and they struggle with blocked and frustrated creative energies. Physical maladies may force them to confront health issues.

Life-Path Issues

Health

Nearly all 37/10s have a sensitive, refined physical nature with a delicate energy field. The base of the spine and the reproductive organs, along with the solar plexus, can be sensitive areas due to the sexual/creative energy of 37/10s. Their heart and knees may be sensitive as well. Whether male or female, these individuals need to be especially conscious of taking responsible precautions to avoid unwanted pregnancy, since they're more likely than many others to have problems in this area.

As it does with other natural but reluctant or insecure healers, life may deliver physical problems so that 37/10s can learn about a variety of healing modalities. Such 37/10s often experience this learning as a refresher course, because their subconscious is already well versed in energetic healing arts.

To open and support their intuitive capacities and sensitivities, 37/10s benefit from a light, primarily vegetarian diet, although they may choose to add occasional fish or poultry in order to stay grounded. Otherwise, they thrive on a simple, pleasurable diet based on sound health principles.

When insecurity blocks their creativity, 37/10s can fall into self-destructive patterns, such as abusing drugs, food, or sex. With their sensitivities, they don't tolerate abuse of anything very well or very long.

Those working 37/10 need regular, moderate exercise or some form of refined physical training, such as dance, tai chi, yoga, or swimming, to keep energy channels open and flowing. They need to trust that whatever they enjoy is perfect for them. Again, as it is for others working 1, the main function of exercise is to ground energy so that it doesn't demand release through less constructive channels, such as addictive behavior.

Relationships

Like most people working 7 in their birth number, 37/10s tend to trust their mind over their heart, because the heart and feelings are associated with pain and mistrust due to perceived betrayals.

Potentially, 37/10s have a deep connection to the love and wisdom of their heart, but to actualize this connection they have to stop hiding inside their mind's defenses and learn to trust their feelings, even if these feelings sometimes involve pain.

Many 37/10s would rather listen than talk because they're afraid they might say the wrong thing. They prefer privacy to company, yet they feel they need to bond with someone. Because of insecurity, however, 37/10s often expect a great deal of love without giving much back, and they may tend to rely on other people for strength. They often depend on a mate to make them feel complete or a job to fulfill them, relying on outside influences. In this way, they resemble 28/10s, but while 28/10s have more issues with control, 37/10s are looking for substitute parents to take care of them, because they often feel unsure about taking care of themselves. They have mixed feelings about relationships with others; this ambivalence reflects their uncertain relationship with themselves.

Sexuality and relationship depend on openness and trust to flourish. The sexual life of 37/10s feels more fulfilling when it's tied to transcending the body rather than just physical release. Many 37/10s may find that a sexuality workshop aimed at emotional sharing or even the practice of tantra yoga, a form of deep communion through sexual energy in relationship, may open new doors to intimacy and meaning.

Once 37/10s open enough to express their feelings and needs and learn to trust their partner, their relationships flourish.

Talents, Work, and Finances

This birth number is a sensitive, highly artistic pattern; 37/10s work with and are inspired by beauty and nature. Nearly all 37/10s find emotional healing and connection through music. They also display a great ability to express themselves through art, acting, poetry, dancing, photography, design, and any other form of creative expression, including teaching.

These individuals are here to create higher forms of healing, beauty, and inspiration. This doesn't mean that all 37/10s are involved in healing professions, fine arts, or spiritual occupations. Higher forms of healing include a very broad spectrum of ways to balance the body, inspire the emotions, or clarify the mind — all of which heal various states of imbalance. For example, designing a serene work environment is one form of healing; artists, musicians, or homemakers who create lovely and comfortable household settings all bring more beauty into the world; teachers, friends, and colleagues can help to inspire and uplift others.

Money doesn't generally play a central role in the life of 37/10s, except as a means of insulation, of not having to depend on someone else. When 37/10s begin to trust their abilities and manifest them in the world, money appears in their life almost by magic.

Some Well-Known 37/10s

Marc Chagall, Charlie Chaplin, Daniel Day-Lewis, William Friedkin, Ernest Hemingway, Aldous Huxley, Earvin (Magic) Johnson, Paul Klee, Katie Ledecky, Jean Renoir, O. J. Simpson, Bruce Springsteen, Leo Tolstoy, Barbara Walters

Keys to Fulfilling Your Destiny

If you're working 37/10, this section can help you manifest your life purpose by focusing your attention on core issues and by generating specific action to transform key areas of your life.

Guidelines and Recommendations

*   Trust your feelings and your inner gifts of sensitivity, strength, expressiveness, and intuition.
*   Develop the courage to express your feelings.
*   When you meet fear, don't back down.
*   Work in a garden; read a book about angels.

Useful Questions

1. Reflect on the following questions:
    *   When it comes to my body, do I trust my instincts and intuition over outside experts or theories?
    *   Can I express my deepest feelings? If not, why not?

- How can I best use my creative energy to bring more beauty into the world?
- When I don't feel trusting, how can I work this through?

2. If these questions generate insights, how might you put these insights into practice?

Deepening Your Understanding

1. Turn back to Part Two, and reread the main sections covering the digits that make up your birth number: 1, 3, 7, and 0.
2. You may wish to review birth numbers of family and friends and, if they're open to it, discuss similar or different issues in your lives.

Spiritual Laws: The Leverage to Change Your Life

1. Read about each of the following laws in Part Four:

   - THE LAW OF CHOICES: We can choose to create and express ourselves in positive or negative ways.
   - THE LAW OF FLEXIBILITY: Staying flexible, we make the best use of changing circumstances.
   - THE LAW OF ACTION: To overcome insecurity or self-doubt, we can accept our feelings yet behave with confidence.
   - THE LAW OF INTUITION: No longer monitoring other people's opinions, we connect with our heart's intuitive wisdom.
   - THE LAW OF RESPONSIBILITY: To find our boundaries, we need to learn when to say yes and how to say no.

2. Do the exercises for each of these laws.
3. Consider how you might apply each law to your life.

46/10

10: Creativity through Security with Inner Gifts
6: Vision through Acceptance
4: Stability through Process

Those on the 46/10 life path are here to work through issues of creativity and high ideals, finding constructive ways to apply their dynamism and their inner gifts, following a practical, step-by-step process to manifest their vision of a better world. They can create a better world in modest ways at home or among a circle of friends, or in the world at large; the size of the arena isn't important.

With 4 and 6 qualities preceding and influencing the 10, 46/10s have challenges, strengths, and issues unlike other 10s. They may be in touch with the level of vitality and strength influenced by 4, but they may *not feel* very creative due to the perfectionist influence of 6.

Using the method outlined in this book for determining birth numbers, we don't add together the final two digits of four-digit birth numbers. However, *if we did* add them together (1 + 0), we would end up with 46/10/1, underscoring the potential influence of double creative energy (1) further intensified by the inner gifts of sensitivity, strength, expressiveness, and acute intuition (0).

Because most 4s have trouble progressing slowly through a step-by-step process, and since most 6s tend toward impatience, wanting the perfect product right now, the 46 combination entails exceptional challenges in learning to follow and enjoy the process involved in reaching goals. While 46/10s may sense their creative potential, in order to actualize it they have to do what they inherently have difficulty doing. They have to slow down, lay a strong foundation of careful preparation, and develop the necessary skills. Then they can engage in extraordinarily creative, indeed brilliant, work in healing, the arts, business, or any other field by combining their high vision, sensitivity, strength, creative energy, and inner gifts.

Those working 46/10 can see beneath the surface of life into its heart and hidden structures. They can become builders and visionaries, but they need feedback, guidance, and support to help them transform their dreams into practical reality. With the high ideals and vision of 6, 46/10s can get lost in schemes and dreams and seem out of touch with reality.

Once 46/10s recognize that they don't need to do perfect work, they'll strive for excellence in using their creative gifts. They need to work with realism and compassion rather than with quick judgments born of their high vision. In other words, they reach their vision one step at a time by building a solid staircase to a better life, not just for themselves but for others.

One way or another, 46/10s make powerful waves due to their powerful combination of strength and sensitivity, vision, and the inner gifts to focus these ideals. Through the intuitive gifts represented by 0 in their birth number, 46/10s are blessed with incredible foresight and insight. They're here to work with their creative energy in a sustained way for a higher purpose. This vision can nourish and sustain them.

Working 46/10 in the Positive

Individuals working 46/10 in the positive have distinctive qualities of strength, sensitivity, vision, and a bright, clear field of energy. They have the intuitive capacity to create a vision or internal ideal, along with the strength to work as long as it takes to help bring that vision into reality. Pioneers who point the way, they meet with success in business and in relationships by accepting people as they are while skillfully moving to uplift and reach out even farther and higher. These 46/10s are literally or figuratively visionary warrior-priests, working for higher justice.

Working 46/10 in the Negative

Impatient, frustrated, insecure, and discouraged because life never meets their expectations or timetables, these 46/10s want heaven on Earth, right now, but they don't appreciate the work required to bring it forth; like Don

Quixote tilting at windmills, they seek "the impossible dream." Sensitive to criticism because they criticize themselves endlessly without realizing it, they don't really hear other people's feedback or advice; instead, they create rationalizations that fool even themselves. Their judgments interfere with their direct intuitive sight. Focusing only on problems, they discharge frustrated creative energy through abusing alcohol, other drugs, food, or sex.

Life-Path Issues

Health

Nearly all 46/10s have a strong, highly refined body. If they're working in the positive, their high-minded lifestyle helps them maintain their health. If they're working in the negative, problems may arise from substance abuse or inappropriate sexual activity. The most sensitive or vulnerable areas of their body include the reproductive area, abdominal region, and, sometimes, the knees.

Many 46/10s don't just eat because they're hungry; they may also study nutrition formally or informally to find the optimal diet. They need to remember that there's no perfect dietary regimen, only the best one for them at the present time. They also need to avoid quick-fix diet schemes and accept that change and adaptation happen over time.

Those working 46/10 tend to search for and find the highest kind of exercise for themselves, one that combines many benefits, such as gymnastics, martial arts, or a balance of other efficient activities.

Relationships

Accepting their so-called lower emotions is a big challenge for 46/10s because they tend to focus on what they believe they "should" feel rather than on what they really feel. Ideal mental images may hide their authentic self in a haze of denial and self-deception. The better 46/10s know and accept themselves, the better their relationships, because then they also accept other people's imperfections more readily. Most 46/10s need to work toward accepting ordinary human emotions.

Talents, Work, and Finances

Although their high standards, strength, analytical abilities, and sensitivity serve 46/10s in any occupation, some particularly suitable occupations include practicing some form of bodywork or serving as a personal or business adviser. In general, 46/10s also excel in any kind of work with structure, such as architecture or design. Other possibilities include gymnastics, martial arts, or dance, creating beauty using their body as the brush and the air as their canvas. They may even create new, higher forms of business that serve others.

These individuals need to avoid the trap of trying to find a perfect career or never feeling satisfied with any job. They need to pursue not just what they think they *should* do, but what *attracts* them. The keys for 46/10s include careful preparation, confidence, and patience.

The financial success of 46/10s depends on and reflects their level of self-worth — how much abundance they feel they deserve — as well as on their willingness to follow a clear process without skipping steps. Overcoming insecurity poses another hurdle, although not to the same degree as for other people with birth numbers ending in 10.

Some Well-Known 46/10s

No well-known 46/10s have surfaced in our records. This birth number appears far less often than many others; as time passes, more 46/10s may show notable accomplishments and appear in future editions.

Keys to Fulfilling Your Destiny

If you're working 46/10, this section can help you manifest your life purpose by focusing your attention on core issues and by generating specific action to transform key areas of your life.

Guidelines and Recommendations

- Recognize that achievement flows from constant practice.
- Treat your vision as a direction, not a goal.
- Keep dreaming, but create in practical ways.
- Prepare before you act; small steps make a big difference.

Useful Questions

1. Reflect on the following questions:

    *   How do I judge myself and others?
    *   How do I express my creative energy?
    *   How do I feel about projects that take a long time?
    *   How do I utilize my sensitivity and strength?
    *   How can I learn to think less and feel more?

2. If these questions generate insights, how might you put these insights into practice?

Deepening Your Understanding

1. Turn back to Part Two, and reread the main sections covering the digits that make up your birth number: 1, 4, 6, and 0.
2. You may wish to review birth numbers of family and friends and, if they're open to it, discuss similar or different issues in your lives.

Spiritual Laws: The Leverage to Change Your Life

1. Read about each of the following laws in Part Four:

    *   **THE LAW OF THE PRESENT MOMENT:** Impatience and regrets dissolve in the recognition that only now exists.
    *   **THE LAW OF CHOICES:** We can choose to create and express ourselves in positive or negative ways.
    *   **THE LAW OF PROCESS:** The best way to reach any goal is one small, sure step at a time.
    *   **THE LAW OF PERFECTION:** High ideals can inspire us, but excellence is the most realistic goal.
    *   **THE LAW OF INTUITION:** No longer monitoring other people's opinions, we connect with our heart's intuitive wisdom.

2. Do the exercises for each of these laws.
3. Consider how you might apply each law to your life.

11: DOUBLE CREATIVITY

We can choose to create of our life
an accident or an adventure.

— Proverb

In the simplest possible terms, when a double 1 (11) appears to the right of the slash mark, as in birth numbers 29/11, 38/11, and 47/11, this signifies precisely the same qualities outlined in Part Two on 1, but all of the qualities, talents, and potential hurdles represented by 1 are present in double-strength.

29/11

11: Double Creativity
9: Integrity through Wisdom
2: Cooperation through Balance

Those on the 29/11 life path are here to combine creative energy with higher principles and integrity, finding ways to apply their creativity in service of others, aligned with higher wisdom. Such higher wisdom is revealed by spiritual laws, especially the laws 29/11s are here to live and learn.

Using the method outlined in this book for determining birth numbers, we don't add together the final two digits of four-digit birth numbers. However, *if we did* add them together (1 + 1), we would end up with 29/11/2, underscoring the double influence of cooperative energy (2) for 29/11s, along with double creativity (11) — creative service.

All 29/11s, along with other double 1s, have tremendous creative potential. But because their primary life purpose represents a kind of mountain to climb, they may not feel as creative as others who aren't working 1 and who have few pressing issues or obstacles in that arena. Some 29/11s are still stuck working the 2 or 9 issues that precede the 11, which may block their awareness of the abundant vitality available to them. Many 29/11s are extremely creative, but they have trouble handling the energy.

Before 29/11s can open the floodgates of their inborn creative potential, they have to find themselves — their center, identity, balance, and boundaries (2 issues). They then need to work through the 9 gauntlet, which includes clearing their dependence on the opinions of others through following the Law of Intuition, then contacting and living in accordance with spiritual law by taking responsibility for their own life.

Some 29/11s come from a background of child abuse or violence; they may need to fight to get their will back and to find their sense of self-sufficient identity. The 2 influence plays a strong role and requires that 29/11s integrate the sometimes conflicting parts of themselves and overcome the tendency toward resistance and rigidity.

Those working 29/11 also face the challenge of insecurity. With the double creativity of 11 comes double insecurity, which manifests in one of two polarities: Some 29/11s act insecure, nervous, fearful, and underconfident; other 29/11s overcompensate for this internal feeling of inferiority by developing a guarded demeanor that can appear aloof or overconfident. For example, although most 29/11s have a very big heart and a genuine desire to serve helpful causes and make a difference, they can become extremely competitive because they fear losing and its consequences, reflecting their sense of inferiority.

The double 1 with the 9 means that 29/11s need to be aligned with a larger will, toward a higher good, a mission or calling. Their creativity tends to be mental rather than emotional, full of meaning but not generally as full of color and feeling as that of 30/3 artists, for example. Their wisdom will develop over time, as they eventually notice the consequences of their actions. Those who will develop great wisdom and perspective also tend to make more mistakes. The differences between individual 29/11s is the degree to which they are willing to learn from their mistakes.

Nearly all 29/11s have a large and powerful energy field, whatever their physical size. When inspired or excited, they need less sleep than most people. When they decide to generate something new, inventive, original, or insightful, they have the dynamism to perform and produce wonders. Their abundant vitality is a double-edged sword, however, with great benefits or equally great liabilities. Energy is a tool that serves both creative and destructive forces; for example, electrical energy can light our cities or electrocute a human body. As 29/11s learn the lessons of life, they can apply their tremendous vitality in more positive ways. Otherwise, they have a strong tendency toward addictive behaviors to discharge a blocked and painful cauldron of constricted creativity.

Along with all of these challenges, 29/11s display extraordinary potential; when they face their issues with awareness and commitment, they're among the most creative people on the planet. The dynamics of 2 entails a form of cooperation with others, and 29/11s are born to support humanity in ways both large and small. Whether businesspeople or healers, construction workers or hairdressers, mail clerks or athletes, they have the potential to bring the spark of creativity to life through their work, their hobbies, or their family life. Overall, 29/11s are destined to direct their powerhouse of creative energy to uplift and inspire, to support and heal.

Working 29/11 in the Positive

Those working 29/11 in the positive feel inspired and inspire others as they follow a clear path of service, the underlying motive in all that they do. Creative strategists, supportive friends, and loyal allies, they attract people with their natural charisma and lead by inspiration. In whatever creative field they choose, they offer something special, showing exceptional vitality and endurance to reach their goals. Relaxed and open, these 29/11s get inspiration directly from Spirit.

Working 29/11 in the Negative

Outwardly insecure and inhibited — or aloof, subdued, and seemingly self-assured — these 29/11s feel haunted by a sense of inferiority that manifests as competitiveness and a fear of losing. Dominant and opinionated, they seem to have a chip on their shoulder and a need to prove something. Stubborn and resistant, bossy and highly opinionated, they have a hard time letting go. Their illusory inferiority inhibits creative risks that would make their life exciting. Lost, without a real sense of themselves, they alternate between bouts of fitful energy and periods of collapse. Their pent-up energy generates addictive or abusive behaviors, and their lessons about spiritual law (especially about actions and their consequences) often get delivered in a court of law.

Life-Path Issues

Health

Individuals working 29/11 often have an unusual appearance due to the influence of powerful vitality. Their energy field is often two or three times the average. When inspired or excited about a creative project, 29/11s don't need as much sleep as most people. Their attractiveness stems as much from a glowing energy field as from physical features.

They have a very sensitive reproductive (sexual/creative) area, including the lower abdomen and lower back. Reproductive infections, cysts, lower back pain, constipation, or excess weight in 29/11s are very often related to blocked creative energy. Those working 29/11 may suffer more broken bones or unusual diseases than people working other birth numbers. On the other hand, they seem to have exceptional luck, such as walking away unscathed from a bad accident.

Most often, physical, emotional, or sexual problems of 29/11s result from blocked creative energy or problems brought on by specific patterns of abuse. Bodywork greatly benefits 29/11s, whether they're getting it or giving it.

The subconscious mind of 29/11s is open and suggestible; therefore, positive thinking, visualization, and other forms of healing that work with the subconscious and the energy body — such as acupuncture, acupressure, shiatsu, laying on of hands, bioenergetics, and nutritional therapy — often yield better results than standard drugs and medicine.

In general, 29/11s need a varied diet that includes denser or more grounding foods than many other people — foods such as grains, beans, or occasional fish or poultry. They need to pay attention to the laws of nutrition and exercise in the same way they need to pay attention to any spiritual law. Even more than most of us, 29/11s become what they ingest. Their sensitive nature doesn't tolerate drugs or alcohol well; they do best to avoid them altogether.

Like all double 1s, 29/11s absolutely need *more* exercise than the average person — not just for fitness reasons but as a means of keeping their energy flowing and grounded. After a period of conditioning, they tolerate exercise well and thrive on it. Exercising daily and finding creative work or hobbies bring a sense of vitality and well-being to 29/11s.

Relationships

While they often have a sentimental side, 29/11s tend to focus their creative energies in their mind, which inhibits their emotional expression. They tend to repress or intellectualize their feelings. Emotional inhibition, or the apparent absence of emotions, often affects their relationships.

Like 27/9s and 25/7s, 29/11s value and seek relationship with others because they lack a sense of relationship with themselves. Most 29/11s appreciate many friends and contacts and also need someone to be there for them as a source of support, but they sometimes get caught in the double bind of seeking relationship while simultaneously trying to assert their independent nature. Rarely joiners, 29/11s generally live as the individualist who marches to a different drummer.

Many people find 29/11s attractive due to their large and stimulating energy field. However, when feeling insecure and inhibited, 29/11s may experience difficulty with relationships. When their creative juices are flowing into projects or work, they may be too busy being creative to have much time for relationships. Their combination of loyalty, insecurity (needing a sense of connection), and an independent streak makes for complex relationships.

Their sex life can be a paradox: On the one hand, with the amount of vitality flowing through them, most 29/11s who aren't blocked have a strong need for regular orgasms unless they're channeling their sexual energy into intense creative projects or hard physical training. On the other hand, their sexuality can sometimes be repressed and inhibited out of insecurity, or they may withhold sexual expression (negative 2 in undercooperation). Overall, the emotional and sexual life of 29/11s reflects how much balance they have created in the rest of their life.

Talents, Work, and Finances

By virtue of their creativity and presence, all 29/11s have within them the archetype, nature, and creative inspiration of the inventor, the artist, the athlete, and the leader. Natural networkers who enjoy many contacts, 29/11s represent the paradox of the strong individualist who's also here to serve the larger good of the community.

In the financial arena, 29/11s attract money because money is a form of energy and like attracts like. As their energy flows, so flows their abundance. To the degree that 29/11s have stepped forth and expressed their creativity in positive ways, they do well financially, achieving the security so important to them (2 influence). When not working in the positive, they demonstrate and experience down-in-the-dumps feelings of insecurity and lack.

For 29/11s, money is just a way of keeping tabs on how their juice is flowing, although in some cases the accumulation of money can become a kind of competitive game or a way to gain other people's respect and approval — a strong motivation for these individuals. As long as they focus on creative service, 29/11s find that abundance comes naturally.

Some Well-Known 29/11s

Ella Fitzgerald, J. Paul Getty, Martha Graham, Bob Hope, Harry Houdini, Wolfgang Mozart, Edward R. Murrow, Barack Obama, Michelle Obama, Edgar Allan Poe, Tony Robbins, Neil deGrasse Tyson, Jules Verne, Alice Walker

Keys to Fulfilling Your Destiny

If you're working 29/11, this section can help you manifest your life purpose by focusing your attention on core issues and by generating specific action to transform key areas of your life.

Guidelines and Recommendations

- Exercise daily; it can change or even save your life.
- If insecurity gets in your way, move through it.
- Practice to become skillful; then rely on your creative energy.
- Take a weekend workshop that attracts you.

Useful Questions

1. Reflect on the following questions:
   - In what ways do I channel my creative energy, and in what ways do I discharge my blocked energy?
   - How can I make the best use of and benefit from my present situation?
   - How would I most like to serve others?
   - How can I begin to trust my heart over other people's opinions?
2. If these questions generate insights, how might you put these insights into practice?

Deepening Your Understanding

1. Turn back to Part Two, and reread the main sections covering the digits that make up your birth number: 1, 2, and 9.
2. You may wish to review birth numbers of family and friends and, if they're open to it, discuss similar or different issues in your lives.

Spiritual Laws: The Leverage to Change Your Life

1. Read about each of the following laws in Part Four:

    *   THE LAW OF CHOICES: We can choose to create and express ourselves in positive or negative ways.
    *   THE LAW OF FLEXIBILITY: Staying flexible, we make the best use of changing circumstances.
    *   THE LAW OF ACTION: To overcome insecurity or self-doubt, we can accept our feelings yet behave with confidence.
    *   THE LAW OF INTUITION: No longer monitoring other people's opinions, we connect with our heart's intuitive wisdom.
    *   THE LAW OF RESPONSIBILITY: To find our boundaries, we need to learn when to say yes and how to say no.

2. Do the exercises for each of these laws.
3. Consider how you might apply each law to your life.

38/11

11: Double Creativity
8: Influence through Authority
3: Expression through Sensitivity

Those on the 38/11 life path are here to combine creativity and material success, learning to apply their power and express their energy with compassion and generosity. They aren't here to achieve wealth or influence for their own sakes, but rather in service of a larger cause, whether a small circle of friends or colleagues, or the community at large.

What we're here to do doesn't come easily; the life purpose of 38/11s is no exception. With a creative drive even more powerful than other double 1s due to the influence of 8, 38/11s have to deal with powerful insecurity and self-doubt, as well as a tendency to give away, avoid, or sabotage their own power or abundance. They often do this with their mouth, since they also deal with expression issues.

On their life path, 38/11s eventually need to get in touch with and express their feelings and sensitivities, overcome self-doubt, and deal with 8 issues related to repressed anger toward authorities so they can take on their own authority.

Using the method outlined in this book for determining birth numbers, we don't add together the final two digits of four-digit birth numbers. However, *if we did* add them together (1 + 1), we would end up with 38/11/2, adding the potential influence of cooperative energy (2) for 38/11s, along with double creativity (11). Until 38/11s mature, their independent, even controlling nature may make them difficult to work with; they may be overly solicitous and helpful at first, but if they overhelp, the 2 quality sends them rebounding into resentment.

These inherently powerful individuals, whose power may alternately feel suppressed or explosive, have the vitality and drive to make money and make waves. Their lifework, in whatever form it takes, involves learning to control themselves rather than others, and directing their considerable power and vitality to creative contributions that uplift and empower those around them, helping others find their own source of vitality and inspiration.

Most 38/11s feel they can't give enough and can't receive enough. Combining emotional sensitivity and raw, though often inhibited, power, they're driven by powerful creative energy. They may spend their life holding a tiger by the tail until they tame that tiger and learn to channel their energy in positive ways. Otherwise, they may suffer addictions to drugs, orgasms, or food.

With the power and authority issues of 8, most 38/11s can get preachy and didactic or bossy and controlling; these attributes can affect anyone working 8, but for 38/11s, the issues of 8 are amplified by the presence of the double 1.

Like everyone working 1 or double-1 energy, 38/11s also have to deal with insecurity issues, which for them are compounded by a tendency to repress or withhold the power associated with 8. The more 38/11s dedicate their life to a common cause or higher purpose that extends beyond them, in accordance with the Law of Higher Will, the more they purify their 8 characteristics and release their creative energy, which generates the courage to step forward into life.

Working 38/11 in the Positive

Brilliant and powerful leaders or dynamic creative advisers, individuals working 38/11 in the positive can solve long-standing problems, create new options, and open doors to a better world. Money isn't the main issue for them; they apply their life force, and there's always enough. They give and receive without keeping track of the score, and they attract others with their powerful energy field. They help empower others, and they share abundantly. They've learned to lead from a position of equality and mutual respect. Driving the material success path with a tidal wave of vitality makes for an exciting, productive life.

Working 38/11 in the Negative

These 38/11s outmaneuver, outcompete, and overcontrol others, often through manipulation. Too unsure to put themselves on the line, they deny their power and sabotage their success or, alternately, they exploit their power and seek to achieve success by dominating or outshining others. Avoiding exercise, they struggle with addictions due to blocked creative energy. Frustrated by pent-up energy, they alienate others due to an aloof, negative exterior, but underneath churn gnawing self-doubts and insecurities.

Life-Path Issues

Health

Those working 38/11 combine a mixture of vulnerable areas and traits associated with 3 (blocked expression affecting the throat area), double 1 (reproductive area, lower abdomen, lower back), and 8 (possible self-sabotage in the form of accidents or, less frequently, burnout from overwork). This doesn't imply that 38/11s necessarily have to suffer illness or accidents; maladies most often come when these individuals work negative patterns, and they can be viewed as life's feedback, signaling the need to change old habits.

The most effective healing methodologies for 38/11s include positive visualizations, work with beliefs, acupuncture, bodywork, or other relatively subtle work with the mind and energy field. As long as they keep their creative energy flowing, 38/11s have sturdy dispositions and enjoy stable, vigorous health. Those working 38/11 like to make their own rules about nutrition. Most 38/11s are too busy to make food a central issue in their life (except for creative cooking); for most 38/11s, food is just fuel for their life and ambitions. A vegetarian or modified vegetarian diet helps balance a tendency toward aggressiveness.

Like other double 1s, 38/11s need a great deal of exercise to release and ground their creative energy. Once in shape, they thrive on a daily routine of aerobic exercise.

Relationships

Even though 38/11s can appear very secure, the double 1 and the 3 mean that they often seek out one or more partners to give them a better sense of themselves. Most 38/11s have paradoxical qualities in that they need a strong person to lean on, and yet they tend to control everybody in their world.

The nature of their relationships and sexuality reveals much about how 38/11s are working through their life issues. Most 38/11s find that issues of power and control, as well as insecurity, may enter the bedroom with them. They may use sexuality and their partner as a means of release without applying sensitivity to their partner's needs; they may give away their power or abuse it. Sexually, they either like to be in charge or they like to be overpowered. Bondage and sexual power games were probably invented by a 38/11.

Of course, when working in the positive, 38/11s can have mutually satisfying relationships, sexual and otherwise. In any case, their personal relationships serve as a mirror to help them understand and balance their life.

Talents, Work, and Finances

Most 38/11s are natural leaders, with the important qualities of authority, sensitivity, and creativity, which can help solve any problem. They can make admirable or despicable politicians, depending on whether they're working their issues with power and creativity in positive or negative ways, applying power wisely and with authority or using power to subjugate others.

While not all 38/11s serve in obvious positions of authority, they may guide others at school, at work, or at home through their innately powerful mind and creative ideas. They make capable inventors, innovators, and leaders in creative fields, such as business or fine arts. Many 38/11s work as business entrepreneurs, empire builders, heads of state, or heads of small businesses. Whether preachers or problem solvers, they stand out in their field.

In the financial area, 38/11s may experience self-sabotage, both desire and fear, and a tendency toward feast or famine. Having a stable, conservative personal or business partner who's good with money can help. When 38/11s dedicate their creativity toward the common good, making a positive difference in the world, money comes to them naturally. The more energy and service they put into the world, the more money comes back.

Some Well-Known 38/11s

Kevin Bacon, Bill Clinton, Madonna (Ciccone), Peggy Fleming, John McCain, Benito Mussolini, Jacqueline Kennedy Onassis, Michelle Pfeiffer

Keys to Fulfilling Your Destiny

If you're working 38/11, this section can help you manifest your life purpose by focusing your attention on core issues and by generating specific action to transform key areas of your life.

Guidelines and Recommendations

- Take back your power, but also learn to let go of control.
- Do vigorous daily exercise to replace addictions.
- Express what you feel, and feel the power of expression.
- Find creative ways to help charitable causes.

Useful Questions

1. Reflect on the following questions:

   - When do I give away my power? When do I overcontrol?
   - How does my creative energy serve others?
   - In what ways am I generous with my money or energy?
   - When I feel insecure or frustrated, do I discharge energy in constructive or destructive ways?

2. If these questions generate insights, how might you put these insights into practice?

Deepening Your Understanding

1. Turn back to Part Two, and reread the main sections covering the digits that make up your birth number: 1, 3, and 8.
2. You may wish to review birth numbers of family and friends and, if they're open to it, discuss similar or different issues in your lives.

Spiritual Laws: The Leverage to Change Your Life

1. Read about each of the following laws in Part Four:

   - **THE LAW OF CHOICES:** We can choose to create and express ourselves in positive or negative ways.

- **THE LAW OF HIGHER WILL:** Our willingness to serve a higher purpose empowers us to inspire others.
- **THE LAW OF HONESTY:** Honesty is founded on self-awareness of our emotional reality.
- **THE LAW OF ACTION:** To overcome insecurity or self-doubt, we can accept our feelings yet behave with confidence.
- **THE LAW OF INTUITION:** No longer monitoring other people's opinions, we connect with our heart's intuitive wisdom.

2. Do the exercises for each of these laws.
3. Consider how you might apply each law to your life.

47/11

11: Double Creativity
7: Trust through Openness
4: Stability through Process

Those on the 47/11 life path are here to combine creativity and trust, learning to trust the creative spirit within them and channel their life force to help build a more stable, peaceful world. Their world may expand to the larger community or may, with equal significance, limit itself to a smaller circle of family, friends, or associates.

Using the method outlined in this book for determining birth numbers, we don't add together the final two digits of four-digit birth numbers. However, *if we did* add them together (1 + 1), we would end up with 47/11/2, adding the potential influence of cooperative energy (2) for 47/11s, along with double creativity (11).

Since our life purpose is an uphill climb, 47/11s face a number of issues and tests related to the chronology of their birth number: First, they need to explore and come to trust their own process of growth over time; second, they need to overcome a fear or expectation of mistrust or betrayal, most often generated by family problems in childhood; third, they need to overcome a profound insecurity that may interfere with their openhearted connections with others.

The central archetype of 47/11s deals with aesthetics, harmony, rhythm, wholeness, and refinement. Trust is a central issue for 47/11s, and the pure vitality they experience is softened by their aesthetic nature, yet strengthened and supported by 4. We can all appreciate beauty, but to *create* beauty and share it with others requires a period of practice and preparation. Following a step-by-step process is essential for 47/11s.

Like those with other birth numbers, most 47/11s experience difficult or negative aspects of their number as well as a more positive fulfillment of their life purpose. The Law of Process helps 47/11s counteract a tendency toward childlike naïveté and impatience, and the Law of Faith serves as an antidote to an inherent sensitivity to betrayal and issues with self-trust. These are important laws for 47/11s, who sometimes experience debilitating bouts of insecurity aggravated by a lack of self-trust. Sadly and ironically, these refined yet strong individuals often feel like failures before they've even begun.

Once 47/11s have had a chance to tackle the issues of process, trust, and insecurity, they come into their own confidence, beauty, and spirit. As 47/11s open to inspiration, they sense Spirit everywhere and in everyone. Once they trust this spirit in themselves, they bring light, dynamism, and magic into the world.

By blending the razor-sharp mind of 7s with the analytical capacities and strength of 4s, then amplifying the volume with two doses of creativity, 47/11s embody a potential that has rarely appeared on the planet before. They come at a time when their refinement and vitality are most needed, not just to help save our world, but to help celebrate it. Following a step-by-step process to reach their goals requires a degree of trust in the process. They need to remember that creativity alone has little force without the time and skill necessary to catalyze it.

Those working 47/11 can build bridges of light through their creative imagination. Their challenge involves expressing their creativity in practical ways while keeping their energy grounded. They're here not to engage in flights of personal fancy, but to bring their creative visions down to Earth to share with others.

With their utopian vision and their gift of foresight, 47/11s can remind us of the beauty that may have escaped our notice, here and now, in the depths of life. One way or another, they serve as a source of light for others, finding their place in the greater order of life.

Working 47/11 in the Positive

The energy field of those working 47/11 in the positive shines with a kind of clear luminosity others sense rather than see with their physical eyes. By their inspiring presence, they remind us of the creative energy and spirit that work through all of us, whether or not we are yet aware of it. Traveling through different dimensions in imagination, they experience life as a spiritual mystery — a living, tacit realization — and they use their analytical skills, lightning-fast mind, and creative energy to share this uplifted experience of life with others. It may be hard for us to fathom the source of their inspiration or to keep up with their pace. It's as if they have an angel on their shoulder; the more they trust and work with their inner guides and subtle intuitions, the more positive vitality and beauty they bring into the world.

Working 47/11 in the Negative

These 47/11s live in a world of their own mind, without a sense of grounding or connection. Isolated and embittered, they lose themselves in the virtual reality of their creative imagination and live like hermits, even when among crowds. They prefer computers to people, and solitude to people they mistrust. Brilliant failures, they want a magical world where things happen quickly and easily, and they don't always want to be here on planet Earth. They're very sensitive to feeling betrayed by others, and they experience conflicting pulls between inner and outer reality. Struggling under the weight of unresolved childhood difficulties, with their emotions inhibited, they're vulnerable to addiction to escapist drugs or experiences.

Life-Path Issues

Health

Most 47/11s have a very refined, sensitive body and energy field. Like other double 1s, 47/11s are vulnerable in the reproductive area (including lower abdomen and lower back), especially if their creative energy is blocked. The heart and, secondarily, the legs may also be problem areas if 7 or 4 issues are unresolved. Their body is strong but also very sensitive.

When 47/11s are ill, working with their mind — on both conscious and subconscious levels, through positive imaging and creating empowering beliefs — can assist dramatically in the healing process.

These individuals definitely benefit from a grounding diet, preferably vegetarian, with little or no dairy products, but the diet mustn't be too light, or they may get so airy they would float away. The main thing for 47/11s to remember is to trust their own instincts and intuition regarding nutrition and exercise.

Those working 47/11 generally prefer aesthetic kinds of exercises in natural settings that generate a feeling of inner balance and peace, such as hiking in scenic surroundings, actively sculpting, splashing paint on canvas, or doing a variety of different calisthenics to music, incorporating breath, movement, and relaxation. Because of the 4, some kind of routine, even if varied, is important to keep their creative energies clear and open. Demanding exercise that requires coordination of mind, feeling, and attention serves to keep 47/11s physically grounded. They're nourished by forests, deserts, and almost any natural setting.

Relationships

Many 47/11s marry, have children, and settle into a stable life. Nevertheless, most don't fall easily into conventional roles; they're too busy being creative, leading people out into nature or into the realm of their own imagination. In any relationship, the process of developing mutual trust through vulnerability and honest communication remains key. Those working 47/11 also need to pay attention to being truly present on an emotional level.

The sexuality of 47/11s may involve creative fantasy, and they generally experience an active drive, including masturbation if their drive outstrips their partner's or if they prefer the safety of their fantasies to the vulnerability of sexual intimacy.

Talents, Work, and Finances

Those working 47/11 manifest mental creativity at its best. Because of their creative imaginations, they make wonderful writers of fiction, creative advertising copy, or inspiring speeches. Enjoying solitary work, they also make good researchers unless they lack patience or shun routine. They apply their creativity to any form of business, working for the larger family of humanity. They could even become, or write about, a brilliant inventor, a forest wizard (or computer wizard), a hermit sage, or a healer who works with spirit guides.

Like 29/11s and 38/11s, 47/11s share double creative energy and tend to attract money from many sources, but for them money is a secondary motive;

they hardly notice when it comes in or goes out. When their juices are flowing, 47/11s create money the same way they do anything else — apparently by magic.

Some Well-Known 47/11s

No well-known 47/11s yet exist in our records. The oldest 47/11 was born in 1989. This birth number reflects a very small percentage of the population; in the future, as more 47/11s appear and make notable accomplishments, names will be added here.

Keys to Fulfilling Your Destiny

If you're working 47/11, this section can help you manifest your life purpose by focusing your attention on core issues and by generating specific action to transform key areas of your life.

Guidelines and Recommendations

- Stay grounded; take small, practical steps.
- Exercise daily through dance or martial arts — whatever encourages you to stretch and breathe deeply.
- Find ways to inspire yourself and others through business.
- Remember to supplement analysis with gut feelings.

Useful Questions

1. Reflect on the following questions:
   - How can I best share my energy with others?
   - Have I supported my creativity by developing my skills?
   - How can I make a strong, heartfelt connection with others?
   - What do I fear about other people, and what do I love?
2. If these questions generate insights, how might you put these insights into practice?

Deepening Your Understanding

1. Turn back to Part Two, and reread the main sections covering the digits that make up your birth number: 1, 4, and 7.
2. You may wish to review birth numbers of family and friends and, if they're open to it, discuss similar or different issues in your lives.

Spiritual Laws: The Leverage to Change Your Life

1. Read about each of the following laws in Part Four:

   - **THE LAW OF CHOICES:** We can choose to create and express ourselves in positive or negative ways.
   - **THE LAW OF FAITH:** Only when we find faith in ourselves can we have faith in others.
   - **THE LAW OF PATTERNS:** Patterns tend to reassert themselves unless we exert strong leverage to change them.
   - **THE LAW OF ACTION:** To overcome insecurity or self-doubt, we can accept our feelings yet behave with confidence.
   - **THE LAW OF EXPECTATIONS:** Our life unfolds according to our hidden expectations and assumptions.

2. Do the exercises for each of these laws.
3. Consider how you might apply each law to your life.

2: COOPERATION THROUGH BALANCE

Those who live in harmony with themselves
live in harmony with the universe.

— Marcus Aurelius

This section features double creativity and the quest for security of 1 combined with 2 in the frequency of 11/2, as well as the pure, undiluted, focused 2 of 20/2, intensified by 0: Inner Gifts. Birth numbers ending in 12 follow, in their own section.

11/2

2: Cooperation through Balance
11: Double Creativity

Those on the 11/2 life path are here to evolve through issues of creative cooperation, learning to work with others in a spirit of harmony, balance, and mutual support while respecting their own boundaries and areas of responsibility. However, since what we're here to do isn't what comes easiest, before 11/2s can fulfill their life purpose, they have to overcome hurdles and negative tendencies in a number of areas.

Like others working double 1, 11/2s need to realize that they came into this world to fully realize their innate and fundamental equality with other human beings, while acknowledging that we each have different strengths and weaknesses, skills and experience, in particular areas of life. So 11/2s need to learn not to let insecurity and the need to look good keep them out of the arena. Those willing to look foolish end up learning and thriving. Everything is difficult until it becomes easy.

We achieve security and confidence by developing competence in a field, not just through our innate charm. As singer-songwriter Cat Stevens once put it, "It's hard to get by just upon a smile." However, those 11/2s who have it, can use it — a smile and their bright energy field can take them a long way.

Like all those working 2, a key to the quality of life for 11/2s depends on cooperating with one or more people. This is true in business or personal relationships, and this challenge is a constant source of growth and maturation — as, for example, when young children finally learn to share and to help classmates without becoming only a helper.

The 11/2 life path isn't about going it alone, but learning to work in collaboration. For some working other birth numbers, this comes easily, but 11/2s find it harder to learn to cooperate with others, with all parties doing their part for the common good, not always trying to gauge who's doing more and who's doing less. With 11/2s, it may seem easier to say, "I'll just do it myself. I'll do this, and you can do that." Such an approach may work well some of the time, but the greatest fulfillment comes in working together.

This need and drive to collaborate with others, and sometimes the challenge in doing so, suggest that 11/2s can learn and thrive (or learn *to* thrive) by engaging in a team sport, which to a degree demands and develops the ability to cooperate with others in a balanced way. Indeed, any sort of collaboration, whether working with lab partners at school, acting or playing music in an ensemble, or engaging in a team project at work, can serve the energetic 11/2.

The positive aspects of 11/2 don't necessarily come easily or naturally, but rather through a patient process of growth, as it may take time for 11/2s to develop and mature.

Working 11/2 in the Positive

Individuals working 11/2 in the positive enjoy collaborating with others, relatively unconcerned about comparing who contributes the most to any partner, team, or group endeavor. With abundant vitality, they're a welcome part of any effort, and show the enthusiasm to begin and the perseverance to see any project through to its conclusion. Although at times feeling a drive to prove themselves and gain the approval of peers, these 11/2s remain secure in the knowledge that they're making a contribution, leading others by their shining example.

Working 11/2 in the Negative

These 11/2s have moments when their abundant creative energy turns inward or outward in self-destructive or destructive ways. If their energy is blocked — that is, if 11/2s feel overwhelmed by insecurity, as if they'll never be good enough — they sometimes decide to be "bad enough" and create problems for themselves and others through addictive behaviors, isolation, or sometimes illegal activities, until awareness of the consequences of their actions creates an opening to change.

Life-Path Issues

Health

Although health issues of double 1, centered around creativity, and associated with a sensitivity around the energy center of the reproductive area, also apply to 11/2, the 2 lends a certain sturdiness to the expanded energy potential of the double 1, underscoring the interaction of the core qualities, potentially in the positive or negative, of both 1 and 2 traits.

Like 4s, resonant 2s tend to feel responsible and therefore stressed whenever a problem arises; in other words, they would feel less stress if they were clearly not responsible for the problem. In any case, 11/2s, with the tendency to feel less than and to have to prove themselves and rise above, combined with the challenges of co-responsibility, are well served by stress-reducing activities such as recreational swimming, meditation, yoga, or tai chi — taking care not to feel driven to be the best or to push themselves past the point of enjoyment.

Relationships

Since the strongest relationship bonds, whether professional or personal, come from mutual support and collaboration rather than competition, 11/2s need to develop the awareness that friendship, loyalty, and mutual support are paramount, especially in intimate relationships with a spouse or partner. These qualities sustain a relationship far longer than good sex or even good communication. Those working 11/2 need to have their partner's back and be in their corner — and expect that their partner also has their back.

Typical of those working any 2 path, 11/2s may find it easier to give than to receive, but they're here to develop the ability to do both. If they're always the giver, or rarely the receiver, they may eventually resent the receiver without realizing or taking responsibility for setting up that very dynamic from the start. It's wise for 11/2s to consider the balance represented by the proverb "If I am not for me, who will be? But if I am only for me, who am I?"

As difficult as it may be, 11/2s need to make their needs as important as the needs of their partner or friends.

Talents, Work, and Finances

Talents of those working 11/2, like those of people working other birth numbers, are nourished, and skills enhanced, through diligent, routine practice — through effort made over time, often entailing two steps forward, one step back. Only through trial and error, allowing for effort and mistakes, and even looking foolish at times, do we grow stronger and gain expertise. Such gradual progress is very much within the reach of 11/2s, though most of these individuals would prefer fast progress, and are likely to devote dedicated effort to shine.

Those working 11/2 can be found in any career or profession, but they feel the most alive when their work allows and even rewards creative thinking. If their job requires routine and sometimes boring work such as data entry, they're likely to need some creative hobby or activity outside of work to let their energy flow.

Energy attracts energy; money is a form of energy; as long as 11/2s are working in the positive and transcending the natural tendency to feel insecure, they strive for and often stand out and thrive in their professional pursuits. Money may not be a central value for them, but security is, so they work hard to achieve it.

Some Well-Known 11/2s

As of 2018, and publication of the 25th Anniversary Edition, the oldest 11/2s are eighteen years old — not generally enough time to become well-known. In later editions of this book, as more 11/2s come of age and make notable accomplishments, names may appear here.

Keys to Fulfilling Your Destiny

If you're working 11/2, this section can help you manifest your life purpose by focusing your attention on core issues and generating specific action to transform key areas of your life.

Guidelines and Recommendations

- Consider the difference between support and servitude; learn when to say yes and when and how to say no.
- Learn to flow with change, relax into life, and stay flexible, letting go of what isn't your responsibility.
- Spend some time each day stretching, meditating, and relaxing.
- To determine a course of action, use your head but go with your gut feelings.
- Do something creative every day, even if it's a sketch or two-line poem.

Useful Questions

1. Reflect on the following questions:
   - How do I use my creative energy?
   - Do I tend to find it easier to give and to serve others than to receive or be served? How might I allow someone in my circle of family or friends to serve me? Am I willing to ask for this?
   - When a problem or challenge arises, or some project isn't going well, is my first impulse to feel responsible even if I'm not? Because of this, am I quick to place responsibility on someone else?
2. If these questions generate insights, how might you put these insights into practice?

Deepening Your Understanding

1. Turn back to Part Two, and reread the main sections covering the digits that make your birth number: 1 and 2.
2. You may wish to review birth numbers of family and friends and, if they're open to it, discuss similar or different issues in your lives.

Spiritual Laws: The Leverage to Change Your Life

1. Read about each of the following laws in Part Four:
   - THE LAW OF RESPONSIBILITY: To find our boundaries, we need to learn when to say yes and how to say no.

- **THE LAW OF BALANCE:** Seeing our tendency to swing from one extreme to another, we find our balance point.
- **THE LAW OF CHOICES:** We can choose to create and express ourselves in positive or negative ways.

2. Do the exercises for each of these laws.
3. Consider how you might apply each law to your life.

20/2

2: Cooperation through Balance
20: Cooperation through Balance with Inner Gifts

Those on the 20/2 life path are here to use their inner gifts in a spirit of service and to establish healthy boundaries and balanced responsibility in order to achieve joyful cooperation and mutual support. From this point of balance, 20/2s can cooperatively serve the common good out of love and caring rather than codependence. Not all codependents work 20/2, of course, nor do all 20/2s behave like codependents, but until they find a balance point, 20/2s tend to feel overly responsible and to overhelp, then feel resentful and withdraw emotionally.

Because 20/2s feel so responsible and on some level blame themselves, even for other people's problems, they quickly find fault with others as a defensive maneuver, as if to say, "It's not my fault!" All 20/2s need to take full responsibility for their own life but not feel responsible for the lives of others, except, of course, in appropriate situations, such as caring for children.

Most 20/2s need to define clearly the difference between service and servitude. In the larger sense, 20/2s can develop the ability to cooperate with life itself, rather than resisting the situations or circumstances they meet.

In their life and relationships, 20/2s start out doing too much; then the pendulum inevitably swings the other way, and they freeze up, resist, or withdraw. They're here to find their comfort zone and define their limits — choosing to do what they feel good about, and, when they don't feel good, knowing when to say "Enough," before they have to say "I'm fed up." As 20/2s get in touch with what they feel rather than what they or others think they "should" feel, they can truly support, and also feel supported by, others.

Those working 20/2, 22/4, and 40/4 have many resonant issues, such as the need to apply a step-by-step approach to problem-solving. Although 20/2s thrive in support positions, they can certainly become leaders or artists in any field. Usually they feel most satisfied if they're supporting others who work toward larger causes.

Similar to 4s, 20/2s have a mind that tends to run in circles when they're making decisions — weighing all the variables, comparing every benefit and liability — in order to feel they're doing what they "should." Most 20/2s are also concerned about stability and keeping everything under control; disorder feels like chaos to them and may bring up childhood fears.

The greatest challenge for most 20/2s is finding their own internal harmony. They thrive when they give their analytical mind some time off and let other people solve their own problems. When 20/2s contact their internal sense of harmony and set their own boundaries, they serve as a standard of balance by which others can set their own internal mechanisms.

Along with innate strength and surprising sturdiness whatever their body type, 20/2s can apply their inner gifts of sensitivity, strength, expressiveness, and refined intuition to their work in the world.

With their extra sensitivity, 20/2s need to remember that if others get themselves stuck in dark or difficult places, they can offer their support if they feel moved to do so, but they're *not* responsible for other people's predicaments. They don't need to get others out of the holes they've gotten themselves into. Sometimes people need to stay in a dark place for a while until they learn what they need to learn. Saving people before they're ready to be saved may not truly help them. It's not for us to decide what others "should" do any more than it is for others to decide what's appropriate for us. Those working 20/2 do best to serve from a centered place of compassionate detachment.

Working 20/2 in the Positive

Those working 20/2 in the positive balance strength and flexibility, home and work, time for others and time for self. Their body stays relaxed and supple, reflecting their internal equanimity, because they worry less and intuit more. Consummate problem solvers and mediators in family or business, they help others reach agreement, just as they've reached internal harmony and integration within themselves. Using both their strength and sensitivity in support of others, they feel useful and appreciated; they support and appreciate themselves as well, honoring their own boundaries, feelings, and limits.

Working 20/2 in the Negative

No one ever knows what these 20/2s want, not even themselves; they're too preoccupied doing what they think they're supposed to do, and they're quick to expect that others do the same. Chronically codependent, they feel responsible for almost everything, keeping the moon and stars in place while meeting everyone's needs. Other people's whims become their demands. They sacrifice for others and then resent it; they tend to give too much, then resist or withdraw completely. Physically, mentally, and emotionally stressed from worrying about everyone else, they suffer from allergies and other ailments.

Life-Path Issues

Health

Their strong, generally vigorous body and robust disposition fight off most illnesses, but 20/2s are prone to tension as their worry and their busy mind impose chronic, thought-produced stress on their body. Allergies may flare up in times of stress, and physical tension may obstruct the efficient working of the lymphatic portion of the immune system.

Most 20/2s (like 40/4s and 22/4s) tend toward either a stocky, wide body, reflecting their strength, or a more wiry body, which is surprisingly resilient. When excessive weight is an issue, 20/2s benefit from aerobic exercise and a low-fat diet, along with stretching, deep breathing, and relaxation or meditation training. Meditation and suppleness are very important for 20/2s, but they tend to avoid both, preferring outward, expansive training for strength — a quality they already have in abundance. Most 20/2s have great potential strength but lack flexibility, so the best kind of exercise for them teaches flow, suppleness, and balance, as do dance, yoga, tai chi, aikido, and other martial arts that emphasize stretching and relaxation.

Nearly all 20/2s have close ties to the subconscious, so they benefit from hypnosis and from positive visualization, in contrast to the negative fantasies and concerns to which they sometimes fall prey.

Relationships

Most 20/2s tend to withhold their real feelings when they're overcooperating because they aren't always sure what they feel — or if it's okay to feel that way. They generally pay attention to their partner's needs and feelings first, but may then feel burdened if they believe they're giving more support than they're getting.

The tendency of 20/2s to overcooperate and then undercooperate reveals itself most clearly in relationships. They put their feelings on the back burner until something inside of them bursts, and then they become reactive and resentful. Anger and resentment are signs that 20/2s have been overcooperating.

They typically start out a relationship in overcooperation, tossing their own values, interests, and needs out the window and, chameleonlike, becoming whatever their partner seems to want. Then, eventually, they swing into undercooperation and withdraw or resist. If their relationship ends, they feel hurt: "I gave so much, and my partner left me!"

The ability to compromise and negotiate is crucial for 20/2s in relationship: "I'll do this much if you do that much." They're here to learn this kind of mutual cooperation.

Sexually, 20/2s follow the same patterns, first doing what they think the other person wants them to do. This period may go on for a short period or for many years — until they become frigid or impotent, or just withdraw sexually. Their subconscious turns off from a sense of having given too much. If this happens, 20/2s and their partners need to see a professional to open up lines of communication and rapport; having "a little talk" won't suffice.

Talents, Work, and Finances

When inspired, those working 20/2 walk a straight path through life — balanced and clear, despite other people's emotions, desires, or opinions. They can excel in many fields due to a balance of strength and sensitivity.

All 20/2s, with their inner gifts, demonstrate a powerful combination of strength and sensitivity, which creates unusual capacities that don't always show on the surface. Like 40/4s, they generally gravitate toward family life and serve as supportive, dependable, caring helpmates and parents when working in the positive. They can also serve as quintessential diplomats in family squabbles or in the larger world of organizations or government.

Those working 20/2 have refined organizing and coordinating abilities and make excellent mediators or negotiators. They often serve as invaluable assistants or support people whose presence and work make a real difference in any enterprise. They don't always work behind the scenes; sometimes they take center stage in front of the cameras, or even in the Oval Office. But for every famous 20/2, thousands work effectively behind the scenes.

Security is very important to 20/2s and entails knowing that the rent or mortgage money is available, with enough left over to put food on the table. Their practical nature will lead 20/2s, quite intuitively, to the secure situation they seek, and to the form of service that suits their abilities and temperament.

Some Well-Known 20/2s

Hans Christian Andersen, Julie Andrews, Joe Biden, Maria Callas, Phil Collins, Norman Mailer, Claude Monet, Debbie Reynolds, Dr. Benjamin Spock, Elizabeth Cady Stanton, Robert Louis Stevenson

Keys to Fulfilling Your Destiny

If you're working 20/2, this section can help you manifest your life purpose by focusing your attention on core issues and by generating specific action to transform key areas of your life.

Guidelines and Recommendations

- When making decisions, write your ideas down and then trust your intuition.
- Learn to say no and feel okay about it.
- Exercise daily, and be sure to include stretching and relaxation in your routine.
- Balance giving with receiving.

Useful Questions

1. Reflect on the following questions:
   - Do I sometimes bend too far backward for people and then feel resentful?

- Where does my responsibility end and other people's begin?
- Do I respect my comfort zone?
- Do I feel trapped in any life situation?

2. If these questions generate insights, how might you put these insights into practice?

Deepening Your Understanding

1. Turn back to Part Two, and reread the main sections covering the digits that make up your birth number: 2 and 0.
2. You may wish to review birth numbers of family and friends and, if they're open to it, discuss similar or different issues in your lives.

Spiritual Laws: The Leverage to Change Your Life

1. Read about each of the following laws in Part Four:

- **THE LAW OF RESPONSIBILITY:** To find our boundaries, we need to learn when to say yes and how to say no.
- **THE LAW OF BALANCE:** Seeing our tendency to swing from one extreme to another, we find our balance point.
- **THE LAW OF CYCLES:** Life brings constant changes, arising and then passing like the seasons.
- **THE LAW OF PATTERNS:** Patterns tend to reassert themselves unless we exert strong leverage to change them.
- **THE LAW OF FLEXIBILITY:** Staying flexible, we make the best use of changing circumstances.

2. Do the exercises for each of these laws.
3. Consider how you might apply each law to your life.

12: CREATIVE COOPERATION

*The time has come
for us to stop tuning separate instruments
and, together, to create a symphony.*

— **Anonymous**

The dynamics of 12 provide an equal synthesis of 1 and 2, resulting in a unique and powerful form of creative cooperation. Individuals working 12, including those with birth numbers 39/12 and 48/12, may demonstrate all of the abilities and face all of the issues of 1s and 2s, but the combination means that their creativity shines most brightly, and manifests most fully, in cooperation with others.

An example of creative cooperation is that of an author and an editor working together to create the best possible book. People who work with or support screenwriters, songwriters, or musicians provide other classic examples. Creative cooperation can appear in any field where people work together to solve problems, do original work, or create sparks together when, individually, neither of them could have accomplished as much.

39/12

12: Creative Cooperation
9: Integrity through Wisdom
3: Expression through Sensitivity

Those on the 39/12 life path are here to work through issues of creativity, cooperation, and integrity, expressing themselves through creative teamwork, aligned with higher wisdom, in a spirit of mutual cooperation. Examples of cooperative teams include the Wright brothers, Gilbert and Sullivan, Barnum and Bailey, Rodgers and Hammerstein, and Fred Astaire and Ginger Rogers. Sports teams also represent a form of creative cooperation, with individuals producing together what they couldn't do as well, or at all, alone.

The life purpose of all working 1 involves creative energy, but most 1s can create in relative independence or even isolation. Because of the combined influence of 2, the abundant creative energy of 39/12s manifests best in cooperation with others, creating a whole greater than the sum of the independent parts.

Using the method outlined in this book for determining birth numbers, we don't add together the final two digits of four-digit birth numbers. However, *if we did* add them together (1 + 2), we would end up with 39/12/3, underscoring the double influence of expressive dynamics (3) for 39/12s.

Although 39/12s share the core 12 with 48/12s, their life path differs considerably because they combine the emotional sensitivity and expressive drives of 3s with strong 9 qualities, including a depth of wisdom and internal seriousness as well as charisma. Because of the strong 9 aspect, 39/12s feel most fulfilled if they cooperate in alignment with higher principles or spiritual laws, and if their work allows them to grow and learn.

People working birth numbers like 20/2, 30/3, or 4 have all of their energetic eggs in one basket; they confront their life path directly early on. But 39/12s, with their issues of expressive energy (3) and integrity and wisdom (9), along with their cauldron of creative energy (1) and associated responsibilities (2), can feel overwhelmed at times. They may take longer than those on different life paths to come into their own, when their psyche finally sorts out and harnesses all of their emerging qualities and drives. Our life purpose isn't what comes easiest, but when 39/12s integrate their insides and find a balance between helping too much and helping too little, and when they learn to give to themselves as well as give to others, they manifest an inherent ability to create extraordinary forms of meaning, inspiration, service, and beauty.

Whether working with another individual or with a group, 39/12s display a depth of emotion and almost religious internalization of meaning and purpose that lets them feel the depths of their soul and the souls of others.

Nearly all 39/12s have abundant vitality. Highly emotional, 39/12s base their intelligence on emotional intuition and sensitivity to the core issues of life. For the most part, 39/12s have little time for frivolous or shallow concerns; they may need to lighten up and act silly on occasion, to remind themselves that life doesn't have to be so serious, at least from a transcendental perspective.

Most 39/12s feel somehow different from other people, almost like outsiders. Due to their emotional sensitivity, combined with the unsettled sense of identity of 9s, 39/12s often suffer from self-doubt and vulnerability to other people's opinions. They may appear subdued or inhibited, but beneath their controlled persona bubbles an inspired passion for life and for making a difference. If withdrawn, 39/12s need to get out into the fray, to stand up inside themselves, and to bring their vitality into life despite what other people think.

Most 39/12s need to pay close attention to how positively or negatively they're using their creative energy in cooperation with others. They need to avoid getting drawn into other people's problems by remembering the difference between sympathy (joining others down in their dark hole) and empathy (throwing others a ladder).

Those working 39/12 come here to find their center and their balance so that they can serve others while also taking care of their own needs. This in turn allows them to regenerate and serve with others even more effectively. If

39/12s feel good about themselves emotionally, they release and enjoy their creative energy to its fullest range and bring their passion and the beauty of their creative energy into the world.

Overall, no matter what form their contributions take, 39/12s feel happiest when working for a higher cause, in cooperation with friends, colleagues, clients, and the world at large.

Working 39/12 in the Positive

The many fine qualities of those working 39/12 in the positive are magnified through their interaction and collaboration with others. They bring passion, presence, and expressive creativity into the world. They respect other people's opinions as well as their own. They know when to hold their ground and when to stay flexible. They make loyal friends, and their relationships are based on heartfelt feeling and deep understanding and respect. They find meaning and enjoyment in their work, which makes use of their creativity and expression, as they help others do their best. These individuals show class and refinement, strength and sensitivity.

Working 39/12 in the Negative

Stubborn and insecure, these 39/12s create in the negative through complaints and cutting remarks, which reflect the depth of overwhelming passions with no outlet. They overgive, and then find fault and withdraw. They have trouble getting along, even with themselves, as their drives compete for priority and attention and their mind whirls as they try to decide what they "should" do and for whom. They feel as if they're living for other people, at the whim of other people's needs and opinions. They have unusual, emotionally generated physical ailments stemming from frustrated expression. They feel lonely and isolated.

Life-Path Issues

Health

Because of the emotional sensitivity and depth of 39/12s, what troubles them cuts deep. Their hypersensitivity is aggravated by the tendency to feel

responsible. When under stress, they're susceptible to psychosomatic maladies and unusual illnesses, not just colds or the flu. This tendency decreases as
39/12s begin to work their life purpose in the positive.

The most vulnerable areas of 39/12s shift based on which part of their
birth number they're working. Their throat can flare up if expression is
blocked. The reproductive area (including abdomen and lower back) is also
sensitive. They're subject to stress-produced allergies. Blocked creativity
and expression underlie many physical symptoms, which serve as signs that
39/12s need to open up their creativity and express inhibited feelings. Physical symptoms also signal the need for 39/12s to bring their life into alignment
with the spiritual laws they came here to live.

Most 39/12s have refined dietary tastes, and food and emotions are in-
terrelated for them. If they're feeling down, they may not want to eat, or they
may pick at food; alternately, they may link food to consolation and overeat.
The more they express their feelings, the more intuitive rather than emotionally dependent their dietary choices become.

They benefit from exercise that combines elements of strength with sensitivity, such as yoga, tai chi, or other aesthetic, even meditative, forms, which
best suit their tastes. They can turn a basketball or volleyball game into an
aesthetic event, but group sports, if they even play them, have more to do
with relationship than with the game itself. More likely, a regular, conscious
routine of movement and breathing brings 39/12s the most benefit and enjoyment.

Relationships

Those working 39/12 are fed, nourished, and guided by their emotions. As
long as 39/12s stay attuned to their feelings, they make good choices in relationships. They generally intuit, although not always consciously, that their
primary relationship serves a larger purpose, beyond companionship or convenient sexual release.

People working certain birth numbers don't require relationships to fulfill
their life purpose, but 39/12s nearly always feel a drive to share their life with
someone, for only in relationship and cooperation does their creativity find
its fullest expression. However, their relationships also serve as clear mirrors
of all of their major issues, including self-doubt and insecurity, vulnerability

to other people's opinions, the need for honest expression, and, foremost, issues of cooperation. All 39/12s in relationship need an understanding and compassionate partner — someone who shares rather than makes too many demands — because even though they have much to give, 39/12s tend to overgive in response to demands and then feel drained.

In the arena of sexuality, 39/12s need to avoid getting drawn into messy situations. While it may not show to others, 39/12s are romantics and feel deep attractions; they develop crushes every now and then. They need to remember not to get involved with anyone who has more problems than they do, and to stay away from married men or women other than their own partner. Spiritual laws apply strongly to relationships; if 39/12s get into problematic situations, they learn painful lessons.

The relationships of 39/12s display depth and passion. As they bring out that passion within the secure bonds of relationship, it nourishes the soil from which their life blossoms. Emotions and mutual support provide the fertilizer and the magic. A fulfilling sexual life, no matter how it is expressed, follows naturally.

Talents, Work, and Finances

Once they find their confidence, 39/12s make natural performers in many fields, whether they act, make sales presentations, tell stories, or give inspired sermons. They also do very well in creative support positions, for example, as book or magazine editors. Their charisma eventually brings recognition, even if they start in the background. They also make very creative therapists who are in tune with other people's feelings. Their multiple abilities and drives lead to varied talents; these individuals can see and feel issues from different perspectives. They can bring forth sensitivity or strength as needed. Their strong opinions are usually well-founded, but they need to stay flexible and open. They do well in any field where their creative mind supports others who are doing their own creative work. They feel most inspired when their work supports a higher cause.

Generally, the financial state of 39/12s reflects the degree to which they're working their life path in the positive — the degree to which they have overcome self-doubt and focused on an area of work that uses their talents. Much of their energy is spent just holding things together, finding their focus with so many competing forces and opportunities within and without. Most 39/12s make good money but usually choose work with other criteria predominating. If they choose to help run a large company, they may earn a high salary; if they choose to be a storyteller in the park, they may make just enough to get by. Once they overcome self-doubt and step forward into the world with their unique combination of talents and drives, their fortunes rise to the occasion.

Some Well-Known 39/12s

Chimamanda Ngozi Adichie, Frank Capra, Emma Goldman, Alfred Hitchcock, Olivia Newton-John, Paul Robeson

Keys to Fulfilling Your Destiny

If you're working 39/12, this section can help you manifest your life purpose by focusing your attention on core issues and by generating specific action to transform key areas of your life.

Guidelines and Recommendations

- Cultivate bridges of empathy with others, not shackles of sympathy.
- Respect your mind, but trust your feelings.
- Focus on one task at a time.
- Notice the creativity you generate with others.

Useful Questions

1. Reflect on the following questions:
    - Do I appreciate my true capacity?
    - When I experience self-doubt, how do I respond?
    - Does my life serve as a good example for others?
    - Have I found a way to use my creative energy in cooperation with others to serve a higher purpose?
2. If these questions generate insights, how might you put these insights into practice?

Deepening Your Understanding

1. Turn back to Part Two, and reread the main sections covering the digits that make up your birth number: 1, 2, 3, and 9.
2. You may wish to review birth numbers of family and friends and, if they're open to it, discuss similar or different issues in your lives.

Spiritual Laws: The Leverage to Change Your Life

1. Read about each of the following laws in Part Four:

    - THE LAW OF RESPONSIBILITY: To find our boundaries, we need to learn when to say yes and how to say no.
    - THE LAW OF INTUITION: No longer monitoring other people's opinions, we connect with our heart's intuitive wisdom.
    - THE LAW OF ACTION: To overcome insecurity or self-doubt, we can accept our feelings yet behave with confidence.
    - THE LAW OF HIGHER WILL: Our willingness to serve a higher purpose empowers us to inspire others.
    - THE LAW OF FLEXIBILITY: Staying flexible, we make the best use of changing circumstances.
    - THE LAW OF CHOICES: We can choose to create and express ourselves in positive or negative ways.

2. Do the exercises for each of these laws.
3. Consider how you might apply each law to your life.

48/12

12: Creative Cooperation through Balance
8: Influence through Authority
4: Stability through Process

Those on the 48/12 life path are here to work through issues of creativity, teamwork, and success, cooperating with others and following a step-by-step process to create a more secure and stable world for themselves and others. Most 48/12s create this process toward stability within their own circle of friends and family; a few do it in the larger society. Either way, 48/12s want their influence felt by others. Because our life purpose poses specific challenges, it may take some time for 48/12s to work through issues of power and process and find the capacity to establish balanced, creative, cooperative relationships with others.

Using the method outlined in this book for determining birth numbers, we don't add together the final two digits of four-digit birth numbers. However, *if we did* add them together (1 + 2), we would end up with 48/12/3, adding the potential influence of expressive energy (3) for 48/12s.

Those working 48/12 come to Earth as bearers of light and creativity. Their appearance signals very practical physical changes and the need for strong leadership and creative cooperation in the times ahead. Many changes are coming to Earth, including major shifts in technology and in consciousness. Amid the changes, we need structure and order, which 48/12s are well suited to help create, as the old forms pass away.

Before 48/12s can serve such lofty purposes, however, they first need to establish their own foundations and accept their own process and power. Not all 48/12s work on a grand scale, but even in a smaller context, within family or local community, they have the potential to share analytical brilliance and creative ideas, along with the power and influence to make these ideas into reality.

Due to their strong power issues, 48/12s need to act in accordance with the Law of Honesty at all times. Because of the influence of 4 and 2, these individuals also have issues with responsibility; they may tend to overwork, driven by strong ambitions. Fortunately, their creative energy helps support their dominant work orientation.

Family are also a high priority for these individuals; they have issues to work out with their parents, and they learn much through their children, if they choose to have them.

All 48/12s need to be cautious about letting their ambitions overreach their level of skill (the process issues of 4s) or their sense of integrity (the honesty issues of 8s). They do well to remember that seeming overnight successes usually take years of preparation and initiation. If willing to follow a careful process, 48/12s have the qualities to succeed at anything they choose — so long as they work in cooperation with others.

The times into which 49/12s are born demand the best of them. Through their own careful work, in the process of overcoming their own challenges they develop the strength and clarity to blaze the trails and build bridges to support others.

Working 48/12 in the Positive

Individuals working 48/12 in the positive learn the lessons of process through their experience: "When in a hurry, slow down," and "Better to do it right than do it over." In working through their own family issues, they develop compassion and understanding. Creative troubleshooters, they eventually find the self-control, the integrated talents, and the drives to support the common good effectively and powerfully. Through creative service, they find the recognition they desire. Happiest where the action is, in the center of the cyclone, they serve where they can, in the way that gives them the most joy, often as pioneers of new frontiers.

Working 48/12 in the Negative

Caught in a maelstrom of change like a rigid tree in a high wind, these 48/12s fight to maintain control in a world that feels out of control, reflecting their inner turbulence and frustrated ambition. Their creative energy demands release, but they withhold it, afraid of what it might do. They bend over backward to help other people and then resent it. Like a tyrant, they may end up "helping by command," even in their own family. They resent other people's authority until they find the courage to apply their own. Ambitious, they want everything now, but they don't understand the time or effort it takes to achieve goals and so end up as brilliant failures. When they compromise their integrity, they meet with short-term rewards but court long-term disaster. When they fall, they fall hard.

Life-Path Issues

Health

In almost every case, the health and vitality of 48/12s depend on the process they follow: If they learn patience and practice a regular regimen of conscious nutrition and exercise, their exceptionally strong disposition sustains vigorous health. They're susceptible to mind-produced stress and corresponding tension if they start to feel overly responsible or concerned with other people's lives. In the worst case, their immune system becomes compromised, with long-term debilitating effects. These symptoms appear, however, only after long-term stress. Meditation practice can serve as a very direct means of reducing stress and enhancing the health of 48/12s by balancing their tendency toward aggressiveness.

Most 48/12s tend to put on weight easily, especially if their creative energy is blocked (due to insecurity or self-doubt). A low-fat, vegetarian or lacto-vegetarian diet works well for them in the long run.

Regular, rather than intermittent, exercise offers a stable process of training very important to 48/12s; otherwise, they may be prone to injuries of knees, ankles, or lower extremities. They may also have congenital or inherited problems to deal with. Pursuing healing for these problems serves to expand their sense of compassion for the afflictions of others. Physical training can also form the foundation of a strong body that takes them far in life and teaches them deep lessons about the process of accomplishing any goal.

Relationships

At their best, 48/12s are strong, loyal, dependable, and supportive, but their life is based more on reason than romance. It's important that their mate or companions understand this and not hold unrealistic expectations of them. Any long-term relationship has to be based on mutual support and cooperation. Feelings alone, or even sexual compatibility, may not be enough to satisfy their greater needs and ambitions. They need a helpmate, not just a lover, or their circumstances may give them plenty of helpmates, and a lover may be all they lack.

Sexuality is important to 48/12s, not just as a means to satisfy their needs and use their creative energy, but also as a point of connection, providing one of the only settings where they show vulnerability.

Talents, Work, and Finances

The 4 means success in business due to a practical nature, as long as 48/12s don't skip key steps; the 8 brings a drive for wealth, power, and recognition that spurs them to their goals. With patience, 48/12s inevitably achieve all they set out to accomplish. Their creative energy and analytical skills make it more likely that they'll form independent enterprises of their own. They can build structures, shape materials, or creatively troubleshoot. They enjoy pioneering new frontiers. Some 48/12s may become skilled mechanics, for example; others found a family or a business empire that supports many people. They tend to be innovators in many fields, from creative athletes to artist-entrepreneurs.

With the blend of 4, 8, and 12, 48/12s experience struggles as they move toward their goals, but with persistence, they see their work come to fruition. If they make a clear commitment, build a solid foundation, and follow their plan step-by-step while staying flexible for contingencies, and if they serve the greater good, they end up using money and authority doing what they love, working cooperatively with others.

Some Well-Known 48/12s

As of 2018, the year of this 25th Anniversary Edition, the first 48/12s — born on 9-29-1999 — are nineteen years old, not generally enough time to become well-known. As more 48/12s come of age and make notable accomplishments, names may appear here.

Keys to Fulfilling Your Destiny

If you're working 48/12, this section can help you manifest your life purpose by focusing your attention on core issues and by generating specific action to transform key areas of your life.

Guidelines and Recommendations

- Remember that self-control is the highest form of personal power.
- Whatever your goal, approach it step-by-step.
- Know when to hold on and when to let go.
- Learn to cooperate with others by treating them as parts of your larger self.

Useful Questions

1. Reflect on the following questions:

    - What is the next step toward my goals?
    - How can I reach my goals with complete integrity?
    - Do I take care of myself and others in equal balance?
    - In what ways do I express my creative powers?

2. If these questions generate insights, how might you put these insights into practice?

Deepening Your Understanding

1. Turn back to Part Two, and reread the main sections covering the digits that make up your birth number: 1, 2, 4, and 8.
2. You may wish to review birth numbers of family and friends and, if they're open to it, discuss similar or different issues in your lives.

Spiritual Laws: The Leverage to Change Your Life

1. Read about each of the following laws in Part Four:

    - **THE LAW OF RESPONSIBILITY:** To find our boundaries, we need to learn when to say yes and how to say no.

- **THE LAW OF HONESTY:** Honesty is founded on self-awareness of our emotional reality.
- **THE LAW OF CHOICES:** We can choose to create and express ourselves in positive or negative ways.
- **THE LAW OF FLEXIBILITY:** Staying flexible, we make the best use of changing circumstances.
- **THE LAW OF BALANCE:** Seeing our tendency to swing from one extreme to another, we find our balance point.
- **THE LAW OF PROCESS:** The best way to reach any goal is one small, sure step at a time.

2. Do the exercises for each of these laws.
3. Consider how you might apply each law to your life.

3: EXPRESSION THROUGH SENSITIVITY

What we can't express runs our life.

— Anonymous

This section includes all birth numbers with 3 as a primary life purpose, including 30/3, 21/3, and 12/3. Even though all three of these birth numbers reflect intense 3 dynamics and issues, 21/3 and 12/3 include other qualities, whereas 30/3 has a strong focus on pure 3, amplified by 0: Inner Gifts.

30/3

3: Expression through Sensitivity
30: Expression through Sensitivity with Inner Gifts

Those on the 30/3 life path are here to work through issues of expression and sensitivity, overcoming self-doubt to express themselves and use their inner gifts to encourage, uplift, and inspire others. Most people come into life to work on a mixture of issues, but for 30/3s, their work and destiny are clear and focused. Those working 30/3 have the support of inner gifts, which include highly tuned sensitivity, inner strength, expressiveness, and intuition. All of these resources complement and support one major life theme: emotional expression.

However, since our life purpose isn't what comes easiest, 30/3s have distinct hurdles to overcome before they can fulfill their destiny. Because 30/3s resonate with the perfectionism of 6s and feel acutely sensitive to the pain and suffering of others, they're prone to feeling disappointed and disheartened at times, and to expressing in negative ways, such as criticizing and complaining.

Those working 30/3 have an inherent drive to express themselves; this expression can come out in either positive or negative ways, but it comes out. Emotional expression may not come easily for 30/3s at first; they may start out inhibited, but once they get rolling, the words flow.

The arena in which 30/3s express may be large, as in performance, teaching, or addressing large groups, or smaller, involving a circle of family and friends. In either case, the challenges and joys of 30/3s arise from expressing their feelings through speech or creative endeavors, such as painting, music, or other media, and from helping others to express their feelings as well. Their expression blossoms with other people, perhaps one-on-one at first. Eventually, if they draw forth the courage, many 30/3s find the opportunity to speak before groups of people. I often recommend public-speaking courses for 30/3s.

Due to their innate emotional sensitivity, many 30/3s go a little numb or put up psychological armor as a defense against the emotional turbulence around them. They may appear unemotional to others, but strong, even passionate, feelings lie just beneath the surface. Those working 30/3 long for passionate involvement and an emotional connection with others, and they often create intense dramas in their life to stir up emotions around them. Many 30/3s like to watch or act in soap operas, because of their drama and emotionality. They make good actors, because they can identify with emotions and model any quality.

The inner gifts of expression, sensitivity, and spiritual discernment amplify the already-existing sensitivity of 30/3s. People working other birth numbers, such as 12/3 and 21/3, are also here to express themselves, but 30/3s combine their innate sensitivity and expressive drive as 3s with the inner gifts of sensitivity and expressiveness. To the degree that 30/3s are in touch with their feelings, they have acutely developed intuitive powers. When they read the newspapers or turn their attention to the world around them, they *feel* what needs to be done, and they express it.

Those working 30/3 need to focus on finding skillful means to express positive ways to deal with problems. They may feel fully justified in complaining, because they usually point out wrongs that do, indeed, need to be addressed, but the challenge for 30/3s is finding ways to channel and release their expressive energy constructively. They need to express themselves honestly and directly but in the most positive and effective ways. They need to focus on the solution, not the problem. This is good advice for anyone, but especially important for 30/3s, for as they describe the world, they see the world.

If 3s in general make the best depressives, 30/3s, with extreme sensitivity and self-doubt, have depression down to a fine art. Flip-flopping between "I can do anything" and "It's just too much for me — I'm not ready," they sometimes slip from confident highs into emotional slumps, feeling the weight of self-doubt, a major issue that sometimes stops them in their tracks just when they're about to succeed. Self-doubt tends to make 30/3s feel unprepared, not good enough, or not up to a task. Self-doubt can discourage and depress 30/3s until they see it as a challenge they're here to overcome, a hurdle for them to leap over as they push onward and upward.

The greatest gift of 30/3s lies in expression and inspired communication. Whether through speaking, acting, writing, or art, they find joy in moving others emotionally, perhaps moving them to action, to change, or to happiness. In the positive, their effectiveness comes from an ability to speak with feeling — not just from the mind, but from the heart.

People working 30/3 have obstacles to overcome before achieving such expressive magic, because our life purpose always holds special challenges. In general, 30/3s start out feeling *less* capable and *more* afraid of self-expression or public speaking than the average person who isn't working 3. When they step into the arena, however, they find great satisfaction; they feel, in some fundamental way, that they're home.

Working 30/3 in the Positive

Individuals working 30/3 in the positive bring enthusiasm, compassion, understanding, and service into the world, in ways large or small, through their creative expression. Whatever their occupation, when they speak, they do so with attunement and sensitivity, and they uplift others. They're enthusiastic and connected to their emotions, and their expressiveness is passionate, forthright, and even inspired. They're honest in communicating their needs and feelings, neither manipulating nor allowing themselves to be manipulated. They manage their life responsibly, not letting their own or other people's emotions run them. They use their inner gifts of expression, sensitivity, and intuition in the service of others, with a joy and altruism that further amplifies these resources, putting 30/3s in touch with the subtle aspects and mystery of existence.

Working 30/3 in the Negative

Depressed about the love they feel they lack from others, these 30/3s complain about the wrongs of society and of their life, feeling justified because there's much to criticize in this world. Needy and hypersensitive, they whine or manipulate instead of stating honestly and directly what they need, who they are, and how they feel. Some are completely blocked in their sexual natures, while others have trouble with emotional or sexual fidelity and often get into promiscuous situations.

Life-Path Issues

Health

Most 30/3s, especially those with suppressed emotions, experience vulnerability in the throat area due to blocked expression. If 30/3s feel a scratchy throat or a blockage there, they need to ask themselves, "What do I need to express that I'm holding back?" Often, once they express what they feel, their throat quickly recuperates. Music that opens the heart, touches the emotions, and enlivens or uplifts is always healing for 30/3s, whose health or illness reflects their emotional state.

Their heart and knees also feel sensitive and vulnerable at times. Those who have problems with misunderstanding, which 30/3s are prone to because of their issues with expression, often get energy blockages around the knees, which over time affect the circulation and eventually the physical structure.

Those working 30/3 need to eat and exercise according to what feels right to them intuitively — what feels emotionally as well as physically good. But they need to take care not to be run by their moods or to seek emotional consolation in the form of food or self-pampering when they're feeling lovelorn. When they're feeling blue, expansive exercise to music lifts their spirits.

Relationships

Nearly all 30/3s have a needy emotional quality that says "Appreciate me"; they look for this emotional support in the outside world rather than in themselves. Although they sometimes expect a lot without necessarily reciprocating, they also have a great capacity to give.

Although 30/3s can appear unemotional, even coldly rational, as a reaction to their sensitivity, they have an extremely large and sensitive emotional energy field. Their voice usually reveals their feeling nature, and their ability to tune into other people's feelings enhances their relationships.

Despite appearances to the contrary, 30/3s are romantics at heart. They love to fall in love, and they periodically get emotional crushes. They need to be very direct and straightforward about this tendency with their partner if they have one. When they feel free to express feeling attracted to someone, this helps clear any obsessive tendencies toward the current attraction. In other words, they can better navigate lasting relationships by acknowledging and expressing, but not acting upon, infatuations that pass through their life. Sometimes their emotions run them, and they get involved in promiscuous situations or infidelities (whether real or imagined) and then wonder what happened.

The emotional aura or energy field of 30/3s is their primary erogenous zone. If their emotions are shut down, sexual technique doesn't help. When in a loving mood, however, they're moved by passion — technique is secondary.

Relationships, for 30/3s, present a monumental opportunity to work through issues of honest expression and emotional vulnerability. They do well to view relationships not only as a form of consolation and nurturance but as a form of spiritual practice.

Talents, Work, and Finances

With their inner gifts of expression, sensitivity, and intuition — and their developed expressive abilities — 30/3s help uplift and nourish others around them in their immediate world or in a larger arena. They may choose to be teachers, salespeople, writers, or lecturers — any role that reminds people of the feeling side of their life. They have inherent gifts in any form of teaching, counseling, healing, performing, or creative expression due to their ability to tune in to people and subtle dimensions. Those working 30/3 can also follow a path of social service, and they tend to make good managers. They can be successful in any field, but they feel most fulfilled if their work offers opportunities for self-expression.

In addition to their emotional sensitivity, those working 30/3 have a superb depth of intuitive intelligence that cuts to the heart of some of life's core issues. Therefore, they do well in any field that involves clear logic and reason.

Any lack of money relates in some way to self-doubt. If 30/3s use their gifts and expression in the positive, money follows.

Some Well-Known 30/3s

Noam Chomsky, Eldridge Cleaver, Hillary Clinton, Bill Cosby, Jodie Foster, Joan Rivers, Carlos Santana, Edward Snowden, John Wayne

Keys to Fulfilling Your Destiny

If you're working 30/3, this section can help you manifest your life purpose by focusing your attention on core issues and by generating specific action to transform key areas of your life.

Guidelines and Recommendations

- Treat self-doubt as a hurdle to be overcome, not a stop sign.
- Give of yourself emotionally, even if you don't always feel you get back in equal measure.

- Allow and express your feelings in the moment.
- Trust and use your refined intuition and special resources.

Useful Questions

1. Reflect on the following questions:

   - Have I held back my drive to express out of self-doubt?
   - Do I express my feelings and needs directly?
   - Am I sensitive to the needs of others?
   - Have I fully utilized my sensitive internal guidance system or other inner gifts?

2. If these questions generate insights, how might you put these insights into practice?

Deepening Your Understanding

1. Turn back to Part Two, and reread the main sections covering the digits that make up your birth number: 3 and 0.
2. You may wish to review birth numbers of family and friends and, if they're open to it, discuss similar or different issues in your lives.

Spiritual Laws: The Leverage to Change Your Life

1. Read about each of the following laws in Part Four:

   - **THE LAW OF CHOICES:** We can choose to create and express ourselves in positive or negative ways.
   - **THE LAW OF HONESTY:** Honesty is founded on self-awareness of our emotional reality.
   - **THE LAW OF EXPECTATIONS:** Our life unfolds according to our hidden expectations and assumptions.
   - **THE LAW OF FAITH:** Only when we find faith in ourselves can we have faith in others.
   - **THE LAW OF ACTION:** To overcome insecurity or self-doubt, we can accept our feelings yet behave with confidence.

2. Do the exercises for each of these laws.
3. Consider how you might apply each law to your life.

21/3 & 12/3

3: Expression through Sensitivity
1: Creativity through Security
2: Cooperation through Balance

Those on the 21/3 or 12/3 life path are here to work through issues of creativity, emotional expression, balance, and cooperation in support of people or causes, applying their energy in positive, constructive ways to teach, uplift, and inspire. To face the inevitable challenges of their life path, 21/3s and 12/3s need courage to overcome the insecurity and self-doubt that may hinder them and need to learn to channel their creative and emotional energy in positive ways. Otherwise, when burdened by doubt or feeling insecure, they may tend to discharge their energy in self-destructive ways, through alcohol, tobacco, or other drugs. If 21/3s or 12/3s suppress their emotional expression, they experience that suppression in their body as physical tension or a variety of other symptoms.

Those working 21/3 or 12/3 are among the most well-rounded, versatile, creative people on Earth. With 2 providing support and strength, both 21/3s and 12/3s can invent, innovate, synthesize, or package impressive works in any field of endeavor. They can express their creativity through any form or material, and the spirit of their message still comes through.

With the first two numbers (1 and 2) in different order, for 21/3s creativity issues (1) are more pressing, whereas for 12/3s cooperation (2) issues predominate, due to the relative position and influence of these digits. Both 21/3s and 12/3s, however, share the same primary issues of sensitivity, self-doubt, and emotional expression, which are so focused in 30/3s. By virtue of their life purpose, they face issues of negative expression, such as criticizing and complaining. In most cases, they express in negative ways when their feelings are hurt.

Even though 21/3s and 12/3s have a high degree of emotional sensitivity, they also have a strong tendency to intellectualize their emotions rather than express their sensitive, and rather insecure, natures. They respond to the feelings of insecurity associated with creative energy either by appearing insecure or, far more often, by developing a courageous but false compensatory persona of dry intellectualism or an overconfident, outgoing bravado to veil a sensitive self, struggling with self-doubt.

In 12/3s, 2 issues predominate over 1 issues; although slightly less insecure, 12/3s have stronger issues with finding a balance between giving too much and then shutting down. Most 21/3s tend toward emotional neediness; they need to focus on letting their emotions flow out to others, as they tend toward emotional stinginess and withholding.

The destiny of both 21/3s and 12/3s involves expressing themselves in their chosen way positively and honestly. When they're dishonest, their dishonesty usually entails holding back their true or authentic feelings rather than outright lying or deceit. They achieve expressive honesty by confronting and revealing their own emotional nature, integrating the sensitive parts of themselves that they have disowned for fear of appearing too weak or needy. Because they feed off emotional connections, they can, indeed, be needy, but they're certainly not weak.

Although they have the internal strength and endurance associated with 2, most 21/3s and 12/3s, like most 30/3s, have very sensitive emotional energy fields as well as creative energy that needs to be moved into the world. They tend to be more constricted than 30/3s, and their sensitive, emotional nature isn't as easy to see as that of 30/3s. Instead of intellectualizing their emotions, 21/3s and 12/3s need to show and express their fears, their anger, their hurt, and their joy, becoming emotionally present and real. When they do, their body also opens up, relaxes, and rejuvenates.

As they discard their false persona, lay their emotional cards on the table, and show their insecurities and vulnerable feelings openly, 21/3s and 12/3s find, to their surprise, a deeper, richer, more nourishing emotional bond with others and with themselves.

Such self-revelation is no small task. Before they can open up, they have to overcome deep-seated fears of rejection, self-doubt, and insecurity. The Law of Action is key in clearing shadows from the subconscious, such as their fear of exploding with anger or collapsing with sorrow, both of which stifle emotional expression. With time and experience, 21/3s and 12/3s develop genuine confidence instead of false bravado and exhibit emotional generosity, which flows out to those around them.

Working 21/3 or 12/3 in the Positive

Individuals working 21/3 or 12/3 in the positive do excellent and sensitive work; they include some of the most creative people on the planet. Their body is relaxed, supple, and relatively free of tension because they express their feelings as they arise, honestly and openly, rather than storing them as neuromuscular tensions. They breathe deeply and easily. Their relationships thrive on honesty and emotional acceptance; when problems arise, they talk those problems over and resolve them. These individuals feel genuine pleasure in uplifting others through their caring words, whether through teaching, acting, singing, writing, or working in a grocery store. The occupation doesn't matter, as long as they have opportunities to reach out to people and build emotional bridges.

Working 21/3 or 12/3 in the Negative

These hypersensitive 21/3s or 12/3s give mixed messages; they act confident and then collapse under the weight of criticism. They come back with cutting remarks and hurt back or withdraw, all without revealing their authentic feelings. Over time, their physical tension and lack of suppleness reflect the degree of emotion they're suppressing. Filled with self-doubt and stifled emotions, insecurity and blocked creativity, stubbornness and reactivity, they fool no one but themselves.

Life-Path Issues

Health

This is one of the physically strongest patterns, with the vigor of 2 and the vitality of 1. Like 30/3s, both 21/3s and 12/3s have a sensitive throat region and may experience occasional flare-ups when their expression is blocked; if this condition is chronic, they may eventually require surgery. If their creative energy is blocked or suppressed, they may encounter issues in the lower abdomen or reproductive areas — for example, stomach problems, hernias, or difficulties with the ovaries in women or prostate in men.

Generally, however, 21/3s and 12/3s are physically strong and robust. If they repress their feelings, this is like corking up a volcano; their body feels the effects of stopping up the energy that's meant to flow freely. As long as they pay attention to expressing their creative energy in the positive and keeping their emotions open and flowing, both 21/3s and 12/3s enjoy exceptional health. When they need healing, they do best to combine whatever treatment they get with some form of emotional healing. Listening to emotional music or even going to emotional movies gives these sensitive, creative people a chance to express themselves. If they can't even cry at the movies, they definitely need to explore the ways they're blocking expression.

For 21/3s and 12/3s, excess weight usually reflects blocked creativity. A two-faceted program of balanced exercise and a creative hobby can bring their body to optimal balance. For these individuals, exercise is a good way to clear suppressed emotions. Because of their creative, emotional nature, 21/3s and 12/3s feel attuned to nature and music, which soothe their sensitive character. Listening to music and taking walks outdoors can help them heal and recharge on emotional and physical levels.

Relationships

The key to relationships for 21/3s and 12/3s entails a willingness to lose face and find themselves by expressing what they feel in the moment. They benefit from asking themselves periodically during the day, "How do I really feel right now?" Once they tune in to how they're feeling, it's important that they express these feelings in some way — not just the safe, okay feelings, but also anger, impatience, shame, embarrassment, jealousy, and competitiveness. This practice begins a process of emotional awakening and physical rejuvenation.

Both 12/3s and especially 21/3s often experience a masked form of insecurity in their relationships. For example, they may flirt to see if others still find them attractive, or they may feel or act competitive with their partner for fear of falling into a subordinate position.

When they're doing creative work, 21/3s and, to a lesser degree, 12/3s may have little time or juice for relationships. Because 21/3s and 12/3s sometimes block emotionally charged negative feelings, such as anger or sorrow, they sometimes withdraw emotionally. The wall they build also keeps out the positive feelings of love, affection, and passion. They may need to take part in some good arguments during which they stay emotionally and physically present. Such an outlet of expression can bring back old passions. The core of a strong relationship for 21/3s and 12/3s is emotional contact, even if this means passionate arguments.

The 2 means that those on both of these similar life paths need to find a balance of giving and receiving so that they don't overgive, only to withdraw resentfully later on. The Law of Balance, which deals with giving and receiving, is key here.

Talents, Work, and Finances

Both 21/3s and 12/3s display a strong combination of creative and expressive energy for writing, designing, speaking, debating, advising, promoting, or engaging in any creative field. Although they're extremely versatile, 21/3s and 12/3s are happiest when expressing and creating while supporting and uplifting others.

No matter what their work, 21/3s and 12/3s generally confront some self-doubt and insecurity. With persistence, they earn positive feedback and support from others, and their confidence grows. The well-rounded qualities of 21/3s and 12/3s make for useful, innovative work. When they get past the double hurdles of self-doubt and insecurity and let their feelings and creative juices flow, so will their finances.

Some Well-Known 21/3s and 12/3s

21/3s: Yul Brynner, Bing Crosby, Salvador Dali, Charles Dickens, Judy Garland, Robert F. Kennedy, Groucho Marx, Margaret Mead, Sugar Ray Robinson

12/3: Helen Hayes

Keys to Fulfilling Your Destiny

If you're working 21/3 or 12/3, this section can help you manifest your life purpose by focusing your attention on core issues and by generating specific action to transform key areas of your life.

Guidelines and Recommendations

- If you want to remain supple and healthy, express your feelings.
- Exercise to release pent-up emotional and creative energy.
- Remember and visualize your strongest qualities.
- Make authenticity — showing what you really feel — a priority.

Useful Questions

1. Reflect on the following questions:

    - Do I fully appreciate my creative abilities?
    - Do I move from overconfidence to self-doubt?
    - Do I intellectualize my feelings, or do I let people know how I really feel inside?
    - What does my body reveal about how I'm using my creative energy?

2. If these questions generate insights, how might you put these insights into practice?

Deepening Your Understanding

1. Turn back to Part Two, and reread the main sections covering the digits that make up your birth number: 1, 2, and 3.
2. You may wish to review birth numbers of family and friends and, if they're open to it, discuss similar or different issues in your lives.

Spiritual Laws: The Leverage to Change Your Life

1. Read about each of the following laws in Part Four:

    - **THE LAW OF HONESTY:** Honesty is founded on self-awareness of our emotional reality.
    - **THE LAW OF FAITH:** Only when we find faith in ourselves can we have faith in others.
    - **THE LAW OF CHOICES:** We can choose to create and express ourselves in positive or negative ways.
    - **THE LAW OF BALANCE:** Seeing our tendency to swing from one extreme to another, we find our balance point.

- **THE LAW OF RESPONSIBILITY:** To find our boundaries, we need to learn when to say yes and how to say no.

2. Do the exercises for each of these laws.
3. Consider how you might apply each law to your life.

4: STABILITY THROUGH PROCESS

Life is a dance if you take the steps:
one step, then another. .

— **Anonymous**

This section includes all birth numbers with 4 as a primary life purpose, including single-digit 4, 40/4, 22/4, 31/4, and 13/4. Even though all of these birth numbers reflect intense 4 dynamics, the qualities, issues, and character of those that contain other digits have a unique flavor due to the influence and interaction of the other numbers, in contrast to the pure, undiluted, single-digit 4.

4

4: Stability through Process

Those working single-digit 4 are here to use their natural strength — inner and outer — and analytical intelligence to establish a solid foundation as a launching pad for their life. However, since what we're here to do isn't what comes easiest, before 4s can fulfill their life purpose, they have to overcome hurdles and negative tendencies along their particular path and process.

For this single-digit life path, please be sure to review the chapter in Part Two that provides a full and detailed discussion of the number 4 and all it represents. Here, I highlight key elements of the path and purpose of single-digit 4s.

As mentioned in Part One, 4 is the first single-digit birth number to appear in the twenty-first century. Because it lacks the multifaceted issues and challenges related to a second, third, or fourth digit, all issues for individuals on the 4 path are consolidated squarely in the domain of values, drives, and challenges of stability, process, and analysis and overanalysis, responsibility, and strength, including stubbornness but also persistence and fortitude.

Single-digit 4s have neither the positive nor potentially negative intensity of the double 4s (40/4, 44/8), nor the double-strength or power of those birth numbers. Single-digit 4s tend to be more subdued versions of those working 40/4 — the most similar birth number, and one also recommended for study. Single-digit 4s tend to be something of a paradox: straightforward but sometimes also stubborn, solid but sometimes wiry, sturdy but not necessarily as powerful as those working 40/4 or 44/8.

Single-digit 4s rise or fall based on how their energy is channeled. They're here to apply persistent effort over time, in a process of small steps in any endeavor, as they establish a solid foundation from which to build the rest of their life; for them, a solid foundation isn't the end of their journey, but a beginning or base camp from which all else follows.

Those working single-digit 4 have a natural penchant for analysis but also a tendency to overanalyze or to rely on analysis until they feel disoriented or confused. Like others working 4, they tend to get overly excited, believing that the sky is falling, before settling back and tackling a challenge. Ironically, since 4s are here to stay grounded, they can occasionally be flighty or even gullible when they tire of endless analysis.

Single-digit 4s need to resign as general managers of the universe in the face of tasks, where they tend toward a default of "I'll just do it myself!" if others don't cooperate or feel the same degree of responsibility. In other words, single-digit 4s need to be responsible, but not overly so. (In most situations, responsibility is something shared by more than one person.) Single-digit 4s also need to be wary of manipulation by those who are only too happy to let them do the bulk of the work. So, like the resonant 2s, these 4s need to find a realistic balance in sharing work with others.

If there's one key to success for 4s, it's the willingness to slow down and follow a patient approach to their goals in small steps, without skipping any. Patience isn't the strong suit for those working 4, so special care is important in developing this virtue.

A master metaphor for single-digit 4s is the process of building a house from a strong foundation and then, in careful layers, using persistence as mortar and resilience as nails, and thus building a life from the ground up. Finally, single-digit 4s can heed the advice of Francis Cardinal Spellman: "Pray as if everything depended upon God, and work as if everything depended upon you."

Working Single-Digit 4 in the Positive

Reliable and loyal, individuals working single-digit 4 in the positive can be counted on when needed. They can take stock of a situation, and through astute analytical intelligence can see benefits and liabilities others might miss. They have, over time and through their own experience, developed perspective and patience. They've grasped the power of breaking down any goal into small, manageable steps. Their sense of success is in the process, not just in reaching the destination. Their birth number points to family as a priority and foundational sense of meaning and purpose. They may travel when young, but eventually aim to put grow roots, and build a home, family, and life through diligent effort.

Working Single-Digit 4 in the Negative

Impatient and confused, these single-digit 4s can't quite fathom that failures have happened as a result of half-baked work, shortcuts, and the belief that things will just work out on their own. Such 4s have occasional but episodic emotional outbursts and feel stressed by a busy, overanalytical mind as they try to figure out a clear path. Although a part of them yearns for stability, when things seem too settled they impulsively decide that it's time for a change in personal or professional relationships. Restless and stubborn, once they decide on something they rigidly "plan the work and work the plan" even if circumstances change.

Life-Path Issues

Health

Conventional health wisdom states that strength serves better than suppleness to support the joints. This principle applies to the stable foundations that are so important for single-digit 4s, but this isn't what comes easiest for them; single-digit 4s who don't prepare well for physical challenges may sustain injuries to lower extremities. Strong legs are important, but in the case of single-digit 4s, flexibility, both physical and psychological, is also critical, to avoid the physical or mental rigidity to which they're prone. (Since stubbornness, the shadow side of strength, is a possible liability for single-digit 4s, they need to be alert for signs of *psychosclerosis* — hardening of the attitude.)

Due to an acute sense of responsibility, single-digit 4s may somaticize stress with various physical symptoms, including allergies and physical tension, especially in the upper back — feeling the weight of the world on their shoulders — until they discover that while stress with tension can be debilitating, stress without tension is quite manageable. Any kind of relaxation or meditation practice serves such 4s well, even remembering to take a deep breath and shake loose in difficult moments. All that said, single-digit 4s are likely to possess a generally sturdy or wiry strength and resilience.

Relationships

The family of birth or their primary caregivers are paramount for single-digit 4s, whether nourishing and supportive or less so; family is an arena where insight and life issues lead to deeper understanding. But as the proverb goes, "Friends are the family we choose," so single-digit 4s may also connect with this larger sense of family through friendships. The 4 is by nature a gregarious, social frequency. Personal and professional relationships and networks can come naturally to these outgoing souls.

Their challenges in relationship may often relate to the innate and overarching sense of responsibility in those working 4. In the negative aspect, they can be among the least responsible types until they gain insight and balance in this arena, similar to those with a single or double 2.

Talents, Work, and Finances

Because of their general ease with people, single-digit 4s can make good managers (moderating that powerful "should" element), sales and marketing people, data analysts, and financial planners (since stability is a key life issue). How successful these individuals are remains largely dependent on their climbing the mountain to master process and their willingness to prepare thoroughly, building a stable foundation and then progressing incrementally.

Some Well-Known Single-Digit 4s

As of 2018, and publication of the 25th Anniversary Edition, the oldest single-digit 4s are eighteen years old — not generally enough time to become well-known. In later editions of this book, as more single-digit 4s come of age and make notable accomplishments, names may appear here.

Keys to Fulfilling Your Destiny

If you're working single-digit 4, this section can help you manifest your life purpose by focusing your attention on core issues and by generating specific action to transform key areas of your life.

Guidelines and Recommendations

* Break down big goals and commitments into small steps; divide and conquer.

- Balance your strength with physical and mental flexibility.
- Whatever you undertake, prepare well, commit, and follow through, step-by-step, remaining flexible and alert to changing circumstance.
- When making decisions, write your choices down — and trust your gut feelings.

Useful Questions

1. Reflect on the following questions:
   - You have beliefs, opinions, expectations, hopes, and desires about what you (or others) might do, but can you know what anyone "should" do, or is this playing God?
   - What are your current goals? Write down small, discrete steps you can take to progress toward each goal, including the beginning small step.
   - When making a decision, have you tried writing down the pros and cons and then checking with your gut feeling?
   - How do you feel and what do you think about the word *stability* as it applies to you?
2. If these questions generate insights, how might you put these insights into practice?

Deepening Your Understanding

1. Turn back to Part Two, and reread the main sections covering the digit that makes up your birth number: 4.
2. You may wish to review birth numbers of family and friends and, if they're open to it, discuss similar or different issues in your lives.

Spiritual Laws: The Leverage to Change Your Life

1. Read about each of the following laws in Part Four:
   - THE LAW OF PROCESS: The best way to reach any goal is one small, sure step at a time.

- **THE LAW OF FLEXIBILITY:** Staying flexible, we make the best use of changing circumstances.
- **THE LAW OF PATTERNS:** Patterns tend to reassert themselves unless we exert strong leverage to change them.

2. Do the exercises for each of these laws.
3. Consider how you might apply each law to your life.

40/4

4: Stability through Process
40: Stability through Process with Inner Gifts

Those on the 40/4 life path are here to establish secure foundations in their life by following a gradual process to their goals, applying their inner gifts in a spirit of service on behalf of people or causes they value. Like 20/2s and 30/3s, 40/4s have a very focused life purpose, undiluted by other numbers and issues, and accompanied by inner gifts. Because our central purpose rarely comes easily, many 40/4s may have trouble feeling grounded or following a long, sometimes arduous process to reach their goals. They may skip or ignore necessary steps, or feel stuck in situations that no longer work.

Individuals working 40/4 need to develop a pattern of success by making short-term commitments and following through, gradually expanding the time frame until long-term commitments become feasible. In the same manner, by breaking down big goals and plans into small steps and focusing on completing one step before going to the next, 40/4s create an inner foundation and process that supports them throughout their life.

When working in the positive, 40/4s combine a superb analytical ability with their inner gifts of profound strength and persistence; sensitivity, which balances their strength; expressiveness; and clear intuition. When 40/4s free themselves from analytical loops and trust their gut feelings, they can make inspired, practical, and even brilliant decisions. Their sensitivity and strength act as powerful, synergistic allies — combining the grace of a ballet dancer with the strength of a bull. However, when stuck in overanalysis, they end up feeling confused and disoriented.

Although 20/2s and 40/4s have many similar strengths, tendencies, and issues, 20/2s deal more with issues of responsibility, internal balance, and cooperation; with 40/4s, a stable foundation and a clear, step-by-step process stand paramount. Once 40/4s ground their energy in practical ways, they can apply their refined intuition to support others and to experience more clarity and fun in life.

All 40/4s have the potential of bringing forth their rich resources, indicated by the 0 in their birth number, but they can only develop their gifts through a process of preparation and practice, which may include some form of schooling.

Like all those with 4 as a life path, 40/4s don't tend to enjoy slow, patient progress; more often, what's in the distance feels too far away and they want it now, or the path to their goals feels confusing. It's especially important for 40/4s to trust their gut feelings (physically based intuition) when making decisions, rather than trying to figure out and weigh everything in their heads, where they go in circles.

Due to an exceptionally strong sense of responsibility that sometimes extends far beyond appropriate boundaries, 40/4s tend to think in terms of what they "should" do rather than what they really desire. Like all 4s, 40/4s can also project "shoulds" on other people.

Most 40/4s are even more stubborn than 20/2s (who have less confusion between mind and emotions). Because of their stubbornness, 40/4s don't want to change, adapt, or move. Life may have to provide hard lessons before they get the message.

Nearly all 40/4s have a hard time letting go of old relationships, past decisions, or prior events — and letting go of the past in general. Therefore, they can suffer from regrets: "If only I had said something." They need to observe this tendency and the pain it brings and come to a point of faith, or trust, in their process; whatever decisions they've made have taught them and brought them to where they now stand.

The Law of Process serves as one key toward the fulfillment of the destiny of 40/4s: First things first, lay the groundwork, and then take one step at a time. The ultimate success or failure of 40/4s in business, relationships, or other areas of life depends largely on whether or not they follow the Law of Process and, secondarily, the Law of Patterns.

Like 22/4s and 20/2s, 40/4s tend to bounce from overanalysis to emotional impulsiveness or hysteria, and they need to balance and integrate mind and emotions. When 40/4s combine their powerful analytical ability with their intuition, they demonstrate unusual clarity and foresight.

Working 40/4 in the Positive

Individuals working 40/4 in the positive prepare thoroughly for any task, and they patiently follow a step-by-step process to reach their goals. They can be counted on to follow through with any commitment, and others perceive them as stable and trustworthy friends and advisers. When making decisions, they consider and analyze their options and also trust their gut feelings. They have worked out any family issues to create the best relationship with parents that's feasible. These 40/4s display exceptional fortitude, but they also make use of their subtle gifts and intuition. They persist through hardships and obstacles, no matter how long it takes, and they remain flexible if they reach an impasse. They have created a stable home situation. Relying on intuition and faith, they eventually find the situations and opportunities to suit their interests and abilities.

Working 40/4 in the Negative

These 40/4s don't trust their intuition, and thus they find decision making a stressful, confusing exercise. Stuck in the mind's never-ending analyses, they go in circles trying to answer questions such as "How can I make things happen?" They end up making impulsive decisions they later regret. Their relationships tend to be unstable and short-lived. They have trouble with commitment or staying put with anyone or anything for very long, so they repeat the same patterns of hello-goodbye. Their stubbornness and unyielding views get in the way of the compromise inherent in any relationship. Impulsive and self-deceiving, they tend to start and stop a task without completing it.

Life-Path Issues

Health

Although 40/4s are usually sturdy and resistant to illness (and practically everything else), they may have problems with their hips, thighs, knees, ankles, or feet — the foundation of their body. Physical constipation often indicates repressed drives and desires, especially when they do what they think they "should" do rather than listening to their intuition. Like 20/2s, they may have allergies, but they're more likely than 20/2s to suffer accidents arising out of impatience or impulsive action. Many 40/4s also have congenital problems or physical issues stemming from childhood.

The body of 40/4s tends to be either stocky or very long. Many 40/4s put on weight easily, so a low-fat, even completely vegetarian diet, along with aerobic exercise, generally works well for them. Especially useful are forms of exercise that counterbalance their strength with stretching and relaxation, such as yoga, dance, aikido, tai chi, or other martial arts.

Relationships

In the negative, 40/4s, like 20/2s, can appear pushy, meddling, bossy, or controlling, when actually they just feel overly responsible for everyone in their universe. They can also have trouble with stability. In the positive, they're as stable and supportive as the Rock of Gibraltar. They also have a strong, even if sometimes subconscious, attraction to raising families. They may bring tensions or energy blocks to their sexual relationship, but yoga or stretching and relaxation exercises help them open up and enjoy the sexual aspects of their nature. The more 40/4s get out of their head — or "lose their mind and come to their senses," as Timothy Leary put it — the better their relationships.

Talents, Work, and Finances

Due to their excellent analytical skills and intuition as well as to their inherent need for secure foundations, 40/4s do well in any form of business. They may feel confused when making their own decisions, but they make excellent advisers, organizers, financiers, or real estate counselors. They feel most satisfied when their business actively helps or supports other people. Service oriented, they do well as caregivers in the fields of nursing or social work, for example, but they also can excel in other fields, including sports and athletics — wherever qualities of persistence, strength, sensitivity, and analytical abilities apply. As long as they follow the Law of Process and use their vitality in practical ways, 40/4s find success.

Some Well-Known 40/4s

Because this birth number is relatively rare in the population, the list of well-known figures is proportionately smaller: Benedict Cumberbatch, T. E. Lawrence (of Arabia), Will Smith.

Keys to Fulfilling Your Destiny

If you're working 40/4, this section can help you manifest your life purpose by focusing your attention on core issues and by generating specific action to transform key areas of your life.

Guidelines and Recommendations

- Appreciate your sensitivities as well as your strengths.
- Follow every step on the path to reaching your goal.
- When in a hurry, take the long, sure way.
- Treat your life as you would build a house, providing a solid foundation and following a gradual process.

Useful Questions

1. Reflect on the following questions:

    - When I make decisions, do I overanalyze or do I trust my gut feelings?
    - How can I use my family challenges as a means of growth?
    - Have I found a balance between supporting others and allowing others to support me?
    - How flexible am I in response to changing needs and situations?

2. If these questions generate insights, how might you put these insights into practice?

Deepening Your Understanding

1. Turn back to Part Two, and reread the main sections covering the digits that make up your birth number: 4 and 0.
2. You may wish to review birth numbers of family and friends and, if they're open to it, discuss similar or different issues in your lives.

Spiritual Laws: The Leverage to Change Your Life

1. Read about each of the following laws in Part Four:

    •   **THE LAW OF PROCESS:** The best way to reach any goal is one
        small, sure step at a time.

    •   **THE LAW OF PATTERNS:** Patterns tend to reassert themselves
        unless we exert strong leverage to change them.

    •   **THE LAW OF FLEXIBILITY:** Staying flexible, we make the best use
        of changing circumstances.

    •   **THE LAW OF HIGHER WILL:** Our willingness to serve a higher
        purpose empowers us to inspire others.

    •   **THE LAW OF CYCLES:** Life brings constant changes, arising and
        then passing like the seasons.

2. Do the exercises for each of these laws.
3. Consider how you might apply each law to your life.

22/4

4: Stability through Process
2: Cooperation through Balance
2: Cooperation through Balance

Those on the 22/4 life path are here to work through issues of cooperation, responsibility, and process to establish a stable and secure foundation, achieving their goals through a patient process involving mutually supportive teamwork. However, since our life purpose entails special challenges, 22/4s have a strong tendency to overcooperate, giving their all and then falling into resentment and withdrawal. Their ambitions can also create blind spots, so they tend to skip necessary steps on the path to their goal. For them, failure is useful feedback if they're paying attention. When 22/4s run into problems, they need to determine which step they skipped and redo it; this releases any pattern of failure. No challenge is too great if 22/4s break it down into small, manageable portions.

For 22/4s, the double 2 has a strong influence in determining the characteristics and issues of the life path. The first 2 deals especially and almost totally with inner cooperation; thus, the fulfillment of the destiny of 22/4s begins with their integration of conflicting beliefs, values, or tendencies. When the life of 22/4s feels problematic, they need to go back to their own inner foundation and, through therapy or other means, harmonize their inner world before trying to organize and control their environment. The second 2 for 22/4s focuses on outer cooperation — relating with others, honoring their own and other people's boundaries, and finding the critical balance between giving too much and shutting down.

Nearly all 22/4s have strong analytical and structuring capacities, but when 22/4s use these capacities to excess, their mind whirls in overanalysis or compulsive worrying until it finally shuts down and reactive emotions or impulsive action takes over. Impulsive actions then lead to regrets. As for all those working 2 energy, balance and integration are key; the aim is to blend mind and emotions, balancing logic with intuition, rather than resorting to extremes. When 22/4s feel confused, they benefit from writing their ideas down and then trusting their instincts — following their gut feeling — for final decisions.

Those working 22/4 need to apply clear, realistic insight and self-compassion in confronting their issues; otherwise, they may react to an over-whelming sense of responsibility by putting on blinders, ignoring feedback, and going into denial, leaving imbalances and problems unacknowledged. Most 22/4s have strong, focused, sometimes rigid opinions, and they don't always listen well to contradictory ideas because they have so many of their own.

When the double 2 and the 4 work together, 22/4s have exceptional vigor and potential. How that potential manifests depends on how they align their life with the spiritual laws key to their destiny. With 4, 22/4s have strength, fortitude, and endurance, but if their life is to proceed toward the fulfillment of their destiny, all depends on making the journey in small, sure steps, and checking to make sure that they have established a solid foundation before proceeding. When this pattern is worked in the positive, 22/4s meet with ex-traordinary achievement.

Working 22/4 in the Positive

Clear-thinking, centered individuals working 22/4 in the positive can accom-plish whatever they set out to do, by a process of small steps, turning stum-bling blocks along the way into stepping-stones. When they fail, they learn from their mistakes and don't repeat them. They've learned hard lessons, but over time the lessons have gotten easier. They've found the balance point be-tween giving too much and giving too little. They live from a stable center of internal harmony and cooperation. These 22/4s serve others only to the point they feel good and clear about their service. Relatively free of worry and stress, they allow their body to relax into life, and their mind focuses on the present as they plan the next small step along the way.

Working 22/4 in the Negative

These 22/4s always seem to verge on the edge of one crisis or another. They're frequently frantic, even hysterical. They experience inner confusion and stress. Making impulsive decisions they later regret, they stubbornly hold their course and repeat the same mistakes. Their forceful, rigid views create anger when others don't do what these 22/4s think they should. As master codependents, they overgive to the point of depletion. They form intense relationships, which they throw themselves into at first and then cut themselves off from, feeling alienated and resentful. Generally impatient, they want to get everything done *now*, without going through the necessary step-by-step process.

Life-Path Issues

Health

Most 22/4s are slim, strong, and wiry, but they're sometimes overweight due to other factors, such as childhood abuse or lack of good education on nutrition. They may suffer accidents because of their impulsive action or mental distraction. When they take responsibility for themselves instead of for everyone else, their health remains strong. As long as they run their life in an orderly fashion and don't get overly stressed, they have one of the sturdier constitutions.

Since the center of their life is service and support of others, 22/4s rarely become too self-indulgent with food; for the most part, they prefer quality to quantity. Food is just something to obtain between tasks and goals, and meals are often catch-as-catch-can.

Nearly all 22/4s do well with exercises and movements that develop flexibility, relaxation, and flow, such as dance, aerobics with stretching, yoga, aikido, tai chi, or other martial arts. These practices emphasize step-by-step skill training and working with partners in a give-and-take way that can help balance their already-strong bodies and their often rigid temperaments better than, say, weight training.

Relationships

As a foundation for all of their relationships, most 22/4s need to clarify their interactions with their parents or primary caregivers. All 22/4s work with foundation energy; their early home life represents the base on which they build. Since our central purpose brings up issues to work through, most 22/4s likely have issues to work out with one or both parents or siblings. Most people have some issues to work out with parents, but it's especially important for 22/4s to deal with these, as it is with any 4s. This doesn't mean getting approval or even agreement of parents, but it does mean talking, sharing views, agreeing to disagree, and being authentic rather than denying or avoiding old resentments. Most 22/4s also learn much through their relationship with their own children or with other children they care for or mentor.

Most 22/4s tend to take care of other people's needs in a functional manner. They tend to be highly responsible and protective caregivers, but they aren't usually sentimental, favoring practicality over emotional nurturance. If their child gets a cut, for example, they won't necessarily fuss over it; they'll efficiently clean the cut and get a bandage.

In other relationships, 22/4s are generally practical, direct, confident, and forthright; to balance these qualities, they also need to take the time to slow down, relax, breathe, feel, and bring sensitivity and empathy into their love relationships. Especially in this arena, 22/4s need to focus on what they really *feel*, not just on what they think they want or think they "should" do.

In the positive, most 22/4s can make extraordinary efforts to serve and support those they love. But when the negative aspects of their strength are activated, their emotional reactivity and strong, often rigid views of how other people "should" behave don't always make for smooth relationships. Also, since their temperament swings from overaccommodating to resistant, they aren't always inclined to compromise or to listen to other people's feedback.

In the positive, however, their intrinsic loyalty and brightness make the effort worthwhile. Having a partner who doesn't have control issues and is easygoing helps the relationship flow more smoothly.

Sexuality for 22/4s tends toward the earthy, vital, and functional; lovemaking may be robust, but not always romantic or slow and sensual. In addition, some 22/4s, like others working 4, have encountered forms of emotional, physical, or sexual abuse that need to be worked through before their sexual life can blossom.

Talents, Work, and Finances

Strength, persistence, common sense, and fortitude can take 22/4s as far as they want to go, as long as they're willing to go through the process to get there. They feel deep satisfaction when using their special talents to support others in service, whether within their family or in teaching, advising, and business enterprises. Their practical organizational and analytical skills help them excel in many other fields. Because 22/4s like to know what's expected of them, they generally feel attracted to anything practical, with clear limits, boundaries, and measures of success.

A strong quality of 22/4s in their approach to work and life involves issues of cooperation. After having their fill of doing what everyone else wanted or expected of them in their childhood, many 22/4s develop maverick qualities later in life and, like 22/4 Frank Sinatra, "do it their way."

Those working 22/4 have a strong orientation toward security, meaning financial stability is a priority; they achieve it through high energy and focused work. As long as they approach their goals step-by-step and remember to enjoy the process, they prosper.

Some Well-Known 22/4s

Woody Allen, P. T. Barnum, Lenny Bruce, Clint Eastwood, Luciano Pavarotti, Ronald Reagan, Frank Sinatra, Margaret Thatcher, Mark Twain

Keys to Fulfilling Your Destiny

If you're working 22/4, this section can help you manifest your life purpose by focusing your attention on core issues and by generating specific action to transform key areas of your life.

Guidelines and Recommendations

- Make friends with yourself first, by integrating your conflicting parts.
- Stay open to feedback from friends; do you give too much?
- Stay flexible in body and mind — resilient, not resistant.
- Structure your life and appreciate each step on the path.

Useful Questions

1. Reflect on the following questions:
   - When I make decisions, do I base them on my authentic needs and values or on what I think I'm supposed to do?

- Do I feel good about what I'm doing for others?
- What's the next step toward my goals?
- Whom do I need to forgive or ask for forgiveness?

2. If these questions generate insights, how might you put these insights into practice?

Deepening Your Understanding

1. Turn back to Part Two, and reread the main sections covering the digits that make up your birth number: 2 and 4.
2. You may wish to review birth numbers of family and friends and, if they're open to it, discuss similar or different issues in your lives.

Spiritual Laws: The Leverage to Change Your Life

1. Read about each of the following laws in Part Four:

   - **THE LAW OF PROCESS:** The best way to reach any goal is one small, sure step at a time.
   - **THE LAW OF RESPONSIBILITY:** To find our boundaries, we need to learn when to say yes and how to say no.
   - **THE LAW OF PATTERNS:** Patterns tend to reassert themselves unless we exert strong leverage to change them.
   - **THE LAW OF HONESTY:** Honesty is founded on self-awareness of our emotional reality.
   - **THE LAW OF BALANCE:** Seeing our tendency to swing from one extreme to another, we find our balance point.

2. Do the exercises for each of these laws.
3. Consider how you might apply each law to your life.

31/4 & 13/4

4: Stability through Process
1: Creativity through Security
3: Expression through Sensitivity

Those on the 31/4 or 13/4 life path are here to work through issues of stability, creativity, and emotional expression, learning to channel their energy in constructive ways and to master a step-by-step process to their goals. Since our life purpose doesn't come easily, 31/4s have to overcome self-doubt and insecurity to develop the confidence necessary to follow a long, sometimes arduous process to reach their goals. Until then, they operate on hopes, wishes, or enthusiastic illusions. Since both 31/4s and 13/4s are here to ground their energy and develop secure foundations, they often confront tendencies toward instability and lack of commitment, which run counter to their life purpose.

To overcompensate for insecurity, many 31/4s develop a highly ambitious persona — a big ego that works to prove their worth as they strive to impress others due to fears of inferiority beneath the surface.

The combination of strong foundation energy, creative energy, and expressive energy gives 31/4s and 13/4s a well-balanced, synergistic blend of strength, sensitivity, and creativity. This blend of qualities, combined with a drive for security and strong ambitions, creates a multifaceted potential for success. When these qualities and drives are working in harmony, 31/4s and 13/4s can accomplish their highest aspirations. But if these same qualities and drives work against one another or manifest in negative ways, then frustration and failures cloud their life.

The willingness to pursue and persist in a gradual process is essential to bringing the highest creativity and expression of 31/4s and 13/4s into the world. Whether their foundation rests on family, home, land, education, or work, this foundation forms the stable base for expanding out into life. A secure home base and a safe, settled, orderly environment amplify their impact many times over. Bursts of inspiration or spurts of energy don't substitute for diligent work over time. The life they build depends on the preparations they make and the process they follow.

The order and relative influence of 1 and 3 result in the only significant difference between 31/4s and 13/4s: With 31/4s, creative energy has a stronger influence than expressive energy; with 13/4s, expressive issues predominate. For 31/4s, strong creative drives, a confident, outgoing persona, and a constant striving for success veil an underlying insecurity. They can be highly competitive because they feel they need to prove themselves to overcome their fear of not measuring up, of inferiority. Most 13/4s, on the other hand, feel more acute self-doubt, which manifests as a fear of insufficient capacity and appears, from time to time, like storm clouds in an otherwise clear sky.

Other than these slight differences in emphasis, 31/4s and 13/4s have nearly identical drives and issues: They both show strong drives for creative expression. They share strength, ambition, and a desire for status. The twin shadows of self-doubt and insecurity confront both 31/4s and 13/4s with worthy challenges on the way to manifesting their strength and achieving success. A key concept for 31/4s and 13/4s is that success in terms of their life purpose lies not so much in achieving the end product as in their ability to go through the necessary process.

Many 31/4s and 13/4s have experienced difficult family histories, sometimes entailing physical abuse by at least one parent or perhaps a military childhood that meant they had to move around and never had a stable home life. Because our life purpose doesn't come easily, they have had hurdles to overcome in the area of establishing strong foundations. Even if they come from relatively stable households, 31/4s and 13/4s benefit from working through issues of animosity, resentment, misunderstanding, or other turmoil to rebuild a sense of stable foundation. They need to express all of their emotions, including anger and resentment, before they can express their love. They don't have to agree with their parents, but they need to bring any issues into the open and express their feelings, even if their parents are deceased.

Both 31/4s and 13/4s can also learn many lessons from their own children or other children.

Because 31/4s and 13/4s tend to experience a division rather than an integration between mind and emotions, they especially need to blend emotional intuition with mental clarity. When making a decision, they can ask, "What would my calmest, clearest, most aware self do right now?" By trusting their gut feelings, they can avoid confusion; otherwise, they tend to analyze everything to death. Once they feel clarity, they can teach it to others.

As for others working 4 energy, the primary challenge or hurdle for 31/4s and 13/4s involves following a step-by-step process — remembering that even the most overwhelming goal is easier when broken down into small steps. Since the life purpose of 31/4s and 13/4s, which involves process, doesn't come easily, a part of them hates things that take a long time and a slow, careful process to achieve. Combining the inherent impatience of 4 with the creative inspiration of 1, many 31/4s and 13/4s like things to happen quickly, even magically. On the other hand, the self-doubt of 3 may slow them down and lead to overpreparation or obsession with one step.

Those 31/4s and 13/4s who have previously moved through a structured process, such as athletes, musicians, or anyone who has stuck with a process of skill training, are way ahead of the game, because they have a template or model they can apply to anything else they do.

Once 31/4s and 13/4s create a stable environment, see past insecurity and self-doubt, and find the patience to follow a step-by-step process to their goals, it's only a matter of time before they reach them.

Working 31/4 or 13/4 in the Positive

Individuals working 31/4 or 13/4 in the positive have developed a sound financial base as well as a personal base of family, friends, and associates. They make decisions by blending head (analysis) and heart (intuition), and they've learned to trust the process of their life. Well-rounded achievers, they've followed goals to completion as they've learned skills, and they use that understanding to reach any goal. Dependable and stable, their blend of strength, flexibility, sensitivity, and creative sparkle serves as a source of practical support and encouragement to others.

Working 31/4 or 13/4 in the Negative

Even if they have a place to live, these 31/4s or 13/4s lack an inner sense of stability; it's as if they were living out of a suitcase. Uncommitted and lacking follow-through, they never feel sure how long they'll stay in one place, in one job, or with one person. Ambitious but impatient, they touch down many places, but they don't put down roots. Confusion underlies their lack of commitment; they don't feel sure of what they're supposed to be doing. They think one thing and feel another, so they don't know what they want. This split between mind and emotions leads to impulsive decisions and then obsessive regrets. They experience more starts and stops than completions. With their unrealistic expectations, they want to be a success without going through the process to get there. Their outward bravado or superior air covers up feelings of self-doubt and insecurity.

Life-Path Issues

Health

The strength of 31/4s and 13/4s, amplified by creative energy, gives them robust appeal, ruggedness, and resistance to everyday illness. Their body type tends to be either wide and bottom heavy or solidly athletic, depending largely on genetics and lifestyle; either way, they're basically strong. However, they're vulnerable at foundation points, such as ankles, knees, thighs, and hips.

Mental stress or resistance can create physical as well as energetic constipation and can compromise the immune system. Forms of meditation, relaxation, suppleness training, and free movement, such as the martial arts of aikido or tai chi, are all useful — as is anything that teaches them to blend, flow, and accept rather than resist. Forms of physical skill training, such as dance or martial arts, offer special benefits because they help turn rigid strength into supple, dynamic power and give 31/4s and 13/4s a direct experience of following a process and experiencing improvement over time. These individuals thrive on exercise and particularly enjoy social sports.

Given the varied 3, 1, and 4 predispositions, 31/4s and 13/4s have no predictable dietary tendencies, but a balanced, low-fat diet serves as a good foundation. If 31/4s and 13/4s are overweight, their success in losing their excess weight depends on their willingness to follow a gradual process toward a more active lifestyle. Fitful, heroic efforts directed toward quick weight loss at best bring only temporary results. The success of 31/4s and 13/4s in this or any enterprise depends on a patient, persistent approach.

Relationships

The easy sociability of 31/4s and 13/4s attracts many friends and admirers. They tend to be gregarious, family oriented, and generally relaxed with people. But their air of confidence often hides an insecurity they're wise to acknowledge to themselves and others in order to achieve a new level of authenticity. In their vulnerability, they can find new strength. Since 4 issues lead them toward self-deception or denial, both 31/4s and 13/4s may discover that confession is, indeed, good for the soul. By confessing their sensitive or insecure qualities, 31/4s and 13/4s find they have less to defend, less to prove, and fewer people they have to impress; this leads to a greater sense of inner solidity.

Most 31/4s and 13/4s are either salt of the earth — a stable, loyal, constant partner — or they have difficulty staying put or making real emotional commitments. Even when they say "I do," they may leave the back door open. Part of them desires stability and security more than anything, but part of them resists that very goal because our life purpose doesn't necessarily come easily. When they see relationship as a process of ups and downs, entailing learning, maturation, and mutual support, 31/4s and 13/4s come to appreciate relationship as a challenging form of spiritual training rather than "the same old thing."

In the sexual arena, 31/4s and 13/4s need to work through the nonsexual issues of self-doubt, insecurity, and lack of commitment. Their past experiences of abuse or their subconscious resistance and physical tension may get in the way of satisfying sexual expression. However, on the positive side, they tend to be strong, vital, earthy, and creative lovers.

Talents, Work, and Finances

Due to their array of creative and expressive drives and their sound analytical abilities, 31/4s and 13/4s find success in a variety of careers, often, but not necessarily, centered in some form of business, advising, or counseling in real estate or investments. However, they also do well in fields as divergent as coaching, service to family, architecture, engineering, or any form of creative communication that supports people. In the positive, their practical creativity, developed over time, leads to the security they desire. If they're patient and thorough, one step leads to the next. But they need to remember that overnight successes can take years — and many small steps — to come about.

Some Well-Known 31/4s and 13/4s

31/4s: Sergey Brin, Marie Curie, Miles Davis, 14th Dalai Lama, Sigmund Freud, Robert Frost, Bill Gates, Hugh Hefner, Ramana Maharshi, Paul McCartney, Babe Ruth, Arnold Schwarzenegger, Donald Trump, Oprah Winfrey

13/4s: No well-known 13/4s exist in our records because relatively few exist in the population.

Keys to Fulfilling Your Destiny

If you're working 31/4 or 13/4, this section can help you manifest your life purpose by focusing your attention on core issues and by generating specific action to transform key areas of your life.

Guidelines and Recommendations

- Remain humble and kind above all else.
- To develop your full creative abilities, first develop your skills step-by-step, over time.
- Exercise your body, your mind, and your emotions.
- Balance your analytical abilities with creative intuition.

Useful Questions

1. Reflect on the following questions:
   - Do I let self-doubt or insecurity stop me?
   - Do I follow a gradual step-by-step process to reach my goals?
   - Have I explored the full range of my creative capacities?
   - Have I worked through early family issues?

2. If these questions generate insights, how might you put these insights into practice?

Deepening Your Understanding

1. Turn back to Part Two, and reread the main sections covering the digits that make up your birth number: 1, 3, and 4.
2. You may wish to review birth numbers of family and friends and, if they're open to it, discuss similar or different issues in your lives.

Spiritual Laws: The Leverage to Change Your Life

1. Read about each of the following laws in Part Four:

   - **THE LAW OF PROCESS:** The best way to reach any goal is one small, sure step at a time.
   - **THE LAW OF PATTERNS:** Patterns tend to reassert themselves unless we exert strong leverage to change them.
   - **THE LAW OF CHOICES:** We can choose to create and express ourselves in positive or negative ways.
   - **THE LAW OF FLEXIBILITY:** Staying flexible, we make the best use of changing circumstances.
   - **THE LAW OF CYCLES:** Life brings constant changes, arising and then passing like the seasons.

2. Do the exercises for each of these laws.
3. Consider how you might apply each law to your life.

5: FREEDOM THROUGH DISCIPLINE

As far as your self-control goes,
as far goes your freedom.

— Marie von Ebner-Eschenbach

This section includes all birth numbers with 5 as a primary life purpose, including single-digit 5, 32/5, 23/5, 41/5, and 14/5. Even though all of these birth numbers reflect intense 5 dynamics, the qualities, issues, and character of those that contain other digits have a unique flavor due to the influence and interaction of the other digits, in contrast to the pure, undiluted, single-digit 5.

5

5: Freedom through Discipline

Those working single-digit 5 are here to experience freedom through both breadth and depth of experience, made possible by discipline — finding a current focus and setting clear priorities. However, since what we're here to do isn't what comes easiest, before single-digit 5s can fulfill their life purpose, they have to overcome a tendency to get scattered due to an innate interest in many topics, pursuits, and facets of life.

For this single-digit life path, please be sure to review the chapter in Part Two that provides a full and detailed discussion of the number 5 and all it represents. Here, I highlight key elements of the path and purpose of single-digit 5s.

Freedom, for single-digit 5s, has little to do with mere self-indulgence or living without any constraints; rather, it entails an expansive love of adventure. Given a choice between money in the bank and a new experience, individuals working single-digit 5 generally opt for the experience, because adventure is coin of the realm in their life.

In a parallel to those working 2, who need to establish a balance between overcooperation and undercooperation, single-digit 5s need to break the tendency to swing from overdependence to extreme independence. It's easy for single-digit 5s to mistake independence and self-reliance for freedom, when they're here to achieve a comfortable state of interdependence — sometimes working with others to achieve goals, and sometimes pursuing do-it-yourself projects. The main thing to avoid is swinging between extremes, as single-digit 5s can find (or put) themselves in situations where they become dependent on others for support or even income until they swing to the other extreme and separate from, or even alienate, those sources of dependence in a striving for total independence and emotional isolation, mistaking such isolation for freedom.

Like all those working with a 5 in their birth number, single-digit 5s feel an innate desire for experience and at least summary knowledge in a wide array of areas. This desire can lead toward pursuing too many things at once, leading to a jack-of-all-trades, master-of-none pattern, which can then lead to exhaustion, disappointment, and burnout. Such individuals do well to explore the saying "When digging a well, it works better to dig one hole a hundred feet deep rather than ten holes each ten feet deep." Otherwise their business card may read like an ensemble, with expertise in gardening and writing, martial arts and computer programming — leading others to wonder exactly what it is they actually do.

This doesn't mean that single-digit 5s can't enjoy varied interests, hobbies, or callings — after all, they're here for adventure and experience. But single-digit 5s need to set priorities and do a psychological or value triage about which activities to focus on now, and which to do later — what to practice for fifteen or thirty minutes, and what to do for hours. They need to grasp that they can do anything, but not everything — at least not at the same time.

These individuals may not need, seek out, or create drama to the degree of 32/5s, but they have an instinctive dislike of boredom or the mundane, and so may tend to fabricate from the cloth of ordinary experience and memory stories that become tall tales, and they may be viewed by friends as unreliable narrators.

Since every tendency bears the seeds of its opposite, single-digit 5s may at times almost obsessively form a narrow focus studying or practicing one thing to the exclusion of all else. Again, balance here is the key, which is what their discipline and challenge is all about.

It's usually exciting, and occasionally exhausting, to be around such individuals, since existence may take on a larger-than-life quality around them, due to their expansive perspectives and possibilities. Those who mature on the single-digit 5 path, developing a sense of discipline, have the potential to enjoy the freedom of good health and financial security, enabling them to travel or engage in trainings and experiences to further expand their broad horizons.

Working Single-Digit 5 in the Positive

Those working single-digit 5 in the positive — the classic Renaissance person — can become a role model of focus and discipline, as well as of adventure and accomplishment. The breadth of experience and interest of these viva- cious souls can lend insight and even depth to any new endeavor, since they've "looked at life from both sides," as the Joni Mitchell line goes. They remind the world that life is an adventure and, like heat-seeking missiles, form goals and do whatever's necessary to accomplish and enjoy them. They take bites out of life, enjoying the feast. They don't just gaze at the view from a cliff over a lake; they leap off and soar into the depths.

Working Single-Digit 5 in the Negative

Feeling stifled and resentful of the very person or people they depend on, these single-digit 5s dream of a future when they're completely on their own and seemingly free. But such plans seem out of reach except in small, fitful gestures, since these single-digit 5s may, early on, lack any sense of focus or priorities. They may play the role of a healer or life coach or financial adviser on sheer bluff, without credentials (if anyone happens to check). They have rich fanta- sies, imagining a life and experience they wish for, but they haven't yet found a way to turn those dreams into reality through actual work and practice.

Life-Path Issues

Health

Beyond standard guidelines of nutrition, exercise, and rest that apply to humans across the board, the aspects of health single-digit 5s can control depend largely on their level of maturity and whether they're working 5 in positive or negative ways. If they follow healthy guidelines, they enhance their underlying genetic potential.

It's likely that single-digit 5s, without the complex challenges of three- and four-digit birth numbers, won't have to confront the degree of insecurity, self-doubt, or stress lurking on other life paths. But single-digit 5s need to stay vigilant and take normal precautions and preparation before attempt- ing athletic feats, and stay wary of bravado or overconfidence in their search of adventure. Varied activities that contribute to health and fitness include martial arts (for its image and adventure), hiking or rock climbing, mountain biking, acrobatics, or other adventure sports.

Some single-digit 5s may prefer a more sedate lifestyle, and find more restful forms of vicarious adventure through reading, movies, or even engaging in cutting-edge research. Yet in every case, disciplined, regular, moderate exercise and balanced diet can provide the freedom of good health. For single-digit 5s, meditation can be profoundly useful, not just for relaxation but in teaching them a simple discipline of confronting boredom while just sitting.

Relationships

A key to any healthy relationship is honesty and authenticity — especially important for single-digit 5s, who have an innate ability to play different roles and see life from many different angles. One friend working 5 as a life path told me that he wasn't sure who he was anymore. "Sure you are," I responded; "it's just that there are so many of you." Anyone who wants to sustain a long-term personal and professional relationship can't always be a moving target. Stable, committed relationships can be challenging if your partner isn't sure who they're married to, or if their single-digit 5 partner is running off on one or another independent relationship — another major relationship challenge if the single-digit 5 continues to yearn for independence. Because single-digit 5s need a long leash or at least a bond of love to bring them back home, maybe someday a single-digit 5 will propose that marriage would best be undertaken for consecutive five- or ten-year terms, renewable on mutual agreement.

Talents, Work, and Finances

Individuals working single-digit 5 are likely to have agile and dexterous manual skills, whether working as a surgeon, juggler, or musician. Due to a wide array of interests, single-digit 5s may display a number of talents or abilities; again, focus is key in the work area, and as in relationships, a sense of discipline and commitment, at least for an agreed-upon duration, is important. Money is likely to be important to single-digit 5s only to the extent that it represents independence, and the ability to finance adventure travel or experiences. Flextime and telecommuting were probably invented (or proposed) by someone with a 5 in their birth number.

Single-digit 5s are likely to be self-starters; they thrive on flexibility and usually get the job done if left to their own clever devices. As with the other single-digit birth numbers, there's no way to suggest a particular type of profession; again, the birth number doesn't point to a given profession, but rather points to how someone might approach and function in that profession. As long as 5s have some wiggle room and space, they can fit in and thrive in many professions, particularly entrepreneurial ventures in which they are their own boss.

Some Well-Known Single-Digit 5s

As of 2018, and publication of the 25th Anniversary Edition, the oldest single-digit 5s are under eighteen years old — not generally enough time to become well-known. In later editions of this book, as more 5s come of age and make notable accomplishments, names may appear here.

Keys to Fulfilling Your Destiny

If you're working single-digit 5, this section can help you manifest your life purpose by focusing your attention on core issues and by generating specific action to transform key areas of your life.

Guidelines and Recommendations

*   Develop some form of simple daily routine to establish discipline; mix variety into the routine.
*   Don't let a feeling of boredom stop you from going deeply into a subject or activity.
*   Find a balance between the extremes of dependence and independence by observing when you swing from one to the other.

Useful Questions

1. Reflect on the following questions:
    *   What are your top three short-term priorities, in order of importance? How about long-term priorities? Are they different or similar?
    *   How do you handle periods of boredom? What's boredom to you?
    *   Do you have a bucket list of things you'd like to do, places you'd like to visit, experiences you'd like to have? If so, how can you arrange to make the first item a reality?

- Do you play different roles in different situations, or do you present the same self to different people? How does that serve you?

2. If these questions generate insights, how might you put these insights into practice?

Deepening Your Understanding

1. Turn back to Part Two, and reread the main sections covering the digit that makes up your birth number: 5.
2. You may wish to review birth numbers of family and friends and, if they're open to it, discuss similar or different issues in your lives.

Spiritual Laws: The Leverage to Change Your Life

1. Read about each of the following laws in Part Four:

   - **THE LAW OF DISCIPLINE:** Discipline generates the focus and depth of experience leading to true freedom.
   - **THE LAW OF HONESTY:** Honesty is founded on self-awareness of our emotional reality.

2. Do the exercises for each of these laws.
3. Consider how you might apply each law to your life.

32/5 & 23/5

5: Freedom through Discipline
2: Cooperation through Balance
3: Expression through Sensitivity

Those on the 32/5 or 23/5 life path are here to work through issues related to independence, emotional honesty, and cooperation, finally experiencing freedom through discipline and depth of experience. Since our life path presents hurdles to overcome, both 32/5s and 23/5s confront internal challenges, tendencies, and conflicts in areas of dependence and independence, responsibility, and honest expression of emotion.

Individuals working 32/5 and 23/5 are nearly identical in terms of the fundamental qualities of their birth number, the only difference being the reversed order of the 3 and 2. Most 23/5s tend to be late bloomers, taking longer to come into their confidence due to the more predominant 3 dynamics, with related issues of sensitivity and self-doubt; they also have stronger fears along with a stronger drive toward expression than 32/5s.

Most 32/5s have deeper issues around cooperation than their counterparts; they tend to give their all for someone, even letting go of their own multifaceted identity and, chameleonlike, adapting to the values, interests, and desires of their partner. Then, somewhere down the line, to the degree they have ignored their own needs, they may withdraw emotionally or become resentful.

This isn't to say that 32/5s don't display the self-doubt of 23/5s or that 23/5s don't have the issues around cooperation of their 32/5 counterparts, but the relative influence of 2 and 3 tendencies differs in each case based on their position in the birth number.

Both 32/5s and 23/5s are here to experience true freedom. The phrase *true freedom* implies the idea of false freedoms — for example, self-indulgence, irresponsibility, or license — when 32/5s or 23/5s insist on doing whatever they want to do, whenever they want to do it. Only those 32/5s and 23/5s who haven't yet matured into a more positive expression of the 5 strive for such "freedom."

The freedom sought by most 32/5s and 23/5s manifests as a drive to experience and know; this freedom entails a sense of mobility in different arenas of life — physical, mental, emotional, social, sexual, and financial. Those working 32/5 or 23/5 seek to explore opportunities and find adventure where they can, whether in life, in books, or at the movies.

Sometimes the drive for experience is so strong that 32/5s and 23/5s end up trying to juggle too many things to avoid missing an opportunity and end up feeling scattered or depleted. Many 32/5s, in particular, burn their candle at both ends. While 23/5s may have less confidence at first and 32/5s are more likely to overreach their limits, both are quick learners, living by their wits, with varied abilities and experience.

Both 32/5s and 23/5s can sometimes focus obsessively on whatever they're doing and lose sight of the bigger picture. Like all those working 5, they need discipline, focus, and a sense of priorities to help free themselves. The ultimate freedom 32/5s and 23/5s seek is internal — the freedom to be themselves, the freedom from self-doubt, the freedom from fear. Only by establishing this internal sense of expansiveness can they feel the fulfillment of their destiny in the external world. However, one way to generate internal freedom is by facing outer experience. Since the external world reflects the world of our psyche, by tackling outer challenges, 32/5s and 23/5s have a chance to confront and transcend the issues of self-doubt and cooperation that bind them. Adventures, whether large or small, serve them well as they stretch their limits, take some emotional risks, and explore their capacities.

The characteristics of 2, which sometimes tends toward overcooperation, combined with the dramatic tendencies of 3 and 5, can generate a kind of martyr complex. These individuals want to save people, save the world, and fight for freedom. The more dramatic the means, the better. Writing to congressional representatives just isn't enough for them. They prefer drama — both on television and in real life.

Since 32/5s and 23/5s tend to be quick-witted, fast learners, they also get bored easily. Boredom is their personal hell. If things get boring, they generally stir up a little drama on their own. Ultimately, the freedom they seek entails illumination and spiritual liberation — expanding their consciousness to the point where the universe becomes their playground. At this point, their body no longer feels like a prison, because they've cultivated their visual imagination and their innate clairvoyant (clear-seeing) abilities and can travel far beyond the confines of their body.

Most 5s have explored many areas of life. The liability is that they get a broad range of experience, but a relatively shallow one. Through discipline and focus, 32/5s and 23/5s enter the depths of experience, going into a few areas deeply enough that they discover the spiritual laws that underlie all aspects of life; in doing so, they find a deeper sense of freedom. Without such discipline, 32/5s and 23/5s tend to skim the surface or get scattered trying to do everything at once. By focusing their attention — by setting clear priorities and sticking with them — they go deeper into the experience of freedom.

Just as 2s tend to swing back and forth between the extremes of under-cooperation and overcooperation, 32/5s and 23/5s tend to swing between the extremes of dependence and independence. Ultimately, they need to find a comfortable balance. They achieve this balance by allowing themselves to explore each extreme, learning about independence through examining their dependency issues, for example. They may find themselves dependent on others as a result of an accident, an illness, or a financial setback, or they may actively create a dependent relationship because of doubts or insecurity about their ability to take care of themselves. Their challenge is to use these experiences to reestablish a healthy balance of independence and appropriate interdependence — in the sense of being able to receive from others.

Out of insecurity, both 32/5s and 23/5s tend to hide behind their social roles. They benefit from remembering that they're more than the roles they play. Their ability to bluff or role-play enables 32/5s and 23/5s to manipulate others consciously or unconsciously, using emotions such as anger to get their way.

Whether they spend their weekends going on safari or watching the soaps, skydiving or taking care of children, 32/5s and 23/5s have a vivacious quality, a Renaissance view of the world. Even if they haven't yet experienced their adventurous or freedom-oriented qualities, sooner or later, in their own way, when they come into their full confidence, 32/5s and 23/5s can discover the potential of their life — the depth, and the boundless state of freedom within.

Working 32/5 or 23/5 in the Positive

Feeling free inside, unbounded by limiting beliefs or fears, the multifaceted individuals working 32/5 or 23/5 in the positive are willing to take emotional risks. Adventurers in daily life, they may or may not choose to go white-water rafting or skydiving, but they've developed the discipline to dig deeply into life, into the heart of experience, rather than just skimming the surface. Passionate and adventurous, like Zorba the Greek they teach by example and excitement. With their quick mind, they see and describe life in new ways. They've formed good habits and enjoy variety within a daily routine. Clever, witty, and fun loving, they make the ordinary into something extraordinary.

Working 32/5 or 23/5 in the Negative

Feeling insecure, these 32/5s or 23/5s manipulate and control others, usually by getting angry or by withdrawing. Or they try too hard to please others and later resent others for their own imbalance. They unintentionally create situations in which they become dependent on someone or something, such as drugs or money. They give away their freedom or limit their experience out of fear and self-doubt. Scattered and quickly bored, they're emotional con artists. Lacking clear boundaries, they play different roles or experience different selves through television or books. Addicted to dramas of one kind or another, they remain at the mercy of their search for varied experience.

Life-Path Issues

Health

Both 32/5s and 23/5s have a sensitive body that tends toward the slim and wiry due to their fast metabolism, which reflects the pace of their life. Even those with a round body don't let that slow them down. Because of their sensitivity, they may use fat or muscle as a psychic buffer. The throat area may reflect issues of withheld expression, but more commonly, 32/5s and 23/5s need to avoid overtaxing their adrenals and nervous system, since they tend to get scattered and stressed or fatigued. If they have erratic or undisciplined habits of diet or exercise, their circulatory system may suffer. In addition, accidents can occur if they physically overextend themselves or overreach their abilities.

If they use drugs as a form of adventure, they eventually come, through hard experience, to learn that drugs can only enslave them.

A balanced, low-fat diet and regular exercise are both very important disciplines for 32/5s and 23/5s. Their exercise regimen needs to include varied exercises that are fun and efficient. Cross-training, moving to music, dancing, martial arts, and hiking are all excellent.

Relationships

Those who travel alone in life, with no responsibilities to spouse, partner, or children, seem to have a kind of freedom in the sense of having no one to answer to and fewer compromises to make. But human beings don't necessarily find freedom in isolation. The influence of 2 means that, at some point, both 32/5s and 23/5s have to work through issues of cooperation with self and others. Committed relationships provide the arena.

Because of built-in challenges in the areas of freedom and independence, some 32/5s and 23/5s may project their own lack of internal freedom onto their partner, companion, or children: "They're blocking my freedom! They don't let me go out and do what I want to do." Some 32/5s and 23/5s do, indeed, attract or choose partners who bring up freedom issues or upon whom they become dependent and whom they then resent. A closer look reveals that 32/5s and 23/5s limit their own freedom. Once they take responsibility for their own life and realize that they can become the writer and director in their own movie, they cease resenting others for stopping them and find more freedom in cooperation rather than in reactive independence or isolation.

Both 32/5s and 23/5s have an emotionally sensitive body and energy field, but both often have some difficulty revealing their feelings. In their relationships, they need to find the courage to express what they feel. They also need to acknowledge a desire for variety and adventure and find a way to fulfill this desire with their partner if they're in a committed relationship. Whether they see their relationship as a doorway to deeper freedom and experience or as a jail determines how the relationship fares.

In the area of sexuality, 32/5s and 23/5s can be very shy and insecure or sensual, adventurous, and passionate — or all of the preceding. They often enjoy fantasies and playing different roles. Their relationships and sexual play present an opportunity to experience new levels of liberation by breaking free of roles to find new dimensions of emotional authenticity and vulnerability.

Talents, Work, and Finances

Individuals working 32/5 or 23/5 appreciate variety as the spice of life, so any occupation that allows them to explore many facets of experience, such as teaching, writing, acting, music, politics, leading trainings, court reporting, or sales work that involves travel and working with a variety of people, can suit their talents and interests. With so many talents, they can do almost anything that appeals to them.

Financially, even though security is an issue, money isn't as high a priority as the experiences it can buy; given a choice between money in savings or a chance for adventure or a learning experience, 32/5s and 23/5s choose the experience, and they may sometimes spend money before they earn it. They appreciate a safe, secure home base (preferably with a fireplace), but when they come into their full confidence, 32/5s and 23/5s tend to trade security for adventure. With the quick wit of the 5 energy, they can usually find or create money when they need it and stay at least one step ahead of any creditors.

Some Well-Known 32/5s and 23/5s

32/5s: Mikhail Baryshnikov, Beyoncé, Mick Jagger, Helen Keller, Coretta Scott King, Steve Martin, Theodore Roosevelt, J.K. Rowling, Sonia Sotomayor, Steven Spielberg, Lily Tomlin, Denzel Washington, Venus Williams, Malcolm X, Mark Zuckerberg

23/5s: Louis Armstrong, Harry Belafonte, Michael Bloomberg, Marlon Brando, Walter Cronkite, Charles Darwin, Ron Howard, Billie Jean King, Abraham Lincoln, Linus Pauling, Sidney Poitier, Franklin Delano Roosevelt, John Steinbeck, Vincent van Gogh

Keys to Fulfilling Your Destiny

If you're working 32/5 or 23/5, this section can help you manifest your life purpose by focusing your attention on core issues and by generating specific action to transform key areas of your life.

Guidelines and Recommendations

* You're more than the role you play; value your essence.
* Remember: Discipline and depth open the doors to freedom.

- Pace yourself, make time for relaxation, and stay healthy.
- Find the courage to be as open and vulnerable as possible.

Useful Questions

1. Reflect on the following questions:

    - When I feel limited or restricted, who can set me free?
    - Have I found a balance between dependence and independence?
    - What's my present level of discipline and focus?
    - Do I directly express what I really feel and need?

2. If these questions generate insights, how might you put these insights into practice?

Deepening Your Understanding

1. Turn back to Part Two, and reread the main sections covering the digits that make up your birth number: 2, 3, and 5.
2. You may wish to review birth numbers of family and friends and, if they're open to it, discuss similar or different issues in your lives.

Spiritual Laws: The Leverage to Change Your Life

1. Read about each of the following laws in Part Four:

    - **THE LAW OF DISCIPLINE:** Discipline generates the focus and depth of experience leading to true freedom.
    - **THE LAW OF BALANCE:** Seeing our tendency to swing from one extreme to another, we find our balance point.
    - **THE LAW OF RESPONSIBILITY:** To find our boundaries, we need to learn when to say yes and how to say no.
    - **THE LAW OF HONESTY:** Honesty is founded on self-awareness of our emotional reality.
    - **THE LAW OF ACTION:** To overcome insecurity or self-doubt, we can accept our feelings yet behave with confidence.

2. Do the exercises for each of these laws.
3. Consider how you might apply each law to your life.

41/5 & 14/5

5: Freedom through Discipline
1: Creativity through Security
4: Stability through Process

Those on the 41/5 or 14/5 life path are here to work through issues related to independence, stability, and creative energy, finally achieving freedom by surrendering to the discipline of a step-by-step process toward chosen goals. Because the mountain path to the fulfillment of our life purpose entails tests and challenges, most 41/5s and 14/5s find a sense of authentic inner and outer freedom only after finding out what freedom isn't; they have tendencies to become dependent on others, then strive for almost aggressive independence. Balancing this tendency with healthy forms of self-reliance, interdependence, and cooperation, these individuals experience freedom only through discipline and focus, taking life one step at a time. It may take a while for them to come to this realization.

While 41/5s and 14/5s share the same drives for freedom, independence, and mastery of experience associated with others working 5, they find this freedom through distinctly different avenues, issues, and challenges due to the influence of 1 and 4 qualities.

All the issues of 5 apply for 41/5s and 14/5s, but these are moderated and balanced by 4 and amplified by the creative drives of 1. Because of the influence of 4, people on both of these life paths often get scattered and go off half-cocked. They also have a strong family orientation, and, in the positive, have more stable energy. Combining a quick mind with creativity, they're here to show people new approaches to life.

Not only do 41/5s and 14/5s differ somewhat from others working 5, they also differ slightly from one another due to the relative nature and order of 4

THE LIFE YOU WERE BORN TO LIVE

and 1. Both 41/5s and 14/5s have significant creative energy to be released and channeled positively, especially 41/5s. Both life paths also share 4 dynamics, dealing with the need to follow a step-by-step process to achieve security.

Since in general those working the 5 path find freedom through discipline, focus, and setting priorities, the tendencies of 1 and 4 can either significantly support or sabotage the quest for inner and outer freedom.

Most 14/5s have an especially strong analytical mind, but they also display a tendency toward confusion and mental stress due to overanalysis. Most 41/5s demonstrate abundant creative energy, but if the flow is obstructed, they, more than 14/5s, may discharge the excess energy through abuse of food, alcohol, tobacco, or other drugs, especially psychedelics. But both of these life paths share the same strengths and potential challenges, in slightly differing degrees, just as they may share scatteredness, or trying to create too much all at once.

In the most positive sense, creative energy adds extra sparkle and juice to the charm and quick mindedness that characterize 41/5s and 14/5s. It also brings a degree of insecurity, especially for 41/5s, and adds a need for innovation and variety, making focus and discipline more difficult. Since 5s already tend to bounce from one thing to another, the influence of 1 has the effect of pouring gasoline on fire.

The movement, evolution, and achievement for 41/5s and 14/5s is best founded on a strong foundation of preparation. Having a stable base, such as committing to a home or family, teaches 41/5s and 14/5s more about inner freedom than traveling around the world and having as many experiences as possible. Most likely, 41/5s and 14/5s have come here to experience both — physically or in their vivid imagination.

The influence of 4 adds needed strength and stability, analytical ability, and grounding to the expansive curiosity and explorative tendencies of 5. However, in its less mature form, especially for 14/5s, the 4 entails a resistance to any regular or diligent step-by-step process and often leads to impatience, the last thing those working 5 need.

In both cases, 1 and especially 4 affect the drive for freedom and independence and add significant challenges. As with those working other birth numbers, to bring their primary purpose or destiny to fruition 41/5s and 14/5s have to climb a steep path, fighting their own dragons as they go, strengthening themselves on the journey.

An example of the mix of magic and chaos that can happen with the dynamic combination of 1, 4, and 5 is the late Thomas Wolfe, 14/5 author of *Look Homeward, Angel,* who delivered his brilliant, sprawling handwritten manuscripts to his editor with the many pages out of order, stuffed into four or five apple crates! Yet many recognize him as one of America's foremost writers.

Working 41/5 or 14/5 in the Positive

Brilliant at structuring and synthesizing, individuals working 41/5 or 14/5 in the positive can use razor-sharp analysis to determine what they need and then follow the steps necessary to achieve their goal. They maintain a balanced body through regular exercise and disciplined diet. Their highly visual imagination, brimming with creativity, is supported by an ability to follow patiently whatever process is necessary to bring their internal images into practical reality. Strong and inspiring, they display a broad grasp of many areas of life, and their outgoing nature makes them enjoyable company.

Working 41/5 or 14/5 in the Negative

Hampered by confusion and insecurity, these 41/5s or 14/5s accomplish little; they get stuck obsessively on one step, or they impulsively drive ahead, skipping steps, so it's halfway to the goal, then back to the drawing board. They feel torn between their desire for security and their need to take risks and explore the unknown. Uncommitted and unstable, they want freedom right now, without applying the discipline or following the step-by-step process to get it. Without a foundation to stand on, they waver and wobble, hoping and wishing, doing many things, but without real effect.

Life-Path Issues

Health

Individuals working 41/5 or 14/5 tend to race around due to their vitality, energy, and thirst for many experiences. When they act impulsively or overextend themselves in a quest for adventure, they may end up with broken bones.

If their creative energy is blocked, 14/5s and especially 41/5s may experience problems in the abdomen, lower back, or reproductive areas.

Meditation is extremely useful for both 14/5s and 41/5s to help calm their mind, which tends to run in circles. Inspiring music also has a balancing, calming effect. The nervous system of 41/5s and 14/5s needs loving care. Generally sturdier and more resilient than 32/5s and 23/5s, they're nevertheless more prone to mental stress.

Both 41/5s and 14/5s benefit from paying attention to regular, stable eating habits, since they have a tendency to skip meals or eat on the run. They tend to prefer a variety of interesting foods, but they require no special dietary guidelines beyond that. If they overeat, they need to explore how their creative energy is blocked and take appropriate steps to express this energy or release it through balanced exercise. They thrive on a variety of activities and may gravitate toward exciting competitive games that take quickness and strength but allow for creativity. They may also enjoy swimming, skin diving, and other water sports, which have a soothing effect on their nervous system.

Relationships

While they experience a pull toward family and stability, less grounded 41/5s and 14/5s have an equal and opposite pull toward a variety of experience and lack of commitment. With so many things to do, they can have trouble settling down, even though the image of a stable home life appeals to them. Insecurity associated with 1 breeds a self-protective, competitive nature, which can also be a factor in relationships. Overall, these individuals display a dynamism that's very attractive, and the only factor limiting their relationships is inside them, at the level of commitment.

Individuals working 41/5 and 14/5 definitely need and value robust, even rambunctious sexual expression, unless insecurity gets in the way; even if insecurity holds them back for a while, eventually they come to express their full sexual drive.

Talents, Work, and Finances

Strength, creativity, and quick mindedness bring 41/5s and 14/5s success in fields that allow both stability and adventure, such as international trade. Any form of creativity or business that demands rapid analysis challenges and satisfies these individuals. They prefer active rather than sedentary work, but writing can also satisfy their restless mind. Clear, creative, dramatic storytellers, they make exceptional writers, but they don't usually want to sit still that long (14/5 Thomas Wolfe used to write standing up, using his refrigerator top as his desk).

Creative visionaries who can see trends before others notice them, 41/5s and 14/5s who do their homework, keep their ideas practical, and have the patience to go through the necessary step-by-step process to complete what they start can create money as easily as ideas.

Some Well-Known 41/5s and 14/5s

41/5s: William Faulkner, Elizabeth Gilbert
14/5s: Frédéric Chopin, Clark Gable, Walter Matthau, Thomas Wolfe

Keys to Fulfilling Your Destiny

If you're working 41/5 or 14/5, this section can help you manifest your life purpose by focusing your attention on core issues and by generating specific action to transform key areas of your life.

Guidelines and Recommendations

- Make peace between stability and freedom; include both in your life.
- Channel your creativity through step-by-step discipline.
- Exercise every day, even if only for a few minutes.
- Find something you can fully commit yourself to and follow through.

Useful Questions

1. Reflect on the following questions:
   - What are the most important steps to create more freedom in my life? Am I willing to take them?
   - Does anyone other than myself really hold me back?
   - How do I use my creative energy?
   - Where do I need to apply more discipline in my life?

2. If these questions generate insights, how might you put these insights into practice?

Deepening Your Understanding

1. Turn back to Part Two, and reread the main sections covering the digits that make up your birth number: 1, 4, and 5.
2. You may wish to review birth numbers of family and friends and, if they're open to it, discuss similar or different issues in your lives.

Spiritual Laws: The Leverage to Change Your Life

1. Read about each of the following laws in Part Four:

   - **THE LAW OF DISCIPLINE:** Discipline generates the focus and depth of experience leading to true freedom.
   - **THE LAW OF CHOICES:** We can choose to create and express ourselves in positive or negative ways.
   - **THE LAW OF PROCESS:** The best way to reach any goal is one small, sure step at a time.
   - **THE LAW OF CYCLES:** Life brings constant changes, arising and then passing like the seasons.
   - **THE LAW OF THE PRESENT MOMENT:** Impatience and regrets dissolve in the recognition that only now exists.

2. Do the exercises for each of these laws.
3. Consider how you might apply each law to your life.

6: VISION THROUGH ACCEPTANCE

It doesn't matter what we do
until we accept ourselves.
Once we accept ourselves,
it doesn't matter what we do.

— Charly Heavenrich

This section includes all birth numbers with 6 as a primary life purpose, including single-digit 6, 15/6, 24/6, 42/6, and 33/6. Even though all of these birth numbers reflect intense 6 dynamics, the qualities, issues, and character of those containing other digits have a unique flavor due to the influence and interaction of the other numbers, in contrast to the pure, undiluted, single-digit 6.

6

6: Vision through Acceptance

Those working single-digit 6 are here to reconcile their high ideals with practical reality and to accept themselves, their world, and the present moment through an expanded vision of life's inherent perfection. However, since what we're here to do isn't what comes easiest, before single-digit 6s can fulfill their life purpose, they have to overcome hurdles and negative tendencies in a number of areas.

For this single-digit life path, in particular, please be sure to review the chapter in Part Two that provides a full and detailed discussion of the digit 6 and all it represents. Here, I highlight key elements of the path and purpose of single-digit 6s.

Along their climb up the mountain path, single-digit 6s need to understand their high standards in perspective, balancing idealism with realism to soften judgments about themselves and others. These visionaries can, at best, contribute to the higher possibilities toward which we're all evolving, but they need to find patience and practicality in what may otherwise be a quixotic quest.

Those on the single-digit 6 path tend to judge how they're doing not only against perfectionist standards, but by comparing themselves to masters in their field, even comparing themselves to their own past best performance.

These individuals, like those working any birth number and life path, may experience repeated lessons when young — lessons that finally penetrate and become an expanded and mature understanding. For example, young single-digit 6s may at first tend to idealize new people or role models they meet, seeing them through a rosy lens, as perfect — or nearly so. But soon, their laser vision detects one flaw, then another, until they become disillusioned after a whirlwind courtship or upon forming a business partnership. Eventually, they come to accept that every teacher, partner, friend, parent, or loved one has flaws, and that they themselves are no exception.

Like all those with a 6 in their birth number, the key problem phrase (like the "should" of 4s) is "if only" — that is, even after doing well in a sports event or stage performance or giving a party, they may still focus or obsess on one small perceived error, thinking, "If only I had (or hadn't) done that, it would have been perfect."

Once they use their high standards instead of becoming the victim of them, single-digit 6s find patience, realism, and flexibility, and continue to strive for excellence (but not perfection). No longer lost in petty details, placing fewer judgments on themselves or others, a warmth emanates from them as they attract others like moths to the flame.

Working Single-Digit 6 in the Positive

The visionaries working single-digit 6 in the positive strive for high standards and call us to do our best and beyond. Accepting the transcendent perfection of imperfection, they have a compassionate, evolutionary understanding of process, finding a heart and patience with both themselves and others in their world. Working diligently for improvement over time, these single-digit 6s, whose eyes are attuned to higher possibilities, serve as a positive counterbalance to cynics and shortsighted pragmatists who only look down at their feet. These bright individuals are sources of light that illumine the lives they touch.

Working Single-Digit 6 in the Negative

Measuring the world against idealistic standards, these single-digit 6s are chronically disappointed in others (and, deep down, in themselves). They feel angry and dissatisfied, because nothing turns out as well as they had hoped or expected. Beginning with enthusiasm, they end with dashed hopes, leading to a cynical disposition. However well they do at any task, and whatever they accomplish, these individuals suffer from a feeling that they could have done better. They tend to compare themselves to the best among them and either drive themselves to measure up or give up since they can't be the best ("I can't fail if I never really try").

Life-Path Issues

Health

High-minded single-digit 6s look to evidence-based, cutting-edge techniques and technologies of physical health and fitness training — not that all of these individuals strive for physical perfection, since different body types and environments influence health beyond the birth number. Due to the purity and goodness they seek — unless they're working in the negative and have given up — there's a bright blue in their energy field, making them attractive to many.

The high standards and the exaggerated pressure single-digit 6s may feel in school or the business world can lead to muscular tension and stress around the chest area, so they need to incorporate full, relaxed (rather than effortful) breathing into any health practices to bypass or relieve asthmatic symptoms. Overall, however, when working in the positive, these individuals strive to live well and do the right thing, forming positive health habits and practicing moderation in all things.

Relationships

Unlike some, who are merely *in* a relationship, single-digit 6s tend to "do relationship" as a project — at best, as a work of art; at worst, as an exam they have to pass. They may reflect on how the relationship is going, think about how to improve it (along with everything else), and have trouble just kicking back and going along for an enjoyable, bouncy ride. In sexual relationships, single-digit 6s may strive to perform well rather than to simply lose themselves in the ecstasy of the experience. One springboard diver friend working 6 reported that his girlfriend asked him if he "made love with his toes pointed." Until they learn the art of relaxation, single-digit 6s can tend toward the uptight, making relationship into an arena of personal growth for all concerned. Nevertheless, others often benefit and learn from their relationship with 6s, because these individuals raise the bar and call us to a higher standard.

Talents, Work, and Finances

Ironically, those with the highest ideals and standards tend to have a lower sense of self-worth, since they rarely meet their own standards, even as they judge others, then judge themselves for judging others. A limited sense of their own worth can lead to subtle forms of self-sabotage. They may not recognize their own talents or their own worth, and even volunteer to work for less than they deserve, only to resent it later when they aren't getting fair compensation. They often have harsh judgments about the fields of advertising and marketing, and are reluctant to promote or market themselves. Since we need two things to succeed — to be good at what we do, and also to be good at promoting what we do — single-digit 6s may find money harder to come by due to a reluctance to promote themselves, which feels beneath them. Still, they may eventually be quite successful as they perform at high levels and people come to recognize their talent and work habits.

Some Well-Known Single-Digit 6s

As of 2018, and publication of the 25th Anniversary Edition, the oldest single-digit 6s are under eighteen years old — not generally enough time to become well-known. In later editions of this book, as more single-digit 6s come of age and make notable accomplishments, names may appear here.

Keys to Fulfilling Your Destiny

If you're working single-digit 6, this section can help you manifest your life purpose by focusing your attention on core issues and by generating specific action to transform key areas of your life.

Guidelines and Recommendations

- When confronting perfectionism, remember the words and the perspective "I am (this is) good enough."
- Remember that it's not what you do that counts; it's who you are.
- Learn to accept and make the best use of whatever happens, and accept your response, no matter what.
- Allow your vision of what you could become to inspire you and call you onward while you enjoy your life here and now.

Useful Questions

1. Reflect on the following questions:

- In what way might *this* moment, *this* circumstance, *this* current challenge, be perfect? (Or at least a perfect part of my/our evolution?)
- What are three small things you can do to bring a little more light into the world? A kind word? A thank-you? An apology?
- What if a voice from the heavens informed you that you have accomplished everything you need to do, and that the rest of your life could be approached as play? What then? And why not?

2. If these questions generate insights, how might you put these insights into practice?

Deepening Your Understanding

1. Turn back to Part Two, and reread the main sections covering the digit that makes up your birth number: 6.
2. You may wish to review birth numbers of family and friends and, if they're open to it, discuss similar or different issues in your lives.

Spiritual Laws: The Leverage to Change Your Life

1. Read about each of the following laws in Part Four:

- **THE LAW OF FLEXIBILITY:** Staying flexible, we make the best use of changing circumstances.
- **THE LAW OF PERFECTION:** High ideals can inspire us, but excellence is the most realistic goal.
- **THE LAW OF INTUITION:** No longer monitoring other people's opinions, we connect with our heart's intuitive wisdom.
- **THE LAW OF PROCESS:** The best way to reach any goal is one small, sure step at a time.

2. Do the exercises for each of these laws.
3. Consider how you might apply each law to your life.

15/6

6: Vision through Acceptance
5: Freedom through Discipline
1: Creativity through Security

Those on the 15/6 life path are here to work through issues involving idealism, independence, and creative energy, finding creative ways to uplift others by first accepting themselves, then sharing their vision with others. Since our life purpose involves challenges, 15/6s confront and have to overcome hurdles of perfectionism, dependence, and an underlying insecurity before they can realize and share their larger vision of possibilities.

This higher vision may cause 15/6s to reject their present reality, but only through acceptance can 15/6s incorporate, embrace, and include all experiences into their understanding and build the necessary bridges between what is and what may be. They may write or dream, lead or follow; they may sing of bygone days or of future possibilities, but only in focusing their creative energy do 15/6s bring heaven to Earth. High ideals are fine, but 15/6s have to ground them in reality if they're to make a difference in the world.

Those working 15/6 don't have to *find* freedom or high ideals; rather, they *create* them. They're originators, innovators, and visionaries of the highest degree. Nearly all 15/6s feel a very strong sense of service, as if they're here on a mission.

Questions such as "What is the ideal?" and "What is authentic freedom?" constantly reverberate within 15/6s as they search for the conclusive experience, the deep and the lofty. Unless they stay grounded, 15/6s tend to create and live in an idealized world of their own, as writers of fantasy and science fiction sometimes do. Isaac Asimov, a 15/6, demonstrated how to create his own worlds in the most constructive way. Others may simply be dreamers who live in castles of their imagination, only occasionally returning to everyday life on planet Earth.

The usual hurdles related to those working 6 energy, such as perfectionistic standards, a tendency toward judging self and others against these standards, and low self-worth, confront 15/6s on the path up the mountain. The quick-minded orientation toward freedom and experience of 6 strongly influences 15/6s, who seek with a deep longing to experience the more perfect life they envision, a better world of perfect justice.

Because of the 5 influence, 15/6s need a practical focus to sort out many interests and tasks — a practice or field where they can focus their high standards. Without a direction, outlet, or goal, they can wander aimlessly in dream worlds; with a clear direction, they open doors to the future and point to our highest potential as did writers Isaac Asimov and Jules Verne.

But for all the high-minded, creative, freedom-oriented individuals born to this life path, others have struggled with obstructed or inhibited energy. Such 15/6s often feel scattered, directionless, trapped, or constantly disappointed; they pursue escapist activities, from reading literature about utopian societies to seeking out self-destructive drug hallucinations.

Along with 5 issues, including the absolute need for discipline, 15/6s have the abundant creative energy of 1, which transforms ideals and visions into some kind of form. For 15/6 Christopher Columbus, the vision was a new land across the uncharted regions of the ocean. For another 15/6, Joan of Arc, the vision was becoming God's knight of peace.

The drives of 15/6s blend qualities of creativity, liberation, justice, and a longing for perfection and form one of the most distinctive, high-minded life paths in modern times.

Working 15/6 in the Positive

Inspired and uplifting, individuals working 15/6 in the positive reveal visions of new possibilities and a brighter future. As high-minded strategists, through focus and discipline they apply active creative energy to awakening people from the mundane into the more sublime, more peaceful, liberated beings that they really are. At their best, these creative visionaries embody and channel the very force of human evolution to help change their world and themselves. Accepting themselves and others, they work with patience to convey positive laws of living through their work. They show the way to perfect freedom.

Working 15/6 in the Negative

Picky, judgmental, and disappointed, these 15/6s search high and low for the right person, idea, system, or scheme to improve themselves, but their search only reinforces their sense of incompleteness. They're unrealistic dreamers and unprepared idealists who often become martyrs to a cause or idea. Frustrated with themselves and others, they misdirect their stifled creative energy, discharging it in self-destructive ways. They use drugs or other means to tune out a world that falls painfully short of truth, justice, honor, or peace.

Life-Path Issues

Health

Due to their creative energy and quick mind combined with their perfectionistic standards, 15/6s tend to be active and high-strung. If they direct this energy into focused work, their hair-trigger energy works in bursts of creativity and productivity. If they misdirect it, they may experience nervous disorders, skin rashes, abdominal problems, and possible burnout.

The body and energy field of 15/6s shine with a bright, even mystical quality and refinement reflected in the music of Jascha Heifetz or the style of actor David Niven, both 15/6s.

Individuals working 15/6 benefit most from evolved and refined methods of healing, such as visualization and hypnotherapy, which draw on subconscious imagery to generate internal self-healing mechanisms, homeopathy, acupuncture, aromatherapy, and color therapy — all forms of healing with the fewest side effects.

Other people can't effectively advise 15/6s about nutrition or exercise because these individuals do better looking to their own internal archetypes and ideals for guidance. In general, they do best on a purifying diet and need less food than many people.

Most 15/6s are drawn to exercise that feels natural and balanced to them; at best, they practice a simple, efficient routine incorporating the essential elements of breathing, stretching, toning, and relaxation, such as tai chi, or an evolved type of light calisthenics that allows for variety.

Relationships

Those working 15/6 tend to idealize people out of proportion to their actual qualities or characteristics. They may also harbor secret disappointments, because others are never quite perfect enough for them. They tend not to perceive the person they're with; instead, they can carry on a relationship, even long-term, with an idealized image they project onto that person; in this sense, they may love the image they've created without getting to know or accept their partner as their partner truly is. Alternately, their idealized vision may quickly wear thin as they discover character flaws in their partner.

In general, 15/6s desire to create something more, or higher, out of their natural sexual drive and out of relationship in general. Since they compare their relationship to an ideal image, their relationship becomes a constant form of self-improvement unless they're so busy dreaming and creating that they don't pay much attention to or invest much energy in the relationship.

Talents, Work, and Finances

Those working 15/6 explore different forms of work before finding a chosen profession or, rather, a high calling. Their ideals and need for variety may direct them to writing, acting, exploring, or coaching, occupations where they feel comfortable being different and can help to shape people and ideas into something more, since reality never seems quite good enough or may fall short altogether. Whatever creative endeavors they pursue, if 15/6s persist and avoid becoming disheartened or impatient, they excel due to their high standards.

The finances of 15/6s reflect their creative output; if 15/6s don't find their focus as they wait for the more perfect opportunity, they feel a lack on many levels. But if they produce something practical and useful — something people can use today, not in the distant future — and if their ideals inspire them to creative ventures, the rewards appear and they prosper.

Some Well-Known 15/6s

Isaac Asimov, Federico Fellini, Richard Harris, Jascha Heifetz, David Niven

Keys to Fulfilling Your Destiny

If you're working 15/6, this section can help you manifest your life purpose by focusing your attention on core issues and by generating specific action to transform key areas of your life.

Guidelines and Recommendations

- Hold to your vision, and reach it through discipline.
- Harness your creative energy with patience.
- Visualize what you want, and let your vision inspire you.
- Find the perfect freedom inside you.

Useful Questions

1. Reflect on the following questions:

   - In what way is my present situation perfect?
   - Can I apply my high ideals and creative vision in practical ways?
   - Where can I find perfect freedom or justice?
   - Can I love and accept myself, my partner, and my world right now?

2. If these questions generate insights, how might you put these insights into practice?

Deepening Your Understanding

1. Turn back to Part Two, and reread the main sections covering the digits that make up your birth number: 1, 5, and 6.
2. You may wish to review birth numbers of family and friends and, if they're open to it, discuss similar or different issues in your lives.

Spiritual Laws: The Leverage to Change Your Life

1. Read about each of the following laws in Part Four:

   - THE LAW OF PERFECTION: High ideals can inspire us, but excellence is the most realistic goal.
   - THE LAW OF FLEXIBILITY: Staying flexible, we make the best use of changing circumstances.

- **THE LAW OF THE PRESENT MOMENT:** Impatience and regrets dissolve in the recognition that only now exists.
- **THE LAW OF DISCIPLINE:** Discipline generates the focus and depth of experience leading to true freedom.
- **THE LAW OF CYCLES:** Life brings constant changes, arising and then passing like the seasons.

2. Do the exercises for each of these laws.
3. Consider how you might apply each law to your life.

24/6 & 42/6

6: Vision through Acceptance
4: Stability through Process
2: Cooperation through Balance

Those on the 24/6 or 42/6 life path are here to work through issues of perfectionism, process, and responsibility, taking life one step at a time, manifesting their vision in practical ways, and accepting the inherent perfection of their life. Since our life purpose doesn't come easily, 24/6s and 42/6s have a hard time accepting themselves, others, and the world *as they are*. Both 24/6s and 42/6s can get lost worrying about petty details — things they said, should have said, or shouldn't have said or done. Regrets and guilt are a familiar part of their life until 24/6s and 42/6s expand their vision to the bigger picture, to the overriding perfection of life. With 4 issues combined with ideals of 6, 24/6s and 42/6s have difficulty with patience; they see their own and everyone else's potential and push to reach the summit, but they would rather make the journey in one leap than follow the step-by-step process they're here to master.

Both 24/6s and 42/6s tend to idealize people they've just met, or new opportunities, jobs, and places; then they feel disappointed because nothing and no one can ever quite meet their expectations. Most 24/6s and 42/6s tend to set themselves up and let themselves down.

They need to balance their native idealism and vision with a strong dose of realism and come to appreciate the imperfections we all came here to work through. Starting out as idealists, 24/6s and 42/6s set themselves up for disappointment as they search for the perfect job, the perfect relationship, or the perfect life. Whatever they're doing or whomever they're with, they have a sneaking suspicion that there may be something or someone better.

Despite this, 24/6s or 42/6s aren't necessarily fickle or promiscuous; for the most part, their high standards and self-image help ensure high codes of behavior. If they do slip, the regrets and guilt they suffer are usually worse than any punishment. Even when doing very good work, they have a little voice inside that says, "It could be better." They try too hard, feel too responsible, and are generally hard on themselves. When they criticize other people, they're likely to judge themselves for judging others.

With the combination of 2 and 4 qualities, 24/6s and 42/6s bring powerful support and service into play. They have the internal strength to bring at least some of their visions into reality as they find the limits of their responsibility, master cooperation, and work toward their goals in small, persistent steps.

With the sense of responsibility that goes with 2, the easy sociability of 4, and the high ideals of 6, 24/6s and 42/6s push themselves very hard in their impatience to reach their goals. They have a vision of everyone's highest potential, including their own, without always appreciating others or themselves *right now*, doing their best.

Because 2s and 4s have more similarities than any two other digits — sharing tendencies toward overanalysis, codependency (a sense of over-responsibility for the lives and feelings of others), strength, and stubbornness — the 24/6 and 42/6 life paths are nearly identical, except for a slightly different emphasis based on the order of the first two digits, 2 and 4.

While 24/6s experience issues with family (4) somewhat more acutely than 42/6s, 42/6s have a stronger tendency toward overcooperation (2), sometimes turning to undercooperation (resistance or withdrawal). But both 24/6s and 42/6s experience both kinds of issues, and they share the same tendencies to push themselves and others, measuring everyone against their high standards.

Both 24/6s and 42/6s, unless they're in a very negative state, are pleasant people to be around; with the support and service characteristics of 2 and the easy sociability of 4, they treat other people like family. Due to the interaction of high standards (like those working 6 they want to "do right" and "be good") and the tendency of both 2s and 4s to do what they think they "should" do rather than what they really feel, both 24/6s and 42/6s tend to be masters of self-deception and denial. They deny their own feelings, deny their situation, and sometimes stubbornly hold to their course even if their ship is sinking. Therefore, both benefit from the Law of Flexibility, which teaches them to flow with what happens in life.

Those working 24/6 or 42/6 are generally very outgoing, gregarious, bright, strong, and vital. They try hard to please others and to do the right thing, so they need to stay vigilant toward those who may attempt to manipulate them through guilt. They need to do the right thing for themselves — to contact their own authentic values and needs.

Since 24/6s and 42/6s appreciate their own and other people's potential, they tend to push themselves and others to fulfill their expectations. These individuals tend toward chronic self-improvement programs until they finally come to accept themselves and others as they are right now, and appreciate that while they aren't perfect, facets of them are very good.

Both 24/6s and 42/6s need to appreciate the difference between true or ultimate perfection and perfectionism — unrealistically high standards that can never be fulfilled and that lead to frustration. As 24/6s and 42/6s mature, they come to appreciate the inherent or transcendental perfection of everything and everyone, while realizing that in this conditional realm, no person, product, or performance is perfect; excellence, not perfection, is the best we can achieve.

Both 24/6s and 42/6s need to understand that excellence comes through following a careful, patient, thorough, step-by-step process. A skipped step can mean failure and having to start over.

Since they compare themselves with their ideals (or with the best people around), 24/6s and 42/6s often feel like failures even when they're doing very good work. They may also lack practical judgment — thinking their cake is done when it's still only half-baked.

As mentioned before, with the strong 4 dynamics, 24/6s and 42/6s tend toward overanalysis, which changes to disorientation as their mind whirls, weighing all the variables. This confusion can result in impulsive or compulsive decisions and corresponding regrets. Since they're here to ground their energy, they also have challenges in this area. If they resist the process, they sometimes encounter difficulties translating their high visions and hopes into practical forms of occupations and service.

Once 24/6s and 42/6s relax into life and into their body, accept and appreciate their own and other people's imperfections, and learn to trust that their life reflects, in some sense, a perfect process of learning, growth, and evolution, they finally feel as if they've come home. The process to realizing this perfection takes time and happens in small increments; it can't be rushed, as much as they'd like to get it all done right now.

Working 24/6 or 42/6 in the Positive

Bright, gregarious, productive, and supportive, individuals working 24/6 or 42/6 in the positive have a good relationship with friends and associates. Their practical analytical ability blends common sense with high vision. They act with strong conscience and want to learn from their mistakes and continue to improve themselves and their world. Strong, healthy, and full of vitality, these individuals can be counted on to get any job done as their work evolves from good to brilliant. They're always improving, always pushing toward perfection, but they accept the step-by-step process from where they are to where they want to be. They have a good sense of balance; they know how to give graciously and how to receive. Practical idealists, they appreciate themselves and others and find joy in the world.

Working 24/6 or 42/6 in the Negative

These 24/6s or 42/6s feel frustrated and impatient with their life because nothing meets their high standards or happens as quickly as they would like. Impractical, impatient dreamers, they start out with a burst of enthusiasm and effort, but if they don't succeed quickly, they soon abandon ideas and plans without really giving them a chance to develop ("What's the use?"). They idealize people they meet, then feel disappointed to learn that those people have their own issues to work through. Hypersensitive to criticism because they're so critical of themselves, they don't listen well to other people's feedback or advice, and they make the same mistakes over and over again.

Life-Path Issues

Health

Most 24/6s and 42/6s have a strong constitution, resistant to illness. If they become ill, they usually heal quickly. If they experience a chronic condition, they usually find they brought it on themselves through long-term resistance to change and associated tension. Accidents, especially to lower extremities, may be more likely if they act impulsively, get distracted, or overreach. Their adult life may entail a process of healing and rejuvenation or a process of degeneration, based on their health habits. Depending on their stress level, degree of worrying, or the pressures of perfectionism, they may develop allergies or use tobacco or alcohol to relieve frustration.

Due to their blend of high standards and impulsiveness, 24/6s and 42/6s tend to strive for ideal dietary or exercise habits for periods of time, followed by vacations or binges. They may alternate between puritan and hedonist tendencies, feeling as if they've blown it, then making new resolutions.

Rather than looking for the perfect diet or the perfect exercise system, 24/6s and 42/6s do best when they gradually refine habits of moderation that reflect the step-by-step process toward excellence they're here to learn. If, for example, they decide to lose weight, the success of going through a patient process is of far more significance in terms of their life path than quickly succeeding with their weight-loss program.

Their already-strong body finds balance in activities that combine mental focus, emotional calm, and relaxation with physical suppleness. They can tolerate and thrive on strong, regular workouts. Rather than just taking up a routine fitness practice, such as running or swimming, both 24/6s and 42/6s gain even more benefits when they include a martial art, yoga, a dance form, or another activity that requires a process of improvement over time.

Relationships

Overall, 42/6s and especially 24/6s can become frantic trying to find the perfect job or relationship. Because of this, they can sometimes encounter difficulty feeling stable or committed to a person or a job. Commitment can frighten them, because for them commitment means forever, but they're never *sure* they've found the "perfect one." They say "I love you," but inside they don't know if they're really telling the truth because they aren't sure if they love enough; they aren't even sure how they feel, because they've only learned what they're supposed to feel, and it takes time for them to contact and accept their genuine feelings, both good and bad.

Because of their gregarious nature, when working in the positive 24/6s and 42/6s make enjoyable company. Concerned and conscientious, they give that extra effort. Their high standards render them enthusiastic, skillful lovers who generally give more than they take, so they need to learn to find a balance of giving and receiving and put more emphasis on vulnerability than on performance.

Talents, Work, and Finances

Strength and precision make bodywork, architecture, or service-oriented professions enjoyable kinds of work for 24/6s and 42/6s. They also make excellent advisers in business due to their analytical abilities and the support capacity of 2. Some 24/6s and 42/6s even end up in some form of planning or politics to help improve the world. They also make natural athletes — gymnasts, divers, tennis players, or skaters. Where strength and form are essential, 24/6s and 42/6s can make some of the best athletes anywhere, whatever the sport.

They aren't limited to such areas, however, and fit into nearly any occupation if it suits their values and sense of meaning. The key for them is to cut through the "shoulds" and ideals and rediscover what they really feel and enjoy.

The finances of 24/6s and 42/6s depend on how practical rather than idealistic they are, and whether they're willing to go through the step-by-step process and preparation necessary to reach their goals — that is, whether they're willing to pay their dues. While they search for the most ideal work for them, they're wise not to give up their day job, which provides the foundation and security that can enable them to move on to something that suits them better.

Some Well-Known 24/6s and 42/6s

24/6s: Jeff Bezos, Warren Buffett, Lewis Carroll, Thomas Edison, Cary Grant, Jesse Jackson, John Lennon, Joe Louis, Eleanor Roosevelt, J.R.R. Tolkien, Stevie Wonder

42/6s: T.S. Eliot, Samuel Goldwyn, Michael Jackson, Pope Paul VI, Christian Slater

Keys to Fulfilling Your Destiny

If you're working 24/6 or 42/6, this section can help you manifest your life purpose by focusing your attention on core issues and by generating specific action to transform key areas of your life.

Guidelines and Recommendations

*   Accept yourself as you are, not as you "should" be.
*   Enjoy the process, not just the product.

- Appreciate this reality: No perfect job or person exists.
- Relax and breathe easy; you aren't responsible for others.
- Stay open to feedback, listen to it, and accept it graciously.

Useful Questions

1. Reflect on the following questions:

    - Do I fully realize my present value and capacity?
    - Am I honest with myself?
    - Does my life feel stable and settled?
    - In what ways are my present circumstances perfect?

2. If these questions generate insights, how might you put these insights into practice?

Deepening Your Understanding

1. Turn back to Part Two, and reread the main sections covering the digits that make up your birth number: 2, 4, and 6.
2. You may wish to review birth numbers of family and friends and, if they're open to it, discuss similar or different issues in your lives.

Spiritual Laws: The Leverage to Change Your Life

1. Read about each of the following laws in Part Four:

    - **THE LAW OF FLEXIBILITY:** Staying flexible, we make the best use of changing circumstances.
    - **THE LAW OF PROCESS:** The best way to reach any goal is one small, sure step at a time.
    - **THE LAW OF BALANCE:** Seeing our tendency to swing from one extreme to another, we find our balance point.
    - **THE LAW OF PERFECTION:** High ideals can inspire us, but excellence is the most realistic goal.
    - **THE LAW OF NO JUDGMENTS:** The universe doesn't judge us; it only teaches us through natural consequences.

2. Do the exercises for each of these laws.
3. Consider how you might apply each law to your life.

33/6

6: Vision through Acceptance
3: Expression through Sensitivity
3: Expression through Sensitivity

Those on the 33/6 life path are here to work through issues of perfectionism, emotional expression, and self-doubt in order to bring forward their inspiring vision of life's possibilities, while appreciating the innate perfection of the present moment. This world contains both beauty and ugliness, kindness and cruelty. Those working 33/6, with their high ideals and acute sensitivity, tend to feel disheartened by the problems and imperfections of the world, but they suppress their sadness and even their anger as they attempt to "do the right thing" due to their high standards. Ironically, even with their depth of emotions, 33/6s can appear cool and unemotional.

When 33/6s displease someone, they may not acknowledge they're troubled by this, but they are acutely sensitive to what they perceive as others' responses to them because they combine the emotional needs of 3 energy with the sensitive conscience of 6 energy. Therefore, 33/6s need to take care not to let themselves be manipulated in their desire for approval and their strong social needs to be liked and respected.

The life of 33/6s grows brighter when they realize that their visions, hopes, and high ideals are here to inspire them, not become the yardstick by which they measure the world. They need to appreciate that in the world of form, no perfect person, performance, or product exists; they also need to appreciate and express their vision of the inherent or higher level of perfection already existing in the world.

Although their basic life purpose is the same as that of others working 6, 33/6s have a distinctly different quality due to the powerful influence of

270

the double 3. As they do for birth numbers 22/4 and 44/8, double numbers represent significant strengths and added challenges.

For 33/6s, the double 3 means that inner expression needs to manifest before outer expressiveness can bloom. Inner expression means that 33/6s are communicating with themselves and getting in touch with their own inner feelings. This poses a clear challenge for most 33/6s because their perfection-istic nature tends to fixate on the best, most ideal way to feel, to be, and to act; they can lose touch with the real, not always nice, feelings that make up the entire complex of their personality. Although 33/6s don't rely on denial as much as 42/6s and 24/6s, it may take time and insight work for them to finally accept their real feelings.

Getting in touch with and accepting their most authentic feelings opens channels to their subconscious wisdom and intuitions, and enables them to form and enjoy a more compassionate, empathic bond with others.

Once 33/6s contact their own feelings, the second 3 involves finding the courage to express their feelings to others; again, this is difficult because they're very sensitive to criticism, and they want to appear in the very best possible light. In some cases, their standards are so high, they just give up. Expressing their feelings entails a certain vulnerability and leaves 33/6s open to others. If they take the risk, they're rewarded with closer relationships with others and with themselves.

Contacting and expressing feelings doesn't end the challenge of double 3s, and 33/6s are prone to disillusion, disappointment, and general frustra-tion when life doesn't meet their high standards and expectations. Because of this, they tend to express themselves in the negative, through complaining, criticizing, gossiping, judging, or name-calling. Of course, 33/6s then turn around and judge themselves for advertising their judgments out loud. But even negative expression is preferable to denial. In the short run, it may be better for 33/6s to express in the negative than not to speak at all — at least until they learn to express their feelings authentically in more positive ways.

Even though many 33/6s feel compelled to complain, judge, condemn, and otherwise express in the negative, they can develop the skill to express the same idea honestly in a positive way. It's very important for 33/6s (or anyone working 3) to realize that anything they express in negative ways, they can also express in positive ways. The Law of Choices addresses this key area.

The destiny of 33/6s relies on their cultivating their natural, high-minded vision of the bigger picture — their ability to see the inherent beauty, opportunity, and teachings of life's ups and downs. Having cultivated their vision, they need to learn to use their expressive drives and abilities in the most constructive, uplifting, even enthusiastic ways. This doesn't mean denying an injustice or problem or seeing only the sunny side of life; it means recognizing and accepting all that happens, whether we like it or not, as fuel for our growth and learning.

With the double 3, 33/6s have two doses of self-doubt, which can drag them down because of the weight of their ongoing, stratospheric standards, unless they recognize that the hurdle for what it is and deal with it. They can balance their perfectionistic tendencies by remembering that every incident reflects the universal teacher, making every circumstance a perfect opportunity to learn.

Self-doubt and perfectionism make up the two biggest hurdles for 33/6s. The combination tends to send them on a never-ending quest for self-improvement; those working 6 love to improve themselves and everything else, and the self-doubt of those working 3 sends them swinging from manic overconfidence to depressive doubt. Very competitive, they constantly judge and compare themselves with others to see how they're doing. If they don't feel like they're doing well enough, they may push themselves, strive for lofty goals, and reach for perfection. If they succumb to self-doubt, they may step out of the game, just get by, or drop out, disheartened and defeated, victim to the logic "If I don't try, then I can't really fail." If they stay in the game, however, they end up doing well because of their inherently bright, sensitive, and intuitive nature.

Nearly all 33/6s are more interested in goals than in the sometimes lengthy process necessary to reach them; unlike those working 4 energy, who have trouble tolerating slow, careful steps, 33/6s are willing to go through the steps, but they want to do it quickly so that they can reach the ideal, the end product. They see the completed vision before them and want to achieve it; they want to arrive almost before they've begun. Like those working 4 energy, 33/6s need to apply the Law of Process, not because they're reluctant to go step-by-step, but rather as a reminder to slow down and enjoy the journey.

Most 33/6s feel a strong need for emotional support and love; even though many people love and admire them, they may not feel it until they come to love and accept themselves and to see their own beauty and light.

Working 33/6 in the Positive

Surrounded by a bright energy field reflecting purity and clarity, the sensitive individuals working 33/6 in the positive have an attractive dynamism and an enthusiastic way of helping others see their own perfection and the positive side of every issue. Their body is strong because they've developed and refined it through proper exercise and diet. They accept their shape whether or not it meets anyone else's idea of perfection. They see the inherent perfection of others, and they've come to accept themselves; self-evaluation has changed to self-valuation. They always have a kind word or good thing to say about others. Their laser eyesight can spot the beauty in anyone or anything; they see the higher beings we're all becoming. With their high standards and sense of fairness, they work for justice, right, and truth in constructive ways.

Working 33/6 in the Negative

Tight-lipped, inhibited outsiders, these 33/6s have down-turned corners of their mouth, indicating their disappointment with most people and their anger and frustration about the world. "It isn't *fair!*" is the battle cry of these harsh critics, as they judge the world against unreachable ideals. They hold in their expression or let it out in negative tirades and complaints as their laser vision points out the flaws in everyone and everything. Their body holds tension within extra fat or extra muscle as body armor to insulate them from a world that feels burdensome due to their own self-imposed standards.

Life-Path Issues

Health

The source of vitality for 33/6s comes from having a cause, an idea, or an ideal that inspires them. Most have a strong, healthy body, but due to their sensitivity and depending on their emotional state, they may sometimes have to deal with sore throats due to unexpressed feelings. When nervous or pressured by feeling that they have to do well, they sometimes experience a nervous stomach. The stress they impose on themselves with their standards can also manifest as muscular tension, especially in the jaw; as occasional skin rashes; or even as asthma if the world seems to press in on them as they try to meet their own impossibly high standards. If working in the negative over time, 33/6s may experience chronic illnesses, including colitis, ulcers, or other abdominal symptoms.

Chronically blocked, suppressed, or unexpressed anger related to judgments they place on themselves or others can turn to arthritis in later years, a form of crystallized anger in the joints, especially for those 33/6s who have a cool, controlled exterior.

All of the preceding problems or conditions reflect those working 33/6 in the negative; these issues are *not* inevitable or necessary. Health conditions can improve significantly once 33/6s (or people working other birth numbers) learn to ease up and go with the flow.

Good advice for any 33/6s would be to eat what they feel good about and to feel good about what they eat. Because of the 3, emotions play an important role in anything they do. They tend to aspire to and work toward an optimal diet, depending on their knowledge of nutrition and their instinctive feel. Although not an issue for most 33/6s, some may be vulnerable to anorexic eating disorders due to a distorted body image of not being slim enough or not being perfect enough.

Most 33/6s do well with clear-cut fitness exercises; they naturally look for the optimal form of exercise for them, even one that fills emotional or social needs. Many also enjoy skill training, such as martial arts, where they can refine and hone skills to perfection. Of the top five martial artists I've known, three happen to work the 33/6 life path.

Relationships

Emotions aren't reasonable, neat, orderly, or predictable, and 33/6s may have difficulty letting their hair down and getting wild and passionate (unless, of course, they're skillful actors like 33/6s Meryl Streep and Robert De Niro). Overcoming self-doubt and the fear of other people's opinions may take a little time for 33/6s. Until they're willing to express their feelings directly — as in "I feel hurt!" — they tend to stifle upsets and keep their cool, at least in public. But among family, if it feels safe to do so, they express themselves more freely.

When emotions are held back, so are relationships. Those working 33/6 need to realize that their partner or spouse wants to love *them*, not somebody with a perfect mask. The more genuine and vulnerable they can act and the more they can feel — "Here's who I am, the good and the bad; take it or leave it" — the better.

Sexually, many 33/6s focus on technique or performance rather than surrender to wild abandon or the pure emotional content of lovemaking. In some cases, if they haven't yet understood their perfectionistic tendencies, their sexual feelings may diminish due to repressed anger resulting from judgments about their lover. In the positive, 33/6s can form nurturing, symbiotic relationships, sexual and otherwise. In the sexual arena as elsewhere, those working (double) 3 need to remember that what they feel they most need is what they most need to give.

Talents, Work, and Finances

Unless 33/6s allow self-doubt to stop them, their high standards make them naturally prone to success, because they do very good work (even though they don't always feel that way). They have a deep emotional sensitivity, whether or not they show it, and a mind that focuses and directs a profound intuitive intelligence. To succeed, however, they need to get a grip on their ideals, stay practical and realistic, and remain positive.

The desire of 33/6s for precision, along with their expressive and intuitive abilities, can shine through many different occupations, such as teaching, training, organizational work, design and architecture, and illustration. Actors, dancers, and athletes who are 33/6s study their craft deeply; they're consummate professionals. Many 33/6s make excellent, prolific writers; they excel at anything having to do with communication, feelings, and expression. They tend to offer that extra touch and to work conscientiously toward high standards.

If any problems arise in the financial arena, self-doubt and perfectionist procrastination probably lie at the source. Whenever 33/6s experience a lack of abundance, this may stem from self-worth issues — from unrealistically devaluing themselves and being afraid to step up and let the world know what they're worth. When they come to know and appreciate themselves — and to express their true emotions — they also express their joy for life.

Some Well-Known 33/6s

Fred Astaire, George W. Bush, Dale Carnegie, Agatha Christie, Albert Einstein, Stephen King, Elisabeth Kübler-Ross, Mary Tyler Moore, Linda Ronstadt, Meryl Streep, H. G. Wells

Keys to Fulfilling Your Destiny

If you're working 33/6, this section can help you manifest your life purpose by focusing your attention on core issues and by generating specific action to transform key areas of your life.

Guidelines and Recommendations

- Reconnect with your real — not your ideal — feelings.
- Express your feelings, not just your thoughts.
- Acknowledge your sensitivity, and let others see it.
- Appreciate who you and others are right now.

Useful Questions

1. Reflect on the following questions:

   - How do I use my expressive energy?
   - Do I sometimes feel burdened by self-doubt and overly idealistic standards?
   - Can I appreciate who I am right now?
   - Do I let people know how I feel?

2. If these questions generate insights, how might you put these insights into practice?

Deepening Your Understanding

1. Turn back to Part Two, and reread the main sections covering the digits that make up your birth number: 3 and 6.
2. You may wish to review birth numbers of family and friends and, if they're open to it, discuss similar or different issues in your lives.

Spiritual Laws: The Leverage to Change Your Life

1. Read about each of the following laws in Part Four:

    •   **THE LAW OF FLEXIBILITY:** Staying flexible, we make the best use of changing circumstances.

    •   **THE LAW OF PERFECTION:** High ideals can inspire us, but excellence is the most realistic goal.

    •   **THE LAW OF CHOICES:** We can choose to create and express ourselves in positive or negative ways.

    •   **THE LAW OF INTUITION:** No longer monitoring other people's opinions, we connect with our heart's intuitive wisdom.

    •   **THE LAW OF THE PRESENT MOMENT:** Impatience and regrets dissolve in the recognition that only now exists.

2. Do the exercises for each of these laws.
3. Consider how you might apply each law to your life.

7: TRUST THROUGH OPENNESS

As soon as you trust yourself,
you will know how to live.

— Johann Wolfgang von Goethe

This section includes all birth numbers with 7 as a primary life purpose, including single-digit 7, 16/7, 25/7, 34/7, and 43/7. Although all of these birth numbers reflect intense 7 dynamics, the qualities, issues, and character of those that contain other digits have a unique flavor due to the influence of the other numbers, in contrast to the pure, undiluted, single-digit 7.

7

7: Trust through Openness

Those working single-digit 7 are here to learn to trust the light in themselves and in others, opening up to share their inner reality with the world. For this single-digit life path, please be sure to review the chapter in Part Two that provides a full and detailed discussion of the number 7 and all it represents. Here, I highlight key elements of the path and purpose of single-digit 7s.

Single-digit 7s have a sharp and insightful intelligence, which enables them to read between the lines. Inward turning, often private, they can become spiritual or scientific seekers. Due to innate trust issues, these individuals may not lay all their cards on the table and thus may experience misunderstandings in their personal or professional life, which they tend to interpret as betrayal.

Since what we're here to do isn't what comes easiest — and since in real life people aren't always consistent or trustworthy — the occasional paranoia of single-digit 7s sometimes seems justified. (As the quip goes, "Just because I'm paranoid doesn't mean they're not out to get me.")

Ironically, some single-digit 7s may be *too* open, sharing their heart early on in relationships only to feel betrayed later on. So, like those working 2 who seek balance between overcooperation and undercooperation, those working 4 who seek balance between taking on too much (or too little) responsibility, and those working 5 who seek balance between abject dependence and total independence, single-digit 7s need to develop the capacity to know how much to trust a given individual in a given situation, rather than extending instant trust or constant suspicion. Mature 7s make sure they get agreements in writing, in this way changing assumptions to verifiable understandings.

Because single-digit 7s are likely to feel a lack of trust in their own independent discernment, they often read widely or follow experts' ideas about diet, exercise, and other systems of personal development. It can take some time to connect with their own inner knower and rely on their sense of discriminating taste — what's most suitable for them.

When single-digit 7s come to trust their own intuitions, ideas, and instincts — and, at transcendent levels, to trust a destiny working through them (and everyone else), they glimpse the possibility that every challenge they meet can ultimately serve their highest good and learning. At best these individuals can evolve from separation and mistrust to a direct and profound sense of the higher energy, love, and trust. Feeling a resonance with certain earth cultures and indigenous peoples, they find this communion among the living things and spirits of the natural realm. The eagle, the brook, and the wind in the trees all speak to them.

Even as they continue to stumble and evolve, single-digit 7s open up to the love, wisdom, and justice operating within every human being. This doesn't mean that they naively allow themselves to be exploited by others; rather, it means that they let their light shine in all their relations, perhaps even becoming insightful guides. Having looked into the depths of their own mind and heart, they can know the hearts of others. Those who have contacted their internal wisdom find out, often to their surprise, that they understand far more than they had once believed.

Working Single-Digit 7 in the Positive

Mature individuals working single-digit 7 in the positive bring fresh insights to nearly any topic due to an incisive intelligence. After cycling between overtrust and undertrusting in their earlier years, these individuals have found a realistic balance. Their trust has to be earned, and agreements need to be clear (and written down). These single-digit 7s have learned to trust reliable sources of knowledge in the world, but always measure what they read or hear against their inner knower — their own judgment and discernment. Former paranoid tendencies have evolved into a discerning wisdom and a healthy capacity for critical thinking. Their daily life balances between teamwork and solitude. At the highest level, they become models of faith (whether religious or secular), with a profound trust in life unfolding; these individuals live the maxim "Trust in God but tie your camel." To the degree 7s achieve this kind of trust — even faith — in a higher order, they can straddle both spiritual and material realms, thriving in both.

Working Single-Digit 7 in the Negative

Ignoring or shutting out the advice or opinions of others, because they feel so vulnerable to other people's ideas, these single-digit 7s are drawn to theories they read or hear, due to a lack of faith in their own inner resources. This leads to a rigidity and a pendulum swing from rejecting all external ideas to embracing theories to the exclusion of their judgment. Self-protective and private to the point of paranoia, they spend a great deal of time in isolation, away from other people, whom they view through a lens of mistrust. Even their wit is cutting, with a cynical edge. They can call forth numerous times when they were betrayed by others, and are ever on the alert for the next betrayal. Such stories seem to justify keeping the world at arm's length, and preferring their own company to that of others. Even if they appear gregarious, they rarely share their inner reality due to fears of being shamed. Or they may lack boundaries and share everything on their mind indiscriminately, then later feel hurt, betrayed, or misunderstood.

Life-Path Issues

Health

Most single-digit 7s need private space and time to recharge. With a deep connection to the natural world, they enjoy and benefit from time in a garden, park, or wilderness area on holiday, or on a smaller scale as a daily respite. These individuals have no specific problems related to health, other than a tendency to think about fitness or wellness activities rather than doing them. But when an active physical passion calls to them, such as hiking, skiing, ballroom dancing, or a sport or martial art, such practice provides an avenue for single-digit 7s to develop deeper levels of self-trust — not only with regard to ideas or philosophy, but also by trusting their training, their instincts, and their improving skills. If they become ill, as we all do on occasion, single-digit 7s need to avoid the tendency to feel betrayed by the body and instead treat the illness as a perfect way to appreciate good health, and have faith in the process of healing and recovery.

Relationships

For single-digit 7s, having a partner provides companionship and a sense of completion, harmony, and balance in their life. But that very companionship means a demand for intimacy, for opening up, and for deeply trusting a loved one to whom they're vulnerable. Whenever anyone lives in a caring, interdependent relationship, the possibility of betrayal exists. Therefore, most single-digit 7s have mixed feelings about intimate relationships; they want them, but they may fear them. They long for companionship, but they can at times act aloof or distant, so with companionship comes a need for their own sanctuary. A room or nook or den, even if it's an easy chair — any space of their own — isn't a luxury or indulgence, but essential. Relationships can become an arena of negotiation if single-digit 7s maintain rigid boundaries. But once they open up enough to find a loving, trusting relationship with themselves, these individuals emerge from their shells to share their wholeness with another instead of looking for completion through another.

Talents, Work, and Finances

The energy of single-digit 7s flows inward. Even though they may find great success in the world in numerous fields, their interests and attention tend to gravitate toward inner processing even when they strive for external achievement. A career is part of a larger, deeper search to understand themselves and the inner workings of the world, whether or not they're fully aware of it. For single-digit 7s a job is simply a means to earn money to pursue other interests; their primary work takes place within. In business dealings, as noted, they're wise to avoid oral agreements; even (or especially) among friends, written contracts establish a basis of trust and understanding. Due to a need for alone time and a comfort in solitude, single-digit 7s can do well in concentrated work alone, whether traveling into deep space or in the solitude of an office doing accounting or pursuing scientific research.

Some Well-Known Single-Digit 7s

As of 2018, and publication of the 25th Anniversary Edition, the oldest single-digit 7s are under eighteen years old — not generally enough time to become well-known. In later editions of this book, as more single-digit 7s come of age and make notable accomplishments, names may appear here.

Keys to Fulfilling Your Destiny

If you're working single-digit 7, this section can help you manifest your life purpose by focusing your attention on core issues and by generating specific action to transform key areas of your life.

Guidelines and Recommendations

• When you have a question, write it down, then let the wiser part of you write an answer.

• Do your best to share what's really in your heart, not just your mind, and form clear agreements with others.

• Honor your need for privacy, but take little risks in sharing your feelings openly.

• Trust your own instinct and intuition; you're the expert on your body and your life.

Useful Questions

1. Reflect on the following questions:

    • When making a decision, ask yourself, "What if I knew the answer?" What follows?

    • Do you trust your inner wisdom? When have you done so with good results? If the results weren't so good, what wisdom did you gain from mistakes or temporary failures that can serve you in the future?

    • Do you avail yourself of solitude when needed, and company as desired?

    • Is it possible that what you perceived as a past betrayal might have been due to a misunderstanding or lack of communication?

2. If these questions generate insights, how might you put these insights into practice?

Deepening Your Understanding

1. Turn back to Part Two, and reread the main sections covering the digit that makes up your birth number: 7.
2. You may wish to review birth numbers of family and friends and, if they're open to it, discuss similar or different issues in your lives.

Spiritual Laws: The Leverage to Change Your Life

1. Read about each of the following laws in Part Four:

    *   **THE LAW OF EXPECTATIONS:** Our life unfolds according to our hidden expectations and assumptions.
    *   **THE LAW OF INTUITION:** No longer monitoring other people's opinions, we connect with our heart's intuitive wisdom.
    *   **THE LAW OF FAITH:** Only when we find faith in ourselves can we have faith in others.

2. Do the exercises for each of these laws.
3. Consider how you might apply each law to your life.

16/7

7: Trust through Openness
6: Vision through Acceptance
1: Creativity through Security

Those on the 16/7 life path are here to work through issues of openness, authenticity, acceptance, and security, learning to trust the creative spirit within themselves and the beauty within others, sharing their ideals and vision in practical ways. Since our life path isn't an easy climb, 16/7s confront specific challenges associated with each digit of their birth number: The creative energy of 1 has to be used for constructive purposes, or it may turn back on itself in destructive ways. This 1 quality often brings a sense of insecurity or a feeling of inferiority. When fueled by the high visions and perfectionistic standards of 6 combined with the trust issues of 7, 16/7s have a deep fear of being shamed or looking foolish and tend to be extremely private people, living within themselves, working to create a better world but somewhat disheartened by this one. They prefer a great deal of privacy; they also have much to contribute due to their incisive mental clarity and awesome creative imagination.

Despite their outward activities — their work, family, and other interests — a conscious or subconscious longing whispers to them, a drive to find safe harbor that offers a sense of communion with self, with others, with the world, and with the Spirit and inspiration that animate us all.

Although many 34/7s, 43/7s, and 25/7s, who are more involved in business or sports or raising children, might not relate to the spiritual language or imagery presented here about 7, most 16/7s resonate with their higher, inner calling, due to their lofty vision.

Two 16/7s, Vladimir Horowitz and Frédéric Chopin, provided a path to a deeper feeling of life through music; 16/7 Fyodor Dostoyevsky offered deeper understanding through the written word. The call to service is key for 16/7s, for without a means to serve others in everyday life, 16/7s might prefer to leave the Earth's physical plane entirely — sometimes literally, as did 16/7 astronaut Buzz Aldrin. They don't leave like the catatonic, whose awareness turns inward in fear, but like the mystic, whose vision turns inward in hope, love, and high aspiration.

The life path of 16/7s, with their intense and active imagination, tends to be one of the least grounded in the everyday realities of life. What discipline it must have taken for 16/7 Chet Huntley, the high-minded journalist, to immerse himself in the daily news!

The challenge for 16/7s, with their high ideals and perfectionistic tendencies, their flowing creative energy, and their desire to know more deeply, is to accept and embrace the everyday world and find within it and within themselves the beauty and perfection they seek.

The 7 influence means that 16/7s long for a more profound connection to life. They achieve this through a primary challenge of those working 7 — learning to trust their inner knower and to trust the world as it unfolds. This may not come easily for 16/7s, but it's what they're here for.

Most 16/7s have significant issues with trusting others and trusting themselves. Few 7s naturally trust themselves, although they may appear to do so to outside observers. They may even state that they do; if they look inside, however, they usually discover that they trust their mind, their knowledge, and the theories and beliefs they have gathered from others.

For 16/7s, trust comes especially slowly because their inherent perfectionism leads to disappointment in self and others who fall short of high expectations. They have trouble trusting their heart and intuition. The 7 tendency to feel betrayed is especially acute and frustrating for 16/7s, and this frustration is fueled by creative energy and aggravated by a tendency toward insecurity and isolation.

However, when 16/7s direct their creative energy toward a vision, a quest, a goal, or a higher purpose, they come to trust the Spirit manifesting in, as, and through them. As their razor-sharp mind begins to grasp and appreciate the inherent perfection of their existence, including their success and failures, their highs and lows, they come to trust the spiritual principles that had previously escaped their notice. The moment they find the bittersweet beauty and transcendent perfection inherent in life, they find safe harbor everywhere and have nothing more to fear.

Working 16/7 in the Positive

Individuals working 16/7 in the positive share their high vision and reveal new possibilities through their creative endeavors as they express truth and beauty. Their intense eyes and sparkling vitality and their crisp, refined qualities reveal them as high-minded angels in human form. Having found unconditional, but not naive, trust in themselves and others, they see the inherent perfection and larger workings of a loving Spirit even in the most difficult circumstances. Inspired by a higher purpose, they find deep meaning in uplifting and moving others to a more refined, elevated sense of their own life.

Working 16/7 in the Negative

Feeling bitter and betrayed, insecure and self-destructive, these 16/7s can have a hard time being here. They feel disappointed in themselves and in others and frustrated that no one has lived up to their expectations, which are now abandoned or turned sour. They long for a more ideal world, but feeling unable to contribute, they've given up hope. Isolated as hermits, they fear other people's criticism and so withdraw from social contacts. Feeling misunderstood and judged by others, they find escape in drugs or in illusory fantasy realms.

Life-Path Issues

Health

If 16/7s experience chronic feelings of betrayal or being misunderstood, the heart and knees become vulnerable. Issues in the abdomen or lungs are also possibilities. Subtle forms of energy work, homeopathy, visualizations, and meditation may work well for 16/7s. They also benefit from any form of meditation or relaxation practice that lets them release random thoughts rather than become absorbed in them.

A satisfying, nourishing, but light diet works well for 16/7s, who usually gravitate toward light eating because, to them, quality is more desirable than quantity. They need to experiment to find the optimal diet, learning to trust their instincts even more than research.

Most 16/7s derive special benefit from more refined forms of conscious exercise, such as tai chi, yoga, and gentle aerobics, including swimming and walking. Exercise keeps creative energy flowing for 16/7s and helps them learn to trust their body's natural wisdom. They enjoy efficient, innovative exercise or simply walking through nature's beauty.

Relationships

If working in the negative, 16/7s confront issues of mistrust and insecurity; in such cases, they find it difficult to express their feelings or show their emotions. Therefore, opening up to genuine intimacy can present a significant challenge. In some cases, their relationships may exist on a fantasy level, as they look for a Dulcinea, a Helen of Troy, a Hercules, or some other idealized figure. Some 16/7s would rather read a book than have a relationship.

When 16/7s are working the positive aspects of this life pattern, their high vision leads them to openness, trust, and sharing, resulting in perfect intimacy. Making love with mindless abandon, letting themselves be seen and known entirely, is both frightening and healing for 16/7s, for whom lovemaking can become a tender and courageous act of accepting the body and earthly life.

Talents, Work, and Finances

Since 16/7s combine creative energy, high standards, and sharp intellect, they inevitably generate exemplary, beautiful work in any field, whether as writers or tile setters, musicians or astronauts. They gravitate toward work that allows a sense of privacy, that challenges their intellect, and that appeals to their high-minded sense of meaning.

The 6 influence raises the possibility that self-worth issues may interfere with their ability to receive and to create abundance. Once 16/7s begin to value themselves and their work and open themselves to receiving, the world gives back to them in return.

Some Well-Known 16/7s

Buzz Aldrin, Fyodor Dostoyevsky, Chet Huntley, Robert Wagner

Keys to Fulfilling Your Destiny

If you're working 16/7, this section can help you manifest your life purpose by focusing your attention on core issues and by generating specific action to transform key areas of your life.

Guidelines and Recommendations

- Come out from hiding behind your polished mask.
- Trust and enjoy the creative process of your life.
- Remember that every mistake is inspired by deeper wisdom.
- Completely accept this moment, and find the perfection in it.

Useful Questions

1. Reflect on the following questions:

    - What inspires me?
    - In what sense have my difficulties been perfect?
    - Have I let insecurity or perfectionism stop me?
    - How have my expectations influenced my experience?

2. If these questions generate insights, how might you put these insights into practice?

Deepening Your Understanding

1. Turn back to Part Two, and reread the main sections covering the digits that make up your birth number: 1, 6, and 7.
2. You may wish to review birth numbers of family and friends and, if they're open to it, discuss similar or different issues in your lives.

Spiritual Laws: The Leverage to Change Your Life

1. Read about each of the following laws in Part Four:

    - **THE LAW OF FAITH:** Only when we find faith in ourselves can we have faith in others.
    - **THE LAW OF PERFECTION:** High ideals can inspire us, but excellence is the most realistic goal.

- **THE LAW OF FLEXIBILITY:** Staying flexible, we make the best use of changing circumstances.
- **THE LAW OF THE PRESENT MOMENT:** Impatience and regrets dissolve in the recognition that only now exists.
- **THE LAW OF PROCESS:** The best way to reach any goal is one small, sure step at a time.

2. Do the exercises for each of these laws.
3. Consider how you might apply each law to your life.

25/7

7: Trust through Openness
5: Freedom through Discipline
2: Cooperation through Balance

Those on the 25/7 life path are here to work through issues of privacy, openness, and independence, finally coming to trust spiritual forces operating through themselves, others, and the world, and to experience inner freedom through a focused discipline. Trusting self and others, along with discipline and focus, are primary life issues for 25/7s, and the quality of their life depends, in large part, on whether they work these areas in positive or negative ways. Because our life purpose rarely comes easily, 25/7s tend toward varying degrees of paranoia; they may begin relationships with an almost naive trust and faith and set themselves up for broken trust, betrayal, or misunderstanding later on.

Most 25/7s need a great deal of privacy and a sense of independence. Due to subtle fears of being shamed or betrayed, they tend to draw back inside themselves emotionally; they don't feel safe enough to let people see their private thoughts or feelings. Some 25/7s have become hurt, bitter, or paranoid and first look out for number one; feeling isolated emotionally or even physically, like the classic mountain hermit, they may seek Spirit but avoid intimate human relationships.

Because of their world-class thinking abilities, 25/7s can find external success, but their life purpose centers more around inner processing than worldly pursuits. Most individuals on the 25/7 life path are involved with work, relationships, family, travel, and any number of ordinary activities in daily life.

Nearly all 25/7s have an appealing lightness and clarity about them; whether or not they're aware of it, they have a close association with the subtle energies some people refer to as "angelic." Even though they may prefer scientific to spiritual models of reality, most 25/7s feel drawn to a sense of beauty and harmony that borders on the mystical.

Something more resides beneath the surface of their life, however, something inside their skin, their heart, and the cells of their body, a kind of longing, perhaps still subconscious, a desire to feel that this is *home*.

The interaction of 2, 5, and 7 gives rise to internal conflicts that send 25/7s on a quest for healing and illumination. These individuals don't necessarily need healing on a physical level; their drive is to heal internal divisions and find the focus, meaning, and purpose they seek.

Most 25/7s have a refined appearance and certain childlike qualities. Children tend to like them because they can play like children. Whether male or female, they have a Peter Pan–like quality; caught between never-never land and Earth, they aren't sure where they belong. They enjoy scenic beauty and find it easier to commune with spirits of nature than with the denizens of the urban world. They like computers and computer art, computer games, scholarly research, reading, and travel in the sea or the sky; they search for worlds of beauty and adventure, where the politics and deceptions of the human world are left behind, or at least held at bay.

Most 25/7s feel caught in a double bind: Not usually trusting of others enough to share their inner feelings, they have few real intimacies; tending to isolate themselves and needing substantial private, independent time, they take pains to protect themselves from a social world that seems, deep inside their subconscious, somehow threatening. Yet they have a desire to help others, to make a difference, to contribute in some way. Like a puppy who slowly approaches a stranger, only to draw back, then approach, then draw back, some 25/7s take a risk and try to establish contact, perhaps through sharing an interest or in structured group settings. Other 25/7s who have felt betrayed draw back into their own independent, uncomplicated, but sometimes lonely world.

With the 2 influence, 25/7s seek internal harmony between conflicting values or ideas; in relationships with others, they seek balance between giving and receiving, and they like to draw clear boundaries around their space. The 5 dynamic creates lessons for 25/7s in the realm of freedom and independence and the discipline necessary to achieve it.

As 25/7s mature through the lessons of their life, they open to deeper levels of self-trust through their own direct experience. Ultimately, even if

25/7s have an interest in spiritual practices or ideas, they don't just want to read about mystical experiences in a book; they want a direct experience of oneness. When they're living in alignment with the Law of Faith, they make contact with the deeper purpose in all that arises. If some people lie to them, cheat them, or betray them in any other form, they may not choose to associate with these people again, but they remain steadfast in their trust of the universal teacher working through these experiences, and they feel gratitude to Spirit for the lessons.

When 25/7s find internal freedom from conflict, they can then focus on a form of service the way Zen archers focus on their archery practice — as a means of transformation and inner awareness. Until they find their focus, however, they tend to remain eternal seekers and spiritual vagabonds, disassociated rather than free, trusting everyone but themselves, searching everywhere but where they stand, trusting only the mind as a repository of information.

Most 25/7s tend toward paranoia. When they feel safe enough to put aside their mental shields and trust self and trust Spirit, they feel the communion they have known from birth but had forgotten; they feel a direct experience of oneness. When 25/7s finally feel Spirit inside, they find Spirit everywhere, in everyone and everything.

Working 25/7 in the Positive

The life of individuals working 25/7 in the positive may or may not appear spiritual or include spiritual practices or inner work. But no matter what field they engage in, these 25/7s are a source of often deep understanding because they look inside to find whatever they need to know. They also learn from others, but they respect their own internal feelings and messages. They're adventurers who bring to light the freedom within; living the liberated life, feeling comfortable and at home almost anywhere, they find satisfaction sharing the truths that experience has taught them. Embodying inner freedom, touched by a sense of oneness, peace, and inner harmony, they go out and touch others. They're grateful for all experiences, because these 25/7s see Spirit everywhere.

Working 25/7 in the Negative

Preferring solitude, these isolated 25/7s avoid people because they don't feel others can be trusted. Aimless seekers of experience, avid readers, or spiritual tramps, they constantly look for the book, training, or teacher who can help them be whole or give them the conclusive understanding they want with their mind. Nevertheless, they don't find what they're seeking because they're searching outside themselves. They're among the paranoids of the world; they assume they're going to be left out, and to the degree they act like a recluse, they do get left out.

Life-Path Issues

Health

The health of most 25/7s depends on the relative clarity of each number: In the positive, the 2 energy brings strength; 5 brings an expansive sense of freedom; and 7 brings a discriminating mind that follows sound health practices. In the negative, however, the 2 means 25/7s get drained and stressed from thinking too much, resulting in possible allergies; 5 means they feel scattered, dependent, and resentful, which compromises the adrenals and nervous system; and 7 means they're sensitive to feelings of betrayal and constricted around the heart area.

For 25/7s, few activities are as healing as drifting down a river, canoeing across a lake, or hiking through the woods. Coupled with meditation and open feelings, these activities work as a positive tonic and rejuvenator.

Most 25/7s need grounding; they need to come down to Earth. They thrive on physical training in sports, dance, and martial arts (as 25/7 legends Muhammad Ali and Bruce Lee exemplify). Any physical training over time helps them find a grounded, experiential degree of self-trust.

Aesthetic forms of healing that focus on the mind, such as visualization, working with light and color, flower essences, and art, are all useful for 25/7s. Like all working 7, 25/7s need to apply regular discipline and not get so involved with the mind that they forget they have a body that requires care.

Relationships

Most 25/7s have clear-cut issues that make sharing their feelings and revealing their vulnerability especially challenging but certainly possible. They experience fears and pain of betrayal, real or imagined, in their heart; so they trust their mind and think their way through emotions, which cuts them off from a sense of connection with others.

Those working 25/7 keep to themselves a great deal, desiring a high degree of privacy and independence, but they still seek to remain connected to their partner, requiring a delicate balance. Most 25/7s seek harmony, balance, and completeness through joining with a partner because they don't feel the harmony and completeness in themselves. To bring more life into a relationship, they do well to practice whatever inner work they choose to enhance their own sense of self-reliance and wholeness. When they come to trust self and Spirit, they open to relationship.

Sexually, the deepest satisfaction for those working 25/7 comes as they emerge from the cave of the mind and trust enough to remove their mental armor and bring emotion into the bedroom.

Talents, Work, and Finances

No matter what their chosen occupation, 25/7s can use their incisive mind in service and support of others. Most 25/7s work well in writing, acting, research, or high-tech fields; they excel as secret service agents, chemists, surgeons, lawyers, and choreographers. Clearly, 25/7s are well suited to any work that requires exceptionally deft thinking ability and skillful hands, especially if that work allows some quiet space. Insightful and private, 25/7s make excellent researchers, scholars, physics professors, and computer whizzes. The 5 quality colors their life path because those working 5 take in many things, while the 7 creates an artistic pattern, seeking rhythm and harmony. Therefore, 25/7s have a strong aesthetic nature, and they're equally at home sitting by a computer or walking along a windblown beach.

These world-class thinkers can do very well financially through a variety of means. Financial lack is usually linked to a lack of self-trust, to the scatteredness of 5, or to spending more than they earn in the quest for experience. But when working their issues in positive ways, 25/7s have a mind that can do whatever they want and a spirit that is there to serve and even, in some cases, to help liberate others.

Some Well-Known 25/7s

Muhammad Ali, Arthur Ashe, Joan Baez, Carrie Fisher, Jerry Garcia, Woody Guthrie, Stephen Hawking, J. Edgar Hoover, Byron Katie, Marilyn Monroe, Vladimir Putin, Gertrude Stein, James Stewart

Keys to Fulfilling Your Destiny

If you're working 25/7, this section can help you manifest your life purpose by focusing your attention on core issues and by generating specific action to transform key areas of your life.

Guidelines and Recommendations

- Trust your instincts and intuition; you're the expert on your body and your life.
- Remember each day to take at least one deep breath and, as you do so, feel as if you're breathing in Spirit.
- Enjoy experience, but focus on relationship.
- Make clear agreements with people to avoid possible misunderstandings.

Useful Questions

1. Reflect on the following questions:
   - How can I make the shift from reliance on outside experts and ideas to trusting my own intuitive body wisdom?
   - To avoid misunderstandings, can I share my real feelings and needs in a given situation?
   - Do I feel safe with people, or do I hide behind a mental shield?
   - What hidden assumptions about trust can I reexamine?
2. If these questions generate insights, how might you put these insights into practice?

Deepening Your Understanding

1. Turn back to Part Two, and reread the main sections covering the digits that make up your birth number: 2, 5, and 7.
2. You may wish to review birth numbers of family and friends and, if they're open to it, discuss similar or different issues in your lives.

Spiritual Laws: The Leverage to Change Your Life

1. Read about each of the following laws in Part Four:

- **THE LAW OF FAITH:** Only when we find faith in ourselves can we have faith in others.
- **THE LAW OF DISCIPLINE:** Discipline generates the focus and depth of experience leading to true freedom.
- **THE LAW OF EXPECTATIONS:** Our life unfolds according to our hidden expectations and assumptions.
- **THE LAW OF PROCESS:** The best way to reach any goal is one small, sure step at a time.
- **THE LAW OF RESPONSIBILITY:** To find our boundaries, we need to learn when to say yes and how to say no.

2. Do the exercises for each of these laws.
3. Consider how you might apply each law to your life.

34/7 & 43/7

7: Trust through Openness
4: Stability through Process
3: Expression through Sensitivity

Those working 34/7 or 43/7 are here to work through issues of trust, patience, and emotional expression and to have faith in the spiritual process operating within their life, establishing security by finding practical ways to contribute to others. Both these life paths present the opportunity of blending the incisive mind of those working 7 with the down-to-earth practicality of mature 4 energy and the sensitivity and expressiveness of 3 energy.

Because of the influence of 4, finding a sense of communion or unconditional trust depends on 34/7s and 43/7s following a step-by-step process of self-discovery. The deeper they go inside, the farther 34/7s and 43/7s see outside.

Since our life purpose always offers some tests and hurdles, 34/7s and 43/7s may feel conflicted, polarized, and pulled in different directions: While 7 tends to pull them upward, into the higher mind or in some cases into metaphysical interests and practices, 4 tends to pull them downward, into daily life, family, and practical business concerns. As these 7 and 4 characteristics mature and integrate, they form a powerful synthesis, enabling 34/7s and 43/7s to build a kind of bridge between heaven and Earth in creative ways, such as making money while bringing more beauty, happiness, or awareness into the world.

Most 34/7s and 43/7s closely resemble one another, except for the reverse order of the first two numbers; while 4 predominates with 7 for 34/7s, 3 predominates with 7 for 43/7s. Because of this, 34/7s experience more acutely issues dealing with stability and process in relation to self-trust; they confront a stronger tendency to skip steps, with secondary drives and issues related to expression and self-doubt. In contrast, 43/7s deal less with process issues and more with emotional sensitivity, including issues of expression and self-doubt, which make them slower to come to self-trust; therefore, 43/7s generally find their confidence later in life. Other than these rising and falling influences, both these life paths include the same fundamental qualities, which interact to form powerful, sensitive, insightful individuals and challenging as well as versatile life issues.

Both 34/7s and 43/7s are here to harmonize apparent opposites and to blend practicality and mysticism, outer and inner experience, flesh and spirit, worldly business and spiritual pursuits. They sometimes accomplish this through launching a spiritual business, whether associated with a particular religion or, for example, selling books or teaching seminars devoted to themes of religion, spirituality, or personal growth.

Whether or not 34/7s and 43/7s work in holistic business enterprises, they're here to bridge two worlds. The 3 indicates a drive for expression, and for uplifting others while living fully in the world rather than in a monastery, ashram, or forest.

Generally, 34/7s and 43/7s feel safer in the realm of the mind because of their exceptional analytical abilities, but they also have powerful emotions. They can act emotionally compulsive or impulsive, but the emotional sensitivity of 3 helps balance their mental energy.

Both 34/7s and 43/7s experience a drive toward security, toward family, and toward business. Confronting issues in the area of foundations (4) means that they have to learn to ground themselves in the practical realities of life, which helps balance the imagination and flights of fancy of 7 and 5. They need to fulfill the practical part of their life and establish a stable base from which to build, step-by-step, a staircase to Spirit. For 34/7s and 43/7s, a step-by-step stairway is a more apt metaphor than a springboard, because their life will rise or fall on the strength of their foundation and the care they take along their journey. A skipped step sends them tumbling back into self-doubt and isolation.

People working these two life paths share 7 with 25/7s, but they have stronger emotional energy because of the 3. Like 25/7s, neither 34/7s nor 43/7s, by tendency, fully trust their feelings. They have fears and expectations that they'll be misunderstood, so they don't share, which in turn creates misunderstandings. By applying the Law of Expectations, they can turn this tendency around, forming positive expectations and working toward positive outcomes.

Working 34/7 or 43/7 in the Positive

Strong, practical, physical, and spiritual, individuals working 34/7 or 43/7 in the positive have learned to trust the mystery and wisdom of life working through them and through everyone else. These freethinkers trust in the process of their life, including the ups and downs, the difficulties and joys. Meditation, which quiets their mind, brings a sense of harmony and peace as a regular part of their life. Combining worldly interests with a commitment toward inner growth, these individuals dedicate their work, relationships, and activities to growth and awakening. They share their insightful nature based on direct experience and feel connected to Spirit even while pursuing the practical concerns of everyday life.

Working 34/7 or 43/7 in the Negative

These 34/7s or 43/7s feel torn between conflicting drives for security and desires to go inward and get away from the material world. Confused and troubled by a human world they don't trust, they see hypocrisy everywhere, reflecting the turmoil they feel inside. Self-doubt only aggravates self-trust issues, so they constantly look for teachers, techniques, and ideas that can help them; they become wandering spiritual vagabonds, seldom putting down roots long enough for anything to grow in their life. Alternately, they want nothing to do with crazy spiritual things. Even though they may appear sociable and gregarious, they're wary of sharing their feelings and end up feeling alone.

Life-Path Issues

Health

Combining the sensitivity of 3 with the sturdiness of 4 and the mental capacity of 7, 34/7s and 43/7s generally have strong bodies, but they still have a hard time trusting their own instincts or intuition. Due to subtle fears that their body may not know how to take care of itself, they seek solutions in either pharmaceuticals, surgery, or subtle medicines, herbs, and food supplements. When they begin trusting their instincts — for example, taking vitamins when their body tells them such vitamins are needed —they know instinctively just what to do and when to do it. Both 34/7s and 43/7s need to pay special attention to their own body's messages. Nutrition is an arena for learning self-trust; they need to listen to the body's wisdom and messages, not just the mind's ideas of what the body needs. They do best to avoid the tendency to follow other people's theories of what's good for them and first confirm the advice with their own insides. Their body works with their higher instincts to maintain the strongest possible constitution.

A low-fat, varied diet that helps maintain a sense of lightness and clarity benefits them, and most 34/7s and 43/7s do well to avoid dairy products. Issues with knees or the throat can appear when they're withholding expression.

Physically strong and rarely ill unless stressed, both 34/7s and 43/7s can experience anxiety or hysteria, which can take the form of nervous break-downs. Those 34/7s and 43/7s who have matured along their path seldom experience such maladies. If they do have a breakdown, however, 34/7s and 43/7s may need to be hospitalized temporarily, although they usually recover quickly. On the rare occasions when they experience a breakdown, it's best for them to accept the process and go through it without resistance. Afterward, they can appreciate all they have learned from the experience.

Those working 34/7 and 43/7 appreciate forms of skill training that have deeper meaning than just doing push-ups to get bigger muscles. Martial arts furnish an exceptional means to develop deeper trust in the body's sponta-neous ability to learn and move. Dance or any free-movement form or sport can benefit them greatly. Routines that combine body, mind, and spirit usu-ally hold their interest longest.

Relationships

In the positive, 34/7s and 43/7s bring stability, constancy, and feeling quality to their relationships. The 3 softens their tendency to stay mental. As long as they've developed open, honest communication and associated trust with their partner, their relationship thrives.

Trust issues for 34/7s and 43/7s center on a subtle, underlying sense of feeling uncomfortable. They're not entirely relaxed when they're with others; it's as if they might say the wrong thing, which they sometimes set themselves up to do.

The quality of their relationships and their sexual life depends on open-ness, trust, and the vulnerability to share their feelings and let go to the point of ecstatic intimacy. Although they enjoy the comforts of home and family, these strong, spiritual personalities won't always stay in relationship for the sake of internal processing and growth.

Talents, Work, and Finances

Multifaceted drives create special challenges, abilities, and opportunities for 34/7s and 43/7s. The blend of 7, 4, and 3 qualities makes for a much stronger, more resilient life path than any single number on its own. Both 34/7s and 43/7s have strong creative and expressive potential, and they excel in a variety of fields, including metaphysics, martial arts, acting or producing, business, and creative writing, especially screenplays, due to their good structural sense. They do well as long as they trust themselves but stay open to feedback and take any project step-by-step.

Many 34/7s, in particular, have compulsive and impulsive spending patterns; both 34/7s and 43/7s can behave frivolously with money. Ultimately, the state of their finances depends on the process they follow and whether they've prepared for an occupation that makes good use of their skills. If not, self-doubt leaves them doing a little bit of this and a little bit of that.

Some Well-Known 34/7s and 43/7s

34/7s: Leonard Bernstein, Michael Douglas, Melinda Gates, Reggie Jackson, Caitlyn Jenner, John F. Kennedy, Golda Meir, Angela Merkel, Elon Musk, Cole Porter, Harry S. Truman

43/7: Sheryl Sandberg; no other well-known 43/7s are listed because there are far fewer 43/7s in the general population than some other birth numbers.

Keys to Fulfilling Your Destiny

If you're working 34/7 or 43/7, this section can help you manifest your life purpose by focusing your attention on core issues and by generating specific action to transform key areas of your life.

Guidelines and Recommendations

- Trust the process of your life.
- Remember, you're absolutely safe; nothing can harm your soul.

- Develop your expressive skills step-by-step.
- To heal your life, share your innermost feelings.

Useful Questions

1. Reflect on the following questions:
   - Do I trust my ability to reach my goals step-by-step?
   - Which do I trust more — my mind or my feelings?
   - Does self-doubt or impatience interfere with my life? If so, how can I change this?
   - Sociable or not, do I share my innermost feelings?
2. If these questions generate insights, how might you put these insights into practice?

Deepening Your Understanding

1. Turn back to Part Two, and reread the main sections covering the digits that make up your birth number: 3, 4, and 7.
2. You may wish to review birth numbers of family and friends and, if they're open to it, discuss similar or different issues in your lives.

Spiritual Laws: The Leverage to Change Your Life

1. Read about each of the following laws in Part Four:
   - **THE LAW OF FAITH:** Only when we find faith in ourselves can we have faith in others.
   - **THE LAW OF PROCESS:** The best way to reach any goal is one small, sure step at a time.
   - **THE LAW OF PATTERNS:** Patterns tend to reassert themselves unless we exert strong leverage to change them.
   - **THE LAW OF HONESTY:** Honesty is founded on self-awareness of our emotional reality.
   - **THE LAW OF EXPECTATIONS:** Our life unfolds according to our hidden expectations and assumptions.
2. Do the exercises for each of these laws.
3. Consider how you might apply each law to your life.

8: INFLUENCE THROUGH AUTHORITY

To do more for the world
than the world does for you —
that is success.

— Henry Ford

This section includes all birth numbers with 8 as a primary life purpose, including single-digit 8, 17/8, 26/8, 35/8, and 44/8. Even though all of these birth numbers reflect intense 8 dynamics, the qualities, issues, and character of those that contain other digits have a unique flavor due to the influence and interaction of the other numbers, in contrast to the pure, undiluted, single-digit 8.

8

8: Influence through Authority

Those with a single-digit 8 life path are here to fulfill an innate impulse to influence others to work with authority, empowerment, and recognition, and to apply whatever degree of financial success they may attain in service of the common good. However, since what we're here to do isn't what comes easiest, before single-digit 8s can fulfill their life purpose, they have to overcome hurdles and negative tendencies in a number of areas.

For this single-digit life path, please be sure to review the chapter in Part Two that provides a full and detailed discussion of the number 8 and all it represents. Here, I highlight key elements of the path and purpose of single-digit 8s.

Like all those with an 8 in their birth number, single-digit 8s have to work through issues related to money, power, authority, control, and recognition. All those working 8 have to reconcile their innate drive to achieve abundance, influence, and respect with fears or negative beliefs that can undermine their efforts or, in some cases, generate impulses to avoid material success through self-sabotage, such as turning down opportunities that come their way.

I have expressed the idea in my books that we can make good money, doing what we enjoy, while serving others. While this applies in principle to all of us, it particularly applies to those working 8 energy, because a key aspect of their path and purpose involves overlapping areas of taking up the scepter of authority, self-control, and empowerment in order to achieve material success — and further, to use that success in service of others and for a higher good. Whether this is accomplished in a smaller circle of family, friends, and associates or extends into the larger world isn't critical. The main thing is for those working 8 to own their personal power and to empower others; they can also fulfill their life purpose by helping others achieve that purpose; that is, helping empower and enrich the lives of others.

The path presents additional complications for 17/8s, 26/8s, 35/8s, and 44/8s, who also have to address issues of insecurity and lack of trust, or idealistic standards, or self-doubt, or lack of focus. But all the challenges for single-digit 8s are contained within the qualities of that one number. So their innate drives for — and avoidance of — influence, authority, power, respect, and even wealth are clear and straightforward. Once single-digit 8s accept their path and consciously see how they hold back, remain passive, or undermine their own efforts, they're ready to step forward and act in alignment not only with their own good, but for the benefit of others in their circle of influence.

No matter what their walk of life, single-digit 8s feel a call to influence family, friends, colleagues, and even those in the larger world through writing, teaching, managing a company, blogging, podcasting, political activism, and any other available means.

These individuals have a strategic intelligence, in the sense that they can see the writing on the wall, where the stream of energy is flowing. In other words, single-digit 8s can see what they need to do to move toward their goals. The challenge is actually *doing* what's needed — taking appropriate action. (Perhaps that's why my old mentor, the man I called Socrates, once told me, "It's better to do what needs to be done than to not do it and have a good reason why you didn't act.") So while the drives and struggles of single-digit 8s for influence, authority, and abundance are straightforward, the key to fulfilling their life path is *action*, in the form of effort over time.

Like those with a 4 whose life reflects whether or not they follow a patient process to their goals, for 8s the question is whether they take action over time, or remain passive for one or another reason. As the proverb goes, "We make zero percent of the shots we don't take."

Working Single-Digit 8 in the Positive

With their powerful, strategic intellect (whether or not they strive in the academic arena), and the authority they project, those working single-digit 8 in the positive can bring extraordinary concentration and focus to present goals and projects. Having learned from their life experience that to reap the harvest they have to sow the seeds, these individuals show dedication and even devotion to the task at hand, and gain recognition for their efforts. Driven not only by self-interest or working for their family, single-digit 8s may also have long-term philanthropic dreams, large or small, and tend to show a generosity and appreciation for the blessings they've earned. These single-digit 8s often stand out and distinguish themselves among family, friends, or the larger world.

Working Single-Digit 8 in the Negative

Passive-aggressive, sending out mixed messages, rambling on or remaining mute, these single-digit 8s haven't yet accepted the innate personal power that's a part of their life path. Feeling impotent, as if others in their world hold sway and have the power, they avoid conflict, stonewall, nominally give in, or overreact in bursts of anger. By their action or inaction, they nonetheless influence others, but consistently underestimate or fail to recognize the impact their words and actions have on others. Whether they're closer to wealth or poverty, or just getting by, they still struggle with or for wealth, feeling conflicted and ambivalent toward money. They resent authority figures yet dream of being an authority. Obstinate, not wanting to be told what to do, these individuals feel trapped in the foothills even while holding a map toward their dreams, since they haven't yet undertaken the arduous journey.

Life-Path Issues

Health

Like those working 4 and resonant 2, single-digit 8s have an innate strength (and stubbornness), which can also manifest as discipline and single-minded purpose. It's especially helpful for single-digit 8s to begin the day well, to set the pace and tone, especially with exercise. Whether that's a four-minute routine (such as the Peaceful Warrior Workout), a yoga class, a workout at the Y, or a two-mile run is less important than *doing something* to begin the day well, before the workaday world monopolizes their attention. This means getting up early enough, which means getting to sleep early enough, setting up a healthful routine on which single-digit 8s can thrive. And since the drive and ambition of single-digit 8s, like resonant 4s, can push the body and joints and result in muscular tension, some self-care in the form of relaxation

— whether meditation or a massage, or therapies such as Alexander Technique, Feldenkrais, and other practices that reduce stress — helps support and balance that drive and ambition.

Relationships

The various digits in the birth numbers individuals are working have an influence over whether their priorities are people, place, or work. For those working 4 issues, people may rank highest; for 7 issues, a sense of place is key; for 8 issues, work is likely to be paramount. So single-digit 8s need to choose not just a mate, but a helpmate and workmate, someone who understands and can accept that work — or a sense of purpose, accomplishment, and drive — is the central pursuit of their partner, and who's willing to support that. Single-digit 8s may seek out, and can thrive with, a patient mate — one who's willing to mind the home fires (male or female) or who has their own independent pursuits and doesn't place an undue emotional burden on busy single-digit 8s, but is present enough to engage them and remind them of the balance between work and family. Single-digit 8s may enjoy and even delight in family (as do those working resonant 4), but raising children at best becomes another project they pursue, fellow humans on whom they can exert a positive influence.

Talents, Work, and Finances

Just as family plays a central role in the life of those working 4, work and career are pivots around which the rest of the life of single-digit 8s revolves — making a good income, doing meaningful work, while serving others can move these individuals to long hours and dedication. Whereas those with 5 energy may work toward independence and an array of experiences, for single-digit 8s the work serves as its own reward. If they gain authority and recognition — and if their work influences others — all the better, since they feel most on purpose when striving toward professional goals. Individualistic, single-digit 8s like to make the rules, not follow them. This quality may lend itself to difficulties with others as they take unilateral action, but may also lead to originality and entrepreneurial success. Single-digit 8s can work with others and thrive in an atmosphere of appreciation for their work, but many find it easier to be their own boss and set their own course.

Some Well-Known Single-Digit 8s

As of 2018, and publication of the 25th Anniversary Edition, the oldest single-digit 8s are under eighteen years old — not generally enough time to become well-known. In later editions of this book, as more single-digit 8s come of age and make notable accomplishments, names may appear here.

Keys to Fulfilling Your Destiny

If you're working 8, this section can help you manifest your life purpose by focusing your attention on core issues and by generating specific action to transform key areas of your life.

Guidelines and Recommendations

- Contact your power and assertiveness through a martial art or another avenue that allows you to express these qualities in a constructive way.
- Take responsibility for any abundance or lack of abundance in your life.
- Consider how you really feel about wealth, power, and high profile.
- Count your blessings, and appreciate the abundance you have in your life right now; share a portion of your blessings with others.

Useful Questions

1. Reflect on the following questions:
   - How do you feel about external authority, and why?
   - Do you follow society's laws and rules, or do you prefer to abide by your own judgment? How has this helped your daily life or made it more difficult?
   - What are your priorities? What are you doing to achieve them?
   - How do you influence others in your family, in your circle of friends, or in the larger world?
   - What does money mean to you?
2. If these questions generate insights, how might you put these insights into practice?

Deepening Your Understanding

1. Turn back to Part Two, and reread the main sections covering the digit that makes up your birth number: 8.

2. You may wish to review birth numbers of family and friends and, if they're open to it, discuss similar or different issues in your lives.

Spiritual Laws: The Leverage to Change Your Life

1. Read about each of the following laws in Part Four:

    *   **THE LAW OF INTUITION:** No longer monitoring other people's opinions, we connect with our heart's intuitive wisdom.

    *   **THE LAW OF HONESTY:** Honesty is founded on self-awareness of our emotional reality.

    *   **THE LAW OF HIGHER WILL:** Our willingness to serve a higher purpose empowers us to inspire others.

    *   **THE LAW OF ACTION:** To overcome insecurity or self-doubt, we can accept our feelings yet behave with confidence.

2. Do the exercises for each of these laws.

3. Consider how you might apply each law to your life.

17/8

8: Influence through Authority
7: Trust through Openness
1: Creativity through Security

Those on the 17/8 life path are here to work through issues related to money, power, and spirit; as they come to trust the creative spirit inside them and share that spirit with others, they realize abundance and inner power. Since our life path always involves challenges, before 17/8s can fulfill their destiny, they have to confront and overcome conflicting drives, fears, and beliefs about money and power, develop deeper trust in themselves and in Spirit, and access confidence and creativity. For 17/8s and all those working 8 energy, sharing abundance doesn't require that they be wealthy; even someone making a modest income can share a few dollars, some time, some energy, or even a bountiful spirit of generosity.

While the more inner-directed 7 and the more outer-directed 8 might seem to pull in opposite directions, no such opposition exists when 17/8s work in the positive. As 17/8s begin to trust Spirit working through them, an underlying burden of paranoia and fear lifts, opening them to an expansiveness that attracts and generates the abundance that flows naturally from their creative energy. In other words, 17/8s must work through the issues of 7 in order to attract a full measure of fulfillment, no matter what the actual scale of their finances.

Although 8 has a certain solidity and grounded materialism about it, the combination of 1 and 7 often gives to 17/8s the charisma of a creative nature spirit — light, airy, imaginative, and glowing. The 8 keeps them grounded and connected to Earth. The more uplifted, inward, and spiritual qualities of the 1 and 7 can serve to balance and complement the 8 drive for recognition, wealth, and power. If 17/8s are working in the negative, however, their inward 7 quality conflicts with and sabotages their energy as they withdraw from life and the outer work necessary to succeed. Most individuals working 8 energy have subtle tendencies to suppress their power; if they don't trust themselves to step forward into the world, they may accomplish nothing.

Nevertheless, 1 tends to attract money; it has a lucky quality about it. When 17/8s let their creative energy flow into the world and begin to have a stronger sense of their spiritual side and the spiritual aspects of the world, money and influence come to them almost as if by magic.

In addition, the creativity of 1 plus the mental acuity of 7, along with the powerful intelligence of 8, serve to create some of the most insightful, original, and even brilliant thinkers around. In the positive, 17/8s have no shortage of ideas to reach their goals.

The 7, however, can exacerbate subconscious fears or avoidance of money or power; if 17/8s don't trust themselves overall, they're less likely to trust themselves with money or power, increasing the 8 tendency toward self-sabotage. Most 17/8s appear upbeat on the outside, but they have a difficult time knowing how to express themselves in the material world.

Whether or not they feel religious or spiritual, 17/8s are here to combine inner growth and inspiration with very practical goals in the material world. For example, some 17/8s might decide to combine their interest in spirituality with material success by opening a bookstore specializing in uplifting, spiritual, or self-help themes and serving as a gathering place for many people. Not all 17/8s run such businesses, of course, but eventually they find the confidence and trust to create *something* that inspires them and others; in other words, they make good money doing what they enjoy in service of others.

All 17/8s need to acknowledge rather than repress the drive they have for recognition and influence; they can enjoy playing in the material realm without losing sight of the reality that material success is empty without a higher purpose.

Working 17/8 in the Positive

The delightful and usually delighted individuals working 17/8 in the positive have bridged the worlds of business and spirit, combining an abiding, transcendental trust in themselves and in the world to direct them wherever they need to go. Trusting a higher power than their own, these spirited innovators find their own power as well, and they help empower and uplift others. They enjoy a sense of abundance that flows forth, attracted by their uplifting energy. As this energy moves into the world in service, and they use mind and money for higher purposes, whatever they do in the name of Spirit comes back in the form of further blessings.

Working 17/8 in the Negative

Insecure, withdrawn, and afraid of confrontation, these 17/8s feel baffled by the world. They want recognition, fear betrayal, and feel that something is missing — the spiritual side of their life. Overcontrolling, they often feel mistrust in business dealings, and they have unexpressed inner conflicts about the morality of money. Pulled between inner and outer drives, they have a hard time being on the planet, in the sense of knowing what to do here. Although they may seem outgoing, they don't really share themselves or their very private inner processes. With the mental qualities of 7 energy and the power issues of 8, they inadvertently talk over people's heads or sound preachy. They lack faith in the powers of self or Spirit.

Life-Path Issues

Health

The heart area of many 17/8s is sensitive to the degree they have unresolved trust issues or charged memories of betrayal. If working the negative aspects of 8, 17/8s may engage in subconscious self-sabotage, which may include physical mishaps. If their creative energy feels blocked or suppressed, the lower abdomen, reproductive area, or lower back may flare up.

A key for 17/8s involves exercise that gives them a sense of personal power and expansiveness, involves some form of skill practice to help them trust themselves, and keeps their creative energy flowing. Meditation also benefits 17/8s as a calming and grounding influence, giving their mind a rest.

With the subconscious close to the surface for many 17/8s, they need to balance physical discipline with a little self-pampering, including indulgent but healthful activities, such as regular massage, swims, or saunas (depending upon the climate), which help nourish and recharge them.

Unless 17/8s feel securely grounded in their physical body rather than identified with their mind, they may not pay sufficient attention to what they eat, although they're likely to be aware of nutritional guidelines. They can get so busy with creative or business projects that they don't make time for regular, relaxed meals. When they do, a light, low-fat, mostly vegetarian diet is optimal for 17/8s, who thrive on such a regimen.

Relationships

The quality of relationships for 17/8s depends on whether they're working in the positive or negative, especially with regard to 7. Most of these individuals require some time to trust and open enough for emotional intimacy. When working in the positive, they can even achieve a spiritual intimacy; until then, their spouse or partner may say, "I never feel like I know who you really are or what you're feeling." But those working 7 and 8 energy can feel uncomfortable revealing their inner life, fearing shame, vulnerability, or both. Power struggles can also arise, because 17/8s often act rigid and controlling when feeling insecure. Most 17/8s, at one time or another, give away their power or assertiveness due to a lack of self-trust and a fear of power; then they want to take their power back, but they aren't always sure how to balance it. They need to learn to share their inner sense of power and empower others.

Sexual issues are highly dependent on how 17/8s manifest 7 — that is, whether they feel open or inhibited. If they feel open, their creative juices translate into active sexual needs, so barring childhood traumas, sex isn't generally a problem for 17/8s; intimacy is. As they refine and transform their trust and power issues, relationships become a stronger priority in their life, furnishing the means to feel a deeper sense of connection.

Talents, Work, and Finances

Nearly all 17/8s have a powerful, insightful mind and inherent drive for success; this, along with their creative potential, provides the fuel for successful endeavors in a variety of fields ranging from sports to politics. They make excellent financial analysts or heads of service organizations, reaching out to many, doing public work in a private way. Eventually, some 17/8s become philanthropists, perhaps even starting charitable foundations, small or large. Or they may open a bookstore or other business that allows them to serve others.

When 17/8s trust their intuition and make creative decisions on that basis, money just seems to show up, and they become extremely successful without knowing why or how.

Some Well-Known 17/8s

Timothy Leary, Mickey Mantle, Adlai Stevenson, Brigham Young

Keys to Fulfilling Your Destiny

If you're working 17/8, this section can help you manifest your life purpose by focusing your attention on core issues and by generating specific action to transform key areas of your life.

Guidelines and Recommendations

- Trust that abundance will flow from your creative efforts.
- Focus on service, not money.
- Find a source of power and abundance through meditation.
- Consider creating a means of livelihood that in some way combines business with personal growth, healing, or spiritual pursuits.

Useful Questions

1. Reflect on the following questions:

   - In what way might my work serve a higher purpose?
   - Do I share my abundance with others?
   - Do I trust my own inner feelings? Do I trust my power?
   - Can I find creative ways to bring people together?

2. If these questions generate insights, how might you put these insights into practice?

Deepening Your Understanding

1. Turn back to Part Two, and reread the main sections covering the digits that make up your birth number: 1, 7, and 8.
2. You may wish to review birth numbers of family and friends and, if they're open to it, discuss similar or different issues in your lives.

Spiritual Laws: The Leverage to Change Your Life

1. Read about each of the following laws in Part Four:

    - **THE LAW OF FAITH:** Only when we find faith in ourselves can we have faith in others.
    - **THE LAW OF EXPECTATIONS:** Our life unfolds according to our hidden expectations and assumptions.
    - **THE LAW OF INTUITION:** No longer monitoring other people's opinions, we connect with our heart's intuitive wisdom.
    - **THE LAW OF HONESTY:** Honesty is founded on self-awareness of our emotional reality.
    - **THE LAW OF HIGHER WILL:** Our willingness to serve a higher purpose empowers us to inspire others.

2. Do the exercises for each of these laws.
3. Consider how you might apply each law to your life.

26/8

8: Influence through Authority
6: Vision through Acceptance
2: Cooperation through Balance

Those on the 26/8 life path are here to work through issues of perfectionism, money, power, and recognition, sharing their abundance in alignment with their highest vision and ideals, in the service of others. Since our life purpose poses specific challenges, the life of 26/8s reflects their conflicting drives and beliefs about authority, money, power, and high profile, and their innate idealism can tend to inhibit the personal power they're here to make manifest. Eventually, 26/8s stand up and assert themselves, and gain recognition and respect within their family, in their community, or in the world at large.

When 26/8s get recognized, it's usually due to the quality of their work. They can work hard for money and recognition, but they have mixed feelings about both due to their inherent idealism. In the negative, the influence of 2 can create inner conflicts, for example, about whether they're undervaluing their service and charging too little or feeling greedy and charging too much. The 6 part of them may say, "Charge less; it's the right thing to do," while the 8 part may say, "I want more!" or may be so afraid of abusing money that they give their skills away for free to avoid the risk of someone being upset or angry with them. Many 26/8s are sensitive to criticism due to the 6 influence, which also can mean they hold back from expressing themselves to maintain their cool.

Those working 26/8 tend to be either passive or aggressive, but in general they tend to be more subdued. Depending on their level of self-worth, which may be shaky due to the high standards of 6, they tend to give away their power and lack self-assertiveness when dealing with emotional confrontations.

Given their high standards, 26/8s often deflect praise and devalue their worth and influence; ignoring their achievements and remembering their mistakes, they have trouble truly enjoying the fruits of their efforts. When caught in repetitive rituals of achievement, 26/8s need to remember the magic words "not perfect but good enough." When they stop holding themselves back, they produce quality work that supports others. Unless they're hiding, 26/8s work hard to rise above the crowd in their immediate surroundings or in the world at large; they strive for security and recognition, although most 8s would deny that they're seeking recognition unless they're willing to take a close look at their life and their actions — for example, when they're in a group of people, they arrange to get noticed. If they're working 8 in the negative, they may be shrinking back from authority, abundance, or recognition — avoiding the very arenas they're here to master.

Most 26/8s tend to compete with and compare themselves to others in terms of levels of recognition, wealth, or influence. Deep down, they want to come out on top, although this desire may be subtle or subdued because of the 6 influence. If they become aware of this tendency, 26/8s generally want to correct it. Their desire for improvement, however, becomes more of the same game of comparison: "I no longer compare myself to others like those *other* people I know do."

Most 26/8s work hard to achieve money and recognition. A core belief generated by the high standards of 6 is that they have to go through difficulty and discomfort to earn or deserve their abundance. Due to their high standards, whatever 26/8s do they feel they could have done better. This can hold them back from stepping forward in their family, among colleagues, or in the world. But when 26/8s get past their issues about money and power, which include negative feelings about wealthy or powerful people, they tend to make good money and use it to bring out a stronger sense of self. When struggling financially, they may feel controlled by others; when successful, they tend to feel expansive and generous.

Those working 26/8 often display a childlike purity stemming from the influence of 6, and they often mature late. The demands and challenges of raising a family as well as working in or creating a successful business provide the initiation to help them feel like competent adults. Without such challenges, they may avoid hard work and recognition and do just enough to get by. Perfectionism, along with fear of money or power, can hold some 26/8s back from getting off the ground; they may feel disheartened, not by life's challenges but by their own unrealistic expectations.

Nearly all 26/8s want to control their own life, but at the same time, they want to do the right thing by others. Therefore, they sometimes give mixed messages to other people; on the surface, they want to please and to be liked, but beneath this, others may sense a powerful, even compulsive, drive for control. When feeling powerless, 26/8s find it hard to stand up for themselves; they typically experience and subconsciously attract subtle or not-so-subtle forms of abuse in their life, ranging from being taken for granted, being taken advantage of, and being verbally criticized, to being physically beaten. They generally seek to avoid social or emotional confrontations, but when pushed to the wall, few people can push back harder.

Although the pure ideals of 6 generally keep 26/8s from abusing power or squandering money, if they don't feel worthy of success they may subconsciously arrange for an accident, a dishonest or incompetent partner, or another form of self-sabotage. The Law of Higher Will helps open the way to a life of abundance and service for 26/8s by reminding them of their higher purpose.

Working 26/8 in the Positive

With their high standards and vision, individuals working 26/8 in the positive make good money, doing what they enjoy, serving other people. They feel a sense of balanced inner power in their relationships, their work, and their life. Out of a sense of expansive abundance, they can hold on or let go as appropriate, without the need to manipulate or control others. They maintain their sense of fairness and integrity and serve as a positive and uplifting influence in the world, using their power and position to help others, perhaps through philanthropy. They hold money and recognition in perspective, focusing on their higher purpose.

Working 26/8 in the Negative

These unassertive 26/8s feel timid, invisible, and ignored. Deeply frustrated in their own endeavors, they resent rich people due to their own negative beliefs about money. They find it difficult to get along with others or to form relationships, and they get into power struggles unless the lines of authority are clearly defined. Overcontrolling perfectionists, they're critical of others, especially those who don't show them respect. They undervalue themselves and their work, judging themselves against unrealistically high standards, and they refrain from taking on challenges in the material world. They not only avoid the fast lane; they don't even get on the highway.

Life-Path Issues

Health

If 26/8s haven't resolved their perfectionistic standards and subconscious negativity about money and power, they may sabotage themselves by getting ill, divorced, or injured to avoid a big success.

If frustrated, 26/8s may experience chronic tension in their solar plexus, inhibiting breathing and draining their energy, or tension around the neck from self-imposed pressure. When they're run down, 26/8s may develop sinus infections, a sure sign for them to ease up on themselves. They tend to drive themselves too hard, then have to recuperate, but a short period of self-pampering is usually all that's required.

Most 26/8s pay attention to laws of good nutrition due to their high standards, but because they work hard, they also like to indulge themselves in ways ranging from having a relaxing drink or taking other drugs to treating themselves to a massage, sauna, and maybe sweets as a consolation for their efforts. The pattern of hard work and then indulgence, along with wanting to maintain a high self-image, means that some 26/8s fall into eating disorders as they overcontrol and then undercontrol themselves, resulting in dietary swings or even bulimia or anorexia. Moderation can be a challenge for 26/8s. With their high standards, 26/8s seek to improve their diet and everything else in their life. As with most people, a varied, low-fat diet works well for them.

Most 26/8s who exercise regularly tend to seek an efficient and balanced form of exercise. Depending on their background and interests, they may pursue sports as a means of achieving recognition or practice weight lifting as a way to feel powerful. Any kind of physical activity that appeals to them works fine, and they usually excel at whatever they do.

Relationships

The standards of 26/8s are so high that they can be hard to live with; either they're judging everyone else by their standards or they're setting an almost impossible example as they strive to be Mr. or Ms. Perfect.

Those working 26/8 may have trouble knowing or expressing how they really feel because they've learned to focus on the best way to feel and then wear that mask. They need to tune in to their authentic feelings and needs.

Many 26/8s have trouble with long-term relationships or making commitments, especially when they're focusing on trying to find the perfect relationship. In other cases, they start out by projecting their idealized image on others and then feel disappointed or even deceived when those individuals turn out to be only human after all. Then they set out to improve them whether they're interested or not. In relationships, 26/8s benefit from applying the Law of Flexibility.

Sexually, 26/8s want to do the right thing, and they often focus on being good in bed and pleasing their partner rather than expressing their own needs and then just letting go. They may tend to maintain control subtly, either of their partner or just of themselves. They need to shift from performance to loving interplay and intimacy. Then their relationship reflects back to them the abundance they feel inside.

Talents, Work, and Finances

When working in the positive, due to their high standards and their drive for recognition and success 26/8s can do almost anything well and tend to rise above the crowd because they work hard and strive to improve themselves. Yet they rarely feel like they're performing as well as they could. They need to feel appreciated for their work, and they tend to strive for a high income. Due to their high ideals, they sometimes have a hard time finding work that feels meaningful enough. Driven toward yet afraid of high profile and recognition, they tend to be late bloomers until, finally, they come to value themselves and the quality of their work, emerging as a positive influence on others.

Some Well-Known 26/8s

James Baldwin, Lucille Ball, Osama bin Laden, César Chávez, Bob Dylan, Jane Fonda, Jack London, Paul Newman, Laurence Olivier, Jesse Owens, Barbra Streisand

Keys to Fulfilling Your Destiny

If you're working 26/8, this section can help you manifest your life purpose by focusing your attention on core issues and by generating specific action to transform key areas of your life.

Guidelines and Recommendations

- Act with quiet power and confidence.
- Find something in which you can excel and persevere.
- Recognize your value, and let your light shine.
- Balance work with personal relationships.

Useful Questions

1. Reflect on the following questions:

    - Do I strive for or avoid money and power?
    - Do I feel I have to do more to deserve success?
    - Do I assert myself in a balanced, consistent way?
    - How have my high standards helped my work, and how have they held me back?

2. If these questions generate insights, how might you put these insights into practice?

Deepening Your Understanding

1. Turn back to Part Two, and reread the main sections covering the digits that make up your birth number: 2, 6, and 8.
2. You may wish to review birth numbers of family and friends and, if they're open to it, discuss similar or different issues in your lives.

Spiritual Laws: The Leverage to Change Your Life

1. Read about each of the following laws in Part Four:

    *   **THE LAW OF HONESTY:** Honesty is founded on self-awareness of our emotional reality.
    *   **THE LAW OF PERFECTION:** High ideals can inspire us, but excellence is the most realistic goal.
    *   **THE LAW OF PROCESS:** The best way to reach any goal is one small, sure step at a time.
    *   **THE LAW OF RESPONSIBILITY:** To find our boundaries, we need to learn when to say yes and how to say no.
    *   **THE LAW OF NO JUDGMENTS:** The universe doesn't judge us; it only teaches us through natural consequences.

2. Do the exercises for each of these laws.
3. Consider how you might apply each law to your life.

35/8

8: Influence through Authority
5: Freedom through Discipline
3: Expression through Sensitivity

Those on the 35/8 life path are here to work through issues of emotional honesty, independence, and power, manifesting abundance, authority, and freedom achieved through discipline and depth of experience. Because our life purpose doesn't come easily, an inherent challenge for 35/8s involves the dynamic tension between drives for wealth, power, and respect and fears of these qualities. This inner conflict frames the life of 35/8s and manifests in both passive and aggressive tendencies; they either behave in a subdued, passive manner, or they act pushy, flamboyant, or even ruthless. One challenge for 35/8s lies in accepting and integrating the passive and aggressive parts of their makeup to form a more balanced and authentic self of acknowledged power and presence.

The life path of 35/8s unfolds in the world of action and influence. Their capacities and genius lie in the areas of authority, leadership, and responsibility. Unless they're inhibited by unconscious fears of their own power, 35/8s can be very dramatic, even ostentatious or flamboyant. When they make a lot of money, they know how to spend it with class.

Wealth, power, and respect fascinate or even preoccupy 35/8s the way a weapon might fascinate a child who's attracted to it but avoids it for fear of doing harm. With their underlying ruthless drive for success, despite their mild exterior 35/8s have a repressed power that can at times make other people uncomfortable even though they don't know why; this power sometimes frightens 35/8s themselves.

The Law of Higher Will can serve to remind 35/8s of their higher purpose and open the way for them to clear subconscious fears and associated tendencies to sabotage themselves. Such self-sabotage can take the form of having physical accidents, alienating other people, forgetting to renew their health or fire insurance, arriving at appointments chronically late, or losing money in speculation or gambling. Self-sabotage ends when they establish a heartfelt commitment to service.

Before 35/8s can truly serve, however, they have to dedicate and use their success for the common good. They need to begin from an assumption of inner power, freedom, and abundance, rather than from a state of need or dependence. In other words, 35/8s experience wealth when they start out feeling their abundance by counting their blessings right now; this gratitude attracts more blessings.

The key to resolution for 35/8s lies not in pursuing or avoiding wealth or authority for their own sakes, but in applying them in the course of providing a valuable service in the world. In fact, 35/8s benefit from visualizing themselves making good money, doing what they enjoy, while serving other people — with the emphasis on service. Such visual images help attract the support of a reluctant or fearful subconscious.

Volunteer work or any gesture of selfless service also helps 35/8s overcome subconscious resistance and self-sabotage. As they come to feel more deserving, they get out of their own way. Since most 35/8s don't tend to give unless they expect to get something back, selfless service can provide powerful leverage for change.

Those working 35/8 share the same life purpose as others working 8, but the influence of 3 and 5 creates very different strengths and hurdles on the path to positive fulfillment of their destiny.

With the quick wit and versatility of 5 come strong issues around discipline; 35/8s have intense ambitions but may not appreciate or be willing to do the work necessary to achieve these goals. Their ambitions outstrip their discipline; they sometimes wait for their ship to come in before they've sent one out.

The positive impact of a healthy discipline and focus in their life can't be overestimated. Discipline leads to personal power and self-control (rather than attempts to control others). When 35/8s practice discipline in their life, they do the work necessary to manifest success. Although they have a steep climb up the mountain — because what we're here to do doesn't come easiest — the rewards are significant, both personally and in terms of their potential contribution to the world.

Even if they're willing to work hard, many 35/8s get scattered trying to do too much, diluting their efforts by pursuing too many opportunities. Discipline in the form of focus responds to and balances this scattering tendency and amplifies their effectiveness. These individuals also need to balance a tendency to swing from extreme dependence when feeling passivity or self-doubt to extreme independence when feeling aggressive; they do this by forming balanced, mutually supportive, interdependent relationships in their personal and professional life.

If 35/8s get stuck in neediness, they tend, almost out of desperation, to use others in their world as means for advancement or learning that may lead to their liberation. When they shift this attitude and see everyone and every situation as an opportunity to serve and share themselves, their life makes a corresponding shift.

With the influence of 3, 35/8s can feel inhibited about expressing their feelings, especially feelings that aren't "nice." This inhibition may manifest, as it does for others working 3, in their talking abstractly or in their not sharing much at all unless someone draws them out. The 3 can also signal a tendency to manipulate or strategize to get what they want without stating their desires directly.

The Law of Honesty applies to 35/8s both in terms of direct and honest expression and also in terms of following the law; 35/8s do best when they follow the highest ethics in business and personal relationships. At first this may seem to go against the grain because they generally don't want to be bound or tied down to conventions; they're used to making the rules, not following them.

The more 35/8s freely share their money, power, freedom, and sensitive heart, the more they get back from the world; the more expansive they are, the more their abundance expands. The fulfillment of their destiny lies not in their awesome mental capacity, but in their capacity to love and sacrifice. Their life path comes to fruition not merely through achieving wealth or power, but through using money and power in self-transcending service to the world.

Working 35/8 in the Positive

Individuals working 35/8 in the positive have achieved a sense of inner influence and abundance through inner discipline, and many blessings have appeared in their life — blessings of abundance they share generously and wisely through their high intelligence and expressive abilities. Others view them as powerful leaders due to their powerful mind, their ability to see the bigger picture, and their genius at getting things done. Emotionally open and vulnerable, they know when to stand their ground and when to let go. These self-made people have a generous, philanthropic nature, taking on positions of leadership and authority. Their relationships are open and mutually supportive.

Working 35/8 in the Negative

People fear these 35/8s without knowing why. Their drive for success, along with dependent feelings and self-doubt, lead them to a tendency toward opportunism as they seek to obtain from others the power and support they haven't found within. They tend to express and control indirectly, through manipulation. They desire wealth and power, but they lack the necessary focus or discipline and tend to sabotage their own efforts because of their inner conflicts. Feeling bad about themselves and powerless and frustrated over their circumstances, they have difficulties with lasting relationships, which degenerate into struggles for control or alternate between aggressive independence and extreme dependence and neediness.

Life-Path Issues

Health

Generally, 35/8s have strong constitutions. However, when they spread themselves too thin, driven by scattered ambitions, they face burnout and possible injuries due to distraction, ignoring traffic laws, or self-sabotage. All 35/8s are wise to wear seat belts and avoid high-risk activities, especially in their late twenties. The preceding problems occur less frequently when 35/8s focus their energy, balance hard work with rest, and commit themselves to working for a higher purpose, thus minimizing the tendency toward self-sabotage.

If 35/8s make work their god, dietary discipline or refinement may take a back seat. Generally, their keen intelligence leads 35/8s to make informed dietary choices. They're wise to treat food as a medicine for optimal functioning. Like most people without specific dietary needs, a balanced, low-fat, primarily vegetarian diet is optimal. *How* 35/8s eat is nearly as important as *what* they eat, and their biggest dietary challenge is moderation, since they may overcontrol or undercontrol in this area.

Depending on their values, background, and lifestyle, 35/8s may or may not make exercise a priority in their life, but they're well suited to forms of exercise that bring a feeling of personal power, such as martial arts, weight training, and individual sports.

Relationships

In many cases, 35/8s have difficulty sustaining long-term relationships until they're thirty or forty years old; before that time, they tend to fall into power struggles. If their passive and aggressive tendencies haven't yet found a balance, they experience subtle or not-so-subtle control issues in their relationships, as well as issues concerning dependence and independence. On the positive side, 35/8s can be exceptionally attentive and enjoyable to be with, and as they begin working their powerful combination of traits in the positive they're able to sustain happy, passionate, mutually supportive relationships.

Although 35/8s can be dedicated parents and loving partners, their work is almost always the center of their life, and it helps if they find self-sufficient partners who understand their dedication to their work from the outset.

Many 35/8s bring the emotional sensitivity and self-doubt of 3 into their relationships. At the same time, their blend of a powerful, versatile mind and wit, along with sensitivity and a strong drive for success, leads them to connect with friends and lovers on many levels. In the highest sense, 35/8s can form lasting bonds based on mutual sharing, mutual sacrifice, and mutual generosity of spirit. Their sexual expression reflects this dynamic.

Talents, Work, and Finances

These individuals are here to use their powerful mind, often bordering on genius, to create wealth through service, to step forward in positions of benign leadership and authority in their family, in their community, or, for example, in the arenas of industry or politics. These individuals make excellent inventors, innovators, or writers; they excel in any field in which a brilliant and curious mind has free rein. In one of the highest aspects of their life path,

35/8s may assume the role of a philanthropist, generously sharing their wealth and influence in service of a humanitarian cause.

Financial issues always have significance for 35/8s, on whatever scale, since money is one of the central themes of their life path. Most commonly, 35/8s pull themselves up by their own bootstraps; among them are many self-made millionaires. If they start out wealthy, they have to learn to use their money and influence wisely and with compassion.

Some Well-Known 35/8s

Melvin Belli, Ingrid Bergman, Usain Bolt, Edgar Cayce, Jack Dempsey, Roger Federer, Buddy Holly, Nelson Mandela, Norman Vincent Peale, Oliver Stone, Aung San Suu Kyi

Keys to Fulfilling Your Destiny

If you're working 35/8, this section can help you manifest your life purpose by focusing your attention on core issues and by generating specific action to transform key areas of your life.

Guidelines and Recommendations

- Combine your brilliance with hard work to find success.
- Own your power, but remember your heart.
- Visualize and then put into practice the good you would like to do for others.
- Find a focus; keep it practical and grounded.

Useful Questions

1. Reflect on the following questions:
    - Have I done the focused work necessary to achieve abundance in my life?
    - Have I found influence and abundance within?
    - Do I uphold the highest ethical standards in my business agreements and personal life?
    - Do I freely share my feelings with others?

2. If these questions generate insights, how might you put these insights into practice?

Deepening Your Understanding

1. Turn back to Part Two, and reread the main sections covering the digits that make up your birth number: 3, 5, and 8.
2. You may wish to review birth numbers of family and friends and, if they're open to it, discuss similar or different issues in your lives.

Spiritual Laws: The Leverage to Change Your Life

1. Read about each of the following laws in Part Four:

   - **THE LAW OF HIGHER WILL:** Our willingness to serve a higher purpose empowers us to inspire others.
   - **THE LAW OF HONESTY:** Honesty is founded on self-awareness of our emotional reality.
   - **THE LAW OF DISCIPLINE:** Discipline generates the focus and depth of experience leading to true freedom.
   - **THE LAW OF BALANCE:** Seeing our tendency to swing from one extreme to another, we find our balance point.
   - **THE LAW OF ACTION:** To overcome insecurity or self-doubt, we can accept our feelings yet behave with confidence.

2. Do the exercises for each of these laws.
3. Consider how you might apply each law to your life.

44/8

8: Influence through Authority
4: Stability through Process
4: Stability through Process

Those on the 44/8 life path are here to work through issues of money, control, responsibility, and stable foundations, following a systematic process to achieve material success — not for its own sake, but in support of other people or causes. Because our life path is strewn with obstacles that test and strengthen us, before 44/8s can manifest their destiny in the positive, they have to overcome negative tendencies, such as a stubborn reluctance to follow through with a gradual, step-by-step process. When mature, 44/8s can show heroic persistence; short of that, however, they want to make success happen right now or give up ("Just forget the whole thing"). They don't usually feel as discouraged or disheartened the way those working 3 do; instead, 44/8s often feel impatient, angry, and frustrated, especially if they haven't yet grasped the absolute necessity of gradual progress over time, broken down into small, manageable steps, as stated in the Law of Process.

Whatever else 44/8s do in their life, they need to spend some time on introspection, so they can come to analyze, understand, and *accept*, rather than resist, the necessary stepping-stones to their destiny.

As with others who have double digits in their birth numbers, such as 22/4s and 33/6s, what 44/8s lack in numerical variety, they make up for in focus and intensity. Take the usual stability, strength, and business acumen of those working 4 and double it; blend the potential qualities of strength and stubbornness, fortitude and rigidity, analytical brilliance and confusion, commitment and instability, ambition and impatience; combine that blend with the drive of 8 for abundance, power, and recognition, and you understand why 44/8s face such a challenge and such an opportunity. As with any life path, the quality of life and the fulfillment of their destiny depend upon whether 44/8s are working the 4 and 8 traits in the positive.

As with every birth number that has twin digits on the left, the first number represents internal challenges — in this case the challenge of inner stability. Individuals working 44/8 need a willingness to introspect and to develop internal processes to strengthen and support the self, such as some form of self-analysis, but they need to avoid getting so obsessed with this process that they go into overanalysis and resultant confusion. As in the case of those working 2 energy, balance is key.

The second 4 in their birth number represents the need for 44/8s to establish an outer foundation within their family — to work out their issues with their parents and their children, if any. Working issues out may mean expressing feelings, positive and negative; it may mean asking forgiveness or offering it; or it may mean finding a common point of understanding or simply agreeing to disagree. In any case, it means communicating and working through issues that might otherwise get swept under the rug.

Most 44/8s share strong concerns and drives in the area of security and stability. Money in the bank, food in the refrigerator, a car in the garage, and clothing in the closet are all essential for 44/8s. Whereas the security of having enough is key for those working 4, the issues of 8 energy involve having *more* than enough. As a result, 44/8s have intelligence, strength, drive, ambition, and desire in abundance.

Given the inherent challenges of their life path, most 44/8s experience issues with family, with security, and, overall, with process. Their willingness to live in alignment with the Law of Process makes or breaks them. In general, 44/8s can reach their goals in relationships, business, health, or spirituality and fulfill their life purpose by following a methodical, practical, step-by-step path. If they skip one step, this usually means they slide back down the mountain and have to start over.

The Law of Patterns can save 44/8s a lot of time by reminding them how to break repetitive patterns of failure or incompletion. If 44/8s ignore or disregard these laws, they learn some hard lessons. Theirs isn't a subtle life path; sometimes life uses high drama to get their attention.

Confusion can plague 44/8s whenever they face an important decision because they tend to analyze everything to death and then feel disoriented.

They often behave very compulsively or impulsively in spending, eating, or other areas of life. Like 2s, they need to find a balance between their mind and their emotions.

With double 4, 44/8s can display extraordinary strength, persistence, and internal fortitude; in the negative, that strength turns to stubbornness and rigidity. Because of the control issues of 8, few people can change the mind of 44/8s unless *they* decide to change, and many 44/8s unduly limit themselves, becoming fixed or rigid in their ideas or approaches due to fear of failure. If they don't listen to feedback from others, they hit brick walls of their own creation. Therefore, 44/8s are wise to remain flexible and stay open to options before becoming set in one direction or burning bridges before they've crossed them. As they integrate the qualities of double 4 and 8, 44/8s reach out to serve others as their sense of abundance grows.

Working 44/8 in the Positive

With the fortitude, perseverance, and analytical skills to take the necessary steps from where they are to where they want to go, no goal is beyond the reach of those working 44/8 in the positive. Their mind approaches any task as a series of component parts, breaking down big goals into small steps. Their health and vitality are exceptional; they take good care of themselves and show necessary caution and care. Loyal and dependable, they form stable and lasting relationships, and they enjoy a sense of family and community with society at large. Powerful and practical, with commonsense business acumen and a drive for success, they allow their strength, their ability to follow a process, and their flexibility to take them to a life of abundance, not just for themselves, but for a larger cause.

Working 44/8 in the Negative

These 44/8s usually manage to maintain control, but they tend to be on the hysterical side. Confused and stressed, when they reach the end of their rope, they may let go in the form of nervous breakdowns. With their stubborn, blind faith in themselves, they seem to repeat the same mistakes again and again. Their relationships are a source of pain and frustration because they constantly engage in power struggles and arguments. They may have made a lot of money and then lost it; they search for a sense of stability but can't make a commitment to anything or anyone. They desire success without being willing to take the steps to achieve it. They feel responsible for too much, yet they try to avoid responsibility for fear they'll fail.

Life-Path Issues

Health

Those working 44/8 don't let anyone tell them how to eat or exercise, or how to do anything else. Nevertheless, a low-fat, efficient, balanced diet is especially important for them, because, with the double 4, unless they pursue regular exercise they tend to put on weight, not just externally but in their internal organs.

Nearly all 44/8s thrive on a regular exercise regimen that emphasizes flexibility, relaxation, balance, and meditation to counteract tendencies toward rigidity, tension, and resistance. Practicing aikido or tai chi, which model the Law of Flexibility, can benefit 44/8s. These arts teach nonresistance — making use of whatever one faces — and they also teach blending, softness, and balance; in addition, both of these disciplines require a patient process to reach mastery. Once 44/8s master such a process, they can then apply it to anything else in daily life.

Relationships

Most 44/8s bring the powerful qualities of loyalty, stability, steadfastness, and support to their relationships. In the negative, they may get caught in power struggles as already mentioned, and their relationships may lack stability if they haven't yet learned the lessons of their life path. When working in the positive, however, 44/8s can maintain a healthy long-term relationship; family and children become priorities in their life, although work remains central.

Although 44/8s certainly possess an emotional life, they're not as strongly centered in the emotions as people working other birth numbers. Their partners may have to appreciate them for their loyalty, strength, and vitality rather than for their sensitivity. It can be hard to get through to them, so subtle hints don't work well.

The approach of 44/8s to sexuality may be lusty, practical, and enthusiastic unless they're dealing with issues of childhood sexual abuse that need to be confronted. They're generally most compatible with someone whose sensitivity balances their strength, but in such a case it's important that both they and their partner appreciate their different styles.

Talents, Work, and Finances

Those working 44/8 often lead or control a business or other enterprise, or they may provide the analytical brains behind the operation. Their success depends almost entirely on whether or not they're willing to go through the gradual or sometimes lengthy process to achieve their goals. In general, 44/8s serve as insightful analysts in the fields of business, psychotherapy, and government intelligence, to name a few.

Financial security is a prime motivator for 44/8s, but whether they gather nest eggs depends on the quality of the nest they build. In other words, they achieve great success in the material realm if they develop their foundation, do their homework and preparation, and pay their dues. Achieving financial stability doesn't usually come easily for 44/8s, but they possess all of the qualities necessary to achieve success. The key for them is to transcend the issue by using their success to serve the community that they've come to perceive as their larger family.

Some Well-Known 44/8s

No well-known 44/8s appear in our records, probably because this birth number appears far less often in the current population than other birth numbers.

Keys to Fulfilling Your Destiny

If you're working 44/8, this section can help you manifest your life purpose by focusing your attention on core issues and by generating specific action to transform key areas of your life.

Guidelines and Recommendations

- When exercising, combine power and strength with flexibility and flow.
- Clarify the sequential steps from here to your goals, and then follow through.

- Talk with your parents, living or not, about how you feel.
- Your greatest power may come from flowing *with* the forces that confront you.

Useful Questions

1. Reflect on the following questions:
    - How can I combine power with flexibility?
    - Do my personal goals serve the common good?
    - Have I sometimes acted too stubborn for my own good?
    - Do I apply both logic and intuition to reach a decision?
2. If these questions generate insights, how might you put these insights into practice?

Deepening Your Understanding

1. Turn back to Part Two, and reread the main sections covering the digits that make up your birth number: 4 and 8.
2. You may wish to review birth numbers of family and friends and, if they're open to it, discuss similar or different issues in your lives.

Spiritual Laws: The Leverage to Change Your Life

1. Read about each of the following laws in Part Four:
    - **THE LAW OF PROCESS:** The best way to reach any goal is one small, sure step at a time.
    - **THE LAW OF PATTERNS:** Patterns tend to reassert themselves unless we exert strong leverage to change them.
    - **THE LAW OF CYCLES:** Life brings constant changes, arising and then passing like the seasons.
    - **THE LAW OF HONESTY:** Honesty is founded on self-awareness of our emotional reality.
    - **THE LAW OF FLEXIBILITY:** Staying flexible, we make the best use of changing circumstances.
2. Do the exercises for each of these laws.
3. Consider how you might apply each law to your life.

9: INTEGRITY THROUGH WISDOM

*Eventually, everyone sits down
to a banquet of consequences.*

— Robert Louis Stevenson

This section includes all birth numbers with 9 as a primary life purpose, including single-digit 9, 18/9, 27/9, 36/9, and 45/9. Even though all of these birth numbers reflect intense 9 dynamics, the qualities, issues, and character of those that contain other digits have a unique flavor due to the influence and interaction of the other numbers, in contrast to the pure, undiluted, single-digit 9.

9

9: Integrity through Wisdom

Those with single-digit 9 as a life path are here to learn and live and lead with integrity, and, through their life experience, connect with others and share their heart's intuitive wisdom.

For this single-digit life path, please be sure to review the chapter in Part Two that provides a full and detailed discussion of the number 9 and all it represents. Here, I highlight key elements of the path and purpose of single-digit 9s.

Since what we're here to do isn't what comes easiest, before single-digit 9s can fulfill their life purpose they learn from failures relating to slips of integrity and lack of attention to how life works. Before they become exemplars of wisdom who may even light the way for others, these single-digit 9s may seem clueless; they just don't seem to grasp the consequences that result from their actions. But those consequences eventually guide them to the higher wisdom they're here to express.

Single-digit 9s, whatever their persona, have a depth of purpose — almost as if they have lived many past lives as monks or nuns in one or another tradition, and carry with them both the weight and wisdom of much contemplation. They might be described, metaphysically speaking, as old souls. But old or not, in *this* lifetime they have to relearn and rediscover these deeper truths. Single-digit 9s, free from some of the distractions and constraints of the challenges faced by other birth numbers working 9 (19/10, 18/9, 39/12, 27/9, 36/9, and 45/9), may find — like the other single-digit birth numbers — a more direct path, and quicker (or at least earlier) lessons leading them to the inescapable truth related to the core of their life path: They're called to live a life of integrity — or suffer the consequences of not doing so. Individuals working some birth numbers seem to bend the rules of life and get away with it for a while, but those working 9 quickly get their hands stuck in the cookie jar — that is, life serves as a speed-reading course in the book of life.

Single-digit 9s are aware of human and social laws, but are more interested in spiritual or universal laws that go deeper and higher than changing customs or precedents. Natural leaders — once they begin working in the positive or mature form of the 9 life path — they lead according to these words of Dr. Albert Schweitzer quoted earlier: "In influencing others, example is not the main thing; it is the only thing." So, like 18/9s, 27/9s, and 36/9s, single-digit 9s need to find their own way before they can lead others. And the best way for single-digit 9s to lead is in being role models of patient wisdom and integrity, bearing in mind the words of James Baldwin: "Children have never been very good at listening to their elders, but they have never failed to imitate them."

Despite the wisdom of influencing through integrity, single-digit 9s have a way of trying to lead via strong opinions, mistaking these opinions for truth. They need to temper their natural zeal and sense of mission in order to avoid becoming too fanatical or fundamentalist. Like anyone working the 9 life path, single-digit 9s not only have strong opinions; they're also sensitive to the opinions of others — though not as much as 27/9s, who face self-trust issues, or 36/9s, with their idealistic standards. Still, single-digit 9s also need the reminder, "What other people think of you is none of your business." Once single-digit 9s are able to follow the Law of Intuition and free themselves from the god of opinion, they can reconnect with the god of their heart, and thereby transcend mere opinions and find true wisdom based on hard-earned, experience-based wisdom. They can then fulfill their destiny and life path by becoming role models of integrity and guide with their deep perspective, the better part of wisdom. They become like lanterns to others on a dark night.

Working Single-Digit 9 in the Positive

Charismatic individuals working single-digit 9 in the positive lead by their example, and are looked upon by others as sources of wisdom. Like exemplar 27/9 Mahatma Gandhi, these single-digit 9s have become the change they wish to see in the world. They have recognized that their opinions are nothing more or less than personal filters through which they see the world — not the equivalent of higher truth — and they have freed themselves from the tyranny of other people's opinions, so they can now hear and reflect on the input of others, but submit any views to the counsel of their own heart. Without hubris, when they feel ready they accept leadership positions and find their path and purpose in service of others. Having learned many lessons, their life quietly or openly reflects those lessons in their actions and through their example.

Working Single-Digit 9 in the Negative

These single-digit 9s live life according to the dictum "Do as I say, not as I do." Out of touch with their own internal wisdom, and supremely susceptible to the views and opinions of others, they defensively shut out or reject advice — even or especially from those closest to them — and instead seek out a method, system of thought, technique, philosophy, or even a spiritual teaching of how to live, and become tunnel-vision devotees. Zealous believers, these individuals mistake their beliefs or opinions for truth, and are quick to impose that truth on anyone in their sphere of influence, whether family or peers. When put in positions of leadership due to a pseudoauthority based on their certainty, they may impose or abuse that leadership, behaving in ways so lacking in integrity that they set themselves up for hard lessons.

Life-Path Issues

Health

At earlier stages of their personal evolution, these individuals haven't yet understood the law of cause and effect, or action and consequence. So single-digit 9s may eat an unhealthy diet, avoid regular exercise, and in adolescent years overuse tobacco, alcohol, or food, or engage in casual but unsafe sex — that is, until they awaken to the truth that we reap what we sow, and then begin to change their behavior. If single-digit 9s are working in the negative, as they age they may experience chronic diseases or rare afflictions, energy illnesses, long-standing suffering, back problems, or arthritis. These maladies may not only stem from external sources, but from their own subconscious, which resonates with themes of sin and repentance.

Keeping a health or exercise journal, noting down their daily diet, exercise, energy level, and hours of rest, can help turn their habits around — a key leverage point for single-digit 9s, who can tend to be out of touch with their body. Meditation may be a useful exercise for many single-digit 9s, to help them get in more conscious touch with, and establish appropriate distance from, the contents of their mind. Since single-digit 9s tend to live up in their head, a good exercise routine helps them lose their mind and come to their senses.

Healing methods and forms of therapy that work with the subconscious, ranging from hypnosis to energy work, can be effective for single-digit 9s, depending on their values and belief systems. As these individuals resolve life issues in positive, uplifting ways, physical maladies may drop away. Rather than obsessive or heroic attempts to heal themselves (breeding more self-involvement), when these individuals turn their attention outward to serve others, and completely accept their condition, their healing begins. By forgiving themselves, they open the door to healing.

Relationships

The relationships of single-digit 9s aren't just personal; they're transpersonal, mirroring their relationship to all things. But they can love deeply, and their loved ones help them connect to a life beyond themselves and into the larger world. For these individuals, relationships can awaken the heart and its deeper wisdom — so friends and families can humanize them, washing away the pull of archetypal memories of solitude and isolation in a hermitage or ashram apart from the world.

Talents, Work, and Finances

Not all single-digit 9s take on roles as teachers or guides; some are cabinet-makers, carpenters, musicians, secretaries, or mail carriers; they follow every walk of life. Yet when they meet with others, whether in the larger society or in the context of family and friends, they naturally gravitate to managerial or other positions of leadership, creating a depth of meaning to their work, no matter how humble. Lacking the constraints or afflictions of those working multiple-digit birth numbers, money flows naturally to single-digit 9s in direct proportion to the service they provide.

In their business dealings, in their personal relationships, and in the areas of diet, exercise, and health, single-digit 9s need to ask internally, "What's the higher principle here?" To put it another way, they might ask, "If I were feeling courageous, altruistic, generous, compassionate, and wise, how would I behave?" The answer reveals the highest direction, whatever their personal preferences or vested interests. Whatever their talents or chosen career, when they work in accord with higher laws they're a light to us all.

Some Well-Known Single-Digit 9s

As of 2018, the oldest single-digit 9s are under eighteen years old. The only well-known 9 we could find is Greta Thunberg, a climate activist from Sweden. In later editions of this book, as more 9s come of age and make notable accomplishments, more names will appear here.

Keys to Fulfilling Your Destiny

If you're working single-digit 9, this section can help you manifest your life purpose by focusing your attention on core issues and by generating specific action to transform key areas of your life.

Guidelines and Recommendations

- Respect the opinions and choices of others, but above all listen to your own heart.
- Before acting or making an important decision, ask yourself, "What would my higher self do?"
- Remember that whatever your role in life, and whether you like it or not, you're leading others by your example.
- Find what inspires you in life, and follow it.

Useful Questions

1. Reflect on the following questions:
   - How might you see and behave differently if, before making a decision or taking action, you asked, "What would my higher self do?"

- In what ways do you lead by example? Consider this carefully, because you may not have realized how much others pay attention to what you do.
- What's your relationship to your own and other people's opinions?
- What do you think of the idea that there's no best book or teacher or philosophy or diet or exercise system or religion, only the best for each individual? Can this idea help you respect the process, the decisions, and the choices of others?

2. If these questions generate insights, how might you put these insights into practice?

Deepening Your Understanding

1. Turn back to Part Two, and reread the main sections covering the digit that makes up your birth number: 9.
2. You may wish to review birth numbers of family and friends and, if they're open to it, discuss similar or different issues in your lives.

Spiritual Laws: The Leverage to Change Your Life

1. Read about each of the following laws in Part Four:

- **THE LAW OF HIGHER WILL:** Our willingness to serve a higher purpose empowers us to inspire others.
- **THE LAW OF INTUITION:** No longer monitoring other people's opinions, we connect with our heart's intuitive wisdom.
- **THE LAW OF NO JUDGMENTS:** The universe doesn't judge us; it only teaches us through natural consequences.
- **THE LAW OF FAITH:** Only when we find faith in ourselves can we have faith in others.

2. Do the exercises for each of these laws.
3. Consider how you might apply each law to your life.

18/9

9: Integrity through Wisdom
8: Influence through Authority
1: Creativity through Security

Those on the 18/9 life path are here to work through issues of honesty, money, control, and confidence, creatively manifesting and applying their vitality and influence in accordance with higher principles of integrity. Most 18/9s can appear expansive, outgoing, even jovial, but there's nothing frivolous about their inner life, which contains shadows of guilt, fear, and insecurity. Given that our life purpose always poses special challenges, 18/9s need to work through deeply rooted, often conflicting attraction and avoidance related to money and power, as well as insecurity issues, on their path to integrity and wisdom.

Because integrity rests at the pinnacle of their life purpose, whether they prefer it or not 18/9s are called to rely on the qualities of high ethics and honesty. They either lead by inspiring example, or they mislead and get made into examples. Like others working 9, 18/9s live a life of truth or consequences. Those 18/9s who live in accordance with higher laws create a very good, satisfying life of honest, diligent work, enjoying the rewards that accrue from their labors. Those who ignore higher laws soon face the law of cause and effect as life gives them feedback they can't ignore.

Most 18/9s have a powerful mind, attractive charisma, and abundant vitality. This combination of the qualities, and drives associated with their birth number makes them extremely powerful leaders who can inspire whole countries, move mountains, and build empires — or who can, with ruthless fanaticism, utterly crush those who oppose them. Demands in the 8 arena of wealth and power and the 9 arena of integrity, amplified by the creative energy of 1, can place heavy internal burdens on those 18/9s who haven't yet recognized and made peace with their inner drives.

The powerful blend of qualities and drives influencing 18/9s tends to attract money and influence and drive them to success unless they sabotage their own efforts. Their veiled insecurity, associated with 1, may be obscured by compensatory behaviors of bluster, competitiveness, and forcefulness, but just beneath the surface of their power and assertiveness lies a certain passivity due to a fear of the surging power of their inner drives.

If 18/9s work their birth number in the positive, they can lead and inspire others by example; their integrity and creativity command the intense respect and loyalty of followers. Therefore, 18/9s most often are drawn to or put in positions of leadership, whether in large or small arenas. If 18/9s work their life path in the negative, their drive for power and wealth becomes obsessive, their opinions become fanatical, and their creative energy becomes destructive to self and others. In other words, 18/9s have the potential to do much good or much harm.

No matter how successful their life may look on the outside, 18/9s face internal issues and conflicts that can generate physical illness or other difficulties, almost as if the subconscious imposes its own internal restraints.

Because the challenges of 18/9s reside in the subconscious, they need to seek their answers within. However, since they tend to focus more on material success in the outside world than on their internal growth, they may resist insight work. And since 8s like to make their own rules, 18/9s can in younger years be especially resistant to learning life's lessons and making appropriate changes. Whether or not they tend toward introspection, 18/9s eventually have to explore the internal weight they carry, a burden of subconscious pain they can heal with the first breath of true forgiveness and self-care.

Self-examination, understanding, and forgiveness can eventually lead 18/9s to a heartfelt connection to the spiritual laws at the core of life, sharing wealth and dedicating themselves to service rather than to the accumulation of material resources or influence. They serve others by inspiration — living as an example of integrity — of power blended with compassion and aligned with a higher will.

All 18/9s need to ask themselves very carefully, "Am I living an exemplary life?" They then need to listen to the answer. If 18/9s don't practice what they preach — and they definitely do preach — life gets their attention in dramatic ways, including illness, accidents, and ruined relationships. There's nothing very subtle about this birth number, and there's nothing subtle about life's feedback.

Sooner or later, one way or the other, when 18/9s have seen enough, felt enough, and learned enough to align their life with the higher laws of integrity, they direct their energies and resources toward the highest good of all concerned. In the process, they transcend their old tendencies and their pain. The stronger their internal commitment to a higher purpose, the more likely that their qualities will manifest in positive ways. The Law of Honesty is key for 18/9s; their deep connection to spiritual laws can help guide them toward their destiny. Due to their natural vitality, charisma, and personal power, 18/9s stand out in any crowd.

Working 18/9 in the Positive

Individuals working 18/9 in the positive have natural depth, charisma, and magnetism. They have an outgoing, charismatic personality that reflects both intelligence and broader wisdom. Their work at home, in their community, or in the world at large reflects their natural leadership by example. Brilliant strategists who know and follow the rules of any game they play, they use their influence and share their abundance to make a difference beyond themselves. With their spiritual power made manifest, they lead by example and by inspiration and provide valuable ideas to others. Life is never boring around them. Hardworking and creative, they subordinate their work to a higher good.

Working 18/9 in the Negative

Although their outer world may look good from the viewpoint of others, the inner world of these 18/9s is filled with turmoil, suppressed fear, and a sense of heaviness, laden with the idea of sin and salvation. They long for health and inner peace, but they get caught up in their own opinions and tend to seek absolute power and control. They preach to others, overtly or subtly, about how life "should" be lived, but they don't follow their own dictates. They resist what arises in their own life and want to control the lives of others. They lose sight of the larger gifts contained in their own challenges.

Life-Path Issues

Health

Many 18/9s experience average or even excellent health; others suffer from asthma, bone or nerve problems, including pain in the neck or lower spine, or other symptoms that reflect and result from long-term (but unacknowledged) fears of abusing power. The suffering they have felt, whether on physical, mental, emotional, or spiritual levels, has sent them deeper and farther on their own journey; in the positive, physical ailments teach 18/9s compassion.

In areas of nutrition and exercise, the principles for 18/9s are very simple and very clear: Learn what is the most healthful, and live that way. Most 18/9s like hard work; when they direct this drive toward any kind of exercise, their life benefits. What kind of exercise they choose is less important than that they do it, because exercise is a simple way to practice alignment with natural law; 18/9s either exercise and feel better or don't exercise and learn the consequences over time.

The same principle applies to nutrition. Rather than following a particular regimen, the key for 18/9s is to eat more of what is enlivening and nutritious and less of what isn't; again, the law of cause and effect operates very clearly for anyone working 9. The more 18/9s practice integrity in the area of health by finding out what is healthful and following through with it, the better example they provide for others to follow.

Relationships

Although 18/9s can be intense and attentive, intimacy and vulnerability may not come easily for them due to latent insecurity and control issues. Nevertheless, 18/9s can offer charm, vital energy, and depth to others. A key is finding a partner who stands up to them and helps them balance power with sensitivity — someone who understands and accepts them as they are so that they can come to accept and even forgive themselves. Although marrying and raising a family aren't usually the center of their life, 18/9s can certainly create a family setting as a backdrop for the larger theater of their life.

With their powerful creative energy and deep-seated need to connect with others, 18/9s have a sexual drive that reflects strong physical, emotional, and spiritual needs, whether or not they're aware of them. When they're working in the positive, they can experience a profound connection through their sexual expression.

Talents, Work, and Finances

The powerful qualities of 18/9s generally take them to positions of leadership. For example, 18/9s are more likely to be attorneys, building contractors, surgeons, or administrators than store clerks. With their dynamic and creative mind, 18/9s are usually one step ahead of most everyone. The significance and potential of 18/9s lies not in what they do, but in how they do it; as long as they reach out to people and live a balanced life of integrity, based on the wisdom of living in accordance with spiritual law, they find deep fulfillment in line with their life path.

Their generally sound financial circumstances reflect their nature and abilities except when they get in their own way with negative beliefs or fears. The important thing for 18/9s is never to strive for money for its own sake, but rather to create money and influence as a natural outcome of useful service. When they're committed to service as their goal, abundance and influence follow naturally due to their creative inspiration and powerful mind.

Some Well-Known 18/9s

Jimmy Carter, Jean Harlow, Rutherford B. Hayes, Burt Lancaster, Charles Lindbergh, Jack Nicklaus, Richard Pryor, Mark Spitz, Kurt Vonnegut, Lawrence Welk

Keys to Fulfilling Your Destiny

If you're working 18/9, this section can help you manifest your life purpose by focusing your attention on core issues and by generating specific action to transform key areas of your life.

Guidelines and Recommendations

*   Focus on *what* is right, not on *who* is right.
*   Don't fear your power; just use it in service of others.

- Ask yourself in what areas of life you serve as a good example and in what areas you don't.
- Apply your creative powers in ways you enjoy.

Useful Questions

1. Reflect on the following questions:

   - Does my sense of security depend on money and power?
   - Do I apply my creative energy in useful endeavors?
   - Have I had problems with people about money or control?
   - Do I place equal value on integrity and on success?

2. If these questions generate insights, how might you put these insights into practice?

Deepening Your Understanding

1. Turn back to Part Two, and reread the main sections covering the digits that make up your birth number: 1, 8, and 9.
2. You may wish to review birth numbers of family and friends and, if they're open to it, discuss similar or different issues in your lives.

Spiritual Laws: The Leverage to Change Your Life

1. Read about each of the following laws in Part Four:

   - **THE LAW OF HIGHER WILL:** Our willingness to serve a higher purpose empowers us to inspire others.
   - **THE LAW OF HONESTY:** Honesty is founded on self-awareness of our emotional reality.
   - **THE LAW OF CHOICES:** We can choose to create and express ourselves in positive or negative ways.
   - **THE LAW OF INTUITION:** No longer monitoring other people's opinions, we connect with our heart's intuitive wisdom.
   - **THE LAW OF FLEXIBILITY:** Staying flexible, we make the best use of changing circumstances.

2. Do the exercises for each of these laws.
3. Consider how you might apply each law to your life.

27/9

9: Integrity through Wisdom
7: Trust through Openness
2: Cooperation through Balance

Those on the 27/9 life path are here to work through issues of balanced responsibility, self-trust, and integrity as they come to trust and follow Spirit manifesting within them and others, living in alignment with the higher wisdom of the heart. Since our life purpose represents an uphill climb, 27/9s eventually confront and have to overcome tendencies to intellectualize experience rather than trust their heart. They also need to work through subconscious issues of mistrust and betrayal and open their guarded heart to find and follow the spiritual laws written there.

In order to access the higher laws of their heart, 27/9s first need to let go of their concerns about other people's opinions and trust their own higher wisdom revealed in their feelings rather than their mental processes. The 7, however, often leads 27/9s to trust everyone *but* themselves — teachers, masters, scientific experts, or advisers — and to live by other people's theories. We can all learn from others, but 27/9s in particular are here to place final authority with the counsel of their heart.

Although integrity and wisdom form the primary life purpose of 27/9s, the 7 is key because 27/9s have to come to trust themselves in order to access the higher principles that will guide them to integrity. Until then, all they can do is what someone else has suggested. Life provides 27/9s with many situations that repeat the same message: "Trust your heart; let your mind surrender to the wisdom of the heart." The term *wisdom of the heart* refers to the feeling dimension, whether we call it conscience, universal unconscious, or intuition.

Like 25/7s, 27/9s can become awareness-training addicts or spiritual vagabonds, going from one workshop, guru, or ashram to the next, looking for confirmation and guidance from teachers, mentors, or others who offer guidelines for living. The more 27/9s monitor other people's opinions, the more difficulty they have getting in touch with their own feeling center.

Since 7 tends to focus in the mind and leads 27/9s to avoid feelings that have in the past brought pain, 27/9s face a significant internal challenge before they can access and live in alignment with the laws of Spirit. One indicator that 27/9s are focused on mental processes rather than connected to their feelings occurs when they use more words than necessary to express what they want to say. When they lose touch with what they actually feel, they talk around issues and engage in social chatter, but they aren't truly self-revealing, even to themselves. Even with their outer social animation, internally most 27/9s feel more like hermits at times, or even look like them, and they definitely need their own private space.

With that need for privacy, imagine how difficult 27/9 Elvis Presley's life must have been; he felt a sense of Spirit that worked through him in his own way, accounting in part for his magic to millions of people, but he let others manage his life rather than following his own heart, and this destroyed him. Errol Flynn, another charismatic 27/9, serves as a pointed example of someone who let his physical desires and impulses predominate over his heartfelt intuitions. Each of these figures, in his own way, lost touch with his own integrity; although exemplary in many ways, these individuals aren't the best overall examples of how to live in accord with higher principles.

Most 27/9s appear self-assured and have a natural charisma associated with the leadership capacity of 9. Their sometimes forceful mental ideas and opinions overcompensate for their lack of trust. These opinions tend to become fanatical beliefs in some idea, person, or method. Because they tie their identity to their beliefs and opinions, their beliefs can become fanatical even when they start out with good intentions. The confident appearance of 27/9s masks a deeper uncertainty; they have a diffuse sense of identity and constantly strive to redefine themselves. Quiet zealots, 27/9s sometimes mistake their opinions for God's will.

Because of the 2, those 27/9s who have awakened to the higher service find meaning in providing support for and in cooperation with others. Such individuals don't need to preach, and they may not look spiritual at all; whatever their role or occupation in life, they teach others by example. Whether they use spiritual language is irrelevant. Leadership and inspiration by example form the keys to their life purpose; they let their life be their teaching. If their life is one of integrity, then no words are necessary; if it isn't, then no words can suffice.

Many spiritual and religious leaders have been 27/9s, including Mahatma Gandhi, Paramahansa Yogananda, Adi Da (Da Free John), Pope John XXIII, Pope Pius XIII, and Kahlil Gibran. In addition, nonreligious leaders who have inspired generations with their own unique charisma include Elvis Presley, Shirley MacLaine, Ray Charles, and Robin Williams.

At the other extreme lies the danger of charismatic teachers, many of whom are themselves 27/9s, who attract groups of followers but who don't practice what they preach and excuse themselves by their higher rank or state of realization. They have their own issues to learn, as do their followers.

Many 27/9s fear spirituality because of subconscious fears of getting too close to the flame (as in burnt at the stake). Whether or not they have conscious awareness of it, if they explore their psyches most 27/9s find an inner resonance with those who were persecuted because their loyalty was to the higher laws of Spirit, not the current ruling order. The archetypes of sin and repentance reside within the consciousness of even those 27/9s who would never use such language.

Whether 27/9s gravitate toward spiritual ideas or avoid them, they feel a longing for higher wisdom, to know and share the guiding principles of life, as well as a deep need for compassion and understanding from others and an ability to give back in equal measure.

Those working 27/9 develop self-trust in their own good time, through direct experience, not just through learning from a wise teacher or reading books. In other words, 27/9s need to *experience* higher wisdom and feel this inspiration directly. They need to know and feel Spirit within themselves and others. Ultimately, no matter how well their external life is going, a part of them won't rest until they've realized this truth.

Working 27/9 in the Positive

Individuals working 27/9 in the positive exude depth and charisma based on their heartfelt trust in Spirit working through them. With their balanced, compassionate wisdom, they have also learned to trust Spirit in the form of other people and in the form of life's circumstances, which, no matter how pleasurable or difficult, they experience as teachings. Although their needs are often met, even in adversity they feel thankful for the lessons they receive. They make natural leaders who teach by example. Committed to service and expressing universal wisdom rather than rigid opinions, they help inspire others through their integrity and their attunement to higher laws. They're natural leaders who teach by example. Maintaining a feeling connection to the higher will within them, they effectively serve others.

Working 27/9 in the Negative

Deluded preachers or eternal seekers, these 27/9s center their world around a particular teaching, method, religion, or philosophy. Quiet fanatics, they live according to the dictates or opinions of others and act as if their own opinions were sacred. Others who don't trust themselves may follow or admire such individuals, mistaking strong opinions for spiritual authority. Deep down, these 27/9s feel lonely and cut off from the world and from true inspiration in their life, because they trust their mind over their heart. They fear and eventually attract betrayal by others, even by their own body.

Life-Path Issues

Health

Most 27/9s have a significant amount of debris floating around in their subconscious, including burdensome guilt from childhood. The 7 means 27/9s may experience a sensitivity around the heart area if they suffer from chronic, unresolved feelings of betrayal.

Feelings of isolation or disconnection can lead some 27/9s to psychological disturbances, as well as to abuse of drugs or alcohol, which numbs their inner pain. The sad irony in cases of drug dependence is that 27/9s are looking to an external source to find the connection with Spirit, which is already inside them.

The key to diet, exercise, and every arena of health for 27/9s is clear: They need to trust their instincts, intuition, and direct experience. They've likely studied theories or research about nutrition or exercise, but they need to take all that knowledge, check it against their own intuition system, and then act.

They do well to recognize the consequences, both positive or negative, of action or inaction, of what they eat or don't eat, and of their habits of exercise. Whatever they do serves as an example to others around them.

Because 27/9s focus their awareness in their head and mental processes, they have one of the least physically grounded birth numbers. Physical training not only provides standard fitness benefits for 27/9s, allowing for a balanced body and clear mind, but also helps them stay in touch with the physically based, practical realities of daily life. The exercise that works best for 27/9s is the form they choose based on their own experience.

Meditation, in whatever form they choose, gives 27/9s a chance to rest their mind and find inner peace. In that peace, their heart speaks.

Relationships

Those working 27/9 may have developed deep empathy and emotional depth, or they may have created an emotional persona to compensate for their mental approach to life. The key for 27/9s in relationships is letting go of mental processes and entering a dimension of feeling untroubled by the turbulence of thoughts, beliefs, and opinions.

Their relationships offer the chance to experience vulnerability, wherein the lessons of trust are learned. For 27/9s, relationships are important not in themselves but as a means of growth and communion; the issues that arise become grist for the mill and lessons on the path.

Good sex for 27/9s is like going to confession. Sexuality for them tends to serve as a means to find harmony, connection, and communion rather than, say, just raw pleasure. They enjoy sexual relations to the degree that they can surrender to and trust their body's mindless wisdom and joy.

Talents, Work, and Finances

Because of an inherent, though not always manifested, love of the outdoors, 27/9s make very good backwoods guides, for example, but they also excel at high-tech careers. Those working 27/9 are creative in terms of finding deeper wisdom. Because they like time alone, they make excellent researchers.

Most 27/9s excel in service and healing-related work, in the broadest meanings of those terms. Their natural charisma, which they don't always appreciate or trust, makes them compelling dancers, actors, or artists, but their art feels more meaningful to them if connected to a higher purpose or motive of service.

Stemming from their subconscious resonance with the vows of poverty taken by monks and nuns, many 27/9s feel a subtle negativity toward or mixed feelings about money and worldly success. If money is scarce in their life, 27/9s may want to reexamine their positive and negative beliefs about money. They also benefit from exploring self-trust issues, which can hold them back in some areas of work. For 27/9s, money, like most things in life, is only a means to learn more about the workings of their own psyche. Their presence and depth pull 27/9s to leadership positions. They most often earn enough money to meet their needs and then some.

Some Well-Known 27/9s

Louisa May Alcott, Carlos Castaneda, Ray Charles, Julia Child, Harrison Ford, Mahatma Gandhi, Jimi Hendrix, Óscar Ichazo, Shirley MacLaine, Thurgood Marshall, Benjamin Netanyahu, Annie Oakley, Elvis Presley, Albert Schweitzer, Gloria Steinem, Henry David Thoreau

Keys to Fulfilling Your Destiny

If you're working 27/9, this section can help you manifest your life purpose by focusing your attention on core issues and by generating specific action to transform key areas of your life.

Guidelines and Recommendations

- Trust that your deepest feelings will guide you precisely to the lessons you're here to learn.
- Every day, remember that Spirit shines through you and through everyone else.
- Forgive yourself for your mistakes.
- Don't take opinions too seriously — yours or anyone else's.

Useful Questions

1. Reflect on the following questions:

- Is my life an example of the highest integrity?
- What inspires me?
- Who's the expert on my life?
- Do I honor my own process and that of others?

2. If these questions generate insights, how might you put these insights into practice?

Deepening Your Understanding

1. Turn back to Part Two, and reread the main sections covering the digits that make up your birth number: 2, 7, and 9.
2. You may wish to review birth numbers of family and friends and, if they're open to it, discuss similar or different issues in your lives.

Spiritual Laws: The Leverage to Change Your Life

1. Read about each of the following laws in Part Four:

    - THE LAW OF HIGHER WILL: Our willingness to serve a higher purpose empowers us to inspire others.
    - THE LAW OF INTUITION: No longer monitoring other people's opinions, we connect with our heart's intuitive wisdom.
    - THE LAW OF FAITH: Only when we find faith in ourselves can we have faith in others.
    - THE LAW OF FLEXIBILITY: Staying flexible, we make the best use of changing circumstances.
    - THE LAW OF NO JUDGMENTS: The universe doesn't judge us; it only teaches us through natural consequences.

2. Do the exercises for each of these laws.
3. Consider how you might apply each law to your life.

36/9

9: Integrity through Wisdom
6: Vision through Acceptance
3: Expression through Sensitivity

Those on the 36/9 life path are here to work through issues of emotional honesty, perfectionist ideals, and self-doubt as they learn to live in accord with the wisdom of their heart, thereby serving as an example of integrity in their daily life. Since what we're here to do doesn't come easily, 36/9s face significant hurdles on their life path and may take years to learn to honor and value their own feelings over perfectionistic ideals or other people's opinions. A major challenge is finding out what they really feel in contrast to what they think they "should" feel.

Even though 36/9s share the same life purpose as others working 9, the 3 and 6 dynamic creates a considerably different life path from the paths of 18/9s, 27/9s, or 45/9s. The perfectionism of 6 influences and intensifies the innate self-doubt of these sensitive and refined individuals. Because 36/9s tend to measure themselves against ideal standards, the idea that they're here to live with the highest integrity may seem impossible or overwhelming, especially since 36/9s interpret this to mean perfect integrity rather than simply following the messages of their own heart.

This dynamic reinforces the strong sensitivity of 36/9s to criticism, since they're already vulnerable to other people's opinions. Given the idealistic standards to which they compare themselves, many 36/9s feel periodically disheartened or discouraged, sometimes giving up even before they begin. They may wear a mask of assurance, but for this confidence to stabilize, they have to balance the tendency to swing from manic overconfidence into doubt and depression by recognizing this as a challenge associated with their life path, a hurdle they're here to overcome. By applying the Law of Action, they learn to acknowledge self-doubt and then move through it.

Most 36/9s feel unsure of their own center or identity; they search not only for how they feel, but for who they are. Because of the combined hurdles of self-doubt, perfectionism, and uncertain identity, 36/9s are highly prone to defining themselves and their worth in relation to other people's opinions and expectations, looking for confirmation that they're behaving in the most ideal possible way or being the kind of person who gains social approval.

Those working 36/9 are here to expand their vision to see that our deepest intuitions may sometimes guide us to make mistakes so that we can learn important, even life-changing lessons. Difficulties due to a certain choice don't necessarily mean that the choice was wrong, that they're off course, or that they can't trust their feelings.

At the same time, 36/9s do need to submit their life to a higher authority — to the wisdom based on their heartfelt connection to spiritual laws — so that they can exemplify the integrity they were born to live. Since 36/9s aim for the ideal rather than for what is real *for them*, the Law of Intuition can help them reconnect with the wisest and most loving guide they can find for their own life, their inner wisdom.

Once 36/9s accept themselves and others as they are, they open themselves to the central challenge of their life: the wisdom to live as an inspiring example to others. Inspiration doesn't require heroics or fame but rather living an ordinary life based on higher laws found in the heart rather than on mental ideas or on physical impulses.

Most 36/9s eventually face situations that reflect to them the need to reconnect with their own needs and desires. As already noted, this represents a major challenge for 36/9s because of the powerful influence of perfectionism in imposing ideals over authentic feelings. Ask 36/9s how they feel, and they most likely answer with their idealized image of what a good, kind, caring, conscientious, brave, upbeat person would or "should" feel. Before they can know themselves or be themselves, 36/9s have to connect with and accept how they truly feel. Then they can be honest with others because they've learned to be honest with themselves — a principle addressed by the Law of Honesty.

With their highly mental pattern and perfectionism, 36/9s want to get everything just right, whether in cooking, sexual performance, or scholastic exams. They tend to be high-strung and nervous, and their health is extremely vulnerable to the state of their mind and emotions. These individuals place pressure on themselves in any group learning situation; they start out okay and then start comparing themselves with others to see how they're doing; usually they end up comparing themselves with one of the most skillful people in the class. Because of such comparisons and because of their own unrealistic standards, 36/9s chronically feel that they're falling short.

Most 36/9s get discouraged and disheartened by their own unreachable standards and judgments, which they often imagine come from other people, until they make a critical leap and discover that they just might be smarter, stronger, and more valuable than they had previously recognized. In making this leap, their sense of self-worth rises, and with it, their enthusiasm for life. They begin to strive *toward* their ideals rather than feeling like a failure for not reaching them.

Until 36/9s connect with the inner wisdom that comprises both their struggle and their birthright, they can tend to be slow to learn the lessons of experience. They end up wondering how they got into their particular situation. When 36/9s make choices without considering consequences, they learn the hard way about the law of cause and effect in the real world. As they learn, they grow wiser, and over time, the seeds of deep wisdom within them start to sprout as they start to see the bigger picture of spiritual law.

Most 36/9s avoid metaphysical or spiritual ideas for a time, based on subconscious resonance with and fear of early mystics or innovative thinkers who were persecuted. As 36/9s clear away at least some of their self-doubt and perfectionism, they begin to appreciate and apply their intuitive wisdom. The world becomes a place to explore and understand; they grow curious about the laws of reality and how things work. They have the ability to seek and find essential truths, ancient secrets, and perennial wisdom.

The high vision of 6, the inherent depth and charisma of 9, and the intuitive sensitivity of 3 give 36/9s an exceptional ability to understand hidden or inner wisdom. Contrast the analytical and creative genius of 31/4 Sigmund Freud, the founder of psychoanalysis, with the deep archetypal discoveries of 36/9 Carl Jung, for example. Freud strongly disapproved of Jung's ideas and criticized him. Jung had to overcome extreme self-doubt and to honor his own inner wisdom despite his mentor's warnings.

Those working 36/9 are here to balance their high vision and ideals with the practical realities of this world, to accept themselves and others, and to share their wisdom with family, friends, or the world at large. But most of all, they're here to align themselves with the spiritual laws revealed through the heart's intuition.

The main teaching device of 36/9s isn't their mouth, but their example. Like all those working 9 energy, they need to remember and embody the earlier cited words of Mahatma Gandhi: "My life is my teaching." By living in accordance with their heart and making peace with their vision, they stand tall and step fully into the life they were born to live.

Working 36/9 in the Positive

Having contacted the core of their true rather than their idealized needs, desires, and feelings, individuals working 36/9 in the positive have wide-open senses and keen intuitive wisdom. With a deep acceptance and knowledge of reality, they can envision the potential of self and world, yet they've learned to appreciate both as they are now — as perfection in an evolving process. While they still may confront self-doubt, they have found the courage to walk a straight line past their doubt, going where Spirit leads them. Whether their life looks conventional or unconventional, they live by higher laws and ideals and see the depths and higher possibilities of life. They connect to this world through service as they express the eternal wisdom they have contacted.

Working 36/9 in the Negative

These 36/9s live to please others. Their expression is blocked as they allow themselves to be defined by other people's opinions. Judgmental about themselves and others, they're quick to spot imperfections but feel hypersensitive to any criticism. High-strung, nervous, and hindered by self-doubt, they play it safe, sticking with the conventional, the routine, and the familiar, since new territory would bring the risk of failure, which would only add to their disappointment in self and world. Reality never seems to meet their expectations or hopes.

Life-Path Issues

Health

No matter what their features, the refined energy field of most 36/9s gives them an attractive appearance that people sense rather than see with physical eyes. Cameras, however, pick up on energy fields, so 36/9s tend to take good pictures, as the example of 36/9 Brigitte Bardot can attest.

Combining the sensitivity of 3 with the high ideals of 6, 36/9s can get discouraged or depressed easily when they or others don't meet their expectations. Chronic depression can compromise their immune system and open the way for colds, stress headaches, or other depressive symptoms.

If working in the negative, 36/9s tend to be high-strung; sensitive areas include the nervous system, the sexual area, and the abdomen. They're also prone to sore throats or chronic jaw tension if they withhold their feelings.

If 36/9s eat food not well suited to their constitution, they're likely to experience digestive symptoms, skin eruptions, or other feedback; over time, they learn to align their diet with their expanding knowledge of what's optimal for them. Nutrition offers 36/9s a fundamental avenue for living by example; they learn what happens when they eat or drink what isn't good for them. As 36/9s learn to follow their own instincts, they're likely to gravitate toward a fresh, varied diet and, over time, eat more of what's good for them and less of what doesn't serve their health and vitality.

All 36/9s benefit from a daily exercise routine, whether a brisk walk, strength exercises, or more sophisticated training. Their physical body needs movement, stretching, and deep breathing each day to relieve tension and stay in balance. The kind of exercise they practice is less important than making sure they do it regularly — a few minutes a day is better than none at all. As in other areas of life, 36/9s can ask themselves whether their exercise habits serve as an example for others. Just seeing someone exercising every day inspires some people. All 36/9s need to avoid making idealistic resolutions they don't carry out or buying equipment they've never used before. Better to start modestly and give themselves a feeling of success and ease; the principle "A little bit of something is better than a lot of nothing" applies strongly here. Most of all, 36/9s need to exercise patience and experiment with what works best for them; in this way, they learn by experience, and then they can share their life wisdom with others.

Relationships

Feeling internal pressure to be good and to improve and to do things right, 36/9s have a nervous hyperactivity and may experience trouble sitting still unless they're tired. They're anxious to please others, and their ideas often go straight from their mind to their mouth as they speak rapidly to keep up with the thoughts that pour forth. This trait affects their relationships, since people sometimes feel uncomfortable around their high-strung energy and sensitivity. When they stay in touch with their feelings, fewer words are necessary.

A major relationship issue for 36/9s involves ideals that block authentic feelings. Because of this, they have a difficult time expressing themselves honestly. Relationships provide a superb opportunity for growth in this area.

The relationships of 36/9s, based on lofty standards, can pose a burden for those they live with. But once 36/9s get past judgments about themselves and others, they open up to relaxed and accepting relationships.

The sexual relationships of 36/9s reflect the issues of their life path — self-doubt, perfectionism with an emphasis on performance, and, for some, issues of morality. The more they work their life path in the positive, the more loving, intimate, and pleasurable their sex life becomes.

Talents, Work, and Finances

Those working 36/9 sometimes live what appears to be a very conventional life and may avoid spiritual or metaphysical ideas due to subconscious fears or self-doubt. Beneath their sometimes conventional appearance lies an ocean of intuitive spiritual wisdom. Even though it might be the farthest thing from their mind, at some point they develop an interest in the deeper aspects of life, even if this doesn't show on the surface. Many, in their own way, bring fresh insights, perspectives, and information into the world, as Carl Jung's life demonstrates. These 36/9s can understand anything and teach it. For example, if they choose to practice bodywork as a profession, their practice leads them to new methods and approaches to get better, deeper results. Many fields, such as acting, teaching, bodywork, writing, psychotherapy, or business, to name a few, can utilize the charisma, high standards, and expressive energy of 36/9s.

Their innate but often hidden wisdom leads 36/9s, despite their own issues and doubts, to make a good living. Their financial problems arise not from having too little, but from wanting more than they have in order to meet their ideals.

Some Well-Known 36/9s

Adele, Isadora Duncan, Dustin Hoffman, Whitney Houston, Carl Jung, Robert Redford, Joseph Stalin, Serena Williams, Malala Yousafzai

Keys to Fulfilling Your Destiny

If you're working 36/9, this section can help you manifest your life purpose by focusing your attention on core issues and by generating specific action to transform key areas of your life.

Guidelines and Recommendations

- Recognize that you have a refined quality; live it.
- Find the beauty that flows from service to others.
- Face self-doubt like a warrior; accept its challenge.
- Accept what you feel, and who you are now, as perfect.

Useful Questions

1. Reflect on the following questions:
    - Do I allow self-doubt or perfectionism to discourage me?
    - What's perfect about my situation right now?
    - Do I have trouble knowing what I really want or feel?
    - Do I base my decisions on higher principles and integrity?

2. If these questions generate insights, how might you put these insights into practice?

Deepening Your Understanding

1. Turn back to Part Two, and reread the main sections covering the digits that make up your birth number: 3, 6, and 9.
2. You may wish to review birth numbers of family and friends and, if they're open to it, discuss similar or different issues in your lives.

THE LIFE YOU WERE BORN TO LIVE

Spiritual Laws: The Leverage to Change Your Life

1. Read about each of the following laws in Part Four:

    - **THE LAW OF INTUITION:** No longer monitoring other people's opinions, we connect with our heart's intuitive wisdom.
    - **THE LAW OF ACTION:** To overcome insecurity or self-doubt, we can accept our feelings yet behave with confidence.
    - **THE LAW OF PERFECTION:** High ideals can inspire us, but excellence is the most realistic goal.
    - **THE LAW OF FLEXIBILITY:** Staying flexible, we make the best use of changing circumstances.
    - **THE LAW OF HONESTY:** Honesty is founded on self-awareness of our emotional reality.

2. Do the exercises for each of these laws.
3. Consider how you might apply each law to your life.

45/9

9: Integrity through Wisdom
5: Freedom through Discipline
4: Stability through Process

Those on the 45/9 life path are here to work through issues of stability, independence, and integrity as they learn to apply a process of discipline over time to experience freedom, and to align their life with higher principles and heartfelt wisdom. Because our life purpose holds special challenges, those working 45/9 may face dramatic life tests to get their attention, help them overcome their negative tendencies, and bring them to maturity. Life provides a curriculum that teaches 45/9s the discipline and focus that lead to inner and outer freedom, and the necessity of following a stable step-by-step process to reach their goals. Above all, these individuals get clear feedback about the wisdom of living in alignment with the laws of Spirit.

Physically strong and mentally quick, with a desire for adventure and excitement, 45/9s often deal with life-and-death issues. Depending on how positively they work out their life-path issues, these individuals evolve through disillusion and difficulty to reach compassion and wisdom. During their lifetime, most 45/9s experience both the upside and the underbelly of life.

The central life challenge for 45/9s entails moving attention from their busy, visual mind to their peaceful inner core, where they can contact their deep intuitive wisdom. At this place of wisdom, all spiritual laws are revealed through the feeling dimension in the moment they need them. When 45/9s have made contact with their inner knower, they can ask an internal question, feel their heart, and *know*.

Even when 45/9s have access to higher laws, they still face the challenge of putting their knowledge into action, thus fulfilling their destiny. Integrity doesn't come easily for any 9s because our life purpose holds our greatest challenge. Those working 45/9 also face challenges stemming from the issues of 4, such as stability and process, and the issues of 5, such as freedom and discipline. The challenges of 4 and 5 will either lead to maturity or continue to pull 45/9s out of alignment with higher laws — out of integrity.

Although most 45/9s aren't necessarily oriented toward inner processing, much happens in their external world that propels them to deeper under-standing. Their life may look dramatic at times, but for the most part they're best served by chopping wood and carrying water, as the Zen masters prac-tice. They may desire extraordinary experiences and quick results, but they're here to learn about being ordinary, direct, and stable; for them, achievement happens only through a gradual step-by-step process.

Those working 45/9 tend to adore the drama and excitement of heroics, but they're here to lead, teach, or inspire others in everyday ways; for example, most of us theoretically know about the importance of eating well and get-ting daily exercise, but we sometimes find it difficult to act on what we know. Those working 45/9 are here to inspire people by acting on what they know in everyday life, even if that entails a long, gradual process.

Before 45/9s can fully exemplify higher laws in everyday life, they have to confront issues related to the challenges of 4s and 5s. The 4 calls for ground-ing and putting down roots, while 5 calls for mobility and exploring options. These dynamics can either pull in opposite directions or balance and com-plement each other.

In the positive, 4 brings stability, security, and a willingness to follow a clear process toward a goal; in the negative, 4 leads to confusion and insta-bility. An individual working 4 in the negative wants everything now or gets frozen on one step of the process. Also associated with 4 is a tendency toward tunnel vision, so 45/9s may end up repeating some tough lessons, such as divorce or health problems or financial crises, until life finally makes its point.

Less sensitive to other people's opinions than 27/9s or 36/9s, those work-ing 45/9 nevertheless have a tenuous sense of identity and often define them-selves in terms of the roles they play. Most individuals working 4 want to *be* somebody without going through a process of becoming, of mastering the necessary preparation. The Law of Process serves such individuals well, in addition to the reminder that we are more than the roles we play.

In the positive, 5 leads 45/9s to feel a constant sense of inner freedom, no matter what the circumstances, with the discipline and focus to generate mobility and a sense of outer freedom as well. In the negative, 5 can make 45/9s feel trapped, a prisoner of circumstance, too scattered to make any significant headway in life.

As 45/9s bring the stable aspects of 4 into maturity, they enjoy the fruits of a clear analytical ability, strength, sociability, diligence, and a mastery of process. When 45/9s bring the dynamic aspect of 5 into maturity, they enjoy the fruits of adventurous qualities, a quick mind, versatility, and authority.

Many 45/9s need to get grounded and stay put long enough to harvest the fruits of their labors. They may want to travel and just touch down in different locations, getting a valuable overview of life but missing the depth that brings wisdom. Eventually they realize that the real work, adventure, and treasure lie here, now, within.

The Law of Discipline addresses potential tendencies of 45/9s to feel scattered and to dilute their efforts. The combined dynamics of 5 and 9 create drives that send 45/9s seeking inner freedom, not mere independence or self-indulgence, due to their intuitive if sometimes unconscious connection to higher laws. No matter what they do, no matter how intelligent, wealthy, successful, or attractive they are, 45/9s don't find peace or freedom until they contact higher laws, experience them, and live them.

The combination of 4 and 9 energies creates drives that send 45/9s seeking inner stability, not merely staying put in one location, but feeling like the Rock of Gibraltar inside. Those 45/9s who have achieved this balance demonstrate sterling qualities, such as loyalty, responsibility, and strength.

Those working 45/9 are here for more than understanding; they come for wisdom, which emerges as they begin to live what they understand; then 45/9s can teach others through their example, without words.

Whether stable and practical or ungrounded dreamers, 45/9s aspire at levels deeper than their conscious awareness to the wisdom or experience that sets them free. Intentionally or not, 45/9s draw to themselves demands and disciplines as a means to discover and embody higher wisdom.

Working 45/9 in the Positive

Individuals working 45/9 in the positive provide an inspiring example of how to follow a careful, disciplined process to reach goals and achieve a sense of inner freedom. Strong, witty, and charismatic, they attract many friends, admirers, and students; whether or not they call themselves teachers, they teach by example, demonstrating true wisdom and inner freedom. Bound by no conventional rules but aligned with higher laws, they live a life that may appear ordinary from the outside, but their influence, even in the midst of ordinary activities, has an extraordinary quality that inspires others around them.

Working 45/9 in the Negative

These 45/9s display strength and cleverness, but they don't know what to do with either. Scattered, undisciplined, disoriented, and sometimes overwhelmed by a sense that they're missing something important, they hide behind the roles they play, seeking security there. They don't live what they profess, deceiving themselves as well as others. Ungrounded and irresponsible, they may feel free and liberated, but they never really challenge or test their own views. Because of this, they face hard lessons about reality.

Life-Path Issues

Health

The health of 45/9s depends almost entirely on whether they're working their life issues in the positive or negative. In the negative, they may have to deal with broken bones, head injuries, or illnesses that affect the brain or nervous system. In the positive, they enjoy robust health. Stubborn 45/9s encounter conditions that force them to reassess their life and make a careful, step-by-step process of recovery.

The foundation of their sense of stability and freedom depends on a strong, healthy body. Because of hurdles associated with 9, 45/9s may ignore the necessity of sound nutrition and exercise and suffer the consequences. Sooner or later, 45/9s start the process of adapting themselves to a healthier lifestyle. The challenge is great; most 45/9s prefer heroic efforts to long, drawn-out processes.

In due time, as a matter of course, 45/9s begin to align their diet and exercise routines as simple, everyday disciplines. However, depending on their lifestyle and background, they may prefer varied, exciting, or challenging exercises, such as martial arts, water sports, and mountain climbing.

Relationships

Depending on their life experience and whether they're working in the positive or the negative, 45/9s may lack sensitivity and compassion or they may have cultivated these qualities through facing their own difficulties.

Their emotional life and relationships are wild cards, however, because of the drive toward stability and family issues of 4 along with the drive toward independence of 5. Most 45/9s, in any case, learn much from their relationship and their family of origin. In family relationships, most 45/9s meet with specific issues, such as leaving home early due to an independent streak or staying at home too long due to dependent tendencies. Most have issues to work out with parents or siblings. In any case, 45/9s are likely to experience their circle of friends or the world at large as extended family.

Part of the emotional maturation of 45/9s entails accepting their feelings and following a process to develop deeper, more intimate relationships. Relationship may well form a key part of the foundation from which they can realize a higher and deeper freedom. Since 45/9s gravitate to new ways of being, living, and doing as they search for the larger picture of life, it's unlikely for them to form totally conventional relationships, although they need to form responsible ones.

Beyond biological drives, 45/9s desire sexual relationships that have an element of adventure or variety, although they also seek a deeper sense of connection. Sexuality can become a joyous part of their life if practiced not for its own sake but within the perspective of higher wisdom.

Talents, Work, and Finances

The sharp analytical abilities and quick mind of 45/9s help them create needed changes in fields such as ecology, psychology, personal growth, and other areas where leadership is needed. Or they may appear conventional and find work that challenges their skills in the changing world of business. As long as they prepare well and develop a solid foundation, their drive for freedom for themselves and others eventually leads them to success.

From a realistic financial base, 45/9s can create the security from which to expand. Money may not be the center of their life, but it provides more options, a sense of security, and the freedom they need. It's important for

45/9s to keep their finances in very good order as a way of staying practical and grounded.

Some Well-Known 45/9s

No well-known 45/9s were found in our records, since this birth number appears far less frequently in the general population than many others; more 45/9s are likely to become well-known in coming decades.

Keys to Fulfilling Your Destiny

If you're working 45/9, this section can help you manifest your life purpose by focusing your attention on core issues and by generating specific action to transform key areas of your life.

Guidelines and Recommendations

- Remember to travel the road to freedom step-by-step.
- Respect your own opinions, and let others respect theirs.
- Base your actions on integrity and inspiration.
- Find ways to help liberate others and liberate yourself in the process.

Useful Questions

1. Reflect on the following questions:
   - Upon what principles do I base my life?
   - Have I established a solid, stable foundation?
   - Can I apply focus and discipline in my life in order to achieve inner freedom and independence?
   - What steps can I take to become an inspiring example of integrity?

2. If these questions generate insights, how might you put these insights into practice?

Deepening Your Understanding

1. Turn back to Part Two, and reread the main sections covering the digits that make up your birth number: 4, 5, and 9.

2. You may wish to review birth numbers of family and friends and, if they're open to it, discuss similar or different issues in your lives.

Spiritual Laws: The Leverage to Change Your Life

1. Read about each of the following laws in Part Four:

    *   THE LAW OF HIGHER WILL: Our willingness to serve a higher purpose empowers us to inspire others.
    *   THE LAW OF PROCESS: The best way to reach any goal is one small, sure step at a time.
    *   THE LAW OF DISCIPLINE: Discipline generates the focus and depth of experience leading to true freedom.
    *   THE LAW OF CYCLES: Life brings constant changes, arising and then passing like the seasons.
    *   THE LAW OF PATTERNS: Patterns tend to reassert themselves unless we exert strong leverage to change them.

2. Do the exercises for each of these laws.
3. Consider how you might apply each law to your life.

Part Four

LAWS THAT CHANGE LIVES

The world is not to be put in order;
the world is order, incarnate.
It is for us to harmonize with this order.

— Henry Miller

THE LAWS OF SPIRIT

*You just give folks a key
and they can open their own locks.*

— Robert R. McCammon

Human laws form a basis of social agreement and social order, but human laws are only pale reflections of a higher order of laws sewn into the fabric of existence. These laws govern the movement of the Earth, the cycle of seasons, the forces of nature, and the structure of the atom itself. Nature didn't make these laws; nature only reveals and demonstrates them. The great laws existed before humanity, before nature. Even the cyclone, the tidal wave, the hurricane, and the raging fire — forces that can lay waste to the highest human enterprise — work under the dominion of these great laws. Whether we call them *spiritual laws, universal laws, natural laws,* or simply *higher laws,* we can't alter or deny them. They humble and inspire those who search for order within chaos, as they point to a greater power and mystery at the source of existence. Even the galaxies dance to their music.

Scientists and mystics both strive to understand these universal laws, but use different methods of exploration. The laws in this book aren't distilled to mathematical formulas (such as $E = mc^2$), but rather are presented as axiomatic statements that express a higher order of reality. Their validity doesn't require or depend on any kind of belief. Like the law of gravity, they apply whether or not we believe in them.

The natural world reveals these universal laws to us. The cycles of the seasons, clouds riding the wind, the currents of the river, and the powers of wind and sea — all teach us how to live by revealing the natural way of life. In this book, I refer to these overriding laws as *spiritual laws* or *laws of Spirit*.

When adapted and applied to the human realm, these laws of Spirit become guiding principles that we can use to steer us through the shallows and reefs of life the way the stars and compass guided ancient mariners on their course. Constant as the movement of the planets, they apply not only to the mechanics of nature, but to the human psyche as well. For example, by observing a tree bending in a high wind and observing that only the rigid branches break, we learn from the tree and wind the secret of yielding and the power of flexibility, or nonresistance.

Jesus, Muhammad, the Buddha, Lao-tzu, and other illumined teachers have taught spiritual laws and principles through the use of parables and metaphors about the natural world that also apply to the human social world. For example, the laws of harvest teach that seeds only reproduce their own kind; that what we sow, we reap; and that a seed dies when it stops growing. Any process of growth follows the way of the seed. In order to grow, the seed needs good soil; it takes time to grow into maturity; and it bears fruit of the same kind and quality as itself. When we gather the harvest, we're wise to save at least 10 percent for the next planting. We have to end one cycle to begin another; all seeds grow and change, and eventually die, to be plowed under for a fresh planting.

Of course, the law of harvest relates to more than farming; it illuminates our life and the laws that govern us. As with seeds and cycles, so with human beings and all the beings of creation.

Ultimately, all spiritual laws reveal themselves as needed — not necessarily in words, but rather through our deepest feelings, through the intuitive wisdom of our heart. Our body, when free of external programming and interference, abides naturally within these laws, which are communicated through our instincts and subtle intuitive feelings. All we have to do is to pay attention to and trust our inner knower. The mind or ego, our isolated sense of separate self, resists the flow of the current of life.

When we align our lives — our habits of diet, exercise, work, and sexuality — with spiritual laws, challenges remain, but we can approach them without struggle, with arms open wide, like peaceful warriors embracing the moment, ready to dance.

Beyond Concepts of Morality

Spiritual laws have very little to do with cultural concepts of right or wrong, or good or bad; rather they teach us about actions and consequences. For example, if I climb a mountain but ignore the law of gravity, this doesn't make me a bad person; it just makes me ignorant, injured, or dead. We can declare gravity illegal or even immoral, but the law of gravity still applies.

Despite moral precepts, which differ among cultures, people still commit crimes. Only seeing the consequences of our actions engenders wiser behaviors. Morality comes from social ideas. Wisdom comes from aligning our life with higher (spiritual or universal) laws of reality. Sooner or later, one way or the other, the challenges and consequences of daily life teach us about cause and effect, action and reaction; we come to respect the powers of nature and to appreciate the inherent justice of spiritual law.

Spiritual Laws and Life Paths

The number of laws that govern the universe may approach infinity; the number of laws humans have already discovered and formulated are legion. This book outlines the key laws most relevant to the birth numbers and life paths described in Part Three.

Spiritual laws apply consistently to everyone. However, because of the individual qualities and issues of each life path, certain laws bring the greatest benefit to those working specific birth numbers. The transformative power of this material resides in working with the laws most relevant to fulfilling our individual destiny.

Archimedes said, "Give me a long enough lever, and I can move the Earth." The laws and principles presented here act as levers to help us move toward the most positive expression of our life path. The degree to which we apply the laws central to our individual birth number can make a day-or-night difference in the quality of our experience and the course of our life.

Specific issues in a variety of areas, such as health, relationships, and careers, rise and fall over time. Although such issues come and go, the laws related to our birth number will remain relevant five, ten, or twenty years from now, and for the rest of our life. These laws apply not only to issues presently demanding our attention, but to any and all issues that may appear. The laws of Spirit not only heal the symptoms of discontent; they also heal and balance the tendencies, drives, and fears that constitute the source of our difficulties, whether manifesting as our relationship problems, our health issues, or whatever else arises.

As we align ourselves with the laws most relevant to our life path, we can, over time, work through our core issues with greater refinement, grace, and ease. These laws can help transform *any* issue in our life, because they dig beneath the surface to the roots, helping us transform ourselves at the source rather than merely struggling with the symptoms.

Even the highest laws, principles, and wisdom can help us only if we remember to *apply* them — to use them as guides for changing our perspectives and our actions. If we wanted to learn how to dive off the high board and someone reminded us to stretch for the water, that guidance might save us some belly flops and help us perform more gracefully. But what do we do with this information? We certainly don't have to think about stretching for the water while brushing our teeth or going shopping. We only need to access and apply this information when we leave the diving board and plummet toward the water. We can apply any useful guidance by remembering and then doing, by turning information into action. As we apply useful guidance in the moments when it's most needed, the quality of our moments gets better and better.

The key to the power of a law lies not just in knowing it, but in applying it. And we can do so in the moments when the laws are most timely and needed. These laws are not magic wands, but needles on a cosmic compass, pointing our way. We apply them by aligning our actions with our heart's wisdom, as expressed by the laws that follow. A change in our actions, feelings, or perspectives indicates this alignment with the laws of Spirit. The exercises in Part Four can help you achieve such alignment through direct experience and application.

THE LAW OF FLEXIBILITY

Flexibility avails us far more
than either passivity or resistance;
by actively using whatever arises,
embracing even the most painful circumstances,
we deal with our difficulties more effectively,
as we begin to see them as a form of spiritual training.

Flexibility involves a pragmatic acceptance of, rather than rigid resistance toward, the present moment — a relaxed, adaptive acceptance of ourselves, others, and current circumstances. This doesn't in any way imply passive toleration for what we don't like, nor does it mean ignoring injustice or allowing ourselves to be victimized. Flexibility requires an alert and expansive state of awareness; it entails not just going with the flow, but embracing and making constructive use of it. Mastering this law, we turn stumbling blocks into stepping-stones and problems into opportunities; when high winds blow, we don't just accept or tolerate these winds, we put up windmills. As poet Robert Frost wrote, "Always fall in with what you're asked to accept. Fall in with it and turn it your way."

The Law of Flexibility may appear unrealistic and idealistic at first, bringing up a variety of questions, such as "What if we're attacked on the street, or a tragedy happens to a loved one? How do we embrace that?" Such questions are fair and important, but the answer comes down to this: Great pleasures and great pain and injustice exist in this world. When something painful happens to a group of people, some of these people mentally resist the experience, in total shock, denial, and fear; they suffer the worst, like the tree with rigid branches that break in the wind. Others in the group of people have developed the ability to bend, to accept and experience the situation fully, while keeping in touch with the bigger picture of life — with a sense of perspective about how things are. They accept their emotions and express them fully, but like the branch that bends, they don't break but snap back. Without mental rigidity or resistance, they can respond in the most effective, creative way. In flexibility lies great strength. With flexibility, we learn to treat sun and rain, heat and cold, as equals. We experience life as less painful, less of a struggle, by responding rather than resisting; we treat pain as a test and make the best use of it we can, if only to learn.

I once saw a humorous bumper sticker that exemplified the Law of Flexibility. It read, "If you don't like the way I drive, get off the sidewalk!" If someone is driving right toward us on the sidewalk of life, instead of thinking, "They shouldn't be doing this; it isn't fair; it isn't right," while the car careens toward us, we can apply the Law of Flexibility and jump out of the way, grateful for the chance to test our reflexes.

The martial arts of aikido and tai chi, which reflect and embody the Law of Flexibility, are founded upon nonresistance: When pushed, pull; when pulled, push; and when a force comes toward you, get out of the way. Everything serves our highest good if we make good use of it.

When we view life only from the personal viewpoint of our conventional mind, we certainly won't always feel grateful for some events, such as financial setbacks or catching the flu. The Law of Flexibility, however, reminds us to expand our vision beyond ourselves to see the bigger picture so we can better appreciate that every circumstance, whether it appears positive or negative to us at the time, serves as an opportunity to strengthen our spirit. Stress happens whenever the mind resists what arises in life — whether situations, people, or emotions. Phrases such as "I'd rather be" or "They should (or shouldn't) be" reflect our resistance to what is. By seeing everything we meet as a potential lesson that may, in the long run, make us stronger, wiser, or more whole, we get past expectations or judgments about what is and embrace life.

Life may not always be fair from the viewpoint of the limited mind, but from a much larger perspective, spiritual laws still hold true. Flexibility involves developing the attitude "Okay, here's where I am and who I am. I'll do the best I can with the situation." Just as opportunities also contain problems, every problem brings an opportunity.

The Serenity Prayer used by Alcoholics Anonymous and other twelve-step programs reflects the Law of Flexibility: "God grant me the serenity to accept the things I cannot change, the courage to change the things I can, and the wisdom to know the difference."

Flexibility enables us to enjoy situations that might once have troubled us, such as changes in fortunes or the ending of relationships. Sometimes flexibility means staying aware of both sides of issues or events but focusing on the more positive side of any difficulty. For example, as painful as the breakup of a relationship may be, it opens up the space for new opportunity, new love.

Cats are masters of the Law of Flexibility: When a cat wants to walk out the door but someone is blocking its way, it tries to go one way, then another, and then another; it's persistent, but it also knows when to sit back, relax, and wait for another opportunity. Like cats, we don't have to waste energy resisting or fretting over circumstances we can't avoid.

Flexibility means total and unconditional acceptance of who we are, whom we're with, and what we're doing in this moment, even as we learn and grow and effectively handle what's in front of us. This may require a shift in attitude, not necessarily a shift in behavior. If we catch ourselves criticizing others or calling them names, it also means accepting and forgiving ourselves on the spot for our mistakes.

Flexibility means staying adaptable; like water, we take the shape of our container — the present moment. We open to life at whatever level we can.

The Law of Flexibility parallels the Law of Perfection but with slightly different emphasis and purpose. By practicing the Law of Flexibility, we stay open to experiencing rather than avoiding the highs and lows. We live more fully.

We can apply flexibility to our work, our relationships, or any other aspect of everyday life. Free of resistance, we learn the art of unreasonable happiness. Master this law, and we've mastered them all.

Experiencing Flexibility

This partner exercise gives a physical experience of acceptance as it applies to the highest martial arts, as well as to any situation in daily life.

1. Stand naturally, with your feet shoulder width apart, and hold one arm out in front of you. Have your partner take your wrist or forearm and smoothly pull you forward, as if trying to get you to go somewhere.

2. As your partner pulls, take one step forward to maintain your balance and resist (pull against) the pull of your partner. Experience what this feels like physically and emotionally.

3. Now, have your partner pull once again, but this time, *just* as your partner begins to pull, while maintaining your balance, take two steps forward and *gently* push your partner in the direction of your partner's pulling. In other words, instead of resisting the force, join it; make it yours. Experience what this feels like physically and emotionally. This time, you didn't accept your partner's pull in the sense of resigned submission or passive toleration, and you didn't actively work against it; rather, you *made use of it*.

4. After allowing your partner to be in the other role, compare your experiences.

Applying the Law of Flexibility

1. Think of a situation or incident that you tend to fight or resist.

2. Consider how you might apply flexibility to embrace and flow with the forces of your life.

3. Notice whenever you tend to contract, tense, resist, pull back, freeze up, or fight when dealing with this situation or incident. Ask yourself, "What if I actively went with the force and made it mine?"

THE LAW OF CHOICES

The most basic choice we have in life
is whether to expand or contract,
whether to bring our creative and expressive energies
out into the world in positive or negative ways.
No matter what our circumstances,
we have the power to choose our directions.

Most creatures on Earth have a relatively narrow range of conscious choices; they work primarily through instinct and adaptation. In contrast, we humans have far-ranging powers of choice. Our daily life consists of a series of choices and exercises in free will — whether to get up or stay in bed, what to eat for breakfast, what to do with our day, whether to change careers, go back to school, or continue a relationship, and so forth.

Depending on our circumstances, we may experience many choices or few choices. Mental illness or other incapacity may distort or limit our power of choice; clarity of mind enhances it. Clearly, we don't all have equal choice over our circumstances; for example, if we have great wealth, we can choose to fly to Europe for dinner; if we live in an impoverished country, we may choose to eat but find no food available. If we're bedridden, we may choose to run through the hills but find ourselves unable to do so, except in our imagination. Physical circumstances can indeed limit our physical options. The Law of Choices, however, addresses our power and responsibility to choose how we *respond* to our circumstances — a power we never lose as long as we live. As the proverb goes, "We have to live and we have to die; the rest we make up."

Sometimes we feel as if our choices are made for us by our family, by our employer, by our friends, by our circumstances, or by God. If, for example, our employer tells us, "You have to work overtime or we'll have to let you go," we may feel that we don't have a choice. But of course we do; we make conscious choices by recognizing that every choice has consequences.

We can each choose an easier path or a more difficult one. We rarely choose to take the more painful path unless we believe it will bring us pleasure in the long run or get us to our goals more quickly. The fewer distorted or limiting beliefs we have, the greater our power of choice.

We also need to trust the intuitive messages from our subconscious, which may choose experiences or attract people into our life with results that we don't consciously want but may need for our highest good and learning. The more we honor the Law of Choices, the more clearly we can live our life on purpose and by choice, taking responsibility for our direction rather than viewing life as something that just happens to us. For example, instead of wandering through life, wondering if we're on the right path or with the right person or in the right job, we recognize that we've chosen these people and circumstances. With that recognition comes the power to accept our choices, take responsibility for our life, and perhaps make new choices. If we ever feel powerless in a situation, that's a key time to remember our power of choice.

In the context of the Life-Purpose System and the life paths it describes, we can choose to expand or contract, build or destroy, in the two key areas of creativity and expression.

Each of us has creative life force. We also have the ability to express ourselves. We can choose to create and express in either more positive or more negative directions. We may not always feel as if we have a choice; sometimes we may feel that our creativity and expressiveness are suppressed or blocked. Yet the more we appreciate the power of choice, the more we take charge of how we channel our creative energy and how we express ourselves.

Creative Choice

Everything that exists is made of energy, and energy can manifest itself along a spectrum from positive to negative. For example, electricity can light a city or take a life. Money is another kind of energy; we can use this energy in positive or in negative ways, such as by donating to a charity, taking a needed vacation, or even hiring someone to perform a crime.

Creative energy has a surging, dynamic quality; it exists to flow toward some purpose. This energy acts as a double-edged sword; if it isn't used for constructive purposes, it gets discharged in destructive ways. If our creative energy gets blocked altogether, like water surging against a wall, it turns back on us and creates pressures that we experience as painful symptoms at physical, emotional, and mental levels. Excessive weight, for example, often reflects blocked creative energy with nowhere to go. We create in constructive ways, or we create in destructive ways; either way, creative energy finds expression.

Examples of creating in the positive include the fine arts — music, painting, sculpture, writing, drama, and so forth — but creative energy can also be expressed fully through having and raising children, coming up with innovative solutions to business problems, working with plants and growing things, or taking care of animals. We can apply creative energy to any field, including healing, crafts, interior design, or a thousand other endeavors.

Pablo may become a creative artist; Theodore may create counterfeit money. Karinna may apply her creative energy and deft fingers to playing guitar; Margarite may become a pickpocket. One person may create with language to tell stories; another may use language to tell elaborate lies. All of these examples reflect creative energy, used in constructive or destructive ways.

Many prison inmates are extremely creative; they can draw, paint, sing, act, and write beautifully, but they directed their creativity into negative directions: They planned creative robberies, conned people out of money, lied, and so on.

Blocked creative energy either manifests as physical maladies and symptoms or gets discharged through abuse of tobacco, alcohol, other drugs, food, or sex. When such release becomes repetitive, compelling, or chronic, it may expand into full-blown addictions.

As we recognize that we have, on some level, chosen how we channel our creative energy, we can learn other ways to open up and channel that energy in directions that inspire or help others and bring rewards instead of punishments. No matter how destructive or blocked our creative energy may have been in the past, this can change once we apply the power of choice. By choosing to express our creative energy in positive, life-affirming ways, including daily exercise, we can change the course of our life.

Experiencing Creative Choice

1. Consider how your creative energy manifests.

    •   Is your energy flowing into creative projects or activities, or is it blocked?
    •   If your energy feels blocked, do you experience physical symptoms?
    •   How might you use this energy in an enjoyable and constructive way?
    •   How do you balance, ground, or release creative energy when pressure builds up? Do you exercise? Do you smoke cigarettes? Do you talk a great deal? Do you drink alcohol or use other drugs? Do you overeat? Do you feel pressure for sexual release?

2. No moral judgments are implied; the above options are neither good nor bad; they're only more or less constructive ways to use creativity.

    •   How will you choose to use your creativity in the future?
    •   Will you apply the power to choose?

Applying Creative Choice

1. Make a list of the more constructive and less constructive ways in which you make use of your creativity.
2. Contemplate your list, and consider the life you would like to create for yourself. You may choose not to make any changes, or you may decide to take a risk and try something new.
3. If you're dealing with abuse of alcohol, tobacco, or other drugs, or abuse of food or sexuality, consider the following suggestions to help you turn around your life:

    •   Find a twelve-step program or other self-help group; in the case of addictions, group support is essential.
    •   Commit to an exercise program to balance and release addictive pressures constructively.
    •   Find a counselor or psychotherapist to help you work through underlying issues.

4. If you've avoided learning creative skills or arts out of insecurity or

the feeling that you might not be good enough, explore new possibilities; take a leap and express your creativity.

- Take an art or drama class; make up short stories or write in a daily journal; take up a craft or hobby; rearrange, redecorate, or redesign your living quarters; help someone solve a problem; work in the garden; or do volunteer work. All of these are positive examples of creativity.

Expressive Choice

We typically express ourselves and our emotions through words or gesture, but also through music, performance, arts, crafts, and other symbolic avenues.

Expression entails more than just talking or passing out ideas or information. Expressive energy is *emotional* energy, or feelings; these feelings may signal anger or sorrow or fear or joy or excitement that's seeking a way into the world. We express ourselves in constructive ways, or we express ourselves in destructive ways; either way, expressive-emotive energy will emerge.

If we deny or suppress the passion within us, this block can contribute to sore throats, ulcers, other abdominal problems, lower back pain, uterine fibroids, prostate problems, headaches, muscular tension and stiffness, or other symptoms and maladies. We can, however, rejuvenate and invigorate ourselves by taking appropriate steps to heal our body and, at the same time, form new habits and create new avenues of free and open self-expression.

Creative energy can be channeled in isolation, such as through painting pictures or building models by ourselves, but expressive energy entails relationship — someone else open to receiving our expression, someone willing to listen, to watch our performance, or to appreciate our expressive crafts. Our audience may be adults, children, or even animals with whom we've established a relationship (and who listen well without judgments or blame).

Expressive energy is so strong in some people that it may come out at first in one-on-one situations, but as confidence rises, the expressive drive often expands to include groups in one form or another. Whatever forms our expression takes — coming out through creating symphonies, speeches, or soap operas — it can convey, stimulate, or inspire feelings, stirring our emotions.

Positive expression manifests as inspiring, enthusiastic, constructive, uplifting communication, such as speaking, singing, acting, music, writing, or expressing through other arts. Negative expression manifests as bad-mouthing, complaining, criticizing, or whining. It tears down, hurts, or destroys, and it can cut people to ribbons.

Those of us who have a great deal of expressive energy have the power to either uplift or tear down. Once we recognize our ability to uplift or tear down, we can learn to channel this energy in responsible, constructive ways.

Whether our feelings seem positive or negative, we can all appreciate the value of expressing them in constructive ways. Getting in touch with and releasing our authentic feelings can generate new levels of vitality, integration, and healing. In valuing positive expression, I don't mean to imply that we need to deny our anger, fear, or sorrow, nor do I recommend repressive strategies in the name of staying cool or above it all. We can express even anger, fear, sorrow, or any other so-called negative emotion in negative or positive ways. For example, if we feel angry, we can call someone names, or we can say something like "I feel really angry right now about what you did, and that puts a wall between us, which I don't want."

The Law of Choices, when applied to expression, reminds us that, in the long run, honest expression of *all* of our feelings benefits both ourselves and our relationships; the Law of Honesty also applies here.

Expression — the pen — is indeed mightier than the sword. Misused expression has allowed dictators to take over and manipulate whole nations; it has slandered and destroyed lives. At the same time, the most moving works of art and the most eloquent speeches of history stand as glowing examples of the power of expressive energy to bring beauty into the world and to inspire us to action and to change.

Even in everyday life, the way we express ourselves can make a tremendous difference in the quality of life for ourselves and those around us. The choice is ours.

Experiencing Expressive Choice

1. Consider the following questions:

   - When did you last express something in a negative way to someone?

   - When you express something in a negative way (for example, a criticism or complaint), do you notice that you feel fully justified at the time?

- How do you feel during and after you criticize or complain, or express in another negative way?
- When did you last express something in a positive way to someone?
- When you express something in a positive way (for example, giving someone a compliment or expressing angry feelings in a constructive way that honors the relationship), do you notice the way positive feelings come back toward you?
- How do you feel during and after you compliment someone or express your feelings in another positive way?

2. As you reflect on your answers to these questions, you might want to imagine or even mentally rehearse more positive ways to express your feelings.

Applying Expressive Choice

1. Write down or recall the last one or two times you expressed something in a negative way.
2. Consider that when we criticize, we don't usually express our feelings; instead, we turn what we feel into judgments. Rewrite how you might have phrased your feelings directly and honestly. Hint: Instead of using "you" or some other pronoun (*"You* make me crazy!" *"They* always…"), use "I feel" ("*I feel* angry when…").
3. The next time you have a chance, put what you have learned into practice.

THE LAW OF RESPONSIBILITY

Once we establish the limits and boundaries of our responsibility,
we can take full charge of what truly belongs to us
and let go of what doesn't;
in doing so, we find more enjoyment supporting others,
as we create more harmonious cooperative relationships.

"United we stand, divided we fall. Many hands make light work. No one is smarter than all of us." The principle has been stated many ways, but each statement expresses the same sentiment: Working together, we can accomplish tasks that would be difficult or impossible without cooperative effort — for example, building a skyscraper or staging a play.

In every endeavor where people work together at different levels of responsibility, some of them may have more visibility, but they're supported by other people without whom their efforts would be unproductive. What would the rock star do without the sound technicians? Could the corporate president or head of the board run a company without efficient secretaries? When achievers rise in politics or industry, they're supported by others who form the foundation of their enterprise.

Families, corporations, or empires rise or fall based on the quality and level of cooperation and responsibility within their boundaries. At the individual level, our own effective functioning as a human being depends in large part on our internal states of cooperation.

Before we can help others, we have to help ourselves — to put our internal house in order — and reconcile our conflicting subpersonalities: those identities, beliefs, values, and ideas that seem to oppose one another or sit on different sides of the fence. We may even need to facilitate active cooperation between the right and left hemispheres of our brain. Before we can find harmony, we have to notice what is out of harmony — the either/or, yes/no, I should/I shouldn't dichotomies that result in confusion since every decision involves pros and cons. A variety of approaches exist to harmonizing our various parts, including subpersonality work, Voice Dialogue, Neurolinguistic Programming, alchemical hypnotherapy, and other educational methods that help integrate various characters of the psyche.

In our relationships with ourselves, with other people, and with our own circumstances, we need to discover our point of balance, define and delineate the limits and boundaries of our appropriate level of responsibility, and recognize that our values, needs, and priorities may rightfully be very different from those of our parents, siblings, spouse, or other people. As Larry Eisenberg wrote, "For peace of mind, we need to resign as general manager of the universe."

Those of us who feel a strong drive to support, serve, and assist others can, in our need to give, sometimes overcooperate to an extent that debilitates both us and those we serve. In extreme cases, this tendency to overhelp degenerates into codependency, where we lose ourselves in obsessive focus on other people's lives, pouring out without receiving in return. Codependents assume responsibility for other people's lives far beyond the normal duties of parents or friends or employees. They base their value, their self-worth, and even their identities on their ability to help other people, obsessively focusing on other people's needs before their own, a form of playing doormat or even slave.

The overcooperation that lies at the core of codependency involves a distorted or exaggerated sense of responsibility, leading us to try to fix other people's mistakes rather than allowing them to learn from the consequences of their own behaviors.

If we overcooperate with other people, they rarely complain about it. Seldom do we hear others say, "You're just too easygoing!" However, we soon discover that when the pendulum of our psyche swings too much into overcooperation, eventually it swings back the other way, into undercooperation. This shift may take a few days, weeks, months, or even years, but sooner or later it happens.

In the case of undercooperation, we either go into complete resistance and resentment or we continue doing things for other people while withdrawing emotionally. Unless we correct this pattern, it can lead to the death of a relationship.

Happily, relationships suffering from traumatic or chronic cooperation issues can be saved or, in some cases, resurrected. The miracle involves finding a new balance between giving and receiving — establishing a mutually supportive relationship. Open communication can lead to a more equal sharing of responsibility, lifting the psychological burden from the shoulders of those with codependent tendencies. The major responsibility for establishing a new balance, however, rests with those who have such tendencies.

Responsibility in itself seems a desirable attribute, but those of us who feel overly responsible — who feel compelled to overhelp — need to shift our attitude and actions and find our balance point in order to achieve a state of true cooperation and balanced responsibility. The most powerful form of cooperation and support may sometimes mean encouraging and empowering other people to do things for themselves. The best assistance often includes making the right demands.

The Law of Responsibility serves as an essential reminder of the value and ultimate necessity of finding, respecting, and working within our own sense of boundaries. While we're all here to stretch our comfort zone, we're not here to ignore it. This law reminds us to respect our internal values and to find our own point of balance.

Let's take the example of Rosalyn and Tanya, each a mother of two young children. Both Rosalyn and Tanya were formerly advertising executives who commuted daily to work in San Francisco. Rosalyn decided to stay home with her children, putting her downtown career on hold; Tanya, on the other hand, continued working downtown and found a good nanny to take care of her children while she was at work. Rosalyn and Tanya made different choices. The issue here is that neither woman chose what she most deeply wanted to do; instead, each chose what she felt she was "supposed" to do.

Rosalyn felt frustrated at home, but she believed that she had to remain with her children all day to be a good mother. Tanya hated leaving her children every day, but she wanted to be a modern woman with equal opportunities, not tied to the home the way she felt her own mother had been.

Both women were, in a sense, overcooperating with someone else's values and ideas of what they "should" be or do rather than listening to their own needs. Happily, each has now found a balance that works well for her. Tanya has found a way to work at home so that she can see her children more, and Rosalyn is back in the office, working part-time and loving it, and she better appreciates the time she has with her children because her other needs are being met.

In applying the Law of Responsibility, we support others, but we also accept support; we find a balance between the two. We find the difference between what we think we "should" do or be and what our heart really desires. We do what we can feel good about inside; if we don't feel good inside, we state our feelings and reach a compromise: "I'll do this much, but you'll have to do the rest." That's the heart of responsibility and the soul of cooperation.

Experiencing Responsibility

Before finding a balanced sense of responsibility to self and others and achieving true cooperation in the world, we need to experience it within ourselves. This visualization exercise works with the subconscious to harmonize conflicting parts. With a little practice, it takes only a minute or two. It also provides valuable practice in conflict resolution and can serve as a template for working out balanced, mutually beneficial agreements with others.

1.   Imagine a safe and special place anywhere in the world or the universe. It could be a granite plateau high in the mountains, a hidden glen, or a quiet meadow — your own private inner space.
2.   Create the image of a table with two chairs, on facing sides.
3.   Invite two opposing parts of yourself to reveal themselves, one at a time, and to sit down, facing each other, across the table. You might invite one part that represents your mind and one part that represents your body, a part you like and a part you dislike, a part from the past and a part from the future, or a judging part and a forgiving part. Whenever you have mixed feelings or feel torn in two directions, you can access two parts to represent these feelings.
4.   Ask each part what positive outcome or intention it has for you. Even if one part seems negative, trust that every aspect of your subconscious exists for a reason and is doing its best to serve the whole.
5.   As each part appears in your mind's eye, note what it looks like, how it moves and sits down, and how it behaves. When both are seated, note how they relate to each other.
6.   Internally ask both parts to express themselves until they find a place

of cooperation, rapport, and communication so that in the future they can work together.

7.   When you feel complete, thank them, say farewell, and leave them to enjoy their meeting.

Applying the Law of Responsibility

1.   Either write or recite to yourself a short list of things you'd be willing to do if someone asked you and a short list of things you wouldn't be willing to do. Where do you draw the line, and why?

2.   Write or recite to yourself a list of things that you feel comfortable doing and things that you don't feel comfortable doing for others at home or work.

   •   How many of these tasks do you continue to do, and why?
   •   Do you do things for people, such as your children, spouse, or relatives, and then complain?
   •   Do you feel responsible for the mistakes or lives of other adults?

3.   Consider briefly the areas of your life where you might be feeling overly responsible and where you tend to overhelp or else withdraw in resentment. If you feel exploited or unappreciated — like a martyr or a doormat — what might you do in your life to find a better balance?

THE LAW OF BALANCE

*Balance applies to us
on cosmic, biological, and personal levels —
to our body, mind, and emotions —
reminding us that anything we do,
we can overdo or underdo,
and that if our internal pendulum swings to one side,
it will inevitably swing to the other.*

If gravity is the glue that holds the universe together, balance is the key that unlocks its secrets. All things exist in a state of balance: high and low, in and out, hot and cold, fast and slow, loud and soft — the interplay of opposites. Between the polarities rests a balance point, a center.

Quite unconsciously, while we eat, sleep, work, and move about our daily affairs, our subconscious works through our autonomic nervous system, our endocrine and hormonal systems, and our circulatory system to maintain a delicate balance of temperature and blood chemistry, which, if drastically altered, ends our life. Not only does our survival depend on balance, so do the quality of our life and the state of our psyche.

The Earth itself, functioning like a single, living organism on whose surface we humans are but cells and the oceans and winds the circulatory system, also exists in a state of balance — one we're all too close to throwing out of equilibrium. In a sense, the global ecological drama we currently face reflects what goes on in our individual life as we mature and learn about our own unique states of balance.

Although our subconscious mind — which I refer to as the *basic self* in several of my other books, and which some might call the mammalian or middle-brain or autonomic nervous system — is largely responsible for internal physiological balance, our *conscious self* bears responsibility for our lifestyle and actions. Thus, the Law of Balance is intimately connected to the Law of Choices as well as to the Law of Responsibility, which addresses the balance between overcooperation and undercooperation and demonstrates how achieving balance in even one area of our life can make a significant difference in our effectiveness.

Our psyches contain archetypal polarities such as the puritan and the hedonist, the believer and the skeptic, the social butterfly and the lone wolf, and other dualities that account for contradiction and turmoil within our mind. To achieve balance — physical, emotional, mental, and spiritual — has been a goal of many global traditions of human potential work. Balance is expressed in another way in the Gospel of Thomas: "When you make the two one, and when you make the outside like the inside, and above like below; when you make the male and the female as one, then you will enter the kingdom of God."

Sages from every culture, from Chinese Taoists to Essene rabbis, from Christians to Muslims, have advocated the middle way, the golden mean, the straight-and-narrow path. Even in the world of nature, most humans thrive by avoiding the extremes of desert heat and arctic cold, finding our life more comfortable in the temperate zones.

Literature, especially children's stories, reveals themes of finding balance; in Western culture, the story of Goldilocks and the three bears expresses this archetype as Goldilocks chooses the chair that's neither too large nor too small, the porridge that's neither too hot nor too cold, and the bed that's neither too hard nor too soft, but "just right."

Balance, however, doesn't always depend on avoiding the extremes; balance also embraces the ability to explore the extremes at times, paying equal attention to both sides to keep the pendulum in balance. For example, sometimes we may want to play the hedonist, staying up late and celebrating, indulging our senses; other times, we may express a more puritan or Spartan disposition, eating well and exercising. Sometimes we overwork; other times we overrest. Over time, we remain in balance as long as we work *both* sides equally and return to center. However, extremes create stress and eventually require a swing in the opposite direction. A measure of our awareness and wisdom is whether our life and our actions center around the middle way. An automobile driven moderately each day lasts longer than a car left idle for weeks and then raced for weeks; just so, balance is key to a long and healthy life.

What constitutes balance differs somewhat for each of us, due to our different temperaments, dispositions, and constitutions. Some people, for example, tolerate and thrive on more exercise than others; even our own needs change over time. Each of us needs to find our own middle ground, defined by our unique physical and psychological qualities and needs, not by someone else's values. How much to exercise? How many orgasms to have per week or per month or per year? How much to eat? All of these questions may have statistical averages, but the only true answer is whatever works best for each of us.

The specific life issues each of us needs to balance depend in large part on our birth number, our overall life path, and our primary life purpose:

- If we're working 1, we need to balance between the extremes of elitist superiority and insecurity.
- If we're working 2, we need to find the middle ground between over-helping and resentful resistance or withdrawal.
- If we're working 3, we need to balance between the extremes of manic overconfidence and depressive self-doubt.
- If we're working 4, we need to find a balance between mind and emotions, and between analysis and disorientation.
- If we're working 5, we need to find a balance between moving from extreme dependence to extreme independence.
- If we're working 6, we search for a balanced realism to avoid swinging from idealism to inevitable disappointment.
- If we're working 7, we need to find a balance between naive over-trusting and fears of betrayal.
- If we're working 8, we need to find a balance between passivity and aggressiveness, and between the extremes of feast and famine.
- If we're working 9, we seek a balance between our puritan and hedonist tendencies, and between rigid integrity and its opposite.

Many of us find our balance point by testing our limits and exploring the extremes on either side, then learning from the consequences. Although this isn't the easiest path, it may be the most common one. All the good advice in the world hasn't changed this pendulum method. The advice and experience of others may not apply to us. Sometimes we need to find out for ourselves; experience may not always provide the easiest way to learn, but it seems to be one of the surest.

The Law of Balance reminds us to look carefully at the areas that may be out of balance in our own life. Whatever our gender or biological sex, do we balance the masculine and feminine sides of ourselves? Do we balance work and family, as well as taking care of ourselves and taking care of others?

Considering our life in light of this law helps us see ourselves with better perspective, make appropriate adjustments, and find a deeper sense of health, harmony, and inner peace.

Giving and Receiving

Although we often give goods, favors, appreciation, or attention in order to receive something in return, the universe reminds us that whatever we feel we most need is what we most need to give. One special application of the Law of Balance applies to those of us who feel so emotionally needy that we want to receive nurturance without necessarily having to give any back. All of us have emotional needs and consciously or unconsciously look for ways to get more love, appreciation, and understanding. But actions based on the desire to receive without giving — using indirect means we learned in childhood to get what we want — don't work over time.

This corollary to the Law of Balance states that we receive what we give. Most of us are familiar with this theme, but how many of us practice it? We may give, but whether we're fully aware of it or not, we usually attach strings or expectations: We spend money, we act kindly, we pay compliments, all so something will come back to us. There isn't necessarily anything wrong with this, except that events don't always unfold the way we'd hoped; conditional giving has a hooklike energy that curtails higher qualities or repels the desired results. The secret of giving and receiving is that whatever we feel we need is really a message from our deeper self, which is telling us what we most need to give.

Balance, the heart of ancient Taoist wisdom, is so critical to our life that it forms a template for much of what we call spiritual development or personal growth. Applying this law isn't easy, but the efforts are always worthwhile and can help us master ourselves and our life.

Experiencing Balance

How do you explore both sides to find the middle in your life? Try this simple exercise:

1. Set a wastepaper basket in the center of the room. Sit or stand about five feet away with some balls made of crumpled paper or other small objects to toss into the basket. Keep careful track of where each object lands as you aim for the basket.

   - For every toss that goes too long, deliberately make the next one too short.
   - For every toss that goes too far left, make the next one too far right.

2. Notice how this process helps you find center.

Applying the Law of Balance

1. Consider how you can apply the Law of Balance through working both sides. Ask the following questions:

   - Do I talk very rapidly or loudly?
     Experiment by talking very slowly or quietly.
   - Do I eat too quickly?
     Experiment by eating too slowly.
   - Do I often feel muscular tension?
     Experiment by becoming too relaxed.

2. Ask someone who knows you well the following questions:

   - Do I work too much or too little?
   - Do I act too rigid or too sensitive?
   - Do I act too dependent or too independent?
   - Do I act overconfident or underconfident?
   - Do I act uptight or self-indulgent?
   - Do I seem more inclined to give or to receive?

3. If you think that person's view has some merit, pointing to an area of imbalance, how might you bring that area back into balance? How might you work the other side?

THE LAW OF PROCESS

On the path to our goals
if we want to get from point A to point Z,
the surest way to get there
is to first go to point B, then C, D, and so on.
Skipping a single step,
even though it appears to be a shortcut,
often results in failure.

Our daily life is filled with goals and achievements. These goals may be large, as in climbing mountains, gaining political office, or forming our own company, or they may be smaller, as in baking a cake, winning a softball game, or doing a homework assignment.

Some of us are so occupied with our goals — leaping ahead of ourselves to the end result — that we ignore the path and the process in-between. On the other hand, some of us get so disoriented or doubtful about how to get from here to there that we have trouble even setting our goals, or we get stuck on one step, suffering from tunnel vision.

It helps to remember that if we want to climb a mountain, we need to form a goal, set out a direction, prepare well, and proceed in small, sure steps. We can break down any achievement, no matter how large or imposing, into discrete, manageable steps. If we want to ford a stream, we find the individual stepping-stones. If we try to leap over too many steps, sooner or later we're going to slip. As author Mildred McAfee wrote, "If you have a great ambition, take as big a step as you can in the direction of fulfilling it. The step may only be a tiny one, but trust that it may be the largest one possible for now."

The Law of Process teaches us not only to break a journey into shorter sections but also to appreciate each step as if it were an end in itself. Every step becomes a small success in itself; that way, we succeed many times, not just when we reach our final goal. What we learn on the journey may turn out to be more important than reaching the destination. For example, if we spend twenty years learning to paint portraits and then all our paintings are destroyed, we've still gained inner qualities on the road to our goal, including an ability to see with different eyes and better appreciate the beauty in every face.

Those of us working through process issues need to ask ourselves whether we want to be like the mail carrier who rushes to complete the shift every day and get off work or the mail carrier who delights in the changing scene of the neighborhoods and weather, saying hello to people on the street while walking at a smooth and measured pace. Many of us live only for the big highs, but forget that each small step up the mountain is higher than the last. Process reminds us, "Do it right or do it over."

Here's another example of the Law of Process: Patrick had just come into some money when he noticed that a neighborhood restaurant was going out of business. "What an opportunity!" he said to himself. He bought the business, hired the existing staff, kept the same menu, and put up a new sign stating "Under New Management," thinking that under his charismatic leadership, business would boom. The business failed again, the way most new ventures fail, and for the same reason: Patrick didn't go through all of the steps of the process. He wanted to get to the end product right away.

Joshua, on the other hand, came into a little money and saw a "Going Out of Business" sign on a local restaurant. He did his homework: He interviewed restaurant owners and learned the pros and cons of the business. He learned that the three most important things for a restaurant to succeed are location, location, and location. He found out that the location for this restaurant wasn't the problem; something else had caused it to fail. So he did a demographic study and called two hundred people in the area, at random, to ask them how often they went out to eat and what types of food they liked. Based on what he learned, he decided to open Joshua's Deli Delights. He then spent some time in area restaurants, offering to help wherever he could; he observed and spoke with dishwashers, food servers, cooks, hosts, and managers so he would know what questions to ask on job interviews. Finally, after finding out where to get the best supplies at the best prices, hiring the best staff he could, and making all the necessary preparations, Joshua had covered all of the steps. His success wasn't merely luck, good fortune, or a surprise.

Joshua had mastered the Law of Process and demonstrated that by building a stable foundation based on careful preparation and following a patient process, we can reach any goal. We can achieve anything if we break it down into manageable parts.

Experiencing Process

1. Reflect on how you learned to play a musical instrument or a sport, drive a car, or walk or talk. Did it happen all at once, or was it a step-by-step, trial-and-error process?
2. Observe how houses and skyscrapers are built from the ground up, a little at a time. Consider how much energy and planning it takes. What does this say about how to accomplish anything in life?

Applying the Law of Process

1. Observe in your own life the many processes you go through each day just in getting dressed, getting the kids off to school, going to work, or going to classes; each of these involves hundreds of small steps.
2. A very good way to reinforce the Law of Process involves building a model plane or model house, or putting together any kind of craft.
3. Pay attention to the many small steps in your life.
4. Break any present goal down into small steps; write them down and make a checklist. See the stepping-stones from where you are to where you want to be.

THE LAW OF PATTERNS

Any habit or pattern,
whether we call it good or bad,
despite our best intentions
tends to reassert itself over time
unless we break that pattern
by doing something different.

We humans have the power of spontaneous action, doing old things in new ways, changing and restructuring our life and our behavior. Yet an innate resistance limits this possibility; this resistance is based on our most fundamental physical and psychological structures, connected to the larger universe and to the ways we learn and adapt to our environment when young. Our tendency to form patterns has survival value.

As children, we learned to make sense of the world by observing patterns. We experienced patterns of hunger and feeding, day and night, waking or sleeping, as we conformed to our parents' schedules and our own internal rhythms. By recognizing patterns in the noises our parents made, we learned the complex association of sound and meaning; through repeated patterns, we learned to speak. We grew to depend on patterns repeating themselves, and we learned to repeat them — brushing our teeth and other nighttime rituals; patterns at home, at school, and at work. By the time we were ten years old, the power of patterns became part of our life. As Eleanor Farjeon wrote, "The events of childhood do not pass, but repeat themselves like seasons of the year."

The functional patterns or habits we've developed in the course of our daily life, such as washing our hands before eating, aren't usually cause for concern, but they're still interesting to observe, because if we consciously do something different just to notice what happens, we may feel strange or out of step — attesting to the power of habits.

The Law of Patterns primarily addresses the habits we consider dysfunctional, negative, or destructive — the patterns we wish to change. As an example, take Tom, who had a problem with alcohol. He stopped drinking, then started, then stopped, then started again. Then, finally, he thought he'd stopped for good. He told a friend, "I haven't had a drink for a year; I've got this licked." Having relaxed his vigilance, the pattern reasserted itself, and Tom started drinking again.

Tom had just experienced the Law of Patterns, first stated, in a sense, by Sir Isaac Newton, whose First Law of Motion asserts, "An object at rest tends to remain at rest, and an object in motion tends to stay in motion, unless subjected to an outside force." In terms of our own habit patterns, in other words, just saying "It's going to be different this time" or "I won't do that again" isn't enough. Or to repeat the Mark Twain quip: "Quitting smoking is easy; I've done it hundreds of times."

A woman named Iris once shared this story of how she had invoked the Law of Patterns: Iris had formed a repetitive pattern of losing and then gaining back a great deal of weight over the years — nearly a hundred pounds. During one of her slimmer cycles, she confided to her friend, Marianne, her fears of gaining back the weight and her resolution to keep it off this time. Surprisingly, Marianne told Iris that she probably would gain it back. "Take a realistic look at your situation," Marianne told her. "Did you want to gain weight the first time, or the second, or the third?"

"No!" Iris replied.

Marianne, who had worked with people dealing with a variety of addictive behaviors over the years, had an intuitive understanding of the Law of Patterns and said, "Your old pattern will tend to reassert itself unless you break it by doing something different to *interrupt* it."

"You can bet I will," Iris assured her.

Marianne shrugged. "Patterns are often stronger than resolutions, Iris. I think you need to examine the pattern. Did you say that you started gaining weight after your mother died?"

"Yes."

"And then the second time, you put on weight when you got laid off?"

"Uh huh."

"And the third time?"

"That was totally different. I had a boyfriend, and we split up."

"Iris, if you don't see the pattern clearly, then you have no way to change it. Take another look: What do all these events have in common? Where's the pattern?"

Iris thought about this. "Well, I felt badly about myself when my mother died; we'd had a bad argument, and I never got to say goodbye. And when I got laid off, and when I broke up with my boyfriend — yes, all of those times I felt lousy about myself!"

"Okay, so when you feel really badly about yourself, you go into the same pattern of overeating. Now you have a handle on it," Marianne said. "I'm going to suggest a way for you to break this pattern. It may sound strange, but I think it will help, if you're willing to do it."

"Tell me!" Iris responded.

"How far have you ever walked at one time?"

"About two miles, I guess."

"Okay. The next time this 'I feel badly about myself and I need to eat some comfort food' pattern comes up, I want you to stop whatever you're doing or are about to do, put on your walking shoes, leave the house, and walk two miles."

"That's it? That's your suggestion?"

"That's it."

Looking puzzled, Iris left.

About eight months later, Iris called Marianne, and without even saying hello, she excitedly declared, "It happened!"

"What happened?" Marianne asked.

"Well, I was feeling really stressed out at work. I felt that no one liked me. I was feeling bad about myself again. Back at home, I happened to have a double-chocolate cake in the fridge for a party I was giving. I felt like having a slice — a big slice. I started telling myself I could get another cake for the party. Then I remembered!" she exclaimed. "I saw what was happening! So I put on those damned running shoes and said to myself, 'I'll walk those two miles because I made a promise to myself. *But I'm ending up right here, at this cake!*'

"I walked my two miles — maybe two and a half miles. And when I got back, I picked up the cake and was about to toss it in the garbage when I shook my head, put it back in the fridge, and left it there. We had a wonderful party. And all the gals from work showed up!"

Iris had broken an unwanted pattern by first recognizing the power of the pattern and then doing something to interrupt it, rather than remaining a victim by repeating it.

The Law of Patterns is important for anyone who tends to break resolutions repeatedly or who has a pattern of incompletions or repeated failures (such as three or four marriages, or quitting smoking five times). Any pattern tends to repeat itself until we closely examine what's going on and intervene to break the pattern by doing something else. This law highlights our habits and tendencies and helps us take responsibility for them — not by endlessly struggling against old habits, but by *doing something different*.

Experiencing Patterns

1. Contemplate the power of patterns in the natural world: how, after a few days of heat, sun-generated winds pull the fog back into coastal cities, how animals live by their own patterned instincts.
2. Take a moment to appreciate how your subconscious has instincts too, and grows accustomed to patterns and routines that tend to repeat themselves.
3. Consider the energy required to change an accustomed pattern. Could failure to break old patterns result from underestimating the force and the time required to shift to a new one?
4. Recognize that changing any pattern entails strong commitment and resolve — and an almost heroic battle.

Applying the Law of Patterns

1. Select a repeating pattern in your life. The pattern might be starts and stops; repetitive failures to follow through with a stated goal, such as stopping drinking, smoking, or overeating; or marriage, divorce, remarriage, divorce.

2. When did this pattern begin? Give yourself some time to see the process clearly, from its start to the present day. Focus on the common threads in the pattern, not the differences (such as the different reasons several marriages ended). Once you see the common threads, you gain some leverage and know what you're dealing with.

3. What might you do differently that would have sufficient impact to interrupt this pattern?

THE LAW OF DISCIPLINE

Discipline is the surest means
to greater freedom and independence;
it provides the focus to achieve the skill level
and depth of knowledge
that translate into more options in life.

Those of us who value freedom, self-sufficiency, and independence tend to enjoy a wide range of experiences and to touch down lightly in many fields of endeavor. We often have issues with and resistance to repetitive or routine tasks.

We may see discipline and freedom as opposites if we perceive discipline as limiting our options or forcing ourselves to do something we don't really feel like doing, such as daily exercise or skipping desserts — the sort of thing that requires will and commitment to accomplish. Freedom, on the other hand, implies a lack of boundaries or restriction, keeping our options open, and remaining spontaneous.

The Law of Discipline points to a paradox. While freedom is our transcendent birthright, it has to be earned in this world; discipline remains the key to freedom and independence. This principle applies to both inner freedom and outer freedom. As actress-singer Julie Andrews said, "Some people regard discipline as a chore. For me, it is a kind of order that sets me free to fly."

Although our outer life may appear to include many freedoms, many of us aren't free inside; we feel enslaved to a whirling, churning, runaway mind, full of desires, worries, and negative images. We may feel dependent on others, subject to restrictions they (or circumstances) require. The focus and discipline of inner practices, such as meditation, exploring our beliefs, and other insight work, can generate a sense of inner freedom and inner peace — breaking the chains of the mind.

Outer freedom expands as a result of disciplined effort over time; such freedoms may include the financial freedom associated with excellence in any field, greater mobility, and the ability to travel; the freedom that comes with a strong, healthy body; the social freedom, self-respect, and satisfaction that come from disciplined labor; and, in general, having more options in life.

Freedom involves more than the ability to experience many things; what we gain in breadth, we may lose in depth. But if we persist through boredom, we don't just go *into* experience, we go *through* it; in the process, we learn far more about ourselves and our capacities than if we treat our life as a sampler course.

Discipline is a habit of doing just a little more, going just a little deeper, staying with something, pushing through it. Discipline recognizes that boredom means we're just starting to get it.

An example from my own experience may help bring this point home: During my college years at Berkeley, I practiced gymnastics nearly four hours each day, six days a week. I trained whether I happened to feel like it or not. Every school day of my college career, I knew where I'd be between the hours of two o'clock and six o'clock each afternoon. I was in the gym while most other students were talking in the student union, going for walks in the Berkeley hills, visiting San Francisco, catching a movie, playing pool or cards, socializing, working part-time, or studying. I had to organize my time and cut away whatever I considered nonessential. That discipline brought me many freedoms: trips across the United States, to Europe, and around the world as an athlete; appointments to coach at Stanford University and later to teach at Oberlin College. Today, thanks to past and present discipline and focus, I can visit San Francisco (or New York City, or Paris), catch a movie, or relax in a café. Applied discipline led to achievement, which generated more freedom.

The Law of Discipline teaches us to set priorities and focus on one thing at a time until we get it right — focusing on the activities we need to do now and setting aside what we can do later.

Commitment involves discipline over time. Sprawling between us and our goals in life, we often encounter a kind of swamp rather than a red carpet. That swamp represents the necessary preparation, whether it's schooling that feels only partly relevant to our life, the detail and sometimes drudgery to get a professional degree, or the sacrifices of time and energy we have to make, maybe while raising children, when we could just kick back and enjoy more leisure time instead. The secret to getting through the swamp is having a goal that inspires us — a goal that fills us with a sense of purpose. The goal needs to be specific. For example, just "making good money" isn't enough; we need to visualize what that money will buy, the pleasure it will bring, and maybe how we'll be able to help out some people we care about. When we find a goal that shines brightly enough for us, it draws us like a beacon through the swamp, reminding us what's waiting at the other end.

Discipline and commitment provide the bridge between here and our goals. When we feel discipline falter, we might ask ourselves, "What do I want to look back on?" We may be able to postpone discipline in our life, but in the end we can't avoid it. Sooner or later, if we want to get anywhere or do anything in depth, we have to practice self-discipline.

Experiencing Discipline

1. Imagine yourself on fairly solid ground but in a place you don't care to stay anymore; you feel the urge to move, to go forward, to expand into greater freedom and independence. In the distance, perhaps nearby or maybe so far away you can barely see it, shines a bright beacon, a gold light that represents a way for you to achieve a greater sense of freedom in your life.

2. Now imagine that between you and that freedom stretches a swamp. It's the in-between place; it appears dark and uninviting, it may have unseen risks, and it's going to take time and energy to pass through the murky water and twisting vines. You may meet discouragement and confusion on the way; you may get sidetracked, temporarily losing sight of the goal; and you may even forget why you started and feel tempted to give up, to lower your sights, to just forget it.

3. Now consider that if your desire to reach that other shore of expanded opportunities is strong enough — if the beacon shines brightly enough for you — it will lead you forward through the swamp between here and there; that bright image will help generate the energy to do what you need to do, over time, to make your goal a

reality. That shining beacon is the key to your journey — the key to discipline.

Applying the Law of Discipline

1. Do you feel a desire for greater freedom and independence in your life? If you do, what specifically is it that you want? What will bring you more options, more fun, and more freedom in life?

2. Recognize that dramatic or heroic gestures, such as extreme effort for a brief time, don't usually avail in terms of long-term goals. Decide whether you're willing to follow the path from here to where you want to go.

3. Write down or consider all of the positives and all of the negatives you can think of around what you want to do — whether it's breaking an old habit (see the Law of Patterns), going back to school, getting a second job, completing a project, or mastering another task that represents a bridge between you and greater freedom and independence.

4. Looking at the list you've written or considered, decide whether the effort will be worthwhile. If you're not sure, or if your goal is something you think you "should" do, reexamine your priorities and values. If you feel excited by the possibility, if your goal stirs your imagination, then all you need to decide is when to begin.

5. If you're already in an ongoing process that requires discipline, remember what you're doing it for, whom you're doing it for, and why you're doing it. Pretend you've already reached your goal. What does it feel like? What are you doing? Let your image carry you through.

THE LAW OF PERFECTION

From a transcendental perspective,
everyone and everything is unconditionally perfect;
from a conventional viewpoint,
perfection doesn't exist —
excellence is the best we can achieve,
and achieving it takes time and practice.

The Law of Perfection presents a paradox because it contains two apparently opposite truths, which operate at different levels of experience.

From a conventional view, this world is a place of suffering: crime in the streets, the hungry, the homeless, the oppressed. Even without the daily news, in our own life, when we get what we don't want, we suffer; when we don't get what we do want, we also suffer; and even when we get exactly what we want, nothing lasts in this realm.

From a transcendental perspective — seeing ourselves and this world with all its difficulties from the all-encompassing wisdom and patience and love and understanding that comes when our heart is open — then all of it, the joys and sorrows, the suffering and pleasure, and everything going on in this moment on planet Earth, is absolutely, completely perfect in terms of a great process of evolution.

This reminder of the bigger picture is key for those of us who have perfectionist tendencies and higher vision, but who often lose perspective and worry about petty details. Leaping back to conventional reality, it's certainly not perfect or okay that anyone is cold or hungry or in pain, but from the larger picture, we're all cells on the great body of Earth, itself a tiny speck floating in the void of space, and our personal dramas and global politics are no more significant than a group of ants who are washed away as someone hoses off their driveway.

Without the ability to leap to the bigger picture and take in all of the justice and all of the injustice — the entire drama of human existence — it can be more difficult to cultivate a sense of humor.

Those of us working with issues of vision and acceptance need to develop the ability to take this leap of faith, this mental shift out of our own body, our own life, our own drama, even our own socially conscious, politically correct psyche, and see, accept, and embrace all that is.

By accepting the ultimate (and evolving) perfection of every speck of matter, every circumstance, and every person, even including ourselves, we can rest easy, remembering that however it may seem and no matter how scary it gets, everything is okay — in some sense — as we struggle painfully toward more truth, more beauty, more kindness, and more love in the world.

This shift of perspective may require an understandable stretch for some of us, especially those who, when they try to make the leap, are pulled back down, with questions such as "Perfect? What about the starving children?"

To such questions I can only answer that by accepting all things as perfect, we also accept our own responses and our own responsibility, which may certainly include doing what we can to help the world, to change things, to donate time or money, to raise awareness, to act. That too is absolutely perfect. If we act out of guilt or out of a melancholy spirit, our actions have less impact than if we hold a larger perspective even while doing our best to help alleviate suffering.

The Law of Perfection expresses the paradox that we're perfect as we are, but not yet perfected. Rather, as individuals and a species, we're engaged in a perfect process of growth and evolution, making mistakes and learning from them.

In general, we can't alleviate suffering in others until we alleviate suffering in ourselves. We may be able to feed people and clothe them and help them be self-sufficient; these are important steps, but they don't alleviate the fundamental causes of suffering or envy or greed in the human psyche. By our willingness to grasp the possibility that life is unfolding perfectly, we have a head start. We come from a place of compassion, having learned, as Joseph Campbell quoted from the Upanishads, "to go with joy among the sorrows of this world."

Even when we accept the perfection of our process of unfolding as we stumble, grow, and evolve, this doesn't mean we're perfected; we still continue to change, to learn, to mature, and to improve our life in functional ways. We can also improve in the sense of expanding our moment-to-moment awareness and realization of ultimate perfection.

But our self-improvement needs to come from a place of prior acceptance and joy of discovery and growth, rather than as a condition of self-worth. No person, performance, or product is going to be perfect; as the Law of Perfection states, excellence is the best we can achieve, and achieving it takes time and practice. No matter how hard we work or how skillful we become, we all continue to make mistakes; improvement just means our mistakes grow smaller. We also need to accept our mistakes as perfect — whether in relationships, work, or any other arena. The Law of Perfection is therefore closely aligned to the Law of Flexibility and the Law of No Judgments.

This understanding of "no perfection" can also help lift a burden from the shoulders of those of us who have extremely high vision and measure ourselves against unrealistic standards. We can learn to appreciate the perfection of imperfection. We can develop the capacity to view the lessons of our daily life as perfect in the way life arranges them at the right time and right place. Our high ideals and vision of what might be or what "should" be, however, are meant as beacons to call to us, to direct and inspire us — not as standards to judge ourselves by.

All sorts of events, both beautiful and terrible, can happen in our world; some we like and approve of, while others we dislike and resist. Perfect faith recognizes that our mind can't know or assume what's for our highest good; this faith inspires us to appreciate the perfection of imperfection. Such a recognition open doors to an expanded sense of life.

Experiencing Perfection

1. Recall a moment when you or your life felt perfect or close to perfect. Maybe it was a beautiful day, and the people around you were happy; maybe you felt good about yourself, your mind felt free of pressures or stress, and you expanded into the moment of pristine perfection.
2. Now recall a recent incident, interaction, or occurrence in your life that felt unpleasant — that seemed far less than perfect.

3. Imagine what it would have felt like to expand into that unpleasant situation with the same sense of perfection you've felt at other moments in your life. This may not feel easy at first, but remember: Practice makes perfect.

Applying the Law of Perfection

1. Practice this simple act of remembering:
   - Ultimately, everything and everyone is perfect.
   - Conventionally, nothing and no one is perfect, except flow, change, and fun.

2. Learn to say: "Good enough!" "I'm good enough." "They're good enough." "It's good enough — for now."

3. Whatever happens to us, or whatever we do, we can apply the Law of Perfection by asking ourselves, "In what way might this be perfect? A perfect lesson? A perfect opportunity? How can I shift my perception to make something perfect out of this?"

THE LAW OF THE PRESENT MOMENT

Time doesn't exist;
what we refer to as past and future
have no reality
except in our own mental constructs.
The idea of time
is a convention of thought and language, a social agreement;
in truth, we only have this moment.

The idea that time doesn't exist may seem like abstract philosophy. After all, in a practical sense, time clearly exists, doesn't it? We have watches and calendars; we have memories of things past; and we can safely assume that certain future events will happen. Meanwhile, the clocks keep on ticking away the seconds and minutes and hours of our life. So it may seem patently absurd to suggest that time doesn't exist.

If we examine our own mind very closely, however, we get a flickering look at another possibility — that only now exists. Our sense of passing time as we wait in line at the post office is only an array of impressions and memories as we exist in one present moment, and the next, and the next.

When we feel regrets about the past, that past doesn't exist except in our mind right now, where we keep the regret alive with pictures we conjure up. When we feel anxiety about the future, that future doesn't exist except in our mind right now, where we keep the anxiety alive with the pictures we imagine.

The Law of the Present Moment isn't an abstract concept; *time* is the abstract concept. This law isn't just for philosophers to appreciate; it's for us all to apply, especially when we get stuck in regrets about the past or concerns about the future. As we get used to the idea of the eternal present, bringing our attention back to *now*, we can change our life forever. Forever, of course, is also now.

Most of our worries, regrets, and problems don't exist in this moment; they're kept alive by the pictures, feelings, and associations stored in our mental files under *past* and *future*. The job interview that's happening tomorrow becomes real as we think about it; the argument with a loved one, with all its tears and guilt, is but a phantom of history, resurrected as we think of it and regret what we said in the *past*.

The Law of the Present Moment can sweep our psyche clear of debris and return us to a state of simplicity and inner peace. It won't help us in the future, however, and it never happened in the past. The Law of the Present Moment reminds us about reality as it is, not as we think it is, wish it were, or hope or fear it may be. Only this timeless moment exists. Everything else is part of the mind's magic lantern show.

Normally, when we have a problem, it involves something that has already happened, whether two seconds or two decades ago, or something that we anticipate will happen in what we call the future. We almost never have a problem in the present moment.

For example, Rudolph is sitting on a park bench, in the middle of his midlife crisis. His wife is leaving him; his daughter is getting her PhD in shopping with his last credit card; the bank just sent someone over to nail a "Foreclosure Sale" sign on his front door; his son needs bail money for driving while drunk in a stolen car. Rudolph's life is in shambles. Or is it? Didn't we begin this little scenario as he sat on a park bench? In the moment, just sitting is Rudolph's reality. He may have to deal with other moments and other problems, but right now he has no problems. He's just sitting on a park bench.

Our body lives in the present moment. Despite all the thoughts we may have about past mistakes or future problems, we can call on the Law of the Present Moment, reminding ourselves that *only now exists*. Applying this law involves the practice of relaxing into *this* moment as we handle what appears right now, one moment, one step at a time. As Goethe put it, "The present moment is a powerful goddess."

Those of us who like to skip steps can learn to rest in the present moment. Those of us who tend to take shortcuts to get where we're going can rest easy, take a deep breath, and remember, in the well-known words of Ram Dass, to "be here now." Those of us who get confused or impatient, who think a lot about future plans, can begin to recognize that plans are thoughts, and thoughts change. They only exist in time, and time only exists in the mind. Applying the Law of the Present Moment takes practice, as does any law. We may feel ourselves getting tense, worried, or upset about a thought of past or future as it passes through our mind; then we remember where we are — here and now; then we forget. Then we remember more and more, so that the quality of our present moments improves.

Experiencing the Present Moment

1. Contemplate the following questions:

    *   Do you actually experience the passing of time or just the passing of thoughts?
    *   Can you live in any moment but this one?
    *   Does the past exist at all, in any sense, except in the form of written records, stored memories, and stored tensions you keep alive in the present?
    *   Does the future exist at all, in any sense, except in your own mind's expectations and projections?
    *   Does your power reside in the past, the future, or the present?

2. Let the questions go, take a deep breath, and relax into the eternal present.

Applying the Law of the Present Moment

1. Bring to mind a memory of a past regret, a past anxiety, or a past impatience.
2. Now ask yourself: Did the feeling stem from something that was actually happening in that moment? Or did the feeling stem from thoughts about the past or future that passed through your mind in that moment?
3. Finally, ask yourself: Do you have any problems or upsets in your life right *now*? Not in general, but *now* — this instant? How many actual moments do you experience this problem?

THE LAW OF NO JUDGMENTS

The universal Spirit doesn't judge us;
judgments are human inventions,
a means to compare, contrast, and control
as we judge ourselves against
artificial, and often idealistic, standards
of perfection, morality, or truth.
As youth fades and time brings changes,
we may change many of our present opinions.
So let us refrain from setting ourselves up
as judge of the highest matters.

— **Plato**

If the universe doesn't judge us, what right or business do we have to judge ourselves? And against whose standards? Those of us with the highest ideals and standards tend to judge ourselves more harshly than others would ever judge us. We judge and criticize not only our actions but also our thoughts and feelings — even our fantasies! We also judge others against our high vision; then we judge ourselves for judging others!

When we measure and compare everything against the yardstick of our own vision and values, everything falls short, because this is the real world with real people — growing, making mistakes, learning, and evolving.

Each of us tends to internalize the criticism or blame we received or imagined from our parents. We project our judgments on others, who then seem to judge us, but who only mirror our own disappointment. We may imagine God as a stern parent who metes out rewards and punishments in this life or the next.

The Law of No Judgments reminds us that Spirit didn't invent morals; people did. This law begins with the premise that Spirit never judges us but only gives us opportunities to balance and to learn. If we make a mistake, our life will provide ample opportunities to balance the scorecard. If we can accept the premise that Spirit doesn't judge us, we can also begin to give ourselves the same consideration and refrain from judging ourselves.

The higher our ideals, the more prone we become to self-judgments. We feel the pressure of our ideals and the constant need to prove and improve ourselves, fearful of falling short, of not meeting our own standards. Ironically, those of us with the highest vision may have the lowest self-worth. The more harshly we tend to judge ourselves, the more people we attract into our life who seem to criticize us, as if they're acting out our own internal impulses (see the Law of Expectations).

Judgments block flow, set up internal defenses and resistance, and tend to hold negative patterns in place. Releasing judgments opens the way for change. In my book *Body Mind Mastery*, I share a story about Sam, a golfer, who sliced his ball way over a high, ivy-covered wall. Since the ball was long gone, he teed up again and continued with his game. As he putted out on the eighteenth hole, he looked up to see a police officer approaching, followed by the fire chief and some other officials, all looking quite upset. Approaching Sam, the police officer spoke first. "Did you hit a ball over the fence on the twelfth fairway?"

"Yes, I did," replied Sam.

"Well, that ball went through the windshield of a car, causing it to crash into a tree and block the road —"

"And the fire engines!" piped up the fire chief.

"And two apartment houses burned to the ground!" said the police officer. "No one was seriously injured, but the property loss probably amounts to several million dollars!"

Sam took all this in, as the policeman and fire chief asked almost simultaneously, "*What are you going to do about it?*"

Without hesitating, Sam replied, "I think I'll have to move my grip a little to the left."

Consider: What would it be like to model Sam the golfer, and see ourselves and life without having to compare, criticize, blame, or judge ourselves? What would it be like to live as best we can, accept our mistakes, learn from them, and do a little better next time? What if we *completely* accepted ourselves and others? As author Brenden Francis wrote, "Once we accept our limits, we go beyond them."

Experiencing No Judgments

1. Take a moment to observe how you measure the world and yourself against the yardstick of your own values rather than according to any universal truth.

2. Reflect on a recent instance when you had a judgment come up about yourself or someone else. Mentally perform this simple ceremony: Say to yourself, "I release all judgments I've placed on myself [or on the other person] for [whatever's coming up]."

3. As you say this to yourself, take a deep breath, and as you exhale, *feel* that you're breathing out all of the judgments you've ever placed upon yourself for similar issues. Releasing these judgments you've placed on yourself or on others, who merely reflect you, you help release your own negative patterns.

Applying the Law of No Judgments

The tendency to beat ourselves up over mistakes happens to most of us when our performance falls short of our ideals. Here's a humorous and almost instant cure:

1. The next time you feel like beating yourself up, actually *do it*, but do it in the open and with a touch of humor. Physically make a fist and beat yourself! (Of course, don't hit hard enough to cause a physical injury.) Hit your head, your chest, and your shoulders, yelling insults, such as "You baboon! Offspring of a mongrel wombat! Pea brain! Lowlife!" Add your favorite epithets. Be sure to make sound effects as you strike yourself. "Oof! Ow! Oh! Gosh, I deserve this! This'll teach me!"

2. While you're doing this exercise, don't fail to strike yourself physically, and make eloquent insults, *every* time you feel inclined to criticize or judge yourself. If you fail to strike yourself, you'll just have something else to beat yourself up about! Exaggerating the tendency

toward self-assault and bringing it out into the open can clear it very quickly through the power of awareness and humor. This process also generates a stronger sense of self-protection and respect.

NOTE: This exercise isn't recommended as a permanent practice, but only as a means to help us see our tendency to beat ourselves up mentally, bring this tendency into the open, and *release* it. If you have masochistic tendencies or already tend to injure yourself, you may benefit from work with a therapist. Only when you can beat yourself up with a touch of compassion and humor are you doing the exercise in the spirit in which it's intended.

THE LAW OF FAITH

*The Law of Faith is founded on the recognition
that we know more than we have read, heard, or studied;
we know more because we are more;
we have a direct link to universal wisdom;
we only have to look, listen, and trust.*

Some of us believe we trust ourselves, but on closer examination, we discover that we actually trust mental knowledge, theories, and beliefs that came from somewhere or someone else — a book, a teacher, a guide. Those of us who have issues with self-trust tend to rely on scientists, experts, psychics, oracles, gurus, or others to advise us and to validate our views; we may search everywhere but within to find ourselves. Just as some people give away their power, we may discard our inner wisdom and then look for it elsewhere, becoming seekers of truth, spiritual vagabonds, or seminar addicts, traveling from one teacher or workshop to the next, looking for new information that may satisfy or fulfill us. But we never find fulfillment until we discover it within ourselves — not as a large storehouse of information, but as a direct channel to the infinite wisdom available to us all.

Expert guidance certainly has its value, especially from the truly wise. No need, for example, to learn tennis by ourselves when a good coach can save some time. But we need to develop more trust in our own deepest intuition and wisdom as the final arbiter and source of our decisions.

The Law of Faith reminds us to trust our innate wisdom and process, and take a leap of faith into the possibility that we may know far more than we now recognize. This law entails far more than raising our self-concept, however; trust cuts across every domain until we see higher wisdom operating at every level, not only within ourselves but within others and in the world.

The Law of Faith involves trusting the process of our life with all its ups and downs — knowing that wherever we step, the path appears beneath our feet.

The Law of Faith, directly aligned with the Law of Flexibility and the Law of Higher Will, reminds us that we are part of the mystery some call God, and the wisdom within each of us.

When we say "I trust myself completely," we're most often referring to our conscious self — our mind or ego. This kind of self-trust won't take us far, because the ego can only access limited data. When we come to consider the possibility that a mysterious quality of infinite wisdom, patience, and compassion is operating in, as, and through us and everyone else, we open doors to a new experience of life — and when we *realize* this level of trust, our life changes forever.

I use the term *Spirit* to refer to this higher force, but whatever name we use, when we *truly* come to trust this higher force working behind the scenes according to its own laws, then we can also trust those parts of Spirit we call *ourselves* and *others*.

We can always feel this connection and this trust in our heart. But first, we have to get out of our head. This means coming to trust our body's instinctive wisdom about how to move, what to eat, when to have sex, and how to heal ourselves — letting the body do the job it's here to do, without the mind's interference with theories and philosophies. For self-trust to reach its most profound degree, it needs to occur on all levels of our being — physical, mental, emotional, and spiritual.

A corollary to the Law of Faith can be stated thus: Self-trust comes through direct experience. This truth reminds us to pay attention first to our own experience, not to advice from a book or teacher. Improvisational dancing, martial arts and other sports, and playing a musical instrument are all good ways to develop a trust in our body's innate ability to move *without thinking*, following its own wisdom. We come to trust that our body can take care of itself very well without philosophies; we discover what our body knows, and we can do what's needed as soon as we let it reveal the best course — which is the essential meaning of the prayer "Thy will be done."

Challenge experiences, such as firewalking or a high-ropes course or vision quests, can demonstrate in dramatic ways that we can do more than we might have believed, leading to higher levels of self-trust. But even in every-day life we meet challenges that test us, and we face similar kinds of opportunities to test and develop our connection to deeper levels of trust.

The Law of Faith also teaches us to trust our mind, not in the sense of its ability to store information, but in its ability to access higher wisdom. We come to recognize that our brain doesn't just operate as a filing cabinet or computer but also as a radio that can tune in to any station. In other words, information doesn't come *from* our brain; it comes *through* our brain.

Trusting ourselves means sweeping our beliefs out of the way and trusting our deepest intuitions. Our feeling sense conveys messages from the subconscious, which can help us make faster, more comprehensive decisions than the conscious mind, with its insufficient data. Beyond that, what we call intuition can draw on the same universal intelligence that manifests as spiritual laws.

Those of us who trust Spirit work with it directly; the more we trust ourselves, the more we feel a higher order of wisdom and love at work in every aspect of our life. Self-trust involves a willingness to make mistakes and learn from them, for our highest good.

We're all being tested by Spirit in order to learn. In every situation, every challenge or difficulty, the universal teacher operates through our life experience to let us see our present levels of trust, faith, and alignment with spiritual law.

Alan Watts once said, "Beware of teachers who pick your pocket and then sell you your own wallet." Ironically, that's all any teacher can do, even the best-intentioned one, because the treasure is already inside each of us; no one can give us anything we don't already have. All any teacher can do is provide some keys to help unlock our own door. Teachers can only point the way; the beginning and end of the journey is inside us.

Those of us with issues around self-trust need to remember that, ultimately, we're the experts on our own life. By trusting the spirit within us, we come to trust the same spirit in others and begin to feel safe in the world.

Ultimately, the Law of Faith reminds us of the transcendent wisdom of the universe reflected in the old religious adage "God works in mysterious ways." Such faith isn't just about believing or hoping that all circumstances serve us, or that divine justice is operating when we skin our knee. Faith is a direct recognition based on higher wisdom; it entails the courage to trust that whatever happens can serve our highest good.

Experiencing Faith

1. Can you recall a specific time, either recently or when you were very young, when you felt very safe, trusting, and open inside, so safe that you could share your feelings without fear or shame or betrayal? (If you can't access such a time directly, imagine strongly what it *might* feel like.)

    • Can you picture or hear what was going on in your life at that time?
    • What did that sense of trust and openness feel like in your body?

2. Notice how this feeling of trust and openness may be different from how you normally feel around people.

    • What would it be like to feel emotionally safe with other people?
    • In what specific ways might you rejuvenate the feeling of loving faith in yourself and others?

Applying the Law of Faith

1. Having accessed the memory of a feeling of trust and openness in the preceding exercise, contrast that feeling to a recent or more distant incident in which you felt less than complete trust, perhaps even betrayal.

2. How might you have unintentionally contributed to the way that incident played out — that misunderstanding or failed trust — by not sharing your feelings clearly in the first place?

3. With the above in mind, trusting that all parties were acting out a scenario that has served your highest good and learning, replay the incident, applying your current understanding. Observe any differences.

4. Stretch yourself a little more each day, opening up, taking a chance, sharing what's really in your heart, creating a deeper sense of trust and connection with others, a bridge from your spirit to theirs.

THE LAW OF EXPECTATIONS

Energy follows thought;
we move toward but not beyond what we can imagine.
What we assume, expect, or believe
colors and creates our experience;
by changing our expectations,
we change our experience of every aspect of life.

Do we form beliefs based on our experience, or do we create experiences based on our beliefs? Experiences and expectations do, of course, influence one another, but while most of us may credit the logical and psychological idea that our beliefs are primarily shaped by our experience, the Law of Expectations states it the other way around: What we believe or expect, over time, tends to shape our external reality.

Everything is a form of energy; our mind shapes that energy into manifest form and colors the filters through which we see the world. Almost since infancy, we've developed certain sensitivities and expectations. Those of us who expect that people can't be trusted, for example, find evidence that supports this belief.

The key to applying the Law of Expectations is to create new expectations, based not on blind faith but on clear intention. This law helps take us beyond our previously assumed limits, themselves generated by earlier beliefs and expectations that may have been formed within the first months of life.

What we expect tends to appear in our life. If we see ourselves as a lucky person, we sort for or notice incidents supporting this expectation. The same would apply to an expectation that we're unlucky. To paraphrase Goethe, we could say that self-concept is a powerful goddess as well. We tend to achieve only to the level of our expected or assumed limits. In psychology, this is called the self-fulfilling prophecy. In one example, three very popular boys in a high school agreed to take part in a psychology experiment: For several weeks, they started acting very attentive and friendly to a girl who was perceived as very nice but extremely shy, plain looking, and unpopular. They treated her as if she were very attractive and popular. As a result, she showed marked, even dramatic changes in the way she dressed and acted.

She had previously expected to be rejected and ignored, and she was; this change in how she was treated changed her expectations, which in turn, created a new experience of life. The three boys initially changed her experience by breaking the old expectations that held her friends at bay; she formed new beliefs about her appeal, which shifted her behavior, so that even when the study ended, her life had changed.

An extensive study conducted by Dr. Kenneth Pelletier on the factors contributing to longevity revealed a list of factors associated with long-lived people, such as fewer illnesses, youthful appearance, a sense of humor, and enjoyable work, along with lifestyle factors, such as diet and exercise. The study concluded, however, that the primary factor in longevity was people's expectations, despite any other factors. This study serves as testimony to the power of expectations.

These observations don't necessarily mean that if we worry about getting cancer or having an automobile accident or losing a loved one that these thoughts are somehow going to make such things occur; such concerns are more based on magical thinking and superstitious fears. Such concerns need to be addressed, shared openly with someone, and cleared, so that our mind can focus on more realistic concerns. Nor does this law imply that if we make affirmative statements a hundred times a day about attracting wealth or people or personal power that we'll suddenly change our life.

The theory of affirmations proposes that by repeating a positive phrase over and over, such as "I attract money and love wherever I go," then our reality moves toward that state. It's a nice idea and a popular practice. But the most effective methods go deeper than the conscious mind, into the subconscious, through visualization, for example (since our subconscious mind does not clearly differentiate between what we see and experience with our physical senses and what we imagine or visualize).

One way to become aware of what we truly expect is to look at our life right now. Our current problems reveal our negative expectations, just as our current blessings reveal more positive expectations. Once we appreciate the influence of our expectations on our present life, we can take steps to change the expectations that no longer serve us. We can set in motion new expectations, beliefs, and assumptions right now; we don't have to wait for experiences to confirm them — we can visualize these experiences using the power of our imagination, opening the door to new possibilities.

Researchers in subliminal messages that play below the level of conscious recognition, with guided imagery and hypnotic suggestions directed to our subconscious mind, have shown that they can influence both our expectations and our experience. As noted, calling forth vivid visual images that include sound and sensation creates impressions within our subconscious mind, which can subtly or sometimes dramatically alter the course of our life.

We also need to notice any contradictory messages that come up when we state what we want or have, then state these contradictory messages, as negative as they may seem, aloud, in an exaggerated fashion. For example, if we state or visualize that we have financial independence but notice a feeling or thought that tells us "This is silly, you're nearly broke," say it aloud. Say it ten times if necessary; wear Groucho Marx glasses, or say it as Mae West or Jack Nicholson might say it. This helps us notice and clear the contradictory messages that get in the way of forming clear, consistent, positive expectations.

Once we change our expectations about ourselves, other people, and the world — not just pretend to change them, but actually change them — we can reshape the course of our lives.

Experiencing New Expectations

1. Think of two activities you do well and two activities that you don't believe you do very well.
2. If you base your views about what you can or can't do well on past experience, when did that experience first take place? Did that incident accurately reflect your inherent abilities, or was it simply based on a lack of experience?
3. Albert Einstein's teachers thought he was "rather dull at mathematics." Might you actually have innate abilities in precisely those areas where you feel weak? Are you willing to open up to new expectations?

Applying the Law of Expectations

Acting can become a transcendental art, not just on the stage of a theater, but in the theater of our life. One enjoyable way to shift expectations involves acting *as if* you already have the courage, love, and wisdom you desire; by looking the part, dressing the part, speaking the part, and acting the part, you can begin to manifest these qualities.

1. When you want to have, achieve, or become anything, ask the questions "What if I could? What would that look like and feel like?"
2. Now, go beyond old beliefs and expectations; act out the role you would like to play until it's no longer a role; try it on until it becomes comfortable. If you don't feel up to a task, play the role of someone who *would* thoroughly enjoy it.
3. This simple exercise can change your life in simple but significant ways. Try assuming a new role of a happier, more open, more positive you today.

THE LAW OF HONESTY

*Recognizing, accepting, and expressing
our authentic interior reality
lies at the heart of honesty;
only when we're honest with ourselves
can we speak or act honestly with anyone else.
In the sense of integrity,
honesty entails acting in line with higher laws
despite negative impulses to the contrary.*

Within the context of our life purpose, as we explore the bigger picture and meaning of our life, the Law of Honesty points to higher laws and inner consequences that are instant, inevitable, and inescapable. It includes, but doesn't focus on, external codes of behavior.

The Law of Honesty centers around honesty with ourselves — our internal integrity. This law is useful for any of us, but especially so for those of us who tend to deceive ourselves with rationalizations — those of us who have issues around honest expression or action. Seeing the truth and inevitable consequences of this law can help us turn our life around.

This law speaks to a larger drama being played out — one where we can't truly deceive anyone but ourselves. If we ever allow impulses of envy, greed, or manipulation to determine our actions or influence our expression, the consequences of these actions are already built into the mechanics of the universe and of our own psyche.

Those of us working with issues of integrity on our life path may tend, at times, to ignore or bend higher laws in the sense of not living up to our inner light. At times we're like a child who furtively takes a candy bar and pockets it, thinking and hoping it will turn out okay, while the child's mother watches from the end of the aisle.

We don't need to be punished for breaking spiritual law or higher laws; the act itself is the "punishment" and sets into motion subtle forces whose natural consequences we can't escape any more than we can escape the force of gravity.

Those of us who slip into lower levels of integrity often don't realize we're doing it. We lie to ourselves before we can lie to others. When we speak with forked tongues or mixed motives, we aren't yet integrated. We have to achieve such integration in order to speak with integrity; we can't have a part of us meaning one thing and another part meaning another. The first step in honesty entails reconciling our own conflicting parts so we can say what we mean and mean what we say (see the exercises under the Law of Responsibility).

When our internal parts work together, when we stop lying to ourselves or deceiving others, when we know deep down that we're acting with integrity despite impulses to do otherwise, we feel gates of higher energy and inspiration open inside of us.

When we speak or act dishonestly, these gates shut; this isn't a punishment but simply the way our psyche works. The saying "Cheaters never prosper" always applies in the long run, because cheaters' own psyches won't let them have inner peace no matter how rewarding their external circumstances may appear to be. Self-sabotage, down the line, is built into every dishonest act — even if we only deceive ourselves.

Some of us imagine that we're getting away with little schemes, maneuvers, and frauds for years while justifying and rationalizing our actions, and then we wonder why our life isn't working out the way we'd hoped. We may imagine that we're getting away with something because we don't get caught, but we're caught every time, by ourselves. As the John Lennon lyric goes, "Instant karma's gonna get you."

To use an extreme example, when we read the newspapers and see millionaire drug pushers living a life of opulence, we may imagine that they're escaping punishment, but we have only to glance inside their psyches to see the internal consequences and causes of their behavior. Bad people don't go to hell; they're already *in* hell; that's why they act so badly.

When we're dishonest in any way, with ourselves or with others, intentionally or not, our internal parts fight one another and our inner sense of spirit or inspiration fades; we feel cut off and alone, and we attract whatever lessons we need to learn. Concepts of morality may change, but consequences are absolute.

Dishonesty tends to take on different forms, such as lying to ourselves and others or seeking money or power for their own sakes, at the inevitable cost of our self-respect. Some of us are used to making rules rather than following them; we forget or ignore our culture's standards of honesty and integrity, bending rules to suit our own desires, turning our backs on the light within us. Whenever we cut corners for expediency, or whenever the ends seem to justify the means, we may not always reap obvious external consequences, but we create inner turbulence that we can't escape no matter where we go.

Others of us who tend toward tunnel vision may put on blinders of self-deception by insisting that "it will work out this time" without our doing anything different. This kind of dishonesty also forfeits a sense of vitality and spirit.

For some of us with expression issues who tend to hint, connive, sigh, whine, or wait for others to read our mind, the Law of Honesty points out that such indirect, misleading, manipulative, or deceitful communication results when we let fear stop us from expressing our true feelings and needs. Whether our actions are deliberate or simply chronic habits, if we manipulate people with an angry face, a sad look, or a sigh, expecting others to know how we feel without actually stating it directly; if we tell people what we think they want to hear, even with the best intentions; or if we use words strategically, hooking into guilt or pushing vulnerable spots to control others or get what we want, we may get what we want for the time being, but forfeit the inner light that we most need in the long run.

Once we find the courage and wisdom simply to state our feelings and say what we want or need, this honesty can bring new life to stale or painful relationships.

Acting with the highest integrity and expressing our authentic needs and feelings can change our personal and professional relationships for the better. Such integrity, honesty, and truthfulness — or the lack of it — form the trail we leave behind us, our personal mark in history. Applying this law, our life changes in simple but profound ways we might not have believed possible, and the very goals we once schemed to achieve begin to manifest in ways we wouldn't have dreamed.

Experiencing Honesty

1. Recall a time you showed high integrity in any area of life:

   - Admitting a mistake
   - Paying a debt
   - Expressing what you really felt or needed
   - Making good on a promise

2. How did it feel?
3. Also recall a time you or others felt you acted or spoke dishonestly. How do you feel about this? How might you now act differently in a similar situation?

Applying the Law of Honesty

1. Can you remember one or two instances in the past when you spoke or acted with less than complete honesty?

   - Did you have a dispute over money or fail to make good on a debt?
   - Did you hide information to protect yourself in the guise of sparing someone else's feelings?
   - Did you say something you didn't really mean?

2. Consider how it would feel to make a call, write a letter, send a check, ask forgiveness, and clean up old business. Follow through if this feels appropriate.

THE LAW OF HIGHER WILL

From the viewpoint of our separate self
and smaller will,
it's normal to act on the basis
of our own desires and preferences;
when we surrender our smaller self and will
to the guidance of a higher will
and dedicate our actions
for the highest good of all concerned,
we feel an inspired glow
at the center of our life.

The Law of Higher Will especially serves those of us who've mistaken our opinions or beliefs for ultimate truth and who've imposed these beliefs on others, forgetting that others have their own paths to follow — not ours. This same law also benefits those of us who tend to sabotage ourselves, who secretly doubt our own goodness or intentions, and who need a way to connect our life to a sense of deeper meaning. The Law of Higher Will also generates a sense of connection for those of us who feel cut off and alone and find ourselves struggling against other egos for recognition or for "the good life."

The heartfelt prayer "Thy will be done" is one way of applying the Law of Higher Will. For some, "thy" refers to God; for others, it applies to the universe, or to infinite wisdom at the core of life. To apply this law in our own life, we have only to ask internally, "If a wise, loving, compassionate, altruistic, all-knowing spirit within me were guiding me now, what would I do in this situation?" The law functions because such a spirit does work through us; we only have to contact it by calling on a part of ourselves, and then we know what to do — then we act in the name of, or as a servant of, the highest and best that's within us.

When we say to ourselves, "Thy will be done," and wait for guidance or direction, we won't get much help from the mind, because the mind plays games, such as "If I'm part of the universe and the universe is part of me, then whatever I want is what the universe wants for me." The Law of Higher Will expands our vision beyond that small self that competes for dominance, moving us into a collaborative vision, based on the recognition that we're all in this (world) together. Thus, this law reflects a profound sense of unity and love.

Calling on a higher will involves contacting motives that go beyond personal preferences and self-interest and acting for the highest good of all concerned — for example, hoping for rain in a drought-stricken area even though our own roof is leaking.

Most of us normally cherish hopes in line with our personal desires, wanting what's good for our smaller self. So we ask, "What are *my* preferences, *my* desires, *my* direction in life?" Or we expand our personal identity to embrace our family, our team, or our community — itself an expansive act of connection, but one that still creates an inner circle of "us" and an outer circle of "them."

We know that a cancer cell reproduces without regard for the whole body. Much of the world's suffering results from a lot of separate little selves unconcerned with the whole. The ego, or separate self, can turn toward or away from higher principles to learn whatever lessons it needs. When we work with the will of the small self, we're limited; we may get results, but if we fall, we fall alone. When we work in line with our sense of the higher will of Spirit, greater inspiration and vitality become available to us.

A woman named Mildred Norman once came to an important turning point while walking in the woods at night. "I felt a complete willingness," she said, "without any reservations, to give my life, to dedicate my life to service. I began to give what I could, instead of to get what I could...my life became more meaningful. I attained the great blessing of good health; I haven't had a cold or headache since." She went on to say, "If your life is in harmony with your part in the life pattern, and if you're obedient to the laws which govern the universe, then your life is full." Mildred changed her name to Peace Pilgrim and went on to walk across every one of the United States and across every province in Canada, expressing her ideas of world peace, peace between individuals, and inner peace. She lived as an inspiring example of integrity and the Law of Higher Will.

When we turn to a higher will for direction, we feel expanded, uplifted, and connected to a larger cause; our life takes on a deeper and higher meaning. When we align ourselves with this inner sense of higher will, dedicating everything we say or do for the highest good of all concerned, more compassion, love, and light flow into our daily life.

The Law of Higher Will serves as a guideline to align ourselves with Spirit, to inspire ourselves, and to help us inspire others.

Experiencing Higher Will

1. Recall a time you wanted something, but another part of you, maybe a higher part, knew that what you wanted wasn't for your highest good.
2. If you did it anyway, you've had a common experience of "my will." If you followed the higher or deeper instinct, you've experienced a connection to higher will.
3. If you followed personal interest, what might it have felt like if you had said internally, with your mind connected to your heart, "Thy Will, not my will, be done"? Might things have turned out differently?
4. Knowing what you know, if you meet a similar situation, what will you do differently?

Applying the Law of Higher Will

1. Select an issue you're dealing with in your daily life, such as deciding between several options or making another kind of decision.
2. Ask yourself, "What does my mind want to do?" Then ask, "What would my higher self, the part of me that's wise, loving, and compassionate, direct me to do?"
3. Holding your decision or the issue in your heart or feeling center, say internally, "Thy will, not my will, be done." Listen. Feel. Then obey the deepest urges of your heart, following your deepest feelings.

THE LAW OF INTUITION

We can only get in touch
with our own source of intuition and wisdom
when we no longer depend on other people's opinions
for our sense of identity or worth.
We all tend to worship something;
the question is,
will we worship the god of opinion,
or the god of our heart?

W e're all here to live in alignment with spiritual laws, but the Law of Intuition is especially critical for those of us with issues of integrity and wisdom as a strong influence in our birth number. Those of us working 9 are here to connect with higher laws, which are accessed through the heart, or feeling dimension. Therefore, although the Law of Intuition benefits anyone, it's critical for those with the digit 9 as their life path, because it enables them to open the primary doorway to their life purpose.

The Law of Intuition can provide needed leverage for those of us who come into this world without a strong sense of identity, center, or inner direction. It also addresses the needs and issues of those of us working 6, who tend to feel very sensitive to criticism and who worry about whether we're doing the right thing, which often gets defined by someone else. In both cases, it's easy to lose touch with our own sense of intuition — the god of our heart — because we're so busy monitoring other people's opinions.

Lacking clear identity, we don't have clear answers to internal questions such as "How do I look?" "Who am I?" "How am I doing?" "How do I appear in your eyes?" "Am I okay?" — so we tend to define ourselves in terms of other people's attitudes and views; we need approval or support from others for a sense of identity. We define and value ourselves based on what others seem to feel about us, we remain at their mercy, open to manipulation by anyone who happens to have a strong opinion about how we "should" act or even who we "should" be. The spiritual teacher J. Krishnamurti observed, "We are raised on comparison; our education is based on it; so is our culture — so we struggle to be someone other than who we are."

There's nothing wrong with getting other reference points as a check and balance, or with asking for someone's opinion; different points of view give us greater perspective, but we can't run our life by committee. The people of this world face food shortages, water shortages, and even shortages of intelligence, but there's an absolute surplus of opinions. People are entitled to their opinions, but what do these opinions have to do with us? What others think of us is really none of our business.

Those of us with an unsure sense of identity innately need something to which we can anchor our identity the way a ship needs an anchor in harbor. Therefore, we tend to find a hobby, a teacher, a system, a method, or a set of beliefs and identify with our opinions with religious zeal or quiet fanaticism. We feel we *are* our opinions, and so we defend them, impose them on others, feel sensitive about them, seek other's approval of them, and mistake our own opinions for truth.

Sensitive to other people's opinions, we monitor them closely and give opinions the power to validate or threaten our own sense of self. We mold ourselves to other people's expectations, or we react to our extreme vulnerability by resisting all opinions of others and, instead, elevating our own opinions as the Truth. In short, we put our own and other people's opinions on a pedestal; we worship the god of opinion. Not all of us call this little god by the same name. For some of us with authority issues, it's the god of authority; for others, it's the god of comparison; for still others, it becomes the god of money. Whatever we put up on that pedestal tends to overshadow the wisdom of our own heart. But as Albert Einstein said, "Whoever undertakes to set himself up as a judge of truth and knowledge is shipwrecked by the laughter of the gods."

We tend to become or take on the qualities of what we worship, so those of us who lack our own center or sense of intuition can come to act like a little god of opinion or god of authority or god of comparison. We may even tend, without realizing it, to dominate others, not respecting the sanctity of their own process.

Some people who engage in inner work or spiritual practices strive to access inner guides or master teachers within, who may offer wisdom, direction, or answers. Other people claim to act as mediums through whom other beings speak — beings they believe are separate forms of consciousness. But perennial wisdom from the global spiritual traditions reminds us that at the level of consciousness itself, we're one and the same, like many drops that return to the ocean, so how can there truly be separate consciousness? The separate guides or inner master teachers are other parts of our larger Self — parts of us that reflect our own innate wisdom. While they can be fascinating, we're wise not to give subtle guides any more power or credibility than we give to people we respect, and all outside opinion is best checked out against our innermost feelings — our own heart wisdom.

More likely, people who have inner guides whom they perceive as separate are accessing what Carl Jung termed the *collective unconscious*, where, in or out of trance, they open to different archetypes or subpersonalities stored within our larger human psyche. Whatever the mechanisms, the wisdom is ours. We can't access this guidance, however, through the logic of our left brain, which stores information and data, not higher wisdom. We access intuition by allowing our heartfelt feelings to link up with and unlock higher mechanisms within our holistic, intuitive right brain. When we make this connection, the combination of feeling and intuition accesses whatever wisdom we need.

The key to the process of gaining access to all spiritual laws resides in making an inspired, *emotional* connection to our heart. But, as already noted, we can't get in touch with our heart while we're monitoring other people's opinions.

In summary, the Law of Intuition reminds us to recognize when we're monitoring the god of opinion and to begin to transfer authority to the god of our heart and our quiet inner voice, the only opinion that ultimately has value for us. Once we contact our feeling center, we can then listen to other people's counsel or opinions without losing sight of our own intuition, the place where we determine what's best for our own life and let others do the same. Then we're free to make use of other people's views without becoming dependent on them; if an opinion doesn't serve us, we can easily let it go.

We don't resist or ignore or seek other people's opinions; we listen to and acknowledge them, take what's useful, and submit all views to the wisdom of our own heart.

Experiencing Intuition

1. Visualize yourself walking along a path through a forest, striding forward with purpose and direction, appreciating the beauty around you, but headed for a specific destination. Feel your sense of purpose and direction.

2. To your right and left, you see people calling to you, criticizing and correcting you: "That's the wrong way!" "You're going too fast!" "You're not going fast enough!" "You look funny!" "You'll never be able to do it!" Feel yourself completely free of all of these opinions. Continue on, your destination clear.

3. You come to a fork in the road. Several people from your present life, people you often rely on, share their opinions with you. You nod in acknowledgment, then wait for a deep inner sense; you look at one path, then at the other, as people yell out their opinions. "Go left!" "No, that's crazy; take the right path!" You receive an internal confirmation, subtle but genuine, to take one path or the other. You take that path, your life path, and walk on, guided by the god of your heart.

Applying the Law of Intuition

Shedding the light of awareness on subconscious tendencies to worship the god of opinion, this exercise provides a path back to center — toward a strong sense of self-direction under the guidance of your own inner wisdom. While some of us tend to live under the tyranny of the god of opinion, others of us worship the god of comparison or authority or money. This exercise works effectively for any of these.

1. In your bedroom or living room, place a cinder block or cardboard box against a wall, cover it with some nice cloth, and add some incense, flowers, or a candle; in other words, make yourself a small altar.

2. Out of Silly Putty or clay, model yourself a little statue of the god of

      opinion (or comparison, or authority, or money). Or if you prefer, buy a doll or character that feels appropriate to you.

3.   Place your god of opinion (or authority, or comparison, or money) on your altar. You can even give it a name. (I like the name *Wuddle*, which stands for "Wuddle they say? Wuddle they think?")

4.   Every morning, just after you get up and before you start your day, get down on your hands and knees in front of your altar; bow down, touch your head to the floor, and say something like "I worship you, great god of opinion. How am I doing? Am I okay? Am I doing the right thing? How do I look?" Or, "Get lost!" Use whatever words feel appropriate to you. Then go about your day.

5.   This exercise can take less than a minute, and you only need to do it for a few weeks, until you become fully aware of this issue as it arises in your life. It happens like this: When others have an opinion about you or you imagine they have an opinion, you can say to yourself, "Gosh, this person looks and sounds like the god of opinion, but it can't be; I left the god of opinion back home on my cinder block. And besides, I already worshipped it this morning. I got that over with. Do I want to worship it *again*?" The next time others have opinions about who you are, how you are, or what you're doing, you can thank them for sharing, acknowledge their opinion, and let them know, "Here's who I am, here's what I need, here's what I'm doing." Taking the god of opinion off the pedestal opens the way to find your own center once again, and trust the god of your heart.

THE LAW OF ACTION

No matter what we feel or know,
no matter what our potential gifts or talents,
only action brings them to life.
Those of us who only think we understand concepts,
such as commitment, courage, and love,
one day discover that we only know when we act;
doing becomes understanding.

Action isn't easy in this world; forces of doubt and inertia are everywhere, even within our own mind and body. Still, we must act. Words may be cheap, concepts and philosophies may be elegant, ideas may abound, and good intentions may sound impressive. Turning all the words, concepts, and ideas into action requires energy; it requires sacrifice. We have to overcome insecurity and hurdle past self-doubt, lethargy, apathy, excuses, and a hundred good reasons not to rock the boat, to stay the course. But we keep getting the same message from life: It's better to do what we need to do than not do it and have a good reason. This states, as well as anything, the Law of Action.

Thousands of motivational speakers thunder out passionate and eloquent ideas like this just to inspire us to get off the couch and make a new life, to put out some effort, some will, some discipline. Still, most of us take action only when the emotional, mental, or physical pain gets so bad that we have to.

Let's change this pattern by acknowledging that no matter what thoughts or emotions may arise (positive or negative), it's our actions that primarily shape our body and life. To paraphrase what I wrote in *Everyday Enlightenment*: To progress toward our goals, we can choose one of the following methods:

(1) We can find a way to quiet our mind, create empowering beliefs, raise

our self-esteem and practice positive self-talk, find our focus and affirm our power to free our emotions and visualize positive outcomes so that we can develop the confidence to generate the courage to find the determination to make the commitment to feel sufficiently motivated to do whatever it is we need to do.

(2) Or we can just do it.

Taking action and making changes do involve initial discomfort, effort, and energy. So how do we get off the couch and take some needed action in our life? It always comes down to this: Just do it.

Most of us wait for permission from our insides to do anything. We wait to feel motivated. We wait until fear is looking the other way, until self-doubt and insecurity step aside and give us permission to act. But action is stronger than subjectivity; there are times when we have to act with strength and courage no matter how we're feeling or what we're thinking. As speaker Vance Havner put it, "Vision isn't enough unless combined with venture. It's not enough to stare up the steps unless we also step up the stairs."

The peaceful warriors of this world don't wait for permission; they know and sense what action to take, and they choose the way of courage and integrity. If the heart confirms it, they act, *despite* any feelings of fear, self-doubt, or insecurity that may arise. They act and let their subjective life — their thoughts and feelings — run to catch up. "Wait, you can't do this! You're not up to it!" our mind shouts, echoing voices from the past. "You'll make a fool of yourself! You'll only get hurt! You'll fail!" All of these voices may pass through our mind, but we act anyway. Soon, these voices or feelings, once so loud and compelling, stop coming around so often.

Once, when I was six years old, I found myself standing on a second-story rooftop of a house under construction. Twenty feet below me was a big sand pile. My older friends had already jumped, but I was only six, and I was afraid. They tried to coax me, tease me, encourage me, and reassure me for about forty-five minutes, when one of the boys finally yelled, "Stop thinking! Just stop thinking and jump!" It struck me in that moment that no matter how frightened I felt, I knew how to bend my knees, I knew how to lean forward, and I knew how to push off. So I stopped thinking, leaned forward, and was suddenly airborne — a *wonderful* feeling — and a valuable lesson I never forgot.

I once coached a gymnast I'll call Jill. She had worked hard on a new dismount from the uneven bars. She'd done it many times in the spotting belt, then with an assist from me. Now, the time had come for her to do it alone.

She was well prepared and ready; she knew it, and I knew it. She got up on the bar and was about to perform the dismount when she stopped. "I can't do it, Coach; I'm afraid."

"Oh, I see," I responded. "Yes, I think I'd be feeling a lot of fear too; after all, it's the first time you're doing it by yourself. Where do you feel the fear?"

"Well, in my stomach and in my muscles; they feel kind of weak."

"So you feel afraid."

"Yes."

"Now that we've cleared that up, let's see you do it."

At first, she looked confused. "But Coach, I told you, I can't — I'm afraid!"

"Whatever gave you the idea that fear was some kind of reason not to do something?"

"Well, I —"

"The only time you have a chance to show courage is when you're afraid. It's fine to feel afraid; it can be a healthy sign that you're not ready for something. But in this case, you *are* ready. Fear is a wonderful servant, but a terrible master. Feel it as much as you want, Jill; experience it completely. Then do the dismount."

Jill hesitated for a moment; then, with a look of determination mixed with just a bit of terror, she swung around the bar, let go, and did a beautiful dismount. She had understood and applied the Law of Action. And as boxing coach Cus D'Amato observed, "Heroes and cowards feel the same fear. They just respond differently."

Every day we all get opportunities to face fear or inertia and act anyway. Not by leaping off rooftops into sand piles or doing gymnastic stunts, but in even more important ways, such as taking the risk to express how we feel, to conquer old habits, or in other ways to experience the power and magic of the Law of Action.

Experiencing Action

1. Imagine yourself standing in your home or office, about ten feet inside the doorway. The door stands open, it's a beautiful day out, and you want to go outside, because "outside" represents reaching your highest hopes and most cherished goals — living the life you were born to live.

2. Now, recall the last time you felt fear or self-doubt or insecurity. Feel the fear, and then translate that feeling into an image, as if the feeling jumped outside you and turned into a being — small or large, male or female, human or not. When the image forms, let's call it Mr. or Ms. Fear (or Self-Doubt or Insecurity).

3. Let yourself create a mental videotape of the following scene: Feel yourself walking toward the open doorway, out into the sunlight, out into your future. You come closer to the doorway, but just as you're about to walk through, Mr./Ms. Fear appears in front of you, and cautions, "Wait, you can't do this! It's too much for you!"

4. Let Mr./Ms. Fear stop you, just the way you've let yourself be stopped or slowed down or confused so many times in your life. Fully experience this.

5. You have now created your video; now *replay* this scene — going to the doorway and getting stopped by Mr./Ms. Fear. Replay it at regular speed or fast-forward, again and again, exactly the same way. Each time, experience what it feels like to let Mr./Ms. Fear stop you. Don't change the scenario; just repeat it, and feel it, until you get angry — not afraid or sad, but *angry*. This may take a while. When you feel really angry, you're ready for the final step.

6. Play the scene once more, but this time, when Mr./Ms. Fear steps in front of you and says, "Wait, you can't…," or threatens you, or pleads with you, or reasons with you, just walk out the door as if Mr./Ms. Fear weren't even there.

7. Remember how much you want to go outside and continue on your way, on your life path. Despite all of the reasons you "can't" or "shouldn't" or "aren't capable enough," follow through; focus on the goal. Walk out the door.

8. Notice how different this feels. Experience the principle and power of pure action.

Applying the Law of Action

Action is stronger than subjectivity. No matter what you feel or think, you can still act.

1. Recall how you feel when fear comes in just as you're about to express how you feel or to take a risk, such as going back to school, taking on a new responsibility, or making a commitment.

2. Recall how you've allowed fear or self-doubt or insecurity to stop you in the past.

3. Consider that if life puts a hurdle in your path, you'd better become a hurdler.

4. To deal with fear, act as if you felt courageous; to deal with self-doubt, act as if you felt fully capable of any such task; to deal with insecurity, act as if you felt centered and confident. Whatever else you do, act! Just do it. Just act, and let the feelings of fear, self-doubt, and insecurity fade in the dust trail you leave behind.

THE LAW OF CYCLES

The world of nature exists
within a larger pattern of cycles,
such as day and night
and the passing of the seasons.
The seasons don't push one another;
neither do clouds race the wind across the sky;
all things happen in good time;
everything has a time to rise, and a time to fall.
Whatever rises, falls,
and whatever falls shall rise again;
that's the principle of cycles.

Different forms of energy vibrate at different rates; like a river, energy flows from a higher to lower level, moving through repeating cycles, expanding and then contracting, like our breathing.

Since everything in the universe is a form of energy, everything falls within the domain of the Law of Cycles: Sunrise and sunset, the waxing and waning moon, the ebb and flow of the tides, and the seasons of the year all reflect this law. It reminds us there is a time for everything under the sun. All things have a most favorable and a least favorable time; all things rise and fall. A thought or action initiated while this pulsing energy is rising and gaining momentum travels along easily toward its success, but a thought or action initiated in a descending cycle has a reduced impact. When a cycle isn't favorable, we wait until it's rising again. There are times for action and times for stillness, times to talk and times to be silent. Few things are more frustrating than doing the right thing at the wrong time.

Appreciating the cycles of our life helps us apply good timing and create better "luck" for ourselves. There are times to work and times to rest, times to take advantage of a building cycle and times to go inside, learn patience, and wait, preparing for the next rising wave.

The lives of Malcolm X and Nelson Mandela provide two dramatic examples of the Law of Cycles. While in prison for many years, they made constructive use of the time. They turned incarceration into a cocoon, where they went through a metamorphosis that would transform their lives and the lives of many others. They studied and read widely, applying the Law of Cycles (and related Law of Flexibility and Law of Higher Will) and emerged to become major leaders of their respective eras.

The Law of Cycles reminds us that as seasons change, so must we. Our old habits don't have to run our life. Our past doesn't have to become our future. Gardening through the four seasons reveals lessons from the natural world: that we need to end one cycle in order to begin another, and that seeds grow and change in their own time, only to be plowed under for the next planting. As seeds go, so do the cycles of our lives. Each season has its gifts. By aligning ourselves with the cycles of time, we can ride the waves of change.

All things have a more or less favorable time. An action initiated while energy is rising travels easily toward completion, but an action initiated in a descending cycle has a reduced impact. So the Law of Cycles reminds us that patience is the better part of wisdom, knowing when to act and when to keep still, when to work and when to rest, when to ride the wave or to go within and wait for the next rising tide.

Each of us has our own rhythms. As we find our own rhythm, we take advantage of whatever point of the cycle we find ourselves; we learn to flow with patience, and in harmony and rhythm with the Law of Cycles. As the Chinese proverb reminds us, "With time and patience, the mulberry leaf becomes silk."

The impulse that sets some cycles in motion may be explosive; some cycles may rise, peak, then fall rapidly, like a heavily advertised bestseller. Like a shooting star, it may have a short but dramatic life. Other books pick up slowly, by word of mouth, rising in popularity for years, and then have a very slow decline. Such cycles apply to the fortunes of individuals, countries, religions, corporations, celebrities, and cultures — rising and falling and rising again as the window of opportunity finally opens, and the timing is right.

Experiencing Cycles

1. Observe how winter brings the cold season of hibernation; spring calls forth warm rebirth; summer calls forth ripening; and autumn brings forth the harvest. In this way, the cycle of the seasons continues in a great circle.

2. Have you observed complete cycles, large or small, in your life?

   • Did your popularity in school have its ups and downs?

   • Do you see cycles of ease and difficulty in your work activities over the years?

   • Have there been times when everything seemed to go smoothly and other times when you felt as if you were pushing through molasses?

3. We can gain a certain security and sense of timing as we realize that life's a circle, and if we have the patience to wait long enough, and prepare for opportunity in the meantime, most opportunities come around again.

Applying the Law of Cycles

Within the great cycle of our life — the spring of youth, the summer of our middle years, the autumn of our later years, and the winter of our final years as our life nears its end — many other cycles flow. Each year brings a spring of new beginnings, a summer of ripening, a fall of harvest, and a cold winter of waiting.

1. Observe the periods of winter, spring, summer, and autumn in your life.

   • In times of winter that called for patient endurance and slowing down, did you use the time for learning and quiet reflection or did you want to rush the coming of spring?

   • When spring arrived, did you take advantage of this new beginning by sowing seeds?

   • Did you allow yourself to enjoy the leisure of summer seasons?

- Did you harvest the fruits of your labors in the autumn cycles, storing, saving, and preparing for winter's return?

2. Consider how your understanding of the Law of Cycles could help you create greater harmony, ease, and natural flow in your life.

3. For more specific applications of the Law of Cycles, see the section in Part Five on nine-year cycles.

APPLIED WISDOM

*It seems essential,
in relationships and all tasks,
that we concentrate only
on what is most significant and important.*

— Søren Kierkegaard

RELATIONSHIPS AND THE
RHYTHMS OF LIFE

All human life has its seasons and cycles,
and no one's personal chaos can be permanent.
Winter, after all, gives way to spring and summer,
though sometimes when branches stay dark
and the earth cracks with ice,
one thinks they will never come,
that spring, and that summer, but they do, and always.

— Truman Capote

To this point, we've explored the heart of the Life-Purpose System and spiritual laws key to overcoming the hurdles we meet along the way. Now, in Part Five, we can apply new insight into two specific areas of life: the dynamics of relationship, and the nine-year cycles of life.

All of us have personal and professional interactions and relationships with a variety of people. Just as individuals have a primary life path and purpose, with associated challenges and gifts, so do relationships in which two people work or live together. The following chapter reveals how to determine and interpret composite issues for any two people for whom you have accurate birth dates. It provides a key to the underlying forces within each relationship and shows how to focus and direct these forces.

Then, in the chapter on nine-year cycles, we review the cycles of life related to our birth number, so we can understand where we are, each year, within that larger cycle. Doing so cultivates patience and wisdom. It also helps us appreciate and make the best use of each passing year. We can apply this knowledge in very practical ways to align our projects and plans with natural cycles, enhancing our timing and increasing the likelihood that we'll be prepared for, and take advantage of, opportunity when it arises.

Readers will undoubtedly find many other positive applications for the Life-Purpose System in diverse areas, such as career counseling, psychotherapy, bodywork, coaching, and teaching; the Life-Purpose System can enable skilled and caring professionals to do even better work.

In addition, parents and teachers can apply the Life-Purpose System to better understand the key issues of the children under their care. It certainly helped Joy and me raise our children with a greater sense of compassion, perspective, and humor. I remind parents that children are both sensitive and impressionable. Their sense of identity is still forming, so in general, I don't recommend sharing this information directly with youngsters. If they're interested, let them read the book when they're old enough and mature enough to do so. Before that time, rather than telling children about their birth numbers, tendencies, or issues, understand these things yourself so you can *encourage* them, with respect to their own issues (which may be quite different from your own), to take the next steps on their own path.

I anticipate that other individuals who study the Life-Purpose System will create additional applications of the material. With that, we turn to the final chapters.

RELATIONSHIP DYNAMICS

Relationship is surely the mirror
in which you discover yourself.

— J. Krishnamurti

Given the richness and complexity of our personal identities and values, no simple formulas or rules exist for successful relationships. However, the Life-Purpose System furnishes keys to understanding relationship dynamics and, as with individual life paths, how to overcome the challenges and enjoy the gifts that manifest between two people.

If we combine two waves of sound or two waves of light, they form a new, composite wave. If we combine the vectors, or direction, of two forces moving together at different angles, they combine to form a new vector — a new force and direction. The same applies to people's life-path frequencies. When working as a unit, two people combine their frequencies to form a new, composite dynamic, usually different from, or greater than, the sum of the parts. Combining the numbers of more than two people makes the interactions so complex that the results become less reliable or useful, but using birth numbers to determine information about any dyad or pair yields valuable insights. The principles described here apply to any kind of relationship between two people, whether personal or professional, whether between friends, partners, companions, lovers, or siblings.

Like the individual life path, the composite relationship path can't be distilled into (or predicted by) numbers alone, since the way these dynamics unfold, in the positive or negative, is influenced by innumerable other factors, including environment, genetics, and life experience.

Following the Life-Purpose System, we can determine a composite number for any two people by adding together the final, right-hand digits of their two birth numbers. For example, adding my final number (26/8) with my wife Joy's (20/2), we get 8 + 2 = 10, indicating creative energy with inner gifts — and together, Joy and I created Peaceful Warrior Services. As a couple, we've accomplished things that neither one of us might have done on our own.

Deriving the Composite Number of a Relationship

As with the individual birth number, you can use one of two methods to derive any composite relationship number and relationship path.

Method One: Use the Life-Purpose Calculator Online

1. Go to peacefulwarrior.com.
2. In the menu, click on Life Purpose to access the Life-Purpose Calculator.
3. Click on the Relationships tab.
4. Enter your day, month, and year of birth.
5. Enter the date of birth of another person, then click Continue. You'll then see the composite relationship number. Make note of that number, return to this page, and read on.

NOTE: If you wish, you can also purchase the Life Purpose App for iOS or Android devices, or find it on the web at lifepurposeapp.com. The app provides the Life-Purpose Calculator as well as key information from this revised edition to have at your fingertips.

Method Two: Do the Math

If you prefer to do the math, you can find a step-by-step method for deriving your composite relationship number with any other individual for whom you have an accurate date of birth in the Appendix at the end of this book. Once you've completed the calculation (and checked your math), make note of that number, return to this page, and read on.

Understanding the qualities of the primary numbers 1 through 9 (plus 0 and the double digits, 11 and 12) helps us appreciate the composite relationship dynamic any two people make together and gives us a sense of what that energy may mean to the relationship.

Composite Numbers of Some Famous Partners

Katharine Hepburn (29/11) and Spencer Tracy (19/10) = 3 (composite)

Lucille Ball (26/8) and Desi Arnaz (23/5) = 4

Mary Tyler Moore (34/7) and Dick Van Dyke (24/6) = 4

Ginger Rogers (26/8) and Fred Astaire (33/6) = 5

Bill Clinton (38/11) and Hillary Clinton (30/3) = 5

Gene Siskel (29/11) and Roger Ebert (31/4) = 6

Richard Rodgers (29/11) and Oscar Hammerstein II (33/6) = 8

P.T. Barnum (22/4) and James A. Bailey (31/4) = 8

W.S. Gilbert (29/11) and Arthur Sullivan (25/7) = 9

John F. Kennedy (34/7) and Jacqueline Kennedy Onassis (38/11) = 9

Prince Charles (29/11) and Princess Diana (25/7) = 9

Elizabeth Taylor (26/8) and Richard Burton (20/2) = 10

Jacob Grimm (26/8) and Wilhelm Grimm (30/3) = 11

Rudolf Nureyev (32/5) and Margot Fonteyn (34/7) = 12

Numbers alone can't explain how or why these famous partners came together or why they became famous. We do know that, in significant ways, they worked their relationship dynamic in the positive in addition to dealing with negative aspects and issues as they arose. To reiterate, whether we're working as individual or in a relationship, we don't just work in the positive or in the negative; we usually work aspects of both. In the long run, it's the proportion of positive to negative that makes a difference.

The preceding examples are, of course, highly selective; readers may want to research the composite relationship between political figures, such as Donald Trump and Vladimir Putin, or crime figures, such as Bonnie and Clyde. (Wikipedia is usually a good source of birth dates.)

Meanings of the Composite Numbers

Two people's composite number reflects the same energy and meaning it would for an individual. Applied to a relationship, however, the numbers may require additional interpretation.

Remember the principle that fulfilling our life purpose isn't what comes easiest. This principle applies not only to individual life purpose, but also to the life of each relationship. If the combined life-path numbers of two people make an 8, for example, their hurdles or negative issues may involve disputes over money or power struggles as they grow into a more positive destiny together, or they may separate if unable to overcome these hurdles. Partners who make a 4 together may learn lessons about the importance of following a process and not skipping steps, or they may establish a solid foundation together. Couples who make a 5 may have to work through issues of dependence versus independence, as well as discipline, before they find a sense of interdependence and freedom within that relationship. Any relationship dynamic implies the same kind of maturation — working through the negative to reach the positive. In this way, we can fulfill the destiny of our relationships. Since relationships provide an important training ground and school for our individual evolution, as we heal our relationships, we heal ourselves.

The following summary of positive and negative aspects of each composite number, like all summaries, can only paint a broad, general portrait. It can't encompass or explain every issue that may arise. But it offers clues and points to typical issues that arise for each number. It reveals some of the internal dynamics, issues, tendencies, and priorities, as well as the higher purpose of the relationship. The composite number can also point to potential traps or hurdles to overcome.

The health and longevity of a relationship depend not on which composite number individuals make together, but on whether or not they're working this dynamic in a positive way. People caught in painful relationships are working these energies mostly in the negative; people with happy, satisfying relationships are working mostly in the positive. As with our individual numbers, most relationships include both positive and negative aspects, sometimes alternating between the extremes.

Understanding Composite Energy

1. Turn to and review the primary digits in Part Two for the composite number you wish to understand. For example, if the composite number in the relationship is a 6, turn to 6: Vision through Acceptance;

read and consider the relationship in that light. If the composite number is a double digit (10, 11, or 12), refer to the appropriate sections for each primary number. For example, if the composite number in the relationship is 10: Creativity through Security with Inner Gifts, look up the material about 1 and then review the material on 0: Inner Gifts.

2.   Read the summary of positive and negative aspects of composite relationship frequencies, which follows these steps.
3.   Answer the questions that follow the appropriate summary as they relate to the relationship.
4.   Review the spiritual laws keyed to the composite number of the relationship.

Positive and Negative Aspects of Composite Frequencies

Note that 1 doesn't occur as a composite number except in the form of 10, 11, or 12.

2: Cooperation through Balance

Positive Aspects and Issues

The 2 relationship can reflect a dynamic of mutual support, loyalty, security, and strength. In this powerful flow of mutual support and cooperation in work and family, each person complements and balances the efforts of the other; a harmony of logic and emotion prevails.

Negative Aspects and Issues

The 2 relationship can suffer from emotional withdrawal and resistance, confusion and imbalance, a struggle between the mind of one person and the emotions of the other. It may lack clear boundaries or areas of defined responsibility. Codependency issues of overhelping, then resentment, may arise.

Key Questions

•   What do we enjoy doing together?
•   Have we found a balance between our different needs?
•   How do we share areas of responsibility?

Spiritual Laws for the 2 Relationship

- The Law of Responsibility
- The Law of Flexibility
- The Law of Balance

3: Expression through Sensitivity

Positive Aspects and Issues

The 3 relationship can create a deep empathic bond through clear expression and shared feelings, so that the two people feel unified in their mutual understanding. Honesty is the touchstone, and conversation is stimulating. The 3 brings romance for lovers and heartfelt friendship between friends.

Negative Aspects and Issues

The 3 relationship can suffer from too much need and not enough giving or from self-pity or depression due to hidden sensitivities and unexpressed feelings, as when one or both people say what they think instead of what they feel.

Key Questions

- Do we subtly encourage each other to overcome our doubts?
- Do we each listen as well as talk to each other?
- Do we honestly and directly share our feelings and needs?

Spiritual Laws for the 3 Relationship

- The Law of Balance
- The Law of Honesty
- The Law of Choices

4: Stability through Process

Positive Aspects and Issues

The 4 relationship serves as a strong foundation for a family or a business enterprise. Each person contributes to a sense of security. Each gives the other honest feedback to clarify and help ensure the success of mutual goals. Whether or not the people are actually related, a sense of family pervades.

Negative Aspects and Issues

The 4 relationship can suffer from burdens of responsibility or obligation and may entail arguments about family or relatives. Unrealistic ambitions and confused plans may produce stress, frustration, or failure. A feeling of stubbornness, conflicting ambitions, or instability pervades.

Key Questions

- What step-by-step process can take us both where we'd like to be?
- What might be the next step toward an even more supportive relationship?
- Have we learned to place equal value on logic and on emotions?

Spiritual Laws for the 4 Relationship

- The Law of Process
- The Law of Cycles
- The Law of Patterns

5: Freedom through Discipline

Positive Aspects and Issues

The 5 relationship can open doors to a sense of adventure, even in the midst of daily life, bringing new experience and mutual interdependence that only draws the relationship closer. There are no assumed limits, and both people experience the freedom to be themselves.

Negative Aspects and Issues

The 5 relationship can suffer from inner conflict and scattered goals, from a pull between dependence and a desire for independence, from underconfidence, from a feeling of going in different directions or in too many directions at once, or from a sense of being trapped.

Key Questions

- What priorities and disciplines are most important to both of us?
- When we want new adventure, who really stops us?
- How can we help each other feel a sense of inner freedom?

Spiritual Laws for the 5 Relationship

- The Law of Discipline
- The Law of Action
- The Law of Balance

6: Vision through Acceptance

Positive Aspects and Issues

The 6 relationship has a purity and clarity, and is usually centered on an intrinsic commitment to growth and evaluation, bringing out the best in both people. There's a sense of optimism and mutual acceptance, where ideals become reality and shared visions of the possible sustain and nourish both people.

Negative Aspects and Issues

The 6 relationship can suffer from disappointment and criticism. The two people may experience failure to live up to each other's ideals; what at first seemed so perfect comes to seem riddled with defects due to unrealistic expectations. They may try to improve each other externally; there is a nitpicking, judgmental quality to interactions.

Key Questions

- What do we appreciate about each other?
- What is our common vision?
- How can we practice unconditional acceptance?

Spiritual Laws for the 6 Relationship

- The Law of Perfection
- The Law of Flexibility
- The Law of Intuition

7: Trust through Openness

Positive Aspects and Issues

The 7 relationship generates a sense of deep trust and openness based on both people's heartfelt sharing and understanding. The two people encourage introspection and inner processing, and the relationship itself is dedicated to mutual growth.

Negative Aspects and Issues

The 7 relationship can suffer from a sense of mistrust based on misunderstanding, emotional pain and paranoia, the fear of betrayal, and a sense of hidden shame or chronic secrets. Both people are dependent on the other to complete or to fulfill them.

Key Questions

- What have we never shared with each other because of fear or shame?
- What might we do to encourage our mutual growth and evolution?
- How can we develop a deeper sense of trust in each other?

Spiritual Laws for the 7 Relationship

- The Law of Faith
- The Law of No Judgments
- The Law of Expectations

8: Influence through Authority

Positive Aspects and Issues

The 8 relationship can reflect benign give-and-take, where power is freely given and shared for mutual benefit, generating a sense and reality of abundance. Here, mental harmony opens the way for love without strings attached.

Negative Aspects and Issues

The 8 relationship can suffer from control or authority issues, such as struggles about who's in charge, leading to a battle of wills. Money may feel scarce. There may be too much desire to get without giving or doing what's necessary; opportunism may undermine a true sense of relationship.

Key Questions

- What can we give to each other?
- Does either of us feel the need to control the other? If so, why?
- How can we together experience a sense of abundance?

Spiritual Laws for the 8 Relationship

- The Law of Honesty
- The Law of Higher Will
- The Law of Action

9: Integrity through Wisdom

Positive Aspects and Issues

The 9 relationship is founded on or develops a deep connection through compassion and tolerance; these individuals are together to teach each other about integrity and life through their differences; this provides a rare opportunity for inner growth and mutual tolerance by respecting each other's differences.

Negative Aspects and Issues

The 9 relationship can entail a lonely, cut-off feeling, a sense of disconnection of the two people from each other, and even from themselves. The two may experience a "can't live with, can't live without" feeling about the other person. Strong opinions clash because these two people see life very differently.

Key Questions

- Do we impose our opinions on each other?
- How do we honor and appreciate our differences?
- Do we remember that each of us knows at some level what's best for ourselves, but not necessarily what's best for the other?

Spiritual Laws for the 9 Relationship

- The Law of Higher Will
- The Law of No Judgments
- The Law of Intuition

10: Creativity through Security with Inner Gifts

Positive Aspects and Issues

The 10 relationship has the closeness and intensity of siblings; it's as if the two people have known each other before; their connection can create passionate vitality they can direct in both spiritual and material realms, manifesting as shared creativity and service.

Negative Aspects and Issues

The 10 relationship can suffer from arguments and hurt feelings due to unspoken sensitivity. Both people may feel suppressed irritation and insecurity due to competitiveness; neither wants to lose face. Stress-related addictions may result.

Key Questions

- What resources do we generate together that we might not generate individually?
- When either of us feels hurt or passionate, do we say so?
- How much energy does each of us bring to the other?

Spiritual Laws for the 10 Relationship

- The Law of Choices
- The Law of No Judgments
- The Law of Higher Will

11: Double Creativity

Positive Aspects and Issues

The 11 relationship produces passionate sparks of creative energy, which, when channeled, generate special magnetism (sexual or otherwise); these people can create anything together. They're like oxygen and fire. The 11 could be added again (1 + 1) for a sum of 2, so balanced and mutual cooperation is also essential here.

Negative Aspects and Issues

The 11 relationship may suffer from blocked or misdirected creative energy that can explode as shared addictions or physical violence. The partners experience a classic love-hate relationship marked by high insecurity and intense sexual chemistry. This dynamic is rarely boring.

Key Questions

- What makes me feel excited about this relationship?
- When we argue, how could we turn the same dynamic into love?
- How do we utilize or inhibit our mutual energy?

Spiritual Laws for the 11 Relationship

- The Law of Choices
- The Law of Responsibility
- The Law of Action

12: Creative Cooperation

Positive Aspects and Issues

The 12 relationship means a productive team wherein each contributes to an interdependent whole. Here we have complementary energies, sharing, and selfless contributions focused on the oneness of partnership — on what's right, not who's right. The 12 could be added again (1 + 2) for a sum of 3, so full and honest emotional expression is key here.

Negative Aspects and Issues

The 12 relationship can suffer from competitive self-interest, resentment, and blocked creativity. "United we stand or divided we fall" applies here; divided, these individuals see only strife and frustration, each self holding on to its own bottled energy. Self-expression is stifled, like a powerful train stuck at the station.

Key Questions

- What can we each do to support the other?
- When do we do the best work together?
- How do we find a balance between giving too much and giving too little?

Spiritual Laws for the 12 Relationship

- The Law of Responsibility
- The Law of Honesty
- The Law of Choices

Understanding Relationships

Spouses, lovers, partners, companions, family members, and business associates who apply their knowledge of the birth numbers can experience a deeper empathic bond that results in increased goodwill, mutual support, loving demands, good humor, and improved communication.

The composite number and associated dynamic between two people shed light on central issues they face together. No system, however, can reach into a couple's private inner sanctuary. Only they can know and appreciate the internal dynamics of their relationship; only they experience the difficulties and the lessons. The innermost thoughts, feelings, and struggles of others are theirs alone to see and theirs to work out in their own way.

Knowledge brings power. It can also bring compassion. Understanding other people's challenges, struggles, and abilities can help us appreciate and understand our own. Often we project our issues onto the mirror of our partner. If we're working 6, our partner may seem to judge us, or maybe we chose a partner who would judge or criticize us so we could work through our issues with judgments. If we're working 9, we may perceive our partner as highly opinionated. For most of us, a good way to understand ourselves is to see which qualities we like or dislike about our partner; the qualities we dislike in our partner may be repressed aspects of our own character.

As we come to appreciate the dynamics of the composite relationship we create with each other, we turn relationship itself into a powerful means of insight, awareness, and personal growth.

Relationships serve mutual needs. In the positive, they bring joy; in the negative, they bring lessons that can't be ignored for long. In these lessons, we find another potential path to illumination, where all paths ultimately lead.

NINE-YEAR CYCLES

The power of the world always works in circles,
and everything tries to be round.
The sky is round, and I have heard
that the earth is like a ball,
and so are all the stars.
The wind, in its greatest power, whirls;
birds make their nests in circles,
for theirs is the same religion as ours.
The sun and moon, both round,
come forth and go down again in a circle.
Even the seasons form a great circle in their changing,
and always come back again to where they were.
The life of a person is a circle from childhood to childhood,
and so it is in everything where power moves.

— Black Elk

The Law of Cycles reminds us how the circles and spirals of time loop back on themselves in endlessly repeating patterns and rhythms. The universe expands and contracts in the rhythm of a cosmic breath that takes billions of years; annually, the seasons pass and return; water falls from the skies, then rises up, condenses, and falls again. Everywhere, we see rhythms and cycles.

We also experience smaller cycles, not often noticed in the business of everyday life — repeating patterns of energy that appear, disappear, and reappear, cycling upward in time, rising ever higher as we learn the lessons of life, rising toward our destinies.

The primary numbers 1 through 9 provide keys to one kind of cycle. The value in observing the rhythms and patterns of our life is that if we can synchronize our personal desires with the larger forces and rhythms, we can harness the power of good timing; we ride the crest of each wave as we swim with the current in the river of time, developing a refined attunement to the natural world.

Even though we retain our birth number and its associated issues for an entire lifetime, we also experience regular, progressive cycles through all of the primal qualities expressed by the numbers 1 through 9. The year we're born relates to our primary life purpose; the following year we experience the qualities of the next higher number, and so on, up through 9, when we begin a new cycle. So in addition to our birth number and life path, we feel a strong influence of the numbers of the years within the nine-year cycles of our life, and each year brings new issues and opportunities.

We can understand the dynamics of each year of the cycle in terms of the rhythms of planting, growing, development, harvest, and plowing under, preparing for the new cycle. This metaphor and image may appear abstract — until we determine our own cycle and notice how it can provide useful, practical guidance about our sense of timing in life.

Nine-Year Cycles

1: Creativity through Security

The first year of a cycle is the year of creativity, of taking the risk to plant the seeds, of newness, of opening to new opportunity and the promise of security. The seed is sown, but it hasn't yet broken through the ground. This may involve a time of planning as well as planting, of resolutions as well as map making. It can also mean going back to school, retraining, or moving to a new location — beginning something anew, forging into the unknown like the lark that sings before the dawn in the days of early spring.

2: Cooperation through Balance

The second year, the seed needs the help and interaction of others — the sun, soil, and water. In our life, the second year of the cycle means working with other people in some form, finding our boundaries, defining ourselves in our new course of work or activity in terms of our relationships with others. We form new ties, alliances, and support networks. The earth grows warmer.

3: Expression through Sensitivity

The third year, the seed breaks through the soil into the sunlight; this may mean a time of visibility and careful growth. The shoot is still green and vulnerable. This time may bring a feeling of vulnerability; doubts may arise: "Can I do it?" Our horizons grow wider; we see and experience more. It's now late spring.

4: Stability through Process

The fourth year, the shoot grows thicker and stronger, extending its roots deeper into the soil. This is time to establish stability: a critical stage, a time not for show but for making sure our roots are strong. This is a time to review and reflect, a time to catch up on anything overlooked, a time to regroup our forces and make sure our preparations are complete. Summer is around the corner.

5: Freedom through Discipline

The fifth year in the cycle, the tree begins to blossom and attract other life — birds, bees, and forest creatures. Just so, if our work has been sound and the soil rich, if we have made good use of the first four years through our labors, now's the time of opportunity, of many options and choices. The orchard bears its first fruit. This is a time of celebration. Summer is here.

6: Vision through Acceptance

The sixth year is a time to give back, to share the harvest with all those who would eat from the fruit of the tree, to pour out, with a sense of duty and high vision, sharing our good fortune. It's a time of generosity and abundance, but also a time to accept and to appreciate the bigger picture of what has been, what is to come, and what lies beyond. It's late summer.

7: Trust through Openness

The seventh year is a time for gratitude in remembering the Source of all the fruit of all the trees. Not as goal oriented, it's a time for enjoyment and ease, a time to look back and learn from the years that have come before: the first year's creative impulse, the second year's teamwork and cooperation, the third year's vulnerability and doubt overcome, the fourth year's regrouping and consolidation, the fifth year's harvest, and the sixth year's sharing. To this is now added the gratitude for it all, seeing how all prior challenges contributed to the present moment. Autumn has come.

8: Influence through Authority

For those who have taken action and done the work of sowing seeds, the eighth year is the time to reap the harvest for the previous seven years. The harvest reflects the quality of all that came before. With deep roots, the tree now stands tall and strong, mature and valued, the fruits ready for harvest. Autumn leaves shower like gold, like rainbows, as the winds of change begin to blow, signaling the later days of autumn.

9: Integrity through Wisdom

This ninth year is a year of completion, of letting go, of quiet reflection that leads to wisdom — a time of looking backward and understanding that all cycles end, then begin again. Attachment never avails here, for all things pass; the fall has ended, and now's the time for plowing under, turning the soil, so that next spring cycle we can plant anew, with renewed hope and vigor, improving on this cycle through the wisdom gained. Winter's bittersweet presence brings a period of inner silence, and stillness, as we wait for the light to come again.

Determining Your Place in the Nine-Year Cycle

You can use one of two methods to derive your place in the nine-year cycle in any current year.

Method One: Use the Life-Purpose Calculator Online

1. Go to peacefulwarrior.com.
2. In the menu, click on Life Purpose to access the Life-Purpose Calculator.
3. Click on the Life Cycle tab.

4.   Enter the day and month you were born. The number that appears (1 through 9) indicates your place within the nine-year cycle. Make note of that number, return to this page, and read on. Remember that the issues of each year in the cycle begin on your birthday. The Life-Purpose Calculator has already taken this into account, so whichever life-cycle year you see is the one you're currently experiencing until your next birthday.

NOTE: If you wish, you can also purchase the Life Purpose App for iOS or Android devices, or find it on the web at lifepurposeapp.com. The app provides the Life-Purpose Calculator as well as key information from this revised edition to have at your fingertips.

Method Two: Do the Math

If you prefer to do the math, you can find a step-by-step method for calculating your place in the nine-year cycle in the Appendix at the end of this book. Once you've completed the calculation (and checked your math), make note of that number, return to this page, and read on.

Retrospective of Major Events in Your Life

1.   Before reading further, write down the year you were born on a piece of paper. Just below that, write the following year. Beneath that, write the next year, then the next, and so on, to the present day. (If you're eighty-six years old, this may take a little time!)

2.   Beginning as far back as you can remember, write down significant events that come to mind, both positive or negative, next to each year. The insight you gain from this exercise is directly related to how many significant events you write down, but even a few events and the years they happened can be eye-opening.

3.   To the left of the year you were born, write your primary life purpose (1 through 9, or 10, 11, or 12); for example, if your birth number is 33/6, write a 6 to the left of your year of birth; then, for the next year, you'd write a 7, then an 8, then a 9, then begin again with a 1, a 2, and so on, for every year of your life, continuing through multiple

nine-year cycles to the present. Now you can see where you were in the nine-year cycle for each year of your life.

NOTE: If your primary life purpose contains two digits (as in the case of 39/12), you need to add those two digits (1 + 2, in the case of 12) to find your place (3 in this example) in the nine-year cycle.

4.   Look back at all of the 1 years, the beginnings of new cycles, and see how this fits; then look at the 2 years (cooperation), and see if this reveals anything related to events in your life. Continue for years 3 through 9.

5.   Were any years particularly memorable? Did you notice any repeating patterns? When an 8 year brought rewards or abundance, what did that tell you about the years leading up to it? If you kept holding on to old patterns right through a nine-year cycle into the next cycle, how did that affect your life?

Learning from the Cycles

Unless your birth number is 10/1, 19/10, 28/10, 37/10, or 46/10, the first year of your life won't correspond to the first year of your nine-year cycle. For example, someone born on 8-23-1992 (34/7) would in their first year be in the seventh year of the nine-year cycle. But the cycle reflects (and is influenced by) our mother's life as much as our own. To clarify: Until children fully individuate, gaining a sense of agency and degree of independent thought and action, then the issues of their first few years on the cycle often reflect what their mother (or in some cases their father or other primary caregiver) is going through, which then in turn influences their own young life due to their developmental dependence.

Looking over your own cycles, you may notice that 1 years often involve some kind of a new beginning and that 9 years most often bring something to a close. The correspondences may or may not be exact or perfectly accurate, but the idea of nine-year cycles helps us appreciate the rhythms of life. You may note similarities between the 1 years, the 2 years, and so on — in other words, you may note comparable kinds of events or influences. With some contemplative analysis, you can begin to understand more about these cycles of life — a perspective that may help you sense what tendencies and opportunities may surface in coming years.

Riding the Cycles

Understanding nine-year cycles brings new appreciation, patience, and wisdom related to the changing opportunities and issues in your current life situation. If you find yourself frustrated by your lack of abundance, knowing that you're still in a 3 year, for example, can help. Rather than expecting an immediate harvest, you can adapt to the dynamics of the year and make the best use of current issues (expression and sensitivity) to open up and develop honest communication, to express what you need and how you feel, laying the foundation for success when harvest time (an 8 year) draws near. Make use of each year for its own purpose; building on each year's essential qualities ensures the richest possible harvest.

Those of us who plant in the spring, cooperating with others, overcoming doubts, and making the best use of each year of the cycle, experience the fullest harvest. Then, when the time comes to let go of what's past, we prepare for the new cycle to come. Whether or not we use these cycles to anticipate or prepare for years to come, we can appreciate the cycles themselves and see the wisdom of riding the rhythms of the seasons of our life.

EPILOGUE

This book shares keys to a sacred teaching that has, for centuries, been veiled in relative secrecy, passed down in a largely oral tradition. The Life-Purpose System deals not so much with self-improvement as with self-knowledge and life improvement. While it may help clarify your path, the timing of your journey and the discipline and faith you apply are yours to choose. By now, you've grasped the essentials of the method and have a feel for the interplay of archetypal patterns that make up your life. You can now more clearly see and appreciate the kinds of issues and the kind of promise your life represents. If you feel a deeper sense of your purpose and direction, then my own purpose for writing this book has been fulfilled.

To put this material in perspective, I close with a final reminder. There's a time for introspection and a time for turning outward; each has its value. We have to know the self before we can transcend it. As we explore the cave of our psyche, we find sparkling jewels of ideas, beliefs, and images, but if we get too fascinated with the facets of personality, we remain within the cave. Remember the light at the end of the tunnel; we need not linger within the caverns any longer than necessary. Self-knowledge isn't the end; it's only the beginning. Let's go deeply into the self, then through it. Once we cross the river of the self, we no longer need the boat. When we've explored our nooks and crannies to the point of becoming transparent to the light of awareness, we finally see the Spirit that shines through us all.

All of the laws described in this book are secondary to the Law of Love. I don't say this merely as poetry or metaphor; I mean it literally. Systems of analysis and introspection tend to put us in our mind as we observe ourselves. Analysis certainly has its place, but it remains subordinate to loving-kindness. If we lose touch with our heart's wisdom, then no method avails; if we love, then nothing else is necessary. This material can help clear away the obstructions that hold love trapped within us and free it to expand into the world as joyous service for the common good.

My highest hope is that you make use of what you've learned. Study this system, apply it, and then throw it away; it's only another step on your journey of awakening. Rest your mind in the eternal present, but open your eyes to the highest possibilities of your life path. Trust the process of your life, keep your sense of humor, and, above all, remember that it's never too late to celebrate the life you were born to live.

Appendix

DOING THE MATH

Although the Life-Purpose Calculator (found at peacefulwarrior.com) makes it easy to calculate birth numbers, composite numbers for the relationship of two individuals, and your place in the nine-year cycle so long as you have accurate birth dates and online access, sometimes it may be more convenient or desirable to do the math yourself.

Manually Calculating Birth Numbers

Anyone who can add a sequence of numbers (such as 2 + 1 + 4 + 5) can determine a birth number in less than a minute by carefully following six simple steps.

1. Begin with an accurate date of birth.
2. Write the full birth date numerically; i.e., 2-20-1985 (or 20-2-1985). **NOTE:** January (1) • February (2) • March (3) • April (4) • May (5) • June (6) • July (7) • August (8) • September (9) • October (10) • November (11) • December (12)
3. Put a plus sign (+) between *each* digit, *including* 0s; then add all of the digits to get a sum.

    •   Using the same example, 2-20-1985 becomes
        2 + 2 + 0 + 1 + 9 + 8 + 5 = 27 — the *original sum.*

4. Once you have the original sum (in this example, 27), if there are two digits put a plus sign (+) between the two digits of the original sum and add them together. In this example, 27 becomes 2 + 7 = 9 — the *final sum.*

- If the first sum ends with a 0 (i.e., 20, or 30, or 40), add the two digits as you would any other two digits to get a final number; for example, 20 becomes 2 + 0 = 2 — the *final sum*.
- For birth dates from 1900 to 1999, you'll always end up with a final sum of 2, 3, 4, 5, 6, 7, 8, 9, 10, 11, or 12.
- Some birth dates after 2000 may add up to a single-digit birth number: 4, 5, 6, 7, 8, 9 — or 10 (resolving to 10/1) or 11 (resolving to 11/2). Other birth dates after 2000 resolve to birth numbers like those prior to 2000, such as 12/3, 13/4, 14/5, 15/6, and so forth.

5. Write the complete birth number as the *original* sum followed by the *final* sum, and separate the final sum from the first two digits with a slash mark (/).

- In the example, the original sum of 27 is followed by a final sum of 9, so the final birth number is written as 27/9.
- I refer to the digit or digits to the *right* of the slash mark (such as the 9 in 27/9) as the right-hand or *final number(s)*.
- For single-digit birth numbers (i.e., 4, 5, 6, 7, 8, or 9), that single digit *is* the final number.

6. Double-check your math to confirm that you've reached the accurate birth number in your own case.

Common Calculation Mistakes

- Putting the wrong digit for the month (for example, writing 8 instead of 9 for September).
- Forgetting to add initial digits individually; for example, for June 10, 1938, incorrectly adding 6 + *10* + 1 + 9 + 3 + 8 = 37, instead of correctly adding 6 + *1* + *0* + 1 + 9 + 3 + 8 = 28.
- Forgetting to write the full year; for example, for March 5, 1963, incorrectly writing 3-5-63 and adding 3 + 5 + 6 + 3 = 17, instead of writing out the full year, 1963, and then adding all of the digits: 3 + 5 + 1 + 9 + 6 + 3 = 27.
- Forgetting to double-check your calculations. It's easy to make mistakes because, as simple as the procedure is, few of us commonly

add a series of single digits. Remember, you can always double-check your math by using the Life-Purpose Calculator at peacefulwarrior .com to confirm that you've arrived at the correct birth number.

Manually Calculating Composite Relationship Numbers

Follow these simple steps to derive the composite number of any relationship for which you have accurate birth dates for both individuals.

1. Using accurate dates of birth, find the birth numbers for both individuals.

2. Add together the final, right-hand digits (to the right of the slash mark) of both birth numbers. If the right-hand digits of one or both of the birth numbers are 10, 11, or 12 (as in 37/10, 29/11, or 39/12), add the digits individually, with a plus (+) mark between each digit as shown. Examples:

    - 24/6 and 35/8 = 6 + 8 = 14
    - 34/7 and 28/10 = 7 + 1 + 0 = 8
    - 29/11 and 33/6 = 1 + 1 + 6 = 8
    - 25/7 and 26/8 = 15

3. After you have added up the dyad's right-hand numbers:

    - If you end up with a sum of 12 or less, stop there.
    - If you end up with a sum of 13 or higher, add these two digits together once again to get a sum of 12 or less. This final sum represents the dynamic of the relationship. Example: 33/6 and 25/7 = 6 + 7 = 13 and 1 + 3 = 4

NOTE: The final, composite relationship number is often different from either individual's final, right-hand number. But in a few cases, the combined dynamic is the same; for example, 27/9 and 27/9 = 9 + 9 = 18 and 1 + 8 = 9. Individually or together, these people are going to be working with integrity and wisdom.

Manually Calculating Your Place in the Nine-Year Cycle

1. Write down your month and day of birth, but substitute the *present* year for your birth year. Example: Let's use 2018, the year of the 25th Anniversary Edition of this book. And let's use Miguel's date of birth

(March 12, 1985). But instead of using his birth year, we substitute 2018, so we work with 3-12-2018 or $3 + 1 + 2 + 2 + 0 + 1 + 8 = 17$ and $1 + 7 = 8$. So, *beginning on his birthday*, March 12, 2018, Miguel would be beginning the eighth year (8) of the nine-year cycle — a time to harvest and all that implies. You, the reader, would of course substitute the current year to determine where you are right now in the cycle.

2. Note that if the birth number is a two-digit number, as in Miguel's example, you'll need to resolve it one more time to derive a one-digit number.

NOTE: Your date of birth does *not* necessarily (or usually) correspond with the first year in the nine-year cycle. For example, Abe's date of birth, 1-11-1940, would resolve to: $1 + 1 + 1 + 1 + 9 + 4 + 0 = 17$ and $1 + 7 = 8$ — the eighth year of the nine-year cycle. How can this be, since on his birth date he was only just born? The 8 (meaning harvest and all that implies) has more to do with Abe's mother's (or primary caretaker's) experience than his own, at least for the first few years of his life, until he gains a degree of agency and independence.

ABOUT THE AUTHOR

Dan Millman — a former world trampoline champion, Stanford University gymnastics coach, martial arts instructor, and Oberlin College professor — has authored seventeen books published worldwide, including his classic *Way of the Peaceful Warrior* (released as a film in 2006). A life-skills teacher and international speaker, Dan has influenced people from all walks of life.

For information about Dan Millman's events, online courses, books, and audios, and to access the free Life-Purpose Calculator:

peacefulwarrior.com

The Life Purpose App is available for iOS or Android devices at
lifepurposeapp.com